Representin

New Persp
Convict Forced L.   ...igration

Edited by

IAN DUFFIELD and JAMES BRADLEY

Leicester University Press
London and Washington

First published 1997 by
Leicester University Press, *A Cassell Imprint*
Wellington House, 125 Strand, London WC2R 0BB, England
PO Box 605, Herndon, VA 20172, USA

British Library Cataloguing in Publication Data
A catalogue record for this book is available from the British Library.

ISBN 0-7185-0075-X

Library of Congress Cataloging-in-Publication Data
Representing convicts: new perspectives on convict forced labour
    migration / edited by Ian Duffield and James Bradley.
        p.   cm.—(New historical perspectives on migration)
    Includes bibliographical references and index.
    ISBN 0-7185-0075-X
    1. Convict ships—Great Britain—History.   2. Prisoners,
Transportation of—Great Britain—History.   3. Convict labor—
Australia—History.   4. Penal colonies—Australia—History.
I. Duffield, Ian.   II. Bradley, James, 1963–   .   III. Series.
HV8950.A855   1997
364.6'8—dc20   96-24610
                                                                         CIP

Typeset by BookEns Ltd, Royston, Herts.
Printed and bound in Great Britain by Biddles Ltd,
Guildford and King's Lynn

Contents

Foreword

The intention of this series is to address the unprecedented mass migrations of the nineteenth and early twentieth centuries that followed in the wake of European imperialism and the globalization of the world economy. The volumes to be published in this series will all assume novel approaches – looking at new types of source or less well-known or previously unresearched labour movements, or adopting new perspectives and methodologies which, for example, cut across the interpretative divide that has often separated white and non-white forms of labour migration. Whilst being rooted in historical problematics, the series will further seek to encourage methods of interpretation which are cross-disciplinary, and which help break down the barriers between historical, sociological, literary and political modes of analysis.

Research into European migrations, and migrations to the New World, has of course long been well established. Global diasporas have impacted hugely upon the making of modern European and American societies, and it is these movements and these societies that have inevitably attracted the most attention. Voluntary and involuntary diasporas elsewhere in the world have by comparison been relatively understudied. In the United States a particular concern has been the slave migrations of the eighteenth and nineteenth centuries, but reference is made to this phenomenon largely in the context of early American social history or Afro-American studies. The lack of a wider comparative literature on non-European migrations has often been lamented. At the same time, interest in non-European labour migrations and diasporas as a field of studies in its own right has been growing for several years, in recognition of the fact that the movements of peoples within Asia, within Africa or between Asia and Africa were a product of the same global forces and had an important impact on just as many people's lives as the movements of peoples that helped populate Europe and North America.

The emphasis in this series is thus on movements of people that have been little researched and written about in the past. This means that by preference and of necessity the emphasis will be primarily on the non-Western, non-European world and on those who have been described as 'the people without history', or in terms of empowerment (and their lack of it) the 'subaltern classes' of the colonial world. Consequently the focus will be primarily on Africa, South Asia, the Indian Ocean, South-East Asia, the Pacific rim and also the Caribbean and Latin America. It is worth recollecting of course that not all subalterns are necessarily African or Asian by descent, and that peoples such as the white convict population of Australia were also at one time a subordinated group, whose history was for long neglected, as were the migrant European populations that helped constitute the present-day societies of Latin America. We do not propose to adopt divisive racist practices in the development of this series. We do, however, intend that all of its volumes should both address neglected fields and offer a non-traditional approach to their subject, and hence represent a departure from the currently available historiography. Above all, it is intended that contributions to the series will describe not only the structure and conditions of these migrations, but the genius of individual migrants, and the variety of ways in which migrants reproduced or reinvented their cultures, adapted and resisted, or otherwise turned their new-found circumstances to their advantage. The emphasis in this endeavour will thus be on primary sources and wherever possible on making use of articulations of those experiences issuing from the migrants themselves.

We hope that the series will have a broad impact and application, and will be of interest not only to scholars of African and Asian history but also to historians and social scientists who teach courses on migrations and diasporas in Europe and the United States. As well as being of interest to those studying labour history, migration, ethnicity and colonial topics generally, it is further hoped that the series will inform the lives of the descendants of migrant men and women, and empower them with a new knowledge about who they are and where they came from.

Crispin Bates
and Marina Carter

Notes on Contributors

Clare Anderson is a graduate of the University of Edinburgh and is a British Academy Research Student, undertaking an Edinburgh PhD. She teaches in the Department of History, University of Edinburgh.

James Bradley has a research post at the Wellcome Unit for the History of Medicine, University of Glasgow, and also teaches in Glasgow's Department of Modern History. He is a graduate of the University of Edinburgh where he later took his PhD.

Ruth Brown is a graduate of both the Victoria University of Wellington, New Zealand, and the University of London. Subsequently she took an MA and a PhD in English Literature at the University of Sussex. She is a widely published independent scholar.

Joy Damousi is a graduate of La Trobe University with a PhD from the Australian National University. She teaches in the Department of History, University of Melbourne.

Ian Duffield is a graduate of University College, London, with a PhD from the University of Edinburgh. He teaches at the Department of History, University of Edinburgh.

Toni Johnson Woods is a graduate of the University of Nebraska, Omaha, and is currently undertaking a PhD in the Department of English Literature, University of Queensland. She has taught literature at the University of Nebraska and currently teaches literature in her department at the University of Queensland.

Hamish Maxwell-Stewart is a Leverhulme Research Fellow at the Wellcome Unit for the History of Medicine, University of Glasgow, and from August 1996 an Associate Research Fellow at the University of Tasmania. He also teaches in the School of History at Glasgow. He is a graduate of the University of Edinburgh where he was awarded his PhD.

Tamsin O'Connor studied as an undergraduate first at the University of Edinburgh, then at the University of Queensland; her University of Queensland Honours thesis has been recognized as of exceptional quality and she is soon to commence a PhD at the University of Edinburgh.

Deborah Oxley studied as an undergraduate at the University of New South Wales, where she subsequently took her PhD in the Department of Economic History. She has held teaching and research posts at the Universities of Melbourne, Sydney and New South Wales and is currently at the Australian National University, Canberra.

Tina Picton Phillipps is a graduate of the University of Edinburgh and teaches in the Department of History and in adult education courses there, while undertaking a PhD.

Kirsty Reid teaches history at the University of Edinburgh, is an Edinburgh graduate and holds an Edinburgh PhD.

Preface

Representing Convicts germinated from a suggestion made by Kate Darian-Smith (then of the Sir Robert Menzies Centre for Australian Studies, University of London Institute of Commonwealth Studies, now of the Department of History, University of Melbourne) for a conference on convicts to be organized by the British Australian Studies Association's History Group. This kicked us into life. James Bradley and Ian Duffield, ably assisted by Clare Anderson and Michael J. Genuardi, organized the event, which was held in Edinburgh, 18–19 March 1995. A team of mainly younger scholars engaged in innovative research, epistemologically as well as empirically, was assembled. There is now a critical mass of such research in the field under way in the United Kingdom, with Edinburgh and Glasgow as its main focal points; of the eleven contributing scholars, seven have a University of Edinburgh connection. Four at the time of the conference were still working there, while two had moved to the University of Glasgow and one to the University of Queensland. However, any tendency to braggart self-regard among the Edinburgh mob has been kept in check by the contributions of scholars from the University of New South Wales, the University of Melbourne and the University of Queensland. Others played a particularly notable part in the conference and we would like to record our warm appreciation of this. They are: Denise Vernon of the University of Salford; Tom Griffiths and Edel Mahoney of the Sir Robert Menzies Centre; Angela Smith of the University of Stirling; and Adrian Graves of the University of Adelaide.

We would also like to offer warm thanks to the following organizations and individuals:

The staffs of the Archives Offices of New South Wales and Tasmania and of the special collections in the State Libraries of those states, for expert and kindly help to most of the contributors to this book

The Queen Victoria Museum and Art Gallery, Launceston, Tasmania, for permission to reproduce the front cover illustration

The British Australian Studies Assocation, for its financial assistance to our conference

The authors of *Convict Workers* and Raymond Evans and William Thorpe and indeed all the scholars subject to our critiques, for scholarship worth engaging with

Crispin Bates and Marina Carter as most supportive series' general editors; and Lara Burns as our equally supportive commissioning editor

Bannerman's Bar, The Cowgate, Edinburgh, for providing the perfect site for an eight-hour post-conference wind-down; after all, the most lively Edinburgh intellectual life was always in its 'howffs'.

Lastly, the editors are extremely grateful to Hamish Maxwell-Stewart, who curtailed his honeymoon to choose and negotiate our cover illustration, produced our map and has offered constructive advice and criticism as well as aiding us in some of the editorial tasks.

Ian Duffield
James Bradley

Introduction: Representing Convicts?

Ian Duffield and James Bradley

Unwilling migrants

How a work on Australia's transported convicts should fit into a series on the history of international labour migration might not be immediately apparent. This remains true even though our perspective is limited to 'unfree' labour migration.[1] Search the extremely rich historical literatures on such 'mainstream' topics as: the slave-trade from Atlantic and Indian Ocean Africa; the Trans-Saharan slave-trade; the international migration of indentured labourers from South and East Asia; the large-scale mobilization of various kinds of 'unfree' migrant labour within colonial Africa and South Asia; the migration of indentured servants from Britain to North America and the Caribbean; and the uses made of all this vast and varied flow of humanity on the one hand and its own historical agency, lived experience and cultural history on the other, in destinations around the world. It will be found that comparative references to the forced migration of convicts to Australia are scant and, indeed, usually absent.

This is even the case with much of the literature on the earlier transportation of British convicts to colonial North America, the most obvious comparative historical precedent.[2] The most recent study cites a limited number of works on convict transportation to Australia in its bibliography, yet its index yields but three brief references to that country.[3] By contrast, historians involved in the long-running 'Foundation of Botany Bay' debate have at least had to grapple with the implications of the cessation of transportation to North America as a factor relational to its commencement to Australia.[4] Indeed, A.G.L. Shaw and Wilfred Oldham, whose studies contribute to that debate but also transcend its usual limits, have made important contributions to the historiography of the transportation of British convicts to both regions.[5]

Generally, however, studies of the transportation of convicts to Australia, and their management and lived experience there, have been light on international comparisons. The implication perhaps is that convict transportation and its downstream consequences were virtually unique Australian historical phenomena.[6] The chief exception to date has been *Convict Workers*.[7] It makes extensive comparative use of the literature on slavery in the Americas (especially North America) and substantial, if more restricted, use of works on international indentured labour migration, as well as devoting an entire chapter to forced convict migration as a global phenomenon.[8] We firmly endorse the principle that the study of convict transportation to Australia needs to be located within the comparative literature of international 'unfree' labour migration. While the particular remits of our authors make the extent to which they do this necessarily variable, as a whole *Representing Convicts* adopts and extends this comparative approach. At the same time, we have taken the opportunity to publish *Representing Convicts* in this series, rather than more conventionally for an exclusively Australianist readership, in the hope that those who study other aspects of international 'unfree' labour migration will grasp that the transportation of convicts to Australia offers rich comparative perspectives to their fields in turn. Indeed, one of our authors, Clare Anderson, has already injected an Australian comparative dynamic into her research on the transportation of convicts from colonial India to Mauritius.[9] A further useful lesson for historians of international labour migration might be this: while 'unfree' international labour migrants have usually had dark skins, this is not an historical invariable and the exceptions, of which the convicts sent to Australia are one of the larger, are significant.[10]

Nor is it always the case that the masters of 'unfree' international labour migrants had white skins. Hamish Maxwell-Stewart, in his chapter on the penal station at Sarah Island, makes comparative use of literature on Allied prisoners of war in Japanese labour camps during the Second World War. A more specific instance can be drawn from Australia. In 1828 William Blue, a black man, former convict and a petty landowner at Hunter's Hill near Sydney, was master of four white men. They were: John Cullen, a gardener, and John Wools, a stock keeper, both former convicts, free by servitude; Patrick Hanley, a convict and labourer, assigned by the government to Blue's service; and similarly Thomas Magrath. Blue's son William, then a baker, employed a white man, William B. Lea (free by servitude), as a housekeeper at his premises in Clarence Street, Sydney.[11] Blue was one of several hundred black convict forced migrants to eastern Australia.[12] It is unlikely that he was the only such to end up the master of whites,[13] although it is not suggested this was a common occurrence. Black convict forced migrants in Australia make another useful point for comparative purposes. Most of those of African or Madagascan origin (whether by birthplace or descent) were slaves or had slave forebears. Additionally, numbers of migrant labourers from South Asia were transported from Mauritius to Australia. Although the total in both categories combined was in all probability under 1000, they serve to illustrate that the different systems of 'unfree' labour migration were, to an extent, permeable. The same point is indicated by the periodic escape by sea of enterprising eastern Australian white transportees to Mauritius; a landfall which was, however, more of a pratfall, as they were regularly rounded up and sent back to face the music.[14]

A wider point can be made by pointing out that the transition in eastern Australia from dependence for labour supply on a sustained flow of convicts to reception of abundant flows of 'free' migrant labour, was profoundly equivocal. According to data provided by Nicholas and Shergold, New South Wales received 45,683 bounty migrants between 1837 and 1850; its Port Phillip Bay district received 25,090 such migrants between 1839 and 1850. Bounty migrants were bonded for a term to the colonial employers who put up part of the costs of their voyage out. Thus these 'free' migrants resembled migrant indentured labourers or, perhaps more closely, the 'headright' system of migration to eighteenth-century colonial North America. Astute colonial capitalists caught on quickly to this means of securing control over nominally free labour in a colony where wages for the genuine article were high and such workers accordingly often footloose. An example is those archetypes of the colonial 'landed gentry', the Macarthur brothers, James and William, who jumped at the opportunity offered by Governor Bourke's bounty scheme (inaugurated in 1835). From 1837 to 1839 they brought out 41 families plus a small number of single men to work on their huge Camden estate and in Camden village.[15] After the cessation of transportation to New South Wales in 1840, the big wool-producing pastoralists of the very recently occupied Northern Districts, which became the separate colony of Queensland in 1859, and Port Phillip Bay District, which became the separate colony of Victoria in 1850, soon found themselves facing an acute shortage of labour. Horrified by the prospect of having to pay spiralling wages to scarce 'free' labour,[16] they embraced expedients to fend off this dreadful fate. They welcomed the 'exiles' that Britain dispatched to these districts from 1844 to 1850. These men were convicts who had served a 'rehabilitary' period in Millbank or Pentonville, and sometimes periods of forced labour on public and defence works, after which they were sent to Australia and on arrival granted tickets of leave to find their own employment so long as they did so in these labour-hungry districts.[17]

Just as Australia's convicts were not always white men, so too its indentured migrants. The Northern Districts' pastoralists added other sources of labour – Chinese indentured labourers and Aborigines who, having been subdued, were allowed to live on their former lands in return for labour services. When the Chinese struck for better wages, these Aborigines were deployed as 'extremely violent action' strike breakers.[18] Thus in Australia, as in other places where there were decisions to abolish a specific form of 'unfree' migrant labour, that abolition was deeply ambiguous, fostering a variety of alternative 'unfree' labour expedients, even before coastal Queensland sucked in a large flow of Pacific Island indentured labourers during the rise of sugar planting in the 1860s and beyond.[19] In this respect, there are some broad comparisons, although a diversity of specific expedients, between the abolition/emancipation histories of convict eastern Australia and, for example, the slave-owning societies in Mauritius, the Cape Colony and Caribbean.[20] To provide another instance, Gyan Prakash has demonstrated for colonial India that what the British billed as the emancipation of slaves ushered in a particularly oppressive form of peonage.[21] Thus David Eltis has argued recently that there is a continuum, rather than an absolute duality, between 'freedom' and 'unfreedom'.[22] In the case of the abolition of convict transportation to Australia and all these other emancipations, one important, if not invariable, factor was certainly the availability of alternative labour supplies in the international labour market.[23]

At this stage, some readers might expect to know where we stand in relation to the heated theoretical debates as to whether 'unfree' labour is incompatible with capitalism (as posited by both Classical Liberal and Classical Marxist Political Economy, though with very different interpretations of the consequences for labour itself). This, however, is a bear-pit into which the book does not descend — failing to impinge, as it does, on the three themes which *Representing Convicts* addresses: the analysis of convict texts; questioning the 'criminal class'; and classifying bodies. Suffice to say that we agree with Tom Brass that 'bonded labour [is] compatible with accumulation'; and that the labour management practices of employers of nineteenth-century 'unfree' labour, plus state action in support of such employers, served to roll 'workplace power back in the direction of capital'.[24]

Convict texts

In the scrutiny of convict texts, *Representing Convicts* urges a resort to theoretical and comparative perspectives which its authors feel have been neglected in most existing work on what we also see as an underexplored field. The four authors who have contributed to this section of the book have their own preferred bodies of theory in relation to their specific tasks and disciplines. Throughout the book, it is not our argument that there is a sole 'true' theoretical position, which indeed would be to reify theory and so nullify its utility, reducing it to mere dogma. We have no wish to reproduce, for example, the excesses in this respect of some 1970s' Althusserians.[25] However, the authors of this and other sections feel comfortable with each other's theoretical stance.

Three genres of convict text are examined in the first section of this book. Duffield and Johnson Woods each address a convict narrative, that is to say, a convict autobiography. It speaks volumes about present understandings of this genre that Duffield's narrative, *Passages from the Life of a 'Lifer'* (serialized in the *Moreton Bay Courier*, Brisbane, April 1859) by a concealed author given as 'Jack Bushman', has only been rediscovered very recently.[26] To the best of our knowledge, Johnson Woods's narrative, Owen Suffolk's *Days of Crime and Years of Suffering* (serialized in the *Australasian*, Melbourne, January to October 1867), has been overlooked in the previous literature on convict narrative. Whatever other response there may be to their chapters, Duffield and Johnson Woods both hope that they may encourage others to note that identifying and evaluating convict narratives is a wide open field with enormous potential. The sharp contrast, of course, is with the huge and theoretically aware literature on American slave narrative and the smaller but equally aware literature on British criminal narrative.[27] The theoretical basis of Duffield's analysis is grounded in these comparative areas of study. Johnson Woods utilizes the work of Egan, Pascale and Sturrock on autobiography.[28]

Superficially, their two narratives appear divergent. Duffield argues that *Passages from the Life of a 'Lifer'* has been subject to heavy intervention by an editor who was a class superior to the original author (or perhaps oral narrator) and who had a quite different agenda from that of an ex-convict. By contrast, Suffolk's narrative appears to have been altered merely to observe the nineteenth-century convention of concealing actual persons under invented names. Much more important, both texts contain extensive and meaningful silences and have been shaped and repackaged, if in Suffolk's case essentially by himself. The emergent point is not that Suffolk's narrative is the more 'authentic' (and therefore, perhaps, important) of the two; but that an unproblematically authentic 'convict voice' does not exist — a generic point in all studies of autobiography and biography. The same arguments underpin Picton Phillipps's chapter. Her target is the Revd Richard Cobbold's best-selling biography of Margaret Catchpole (a former servant of his mother's) and the many texts, up to the 1990s, which provide variations on his original melody. Picton Phillipps's finding is ironic. Catchpole is one of the few female convicts of whom 'everybody' has heard.[29] Nevertheless, our 'knowledge' about her remains captive to Cobbold's characteristic mid-nineteenth-century under-standing of proper and improper gender roles. If all this makes some think the game is not worth the candle, they mistake our drift and purpose. For us, a richer, not an impoverished, understanding of these kinds of sources results. They are not to be discarded as 'biased', 'inaccurate' or 'inauthentic' but analysed for their meaningful contradictions and contestations, pregnant silences, revelatory repackagings. Then, history ceases to be that 'shallow village tale',[30] metaphorically speaking, that in conventional practice it has so often been.

Indeed, the only readers who need be unduly alarmed are those who are wedded to the idea that historical writing should perpetuate 'a conception of history as fact' and make 'readers, even sophisticated ones, susceptible to the lure of an authoritatively shaped past'.[31] This position is placed under heavy fire by Ruth Brown in her study of two modern fictional representations of the First Fleet officers, convicts and marines.[32] Using the theoretical stances of Lyotard, Jameson and Anderson,[33] she reveals that Keneally's novel *The Playmaker* and Timberlake Wertenbaker's play *Our Country's Good* (based on *The Playmaker*) are essentially conservative texts, though neither was intended nor generally received as such. Both treat their sources, whether primary or secondary, '[as if] historical knowledge is a given fact to be esteemed, not a process to be questioned'.[34] Concede that point, and the usual gatekeepers of historical 'knowledge' will soon enough tell us all what to think about the past. Our purpose, by contrast, is to present a spectrum of broadly compatible interpretations of how the Australian convict past *might* be understood, allowing space for other readings to follow. Our slogan might be formulated as 'down with "definitive" history!' – whose definitions are they anyway and by whom are they intended to be received without question? Brown is aware of a pitfall here for any shallow post-modernist practice; for her it is 'untenable' to reduce everything to an 'exercise of power and language games'. A way out is provided by Lyotard's statement that 'the impossibility of proving that justice exists is matched by an urgent need to behave as if it does'.[35]

Questioning the 'criminal class'

Some of the themes addressed in 'Convict Texts' carry over into the following sections – questioning the 'criminal class' and 'classifying bodies'. The authors of these sections persistently problematize the historiography and primary sources which they address. O'Connor continues the practice of exploring the meanings of silences, in her case in the historiography of the penal settlement at Moreton Bay. Indeed, in having two contributions on penal stations we not only address an empirically 'neglected' topic but also one which a powerful recent study, *Convict Workers*, has further marginalized by declaring it of little importance.[36] We do not, however, align at all with the mainstream hue and cry against *Convict Workers*. Maxwell-Stewart shows that its representation of the convicts as ordinary workers (albeit convicted ones) can be applied to supposedly the worst of the worst, the convicts sent to the ultra-notorious penal settlement at Macquarie Harbour. His chapter not only serves further to undermine the myth of 'Vandemonianism' (that the worst convicts were sent to Tasmania) but also is a reconciliation of the apparent (but false) contradiction between penal settlements as sites of extreme punishment and of productive labour.[37]

Representations of female convicts have been sexualized as well as criminalized in the sources produced by their contemporary class superiors. Reid and Oxley add new fronts to ongoing assaults on these positions. Much of the literature takes another tack too; that the female convicts were marginalized in the labour force of the Australian penal colonies. By contrast, Reid explores a world of convict workplace power where women enjoyed some success in subverting the disciplinary regimes of the settlers to whom they were assigned. A crucial factor here was the high demand for their labour, but it was not the only one: the women developed channels of mutual advice and communication, thus equipping themselves with knowledge about potential employers. Oxley's chapter looks at the symmetry which exists between the representations constructed by nineteenth-century moral entrepreneurs and twentieth-century historians of convict women. She suggests that the reason for the neglect of the role of the women as workers lies in 'history politicized' – the sexualization of convict women within the historiography. Damousi's chapter in the final section of our book and Oxley's study are mutually reinforcing, for they both identity the female convict body itself as a site for the infliction of dehumanizing punishment and restraint.

Classifying bodies

Representations of 'unfree' migrant labourers, whether convicts or slaves, rest upon the reification and then internalization of 'deviancy' or 'inferiority' within their bodies. The bodies of slaves were constructed from a racist discourse drawing off a spectrum of ideology with the physically sculpted noble, natural and pre-lapsarian savage at one end, and the debased and subhuman 'Sambo/ Quashie' at the other. With convicts, representations of the body intersected with wider discourses of gender, class, race and criminality. Few, however, have focused on the relations between the body and its representations. This is hardly surprising. It is only recently that sociologists have problematized the body.

Chris Shilling noted that the body has always occupied an implicit but marginal space in sociological theory. The discipline has, on the whole, unthinkingly accepted the Cartesian mind/body dichotomy – the existence of the body is recognized, but the functions of the mind and consciousness are privileged over it. The body recedes from vision, transformed into an *absent presence* – sociology has taken for granted the problem of human embodiment. Thus Marxist theory, for example, is concerned with the integration of the human body and capitalist technology. Without the finite productive capacities of both machines and the body, surplus value would have no logical basis.[38] Yet the body remains in Marxism, as in the sociologies which oppose it, an unspoken and unwritten entity.

The body in the historiography of Australian transportation has also been an absent presence. It has possessed life as a passive surface on which brutal punishment was inflicted and as a cipher for the moral degeneracy of the criminal. The entrance into the historiography of cliometricians helped invest convict bodies with new meanings. Now, they contained productive potential and had to be assessed in terms of their place among the other factors of production. These approaches open up ways of seeing the body both as a site for the construction and deconstruction of meanings (whether class, race or gender) and as the main link between the outside world of the convict system and the inside world of the individual convict.[39]

Contributors to the 'Classifying Bodies' section demonstrate this. The practice of shaving the heads of convict women is revealed by Damousi as an attempt to inscribe punishment upon their bodies by undermining their own conceptions of femininity. At the same time, the women's bodies became sites for the reproduction of masculine versions of appropriate feminine behaviour and as locations for resistance to the dominant male gaze. Similarly, Anderson's exploration of representations of Indian convicts, transported to early nineteenth-century Mauritius for use as infrastructural labour, illustrates the nature of bio-power – the classification of individual bodies within an enmeshment of colonial power/knowledge discourse. The Indian convict body was measured and described through utilitarian and racial discourses, but the colonial gaze was undermined by its failure to understand Indian cultural practices, resulting in imperfect 'knowledge' of the convicts themselves. Analysis by Bradley and Maxwell-Stewart of the tattoos sported by convict men likewise challenges the colonial state's ability to know its subjects. While the state collected detailed descriptions of individual convicts for surveillance purposes, these revealed the culture and agency of the prisoner beyond the boundaries of unfreedom. The existence of the tattoo descriptions challenges colonial and historical representations of convicts as members of a 'criminal class', uncovering instead members of the nascent British working class, ripped from the moorings of their families and culture.

Representing convicts?

Representing convicts? This book, then, adopts a critical stance towards how the men, women and children transported to Australia have been represented, both in the historical record[40] and in historians' accounts. Our title itself cannot be exempt from this treatment. In using the word 'convicts', we are following an established historiographical tradition. *The Convict Settlers of Australia, Convicts and the Colonies, Convict Society and its Enemies, The Fatal Shore: The Transportation of Convicts to Australia, 1787–1868* and *Convict Workers*[41] are certainly among the best-known titles in what is now an impressively extensive historical literature. Yet 'convicts' is what the transported generally shunned calling themselves. As the novelist Charles Rowcroft wrote in 1843:

> But I must warn you ... in this country [Australia] ... we always use the term 'government men', or on some occasions, prisoners; but we never use the term 'convict', which is considered by them an insulting term, and the expression therefore is, by all right-minded persons, carefully avoided.[42]

Rowcroft, a free man of gentlemanly origins, was in Australia from 1820 to 1825 and so appears to be conveying a usage established at an early stage in Van Diemen's Land, where he spent these five years.[43] It therefore appears that the agency of 'degraded' convicts affected how their social superiors usually addressed them, unless (by implication) superiors wished to precipitate confrontation. Of course, in a positive sense, the men and women penally 'transported' to Australia (or anywhere else) *were* convicts. That is, they had been convicted in criminal, military or naval courts and sentenced to terms of transportation. We reproduce this terminology in our title, not because we embrace a ploddingly literal historical positivism, which privileges past official usages, nor to conform to an historiographical tradition. Instead we acknowledge that, try as we might, we are not the 'transportees' – to use an available term which is perhaps neutral. Why not empathize a little by using one of the terms the 'convicts' themselves successfully insisted on, it might be asked? The answer is that generous-hearted though the 'empathetic' approach to social history might be, it has an inevitable tendency to theoretical naïveté, especially in defining all self-representations constructed by the dominated as above and beyond critical scrutiny. This methodological pitfall, Alistair Thomson indicates, is finely illustrated in the historiography of pioneer days of the Oral History movement in Britain.[44] We have retained the term 'convicts', not because we suppose for a minute that it is neutral and magisterial, but as an exhibit of what also requires deconstruction. It is an open invitation for readers to continue the process with this book itself.

William B. Gould's *Man with Pipe* – from which a detail has been taken for the cover of this book – is an illustration of the tensions inherent in representing convicts. Gould was a Van Diemen's Land convict: variously described as 'a painter and drawing master' or 'painter, glass stainer & portrait painter', he was sentenced in 1827, aged 26, to seven years' transportation for stealing a 'great coat value £2 silk handkerchief value 4/- 3 gloves value 2/-'.[45] He was, by most accounts, dedicated to inn and alehouse, a fact illustrated in a verse painted at the bottom of *Man with Pipe*: 'The landlord came, and down he Sot, / As happy, as you please, / Said Will, I think you pay^d your Shot / To be sure, and I said Yeas'. It is, almost certainly, this which has led to the painting being commonly entitled 'The Landlord'.[46]

It is, however, the ambiguities, both textual and figurative, embedded within *Man with Pipe/The Landlord* which make it a fine metaphor for the task of deconstructing/reconstructing convicts. The conventional reading of the portrait imagines the raffish gap-toothed, sly smiling, narrow-eyed rogue, pipe in mouth, to be the landlord who has sold his wares to Gould for the price of pictorial immortality. This reading is adequately reinforced if we ignore the erratic use of commas in the verse and assume that the landlord is saying 'Will, I think you payed your shot to be sure', that is, 'you've paid your tab', with Gould replying 'yeas'. But, when we consider the painting's position within the eighteenth and nineteenth-century tradition of portraiture, awkward questions are posed. Painters usually adhered to the classical aesthetic which emphasized beauty above realism. Skin blemished by the pockmarks of smallpox or other diseases became a vision of unmarked purity. Ugliness was transformed into dignity, while humanity metamorphosed into otherworldliness.[47] But humanity is almost the defining feature of *Man with Pipe*, and it is this which undermines conventional painterly aesthetics. Of course, the tradition of caricature inverted the classical aesthetic, heightening the effects of human decay, overconsumption and greed. Yet, it would be equally difficult to place *Man with Pipe* in the same tradition as Hogarth and Rowlandson. It is, quite simply, too realistic. It is this inability to place the portrait which opens the way for alternative, but contestable, readings.

Comparison of *Man with Pipe* with a miniature portrait of Gould by his fellow convict-artist, Thomas Bock, reveals a facial resemblance between the two images. There are also similarities with a rather stiff and formal self-portrait by Gould himself.[48] In all three pictures the aquiline nose is strikingly similar, a feature of Gould's physiognomy which was also noted at the time of a second conviction in 1846.[49] Is it possible, then, that rather than being a picture of an unknown landlord, *Man with Pipe* is a self-portrait of Gould? If this is the case, a whole range of new meanings can be constructed.

Perhaps it is the question of identity which arises most forcibly from Gould and his (self-)representation. This is reinforced by the interaction of verse and image. The word 'sot', for example, is commonly defined as being 'stupefied by drink' – or in Scots, 'fleein' – but also 'a foolish or stupid person, a blockhead or a dolt'. As far as we know, there is no understood meaning of 'sot' referring to the act of seating oneself — although a pun is clearly intended. There is also a teasing tension between the 'landlord', 'Will', which alerts (directs?) us to Gould's forename, and the 'I' of the toper's response. If we accept the least obscure semantic interpretation, that 'Will' and 'I' are one and the same, the likelihood of this being a self-portrait increases. However, the text is dense enough to baffle meanings. Even the word 'yeas' leads into the tortuous maze of language. On the face of it, it is a simple affirmative, but it can be interpreted as 'indeed?' or 'Oh, I have, have I?'[50] It is quite clear that whatever the verse means, a complex language game is under way.

At the same time we have to ask what purpose such a realistic representation served? Why, for example, would a landlord want to possess such an unflattering image? If this was part of an economic transaction (bar tab[51] for painting) why should Gould have so knowingly ribbed the buyer by punning on 'sot'? One of our favoured interpretations is that this was part self-portrait and part joke. The joke is the interaction of verse and payment of 'tick'.[52] At the same time, if self-portrait, this is a very empowering image. It is almost as if Gould is saying 'this is me, warts and all'. The state may have taken his freedom, but *Man with Pipe* is an attempt by Gould to recapture his alienated body.

We have landed ourselves with a highly problematic cover illustration, which is of a piece with the methods of the book as well as an apt illustration of the rich complexity of the materials available for the study of transported convicts. It is the ability to take a convict representation and create from it many different narratives which makes the illustration so powerful. It is also this sense of story-making, with a creative historical edge, which has driven the contributors to *Representing Convicts*. William Gould's *Man with Pipe* stands both for the impossibility of knowing the past, in an objective way, but also for the possibility of a meaningful and theoretical dialogue with traces of that past. This book is therefore an exercise in imagining convicts.

Notes

1. 'Unfree' is placed in inverted commas as an indication that it is, to us, a highly problematic concept.
2. Examples are: James D. Butler, 'British Convicts Shipped to American Colonies', *American Historical Review*, vol. II (1896), pp. 12–33; Peter W. Coldham, 'Transportation of English Felons', *National Geographic Society Quarterly*, vol. LXIII (1975), pp. 172–5; A. Roger Ekirch, 'Bound for America: A Profile of British Convicts Transported to the Colonies, 1715–1775', *William & Mary Quarterly*, 3rd ser., vol. XLIII (1985), pp. 184–200 and *Bound for America: The Transportation of British Convicts to the Colonies, 1718–1775* (Oxford, Clarendon, 1987); Ekirch, 'Great Britain's Secret Convict Trade to Maryland, 1783–1784', *American Historical*

Review, vol. LXXXIX (1984), pp. 1285–91; Ekirch, 'The Transportation of Scottish Criminals to America During the Eighteenth Century', *Journal of British Studies*, vol. XXIV (1985), pp. 366–74; Kenneth Morgan, 'The Organization of the Convict Trade to Maryland; Stevenson, Randolph and Cheston, 1768–1775', *William & Mary Quarterly*, 3rd ser., vol. XLII (1985), pp. 201–27; Basil Sollers, 'Transported Convict Laborers in Maryland During the Colonial Period', *Maryland Historical Magazine*, vol. 2 (1907), pp. 17–47.

3. Ekirch, *Bound for America* (1987). This is nevertheless an important work in its own right.

4. See: G.J. Abbott, 'The Botany Bay Decision', *Journal of Australian Studies*, vol. 16 (May 1985), pp. 21–41; K.M. Dallas, *Trading Posts or Penal Colonies: The Commercial Significance of Cook's New Holland Route to the Pacific* (Hobart, Fuller's Bookshop Publishing Division, 1969); Alan Frost, *Convicts and Empire: A Naval Question, 1776–1811* (Melbourne, Oxford University Press, 1981); Mollie Gillen, 'The Botany Bay Decision: Convicts not Empire', *English Historical Review*, vol. XCVII (1982); Gillen, *The Founders of Australia: A Biographical Dictionary of the First Fleet* (Sydney, Library of Australian History, 1989), 'Introduction'; Ged Martin (ed.), *The Founding of Australia: The Argument About Australia's Origins* (Sydney, Hale and Iremonger, 1978); Martin, 'The Founding of New South Wales' in Pamela Statham (ed.), *The Origins of Australia's Capital Cities* (Cambridge, Cambridge University Press, 1989), pp. 37–51; David Mackay, *A Place of Exile: The European Settlement of Australia* (Melbourne, Oxford University Press, 1985).

5. A.G.L. Shaw, *Convicts and the Colonies: A Study of Penal Transportation from Great Britain and Ireland to Australia and Other Parts of the British Empire* (London, Faber, 1966); Wilfred Oldham, *Britain's Convicts to the Colonies* (Sydney, Library of Australian History, 1990).

6. To illustrate, two 1980s studies follow a mainstream of practice. Robert Hughes's internationally acclaimed book *The Fatal Shore: A History of the Transportation of Convicts to Australia, 1787–1868* (London, Collins Harvill, 1987) is light on comparative references to slavery in the Americas and has no references whatsoever to indentured labour migration; the same is true of J.B. Hirst's well-received work, *Convict Society and its Enemies: A History of Early New South Wales* (Sydney, Allen and Unwin, 1983). One supposes that part of the mass appeal of Hughes's book in the United States was its 'otherness', providing an Australian history which was exotically appealing and thus seemingly authentic to American readers. Shaw, *Convicts and Colonies* (1966), by contrast, is one of the few earlier studies which at least locates transportation to Australia within the wider context of transportation to many other British colonies and from other British colonies as well as from Britain and Ireland, thus introducing an element of 'globality' albeit on an 'imperial preference' ticket.

7. Stephen Nicholas (ed.), *Convict Workers: Reinterpreting Australia's Past* (Cambridge, Cambridge University Press, 1988).

8. Stephen Nicholas and Peter R. Shergold, 'Transportation as Global Migration' in Nicholas (ed.), *Convict Workers* (1988). Admittedly, all this is done with a cliometric slant which has not proved palatable to all tastes. We neither slavishly follow nor

shun this comparative methodology – although the insights it provides through its use of modelling have influenced contributions to this volume, particularly the chapters of Deborah Oxley, who was part of the *Convict Workers* team, and Hamish Maxwell-Stewart.

9. This is a doctoral research project at the Department of History, University of Edinburgh. The main published text on these convicts to date is Edward Duyker, *Of the Star and the Sea: Mauritius, Mauritians and Australia* (Sylvania, NSW, Australian Mauritian Research Group, 1988), which provides a basic introduction to the Mauritian convicts.

10. Nor are the exceptions exlusively a matter of indentured servants sent to Britain's older colonies in North America and the Caribbean plus the convicts sent to Australia. Nicholas and Shergold, 'Transportation as Global Migration' (1988), pp. 30 and 34–6, outline and discuss the transportation of convicts from Spain, colonial Mexico, France and Prussia. The flows involved were not petty; in the case of Cayenne, no total is available but a maximum 'stock' (prisoner population) of 14,000 is given, which predicates a sizeable flow; while New Caledonia received 24,000 *insurgés deportés* (political prisoners), *transportés* (convicted criminals) and *relégués* (petty recidivists) from metropolitan France between 1865 and 1897 (see pp. 30 and 34–5). Whether, however, the enormous numbers of people exiled by Tsarist and Soviet Russia to Siberia can be regarded as *international* 'unfree' labour migration is a moot point – long-distance 'unfree' labour migration it certainly was.

11. See entries for the two William Blues and the other named individuals in Malcolm R. Sainty and Keith A. Johnson (eds), *Census of New South Wales November 1828* (Sydney, Library of Australian History, 1985).

12. See Ian Duffield, 'Skilled Workers or Marginalized Poor? The African Population of the United Kingdom, 1815–1852' (based on Africans transported from Britain and Ireland to Australia) in David Killingray (ed.), *Africans in Britain* (Ilford, Frank Cass, 1994); Duffield, 'Alexander Harris's *The Emigrant Family* and Afro-Blacks in Colonial Australia' in David Dabydeen (ed.), *The Black Presence in English Literature* (Manchester, Manchester University Press, 1985), pp. 68–95; Duffield, 'Constructing and Reconstructing "Black" Caesar' in Paul Hulla (ed.), *Romanticism and Wild Places* (Edinburgh, Quadriga, 1996); Duffield, 'Martin Beck and Afro-Blacks in Colonial Australia', *Journal of Australian Studies*, vol. 16 (May 1985), pp. 3–20; Duffield, 'From Slave Colonies to Penal Colonies: The West Indian Convict Transportees to Australia', *Slavery & Abolition*, vol. 7, no. 1 (May 1986), pp. 25–45; Duffield, 'The Life and Death of "Black" John Goff: Aspects of the Black Convict Contribution to Resistance Patterns During the Transportation Era in Eastern Australia', *Australian Journal of Politics and History*, vol. 33, no. 1 (1987), pp. 30–44; Duffield, 'Identity, Community and the Lived Experience of Black Scots from the Late Eighteenth to the Mid Nineteenth Centuries', *Immigrants and Minorities*, vol. 11, no. 2 (1992), pp. 105–29; L.C. Duly, '"Hottentots to Hobart and Sydney": The Cape Supreme Court's Use of Transportation', *Australian Journal of Politics and History*, vol. 25, no. 3 (1979), pp. 39–50; V.C. Malherbe, 'Khoikhoi and the Question of Transportation from the Cape Colony', *South African Journal of History*, vol. 17 (1985), pp. 19–39; Malherbe, 'David Stuurman, the Last Chief of

the Hottentots', *African Studies Quarterly Journal* (Johannesburg, Witwatersrand University Press, 1980), pp. 47–64.

13.   A prime candidate must be the Van Diemen's Land convict, Richard White, who over time accumulated land and stock on a substantial scale, owned an hotel in Launceston and was rich enough to become a racehorse owner. It seems highly likely that a property owner on this scale would have been assigned convict labour and would have employed others who were free-by-servitude or on ticket of leave. For an account of White's life, see H.B. Holmes, 'The Claytons of Wickford', unpub. MS in Alport Library, State Library of Tasmania, Hobart.

14.   Information gathered by Clare Anderson in the Mauritian Archives and kindly sent to Ian Duffield.

15.   See Alan Atkinson, *Camden: Farm and Village Life in New South Wales* (Melbourne, Oxford University Press, 1988), pp. 38–41.

16.   These colonial workers were 'free' in at least an experiential sense, as they felt confident enough to walk off the job and find a better if they found wages inadequate and work discipline irksome. At times they were able to accumulate savings and acquire petty property, such as a dray and a team of oxen, and so become self-employed. Some, especially former convicts, experienced this life-style liberationally; for a contemporary account, see 'Jack Bushman', *Passages from the Life of a 'Lifer'*, ch. 5, in *Moreton Bay Courier* (Brisbane, 23 April 1859).

17.   Accounts of this system occur in Hughes, *The Fatal Shore*, pp. 551–7; Shaw, *Convicts and the Colonies*, ch. 14.

18.   The mix of exile, Aboriginal and Chinese indentured labour resorted to by the Northern District pastoralists is well described and analysed in Jan Walker, *Jondaryan Station: The Relationship Between Pastoral Capital and Pastoral Labour 1840–1890* (St Lucia, University of Queensland Press, 1988), Part 1.

19.   For a recent in-depth critique of the now extensive literature on Islander labour in Queensland, see Tom Brass's review article, 'Contextualising Sugar Production in Nineteenth-Century Queensland', *Slavery & Abolition*, vol. 15, no. 1 (April 1994), pp. 100–17. The work reviewed is Adrian Graves, *Cane and Labour: The Political Economy of the Queensland Sugar Industry 1862–1905* (Edinburgh, Edinburgh University Press, 1993). For the question of 'unfree' labour in Queensland more generally, see Kay Saunders, *Workers in Bondage: The Origins and Bases of Unfree Labour in Queensland* (St Lucia, University of Queensland Press, 1982).

20.   For Mauritius (and the Mascarene Islands more generally) see: Marina Carter, 'The Transition from Slave to Indentured Labour in Mauritius', *Slavery & Abolition*, vol. 14, no. 1 (1993), pp. 114–30; Marina Carter and Hubert Gerbeau, 'Covert Slaves and Coveted Coolies in the Early Nineteenth-Century Mascareignes' in W.G. Clarence-Smith (ed.), *The Economics of the Indian Ocean Slave Trade in the Nineteenth Century* (London, Frank Cass, 1989); Nigel Worden, 'Diverging Histories: Slavery and its Aftermath in the Cape Colony and Mauritius', *South African Historical Journal*, vol. 27 (1992), pp. 3–25. For the Cape Colony, see: Andrew Bank, *The Decline of Urban Slavery at the Cape, 1806 to 1843* (Cape Town, University of Cape Town Communications no. 21, 1991); Clifton C. Crais, *White Supremacy and Black Resistance in Pre-Industrial South Africa: The Making of the Colonial Order in the*

Eastern Cape, 1770–1865 (Cambridge, Cambridge University Press, 1992); Elizabeth A. Eldredge and Fred Morton (eds), *Slavery in South Africa: Captive Labour on the Dutch Frontier* (Boulder and Oxford, Westview Press, 1994); Patrick Harries, 'Slavery, Social Incorporation and Surplus Extraction: The Nature of Free and Unfree Labour in South-East Africa', *Journal of African History*, vol. 22 (1981), pp. 309–31; Robert Ross, 'Emancipation and the Economy of the Cape Colony', *Slavery & Abolition*, vol. 14, no. 1 (1989), pp. 131–48; R.L. Watson, *The Slave Question: Liberty and Property in South Africa* (Hanover, University Press of New England, 1990); Worden, 'Diverging Histories'. For the Caribbean, there is an excellent summary of the literature to 1992 in Michael Craton, 'The Transition from Slavery to Free Wage Labour in the Caribbean, 1790–1890', *Slavery & Abolition*, vol. 13, no. 2 (Dec. 1992), pp. 36–67. For an African–Caribbean–British perspective, see Michael Twaddle (ed.), *The Wages of Slavery: From Chattel Slavery to Wage Labour in Africa, the Caribbean and England* (London, Frank Cass, 1993). This is merely an indicative sketch of some of the more important recent literature in the field.

21. Gyan Prakash, *Bonded Histories: Genealogies of Labor Servitude in Colonial India* (Cambridge, Cambridge University Press, 1990). Two important recent collective works explore bonded labour in colonial India: Gyan Prakash (ed.), *The World of Rural Labourers in Colonial India* (Delhi, Oxford University Press, 1992); Peter Robb (ed.), *Dalit Movements and the Meanings of Labour* (Delhi and Oxford, Oxford University Press, 1993). These two works in turn reveal, through the works their authors cite, a massive and impressive recent South Asianist literature on 'free' and 'unfree' labour.

22. David Eltis, 'Labour and Coercion in the English Atlantic World from the Seventeenth to the Early Twentieth Century', *Slavery & Abolition*, vol. 14, no. 1 (April 1993), pp. 207–26. Paul Craven and Douglas Hay, 'The Criminalization of "Free" Labour: Master and Servant in Comparative Perspective'; Nicholas Rogers, 'Vagrancy, Impressment and the Regulation of Labour in Eighteenth-Century Britain'; Elizabeth Elbourne, 'Freedom at Issue: Vagrancy Legislation and the Meaning of Freedom in Britain and the Cape Colony, 1799-1842'; and Martin Klein, 'Slavery, the International Labour Market and the Emancipation of Slaves in the Nineteenth Century', all in Paul E. Lovejoy and Nicholas Rogers (eds), *Unfree Labour in the Development of the Atlantic World*, special issue of *Slavery & Abolition*, vol. 15, no. 2 (Aug. 1994), pp. 71–101, 102–13, 114–50 and 197–220, further extend this important point.

23. This point for slaves is well made by Klein, 'Slavery, the International Labour Market and the Emancipation of Slaves'. The variable cases include the well-known one of Jamaica, where the plantocrats were so wedded to slavery that they refused effective imperial assistance to provide adequate alternative labour supply in the form of Indian migrant indentured labour.

24. Brass, 'Contextualising Sugar Production', p. 109. For more on this issue, see Tom Brass, 'Review Essay: Slavery Now: Unfree Labour and Modern Capitalism', *Slavery & Abolition*, vol. 9, no. 2 (Sept. 1988), pp. 183–97; also Clare Anderson's chapter in this volume. Kirsty Reid's chapter in this volume reveals that unfree labour might sometimes contest the redistribution of workplace power towards capital with considerable success.

25. Famously (and controversially) such were rebuked in E.P. Thompson, *The Poverty of Theory and Other Essays* (London, Merlin Press, 1978).

26. By Raymond Evans and William Thorpe in their important article (much cited in this book), 'Power, Punishment and Penal Labour; *Convict Workers* and Moreton Bay', *Australian Historical Studies*, vol. 25, no. 98 (1992), pp. 90–111.

27. See chapter by Duffield in this volume, notes 46 and 36, pp. 38–9 and 37.

28. Susanna Egan, *Patterns of Experience in Autobiography* (Chapel Hill, University of North Carolina Press, 1984); Roy Pascale, *Design and Truth in Autobiography* (London, Routledge and Kegan Paul, 1960); John Sturrock, *The Language of Autobiography: Studies in the First Person Singular* (Cambridge, Cambridge University Press, 1993).

29. Not literally, of course, but she is a strong candidate for an answer to the question 'Name one female convict transported to Australia?' She is one of the very few convict women who have an entry in the *Australian Dictionary of Biography*.

30. Ralph Waldo Emerson, quoted by George Shepperson in his foreword to Jagdish S. Gundara and Ian Duffield (eds), *Essays on the History of Blacks in Britain: From Roman Times to the Mid-Twentieth Century* (Aldershot, Avebury, 1992), p. ix. We understand Emerson's metaphor as especially apt for the parochialism masquerading as universalism of much Western history.

31. Ruth Brown, chapter in this volume, p. 79.

32. Thomas Keneally, *The Playmaker* (London, Hodder and Stoughton, 1987); Timberlake Wertenbaker, *Our Country's Good* (London, Methuen Drama, 1991).

33. Jean-François Lyotard, *The Postmodern Condition; A Report on Knowledge* (Minneapolis, University of Minnesota Press, 1988); Lyotard, *The Differend: Phrases in Dispute* (Manchester, Manchester University Press, 1988); Fredric Jameson, 'Marxism and Historicism' in Jameson, *The Ideologies of Theory: Essays, 1971–1986*, vol. 2, *Syntax of History* (London, Routledge, 1988); Benedict Anderson, *Imagined Communities: Reflections on the Origin and Spread of Nationalism* (London, Verso, 1983).

34. Ruth Brown, chapter in this volume, p. 78.

35. Ibid., pp. 81–2, paraphrasing Lyotard, *The Postmodern Condition*, p. 77 and *The Differend*, pp. 165–71.

36. On the grounds that only a limited minority of convicts were sent to such places; this position is criticized very effectively in Evans and Thorpe, 'Power, Punishment and Penal Labour'. Evans and Thorpe, however, do not join the many reviewers who have rubbished *Convict Workers*; for these see Duffield below, Chapter 1, note 13, p. 35.

37. Here, Maxwell-Stewart takes issue with Evans and Thorpe's 'Power, Punishment and Penal Labour', whose proper concern with power relations is allowed to preclude other functions of penal settlements.

38. Chris Shilling, *The Body and Social Theory* (London, Sage, 1993), pp. 8–15, esp. 8–11.

39. The contributors to this section generally follow the theoretical innovations of those who have applied a social constructionist perspective in relation to the interpretation of the body. Shilling, in *The Body and Social Theory*, rightly criticizes

those who see the body as a socially constructed object for perpetuating the body as an 'absent presence' in social theory. Thus, the work of Foucault and Turner 'ignores the *phenomenology* of embodiment' (p. 80). Indeed, with Foucault, the body '*disappears* as a material or biological phenomenon' (p. 81). The contributors to 'Classifying Bodies' might be open to such criticism, influenced as they are by Foucault. However, all four are extremely conscious of the physicality of convict embodiment and the ability of convicts to use their bodies as a means of resistance.

40. Here, we mean the vast accumulation and variety of what are traditionally called 'primary sources' available for the study of what are perhaps the best-documented ordinary men and women in all history to their time. However, in approaching these sources it is advisable, as Tamsin O'Connor points out in her contribution to this book, to bear in mind the admonition in James C. Scott, *Domination and the Arts of Resistance: Hidden Transcripts* (New Haven, CT, Yale University Press, 1990). For Scott, the 'transcript' of colonialism – its historical records – cannot be regarded as neutral. A similar point is made in Ranajit Guha, *Elementary Aspects of Peasant Insurgency in Colonial India* (Delhi, Oxford University Press, 1983), ch. 2; and 'The Prose of Counter-Insurgency' in Ranajit Guha (ed.), *Subaltern Studies: Writings on South Asian History II* (Delhi, Oxford University Press, 1983), pp. 1–42.

41. Lloyd L. Robson, *The Convict Settlers of Australia: An Enquiry Into the Origins and Character of the Convicts Transported to New South Wales and Van Diemen's Land 1787–1852* (Melbourne, Melbourne University Press, 1965); Shaw, *Convicts and the Colonies* (1966); Hirst, *Convict Society and its Enemies* (1983); Hughes, *The Fatal Shore* (1987); Nicholas (ed.), *Convict Workers* (1988).

42. Charles Rowcroft, *Tales of the Colonies, or, the Adventures of an Emigrant, Edited by a Late Colonial Magistrate* (London, 1843) quoted in Russel Ward, *The Australian Legend* (Melbourne, Melbourne University Press, 1958), p. 35. The general point is also made in Hirst, *Convict Society and its Enemies*, p. 107.

43. Rowcroft arrived at Hobart in 1820 as a gentlemanly free emigrant and left Australia in 1825; see C.J. Horner and Cecil Hadgraft, 'Rowcroft, Charles, 1798–1856' in *Australian Dictionary of Biography*, vol. 2, *1788–1850, I–Z*, p. 402.

44. Alistair Thomson, *Anzac Memories: Living With the Legend* (Melbourne, Oxford University Press, 1994), Appendix 1, 'Oral History and Popular Memory', pp. 225–39, esp. pp. 227–9.

45. All information on Gould was collected by Hamish Maxwell-Stewart. William Buelow Gould's transportation record was drawn from Archives Office of Tasmania (hereafter AOT), CSO1/217, 5237 and MM 33/1. We are also extremely grateful to Diane Dunbar, Curator of Art at the Queen Victoria Art Gallery and Museum, Launceston, Tasmania, for giving us information about the Gould painting.

46. Henry Allport, 'Gould, William Buelow (1801–1853)' in *Australian Dictionary of Biography*, vol. 1, *1788–1850, A–H*, p. 467, characterizes Gould as a 'confirmed drunkard'. Garry Darby, *William Buelow Gould* (n.p., Copperfield Publishing Proprietary Co., 1980), p. 15, states 'throughout his adult life he was a heavy drinker'. The first entry on Gould's conduct sheet – 21 Jan. 1828 – notes a sentence to the chain gang for 14 days for 'Being in a Public House called the Jolly

Sailor in a state of Intoxication after 9 o'clock on Sat'y night'. There were a further four charges of drunkenness and many more for absences without leave. See AOT, Con 31.

47. See Barbara Stafford, *Body Criticism: Imaging the Unseen in Enlightenment Arts and Medicine* (Cambridge, MA, MIT Press, 1991), ch. 4, 'Marking'.

48. Thomas Bock, *W. Gould*, n.d., miniature in oils in Tasmanian Museum and Art Gallery, Hobart; Gould, *W.B. Gould – Self-Portrait*, 1838, oil on canvas, 70 cm x 59 cm, Tasmanian Art Gallery, Hobart: for reproductions see Darby, *Gould*, pp. 81 and 112. We are extremely grateful to Hamish Maxwell-Stewart for pointing these similarities out.

49. Information contained in AOT, W.B. Gould file. His initial description from 1827 has been lost.

50. All definitions are taken from *The Shorter Oxford English Dictionary* (1983). One of the many definitions for 'yea' is 'expressing either vague assent or (more commonly) opposition or objection: = "indeed?"'

51. 'Shot', according to *The Shorter Oxford English Dictionary*, can have the meaning 'the reckoning, amount due or to be paid, especially at a tavern or for entertainment'. We would, however, reject the definition 'a corpse disinterred by body snatchers' as unlikely.

52. Hamish Maxwell-Stewart is quite right in pointing out that one of the more teasing aspects of this 'conundrum' is that if *Man with Pipe* was produced as a means of paying his tab we will never know whether it succeeded as a strategy! It is possible that the verse to *Man with Pipe* was added as an afterthought to the painting. It is quite feasible that Gould produced a self-portrait and later decided that it might solve a credit crisis – adding the words as the occasion required.

Part 1

Convict Texts

CHAPTER ONE

Problematic Passages: 'Jack Bushman's' Convict Narrative

Ian Duffield

In search of the narrator

'Jack Bushman', apparent author of this short, intense convict narrative, is evidently an invented identity. The text of 'his' *Passages from the Life of a 'Lifer'* (hereafter *Passages*) appeared in the *Moreton Bay Courier* (hereafter the *Courier*) in 1859,[1] shortly before Queensland was separated from New South Wales. As a penal station from 1824 to 1842, 'Moreton Bay' became, as well as a place name, a metaphor for brutality and convict degradation beyond that already signified by 'Botany Bay'.[2] Subsequently, 'Queensland' generated counter-meanings of a reconstructed and 'untainted' colonial history, excluding convicts.[3] In 1859 Brisbane, therefore, it was prudent to publish a convict life pseudonymously, for such lives were now skeletons in the colonial cupboard. Convicts were the pioneer colonial settlers of Moreton Bay, as of much of Australia.[4] The word 'pioneer', however, through an exclusivist socio-linguistic practice, is generally appropriated in Australian usage to the free founders of great pastoral enterprises and associated colonial fortunes and gentries.

Raymond Evans and William Thorpe, rediscoverers of this narrative, have identified 'Jack Bushman' as the convict Thomas Brooks.[5] He appears to have arrived at Sydney aboard the *Grenada* on 21 October 1819.[6] That ship's indents state he was tried aged 27 at Lancaster Assizes on 15 August 1818; received a life sentence; was born in Yorkshire; was a collier by trade; and was granted a ticket of leave in 1843, a conditional pardon in 1852.[7] This indent, however, records a collier while the narrative (chapter I) has 'Jack Bushman' abandoning handloom weaving for fly-boat driving.[8] Handloom weaving was then so depressed that many Northerners were adopting other trades,[9] while coalmining was then an expanding sector of the economy. Brooks's apparent occupational transitions are plausible.

Most Australian historians, however, have regarded the convicts as members of a deviant 'criminal class' who lied about their occupational history: through congenital habit, to conceal lack of honest work experience and to secure cushy penal work tasks.[10] Indent information on prior occupations, supplied by convicts on arrival, was crucial to their colonial labour allocation. Did Brooks lie then, on arrival? Minimal colonial demand existed for textile workers. In a colony lacking navigable inland waterways with towpaths, demand for fly-boat drivers was zero. Although coal was produced at the Newcastle penal station (also known as Coal River), Brooks had no obvious incentive to desire allocation to a place reputed harsh.[11] Positing that incoming convicts lacked information on colonial labour demand subverts their alleged manipulation of labour allocation, which predicates such knowledge. Indeed, like Brooks, many arriving convicts volunteered occupational information unsuited to such manipulative practices. Trades in scant colonial demand frequently occur in the indents. Conversely, many convicts admitted to being construction artisans or related specialist labourers, highly likely to be allocated to hard work on government infrastructure projects and their back-and-front linkages. Common labourers also abound in the indents; hardly an occupational ticket to easy street. Here, this chapter follows that controversial publication, *Convict Workers*,[12] whose curt dismissal of all work representing the convicts as 'criminal class' deviants earned hostile reviews by affronted scholars.[13] Nevertheless the strong scholarly consensus concerning eighteenth and nineteenth-century British criminal offenders finds them predominantly ordinary workers who committed crimes.[14] Dualizing 'workers' and 'criminals' is a false premiss. Workers commonly then lived rough, insecure lives in which opportunist crime could meet both necessities and *desires*.[15] Many were transported for work-related thefts,[16] a common practice, and to many workers evidently morally acceptable. From the early eighteenth century, proliferating legislation criminalized workers' older customary perquisites.[17] Denial of these was experienced as imposed wage cutting and countered by what the law redefined as thefts. Subversive plebeian radical ideologies articulated the connection.[18]

Thomas Brooks very possibly had been variously a handloom weaver, fly-boat driver and collier. In a rapidly restructuring British economy, such occupational flexibility was a survival imperative.[19] From 1827, from which time New South Wales indents of convict ships recorded greater occupational detail, all three of Brooks's occupations might have been listed. In 1819, recording only one occupation was usual.[20] Thus the discrepancy here between indent and narrative is explicable. Apparently the Convict Department, which was not noted for its gullibility concerning felons, believed Brooks had been a miner. It found a reasonable fit for his alleged coal-hewing experience. *Passages* (chapter II) places his first two years' service in Australia as at the government stone quarries outside Sydney. These produced materials for the capital's public construction boom, rightly mentioned as then under way. Sydney's government convicts were housed from 1819 in a barracks,[21] as this chapter states. With Governor Macquarie's departure in 1821, a harsher regime, geared to supplying the labour needs of wealthy settlers rather than government, was implemented by Governor Brisbane, following the recommendations of Commissioner H.T. Bigge.[22] Now assigned to much disliked private service, Brooks absconded and as a punishment was sent to Newcastle to hew coal (*Passages*, chapter II). Colonial records list Brooks as subsequently at Port Macquarie then Moreton Bay penal stations, again corroborating the narrative.[23] Further verification is offered by Evans and Thorpe.[24] More such verification could be pursued. It is not, however, necessary here to verify the narrative *in toto*. More relevant in pursuing the narrative's problematics is this broad hint:

> I muse over the strange story of my life, as Jack Bushman reads me page after page ... I have many stories to recount of the scenes I have witnessed at Moreton Bay, which shall be offered when opportunity offers for Jack Bushman to yarn with old Tom, the L f r [*sic*]. (*Passages*, chapter VI)

This reveals that a dialogue occurs in the text between an overt free bushman's narrative voice ('Jack Bushman') and its *alter ego*, a covert, resistant convict's narrative voice (Thomas Brooks). This device requires scrutiny.

Problematics of the 'convict voice'

For Evans and Thorpe, convict narratives 'amplify accurate, authentic convict voices'.[25] This pitches a higher claim for *Passages*' importance than empirical verification can. Verification through correspondence – convergent information from diverse sources – has its own problematics. Numerous older European sources affirm the Devil's bodily presence at historical actors' satanic transactions. Taken literally, this is now unconvincing but interrogation usefully reveals an historically meaningful *mentalité*. Likewise *Passages* requires interrogation of its ambiguities to extract its rich hidden meanings, not just pedantic testing of its positive accuracy. Evans and Thorpe implicitly regard *Convict Workers* as practising the latter in its representation of the convicts. *Convict Workers* contrasts an alleged dearth of 'firsthand' convict accounts[26] with the 'wealth of personal information' on convicts in its chief source, the indents of 19,711 convicts arriving in New South Wales between 1817 and 1840, and so claims to be 'history written from the bottom up'.[27] By implication convict lived experience, a kind of 'virtual voice', is extractable from indents. Hughes's book *The Fatal Shore* asserts: 'the missing element in most accounts of the System has been the voices of the convicts themselves' and proclaims itself uniquely contrary in this respect.[28] It is fruitless, however, simply to intrude the 'convict voice' within an historical practice that has marginalized it by privileging state archives and accounts by the convicts' superiors. An analogy is useful here. Most gender and feminist historians do not slot their work into a prevailing historical practice which assumes that male importance and female insignificance are natural features. They restructure the historical agenda.[29] Likewise, 'convict voice' history, to be effective, must contest everything resting on older prioritizations, especially where privileged sources, however carefully 'verified', are deemed incontestable 'truths'.

No boycott of state records or dominant class accounts is required. Evans and Thorpe, Hughes and the *Convict Workers* authorial team all use them, as does this chapter. Following Foucault, Evans and Thorpe's charge against *Convict Workers* is not its extensive use of indents but its claims that they reveal the convicts' essential nature. To Foucault, systematic state recording from the late eighteenth century of positive empirical data (such as on crime and punishment) created novel power/knowledge relations.[30] For him, such knowledge cannot objectively describe; it classifies according to categories of its own devising and empowers the classifiers. To Foucauldians, such sources cannot tell us who the convicts were *to themselves*, even if subjected *Convict Workers*-style to massive statistical interrogation. Indent data are not sheer fictions but neither are their instrumentalist privileging and ordering neutral.[31] Other charges made by Evans and Thorpe against *Convict Workers* need not concern us here. Their study provides, however, an unusually effective critique of the book, while properly conceding its importance.[32] They understand that to ignore Foucault's critique of the nineteenth-century state's 'authoritative' typologies, taxonomies and statistics, is to occupy an exposed position.[33] For them, *Convict Workers* is 'innocent of any analysis of ... power',[34] a charge hard to refute. Unfortunately, they are open to similar counter-criticism. They hail *Passages* as incontestable historical truth *because* it exhibits the 'convict voice', thereby exhibiting 'innocence' concerning the problematics of convict narratives. Nevertheless, their article, like *Convict Workers*, contributes valuable new understandings of the convict system.

Known examples of convict narratives are quite numerous yet the analytical literature on them, as distinct from empirical quarrying, is limited.[35] As a genre, they somewhat resemble those cheap, racy yet moralizing criminal lives, eagerly devoured by eighteenth and early nineteenth-century British readers. The best scholarly literature on these challenges the dubious authenticity claimed for them by their authors to boost sales.[36] Philip Rawlings highlights these authors' access to the capitally condemned immediately before execution. Confessions of those about to face eternal judgement were represented as *ipso facto* truthful, their biographers as amanuenses to the incontestable. Why should the condemned co-operate with these moral entrepreneurs, Rawlings enquires? He understands the tension between reader demand for salty detail and the imperative to provide moral uplift, especially among the many entrepreneurial clergy who were criminal biographers. He is interested in 'repackaging' of the capitally condemned's orature; equally of their rarer literature as 'even if the involvement [in authorship] of the biography's subject could be demonstrated, it is still necessary to consider the relationship between the biography and the life'.[37] He considers readers, how they read,[38] and in what sense these texts are either 'literature' or 'history'.[39]

By contrast, Evans and Thorpe counter-privilege 'Jack Bushman's' narrative, opposing an 'authentic' convict voice to the pretensions of official record power/ knowledge discourse and all scholarship reproducing it. Rawlings's cautions should be noted before following suit. He challenges belief in any clear distinction between 'fact' and 'fiction', aptly remarking 'the mediaeval belief that the world is flat was as true then as our belief that it is round today'.[40] Evans and Thorpe, however, appear to invite reception of *Passages* as empirical gospel truth. Such secular fundamentalism is methodologically flawed and surely unintended.

It is highly doubtful that Brooks was the direct author of *Passages*. The second sentence of chapter VI significantly states 'I muse over the strange story of my life, as Jack Bushman reads to me'. This instance of the teasing tension maintained between 'Jack Bushman' and 'old Tom' reminds us that many convicts could neither read nor write, or could only read. Others who could nominally write could only scrawl their signatures.[41] Certain artisan trades enjoyed high literacy rates. Handloom weaving's work process, however, did not require literacy. As direct producers, handloom weavers could normally only afford unpaid family labour, commonly employing their children, as in Brooks's case (*Passages*, chapter I), thus obstructing formal schooling. Brooks's literacy is a textual zone of silence. Nothing is said concerning maternal teaching of the alphabet and Bible reading, then common plebeian practices, or childhood school attendance; nothing on schooling in the hulks or aboard the *Grenada*; nothing suggesting opportunities in Australia to become literate. None, indeed, of the colonial work Brooks undertook required literacy. In all probability, he was illiterate, or functionally so.

Passages contains scattered dialogue representing English northern dialect common speech. Nevertheless, its usual style suggests highly literate authorship. Elaborate mid-nineteenth-century prose, larded with fancy literary quotations, predominates; circumstantial evidence of a bookishly fluent author, who had listened to and interrogated Brooks. The narrative's conclusion hints as much; 'may the perusal be productive of as much good as the spirit desires which collated them for the public'. This collating spirit is surely an interventionist author who, as in eighteenth-century criminal biographies, repackaged the tale. Thus a putative third and hidden 'voice' emerges, veiled by its fake authentication via seeming convict authorship. Theophilus Pugh, then printer and editor of the *Courier*, must be a suspect.[42] The sententiousness, elaborate sentence structure and self-consciously literary vocabulary of the narrative resemble much contemporary journalism. The narrative's conclusion, previously quoted, is a fair specimen. It beggars belief that these are the actual words of a rough convict and working man.[43]

Assuming Pugh or someone similar repackaged an oral account, then presumably this person invented 'Jack Bushman' to cloak both Brooks's and his own identity. The line between fact and fiction now blurs. Even if, against all likelihood, Brooks authored the narrative, writing is always interventionist for 'even if a writer attempts to describe something, the description will never be the thing itself'.[44] Self-representations require interrogation as much as any other. Returning to the more plausible alternative of a repackaged narrative, Pugh (or whoever) was no mere amanuensis but, as a (presumed) social superior and thus a patron-editor, intervened powerfully. The medium of publication itself imposed certain proprieties. The *Courier* had persistently attacked the perpetuation of convictism via the exile labour clamoured for by pastoral capital, and was *the* press voice in promoting the cause of a free labour Queensland Colony.[45] April 1859 was perfect timing for an anti-transportation standard-bearer to obituarize the penal past in the interests of its free settler constituency.

Here, comparative recourse may be had to slave narratives, of which hundreds survive, and to the formidable scholarly literature on them.[46] Slave narratives pose similar problems to convict narratives. Many slave narrators were illiterate. Their orature was converted into literature by 'sympathetic' race and class superiors, often abolitionist clergy. Even highly literate slave narrators, such as Olaudah Equiano, needed white patrons to ensure publication and distribution. These patrons wanted slave narratives that proclaimed humble gratitude to divine providence and white benefactors, not individual merit; that were long-suffering of wrongs inflicted and penitent for past sins, not resentful or rebellious. Repackaging created tensions between slaves' aspirations to autonomous liberational expression and these intrusive patronal agendas. Regrettably, studies of convict narrative have drawn little on the rich literature on slave narrative for methodology and comparative perspectives. Both genres could be understood variously: as sado-pornographic titillation; as morally uplifting accounts of salvation from degradation and sin; or, by black or convict readers/audiences, subversively, through identifying with the narrator's concealed liberational desires. Rawlings makes a related point concerning English criminal biographies. Drawing on Gramsci, he argues that 'it is the realisation that the texts may be shot through with contradictions which provides a way out of the difficulties with them'.[47] Convict narratives too are texts in which dominant class power is often both asserted *and* clandestinely contested. Hegemony seeks the assent of the dominated to existing power relations, not open battle. A narrative that simply vilified its subject would fail in this task; one which too openly expressed its subject's liberational desires would normally remain unpublished for the same reason.[48]

Identifying the main body of *Passages'* original readers is easy – the *Courier's* readership. The paper eventually triumphed over its less successful pro-pastoralist and therefore pro-coerced labour rival, the *Moreton Bay Free Press*, which was founded in 1850 and foundered in early 1859.[49] By 1857 the *Courier* had achieved a circulation of over 1000 copies, with three issues a week, as opposed to its puny rival's one.[50] It can be assumed that by 1859, most literate Moreton Bay whites were exposed to the *Courier*. *Passages*, therefore, had the widest possible readership (plus audience, as it will have been read to household groups and the less literate) for the time and place. In view, however, of the close political relationship between the *Courier's* first proprietor, James Swan,[51] and his fellow Scotsman, the Revd John Dunmore Lang,[52] the most formidable of colonial anti-transportationists, a core readership can be identified. This consisted of the small and middling free British immigrants, such as those who had emigrated to Moreton Bay, through Lang's efforts, on the ships *Fortitude* and *Chasely* in 1850. Such people opposed coerced immigrant labour (Lang's unholy trinity of convicts, coolies and Chinese) and were far more numerous than the big pastoralists and their straphangers. Despite unsatisfactory aspects of Lang's 1850–51 emigration project, the *Courier* defended him against his critics and his immigrants stood by him too.[53] Cryle has identified the *Fortitude* and *Chasely* immigrants as 'small capitalists, clergymen and low income families ... predominantly British dissenters', with family groups 'the prevailing feature of the scheme'.[54] One of the *Courier's* strengths, compared with the *Free Press*, was its healthy subscription income;[55] a reflection of its support among successful small and middling immigrants.

It is inconceivable that the *Courier* set out to affront this valuable core of subscribing readers (and advertisers, in the case of those who had successfully established businesses), by serializing over five consecutive issues an open apologia for the felonry of Moreton Bay. In crucial respects *Passages* catered to the ideological interests of these readers, while allowing them a ration of titillation by exhibiting 'deplorable' scenes of vice, degradation and violence in a safely distanced bad old days. The trick is just that of the hellfire preacher who dwells on the engrossing topic of sin to the 'shocked' delectation of the good folk in the pews. As will be seen in the following section, the narrative is redolent with respectable middle-class understandings of such juicy topics as proper and improper gender relations, crime and punishment, and the salutary role of free settlers in sterilizing the infection of Moreton Bay convictism. One can imagine the *Courier's* core readership nodding and musing 'how very right and true' when salivating over this tasty concoction. For these people, the convict past was not to be exonerated, still less was convict resistance celebrated; on the contrary, the convict past was best exposed as hellish and then buried. Had they thought of it, they might have drunk a toast at a public meeting, perhaps in a respectable non-alcoholic beverage: 'To History! The History we need, not the History we don't need!'[56]

Contesting gender, race and class

Embedded in its masculine social context, *Passages* sustains a trope concerning good and bad women. White women (exclusively plebeian in this narrative) are dualized as angels or devils; 'when the angel is taken from the home, the devil soon enters' (chapter II). The *only* angel is Brooks's first wife, his moral lodestone while alive and thence from the grave still guiding him towards virtue. Alive, she inspires him to honest toil, though only arousing such imperfect love 'as my mind was capable'. Her memory is a moralized metaphor of an idealized lost 'home'. Brooks's mother, by contrast, implicitly neglected the maternal duty of 'moral or religious training' (second paragraph, chapter I). This is represented as the doorway to Brooks's wrongdoing and so by implication devilishly negligent, a point many pious Dissenters among *Courier* readers will have picked up.

Widowed, the narrator makes thievish alehouse friends, the worst of whom is the woman he next marries, not for love but 'from a feeling I cannot now describe' (chapter I). This 'indescribable' feeling is certainly lust. Thus *Passages* dualizes sexual desire and morally pure love; devilish women arouse the former, angelic ones the latter, making male sexual morality women's responsibility. Soon, 'little stories of her inconsistencies' and 'old memories' (chapter I) are related to the husband by his new cronies. His second wife is represented, via such hints, as a nasty slut who has been, and perhaps still is, their common doxy. The formula matches a middle-class moral agenda within English criminal biography: that 'unnaturally' autonomous, sexually deviant women seduce susceptible men into crime.[57] When Brooks is on trial for his first offence, this 'devil's' sole concern is the whereabouts of the loot. In chapter II, reports reach Australia that her new child is not the narrator's, precipitating his definitive estrangement. Chapter V offers more devilish women, 'old hags of vice' in the female barracks at Moreton Bay, who corrupt comparative innocents into receiving garrison troops, including officers, for illicit night visits. It is conceded here that Moreton Bay's male convicts delighted in 'making "one as bad as another'" but the passage reeks of the gendered double standard, in which female depravity is far worse then male.

Various analytical strategies have interpreted such representations. Miriam Dixson accepted convict women's ultra-degradation but attributed it to their being 'victims of [male] victims'.[58] The narrative's meta-text concerning lower-class white women could be inserted into this framework. Likewise, Anne Summers could have utilized *Passages*' account of a female convict barracks operating as an army brothel, since for her, 'women were transported solely as sexual commodities and the British Government acted as imperial whore-master'.[59] Woman as devil or angel approximates to Summers's *Damned Whores and God's Police* duality. Dixson and Summers have accepted the empirical accuracy of the degraded representations of female convicts made by Lloyd Robson, Manning Clark and A.G.L. Shaw but offered impassioned pleas in mitigation. Their women are therefore largely powerless creatures, abused, dominated and despised objects of male desire. These views, however, whilst still influential, are contestable.[60]

A more sophisticated analytical stance occurs in Davidoff and Hall's *Family Fortunes*.[61] This identifies the origins, nature and operation of the ideology of femininity, as a British middle-class project of the late eighteenth to mid-nineteenth centuries, remodelling the proper relations and duties of men and women. *Family Fortunes* contrasts all this with the very different gender relations operating amongst workers and suggests that 'femininity' was defined through their negation. Middle-class 'feminine' women were segregated from the morally contaminating workplace. In the sanctity of secluded domesticity, they were to provide attractive moral oases to lure their husbands from the immoral enticements of the *demi-monde*. The truly feminine woman was supposed without sexual desire, a passive lightning conductor for her husband's sexuality, preventing it from striking promiscuously.[62] The doctrine of the two spheres — moralized, desexualized domesticity for women; worldly work for bread-winner men — displaced middle-class women from former roles in managing family businesses. The middle-class woman was to be modest, meek and temperate. For her, tobacco was now anathema, in contrast to the snuff-taking of fashionable eighteenth-century women. Her leisure resort to inns became unthinkable. The feminine woman would be deeply pious but passive in church affairs. Even her charitable activity should be under the guidance of male clergy. She would be a passive moral angel, recalling the representation of Brooks's first wife.

However, the first Mrs Brooks is ill-placed among her class superiors, for almost none of their proprieties was feasible for most working women.[63] Their male partners, through work-related necessity or irresponsibility, were often absent. Thus flexible informal relationships were commonly preferred, avoiding the costs of formal marriage and unthinkably expensive divorce. Such practices damned many plebeian women, especially those who cohabited sequentially, as whores in the eyes of their class superiors. Working-class women also knew that even long-term partners could guarantee neither adequate nor secure earnings to support family dependants. Their own earnings were therefore essential to personal and family maintenance. By entering the workplace, they were regarded by class superiors as morally tainted. If in their free hours they dressed in cheap finery for convivial leisure in street or tavern, they were considered coarse and again whorelike. Many working women smoked pipes; how unfeminine! Female criminal offenders were regarded as doubly guilty – of crimes against the criminal law and their own femininity.[64] *Passages* exhibits such middle-class negation of plebeian and especially convict women. If it is an 'authentic' convict voice, logically Brooks wholly shared these views. Such a position contradicts working-class people's pragmatic, non-judgemental gender relations.[65] Convict agency in opposition to official instrumentality concerning convict gender relations also disappears. Far more likely, in these matters *Passages* hawks a patron-editor's agenda which catered to the *Courier*'s core readers. Brooks may have supplied what he knew was wanted but this too would illustrate patronal power. Significantly, however, *Passages* reveals Brooks as, in reality, pragmatically content with an available woman, outside the angel/devil duality.

The account of Brooks's easy-going life with the Aboriginal woman Susey, after at last regaining liberty, is revealing. Whether the relationship is, by implication, sexual as well as an exchange of maintenance and rum for socially reproductive labour needs pondering. The text (chapter V) coyly describes Susey as 'faithful', which blurs the line between helpmate and bedmate. Brooks's relations with Susey are extenuated; 'if you had served twenty-one years as a slave, and six years as a ticket-of-leave man ... the contrast would take a favourable side for my picture, with the black gin into the bargain' (chapter V). Why extenuate employing an Aboriginal servant? Sexual relations between bushmen and Aboriginal women were an open white male secret but plainer speaking was tricky in a respectable newspaper. Through sly hints, knowing male readers might inwardly relish the implications, without affront to respectable family proprieties.

The relationship commences authentically through violence. White vigilantes shoot up an Aboriginal camp in indiscriminate retaliation for a petty theft (chapter V). Here, the narrative voice openly sympathizes with the Aborigines. Brooks and a workmate are saved by Susey and another Aboriginal woman from retaliatory slaughter, though two other white men are later killed. Mid-century, the region was indeed very violent; for example, in 1843 perhaps as many as 50 Aborigines were deliberately poisoned at Kilcoy Station.[66] In the same year James Demarr, travelling from Sydney to Moreton Bay, noted heavily armed pastoral stations and looked to his firearms for security from hostile

Aborigines.[67] Aboriginal women and girls were frequently abducted by white bushmen to provide coerced sexual and domestic services as virtual slave concubines.[68] Perhaps Susey's lived experience of such coercion was repackaged by Brooks himself as give-and-take consensuality. Either way, the arrangement evidently suited Brooks, yet Susey is represented as neither angel nor devil. This recalls the widespread colonialist representation of 'native' women as offering easy sexuality outside conventional moral boundaries, for white men.[69] To prevent sailing too close to the wind for colonial respectability here, chapter V veers nicely (the patron-editor at work?) by representing the bushman and his 'gin' as bush 'characters'. Impossible parlour guests for *Courier* readers, they were safely picturesque when framed in a distant bush scene.

Turning to other aspects of how Brooks's relations with Aborigines are represented, further problems emerge. A convict who frequently escaped from remote penal stations had reason to dislike and fear Aborigines. From early days the New South Wales authorities used Aboriginal trackers to recapture convict absconders.[70] Around isolated penal stations set among substantial Aboriginal populations, this provided one basis for frontier exchange. At Port Macquarie, in return for such services, Aborigines received blankets, slop clothing, hatchets, fishing tackle and, as incentive payments for 'meritorious work', alcohol and cash.[71] At Moreton Bay, Aborigines had strong reasons to dislike absconding convicts, providing a motive for tracking them beyond the rewards on offer. Under the ultra-harsh regime of Commandant Patrick Logan, as many as 330 convicts absconded into the surrounding bush,[72] a running intrusion inviting strong retaliation.

Penal station absconders lacking bush skills or guns and hunting dogs probably had little option but to steal food from Aborigines' camps.[73] Those who acquired bush skills — as *Passages*, chapters III and IV, indicates Brooks eventually did — might sustain themselves. However, in so doing they appropriated Aborigines' potential food resources. Unless offering reciprocal benefits in return, this too could provoke retribution. On 1 February 1825 Andrew Hynes, an overseer, escaped from the Plantation Establishment at Port Macquarie, with four other convicts. They took most of their gang's weekly ration, a musket, ammunition and some kangaroo dogs. The gun and dogs ensured effective hunting of large game. When Commandant Gillman first reported this event, these men, significantly, had yet to be caught.[74] The longer they were at large, the more surely they were killing game on a significant scale. The narrative's silence about such problems suggests production of a sanitized version of relations between absconders and Aborigines. As it was highly convenient for everyone else to blame violence against Aborigines on brutal convicts, Brooks himself must be the suspect here. Doubts are further aroused by *Passages*' account of Brooks's June 1825 escape with John Goff and others from

Port Macquarie.[75] The five Aboriginal police trackers who located the ringleaders, including Brooks, are not mentioned.[76] Attention is entirely on the horrors of being hunted and fired on by troops, who killed one convict and wounded another.[77] They would have found it far harder, unaided, to locate their quarry. On 2 February 1825, two soldiers plus a 'native bush constable' pursued six Port Macquarie absconders. This tiny force killed one escapee outright, mortally wounded another, while of the remaining four, two were believed killed or wounded. Such combined operations were literally lethal for escaped convicts.[78] These odds, however, confirm Brooks's determined pluck and growing bushcraft.

The account of his second escape, from Newcastle, acknowledges 'fear of the natives'.[79] Escaping later from Moreton Bay with a fellow convict, Charley Boggs, this fear begins to subside. Left alone by his inability to swim a river, losing vital bush kit in the attempt, Brooks 'expected to be used roughly' when Aborigines appeared. Instead, they retrieve his equipment, only keeping an axe (a reasonable toll), and show him where to cross safely. These people, and two Aboriginal women who later give him some shellfish, are 'hospitable blacks' not savage enemies.[80] During his most successful escape, which takes him to Sydney, he avoids whites as 'thugs' who might strangle him[81] but camps with 'blacks', now unquestionably trustworthy friends, and carries a fire stick, the indigenous technology ensuring fire for warmth and cooked meat.[82] By contrast, during his previous escape, Boggs had abandoned him; reunited and reaching Port Macquarie, they had been betrayed by false white friends. Portraying lack of honour among thieves might have its uses for the patron-editor but the text also subverts the colonial image of Aborigines as treacherous. The narrator's friend Banks, tried for the June 1825 Port Macquarie outbreak alongside John Goff and Brooks himself, is reported as eventually escaping to live for 14 years among Aborigines, at last to be shot dead by whites 'out after the blacks', who mistook him for one.[83] This intensifies the unfolding representation of Aborigines as trustworthy and humane, whites as bloody-handed and treacherous. Eventually, the narrator openly embraces Aboriginal society:

> I have plenty of work, do not know what it is to want for food, drink or money, have plenty of blackfellows who are pleased to serve me, because I always perform what I promise them; and for aught I know, my life will conclude in the same society, as that I have chosen from gratitude for having a life preserved, which to many, may not appear to be worth keeping.[84]

Is this the subversive outburst of an outcast, aware that the 'convict stain' permanently excludes him from respectable settler society? Or does it insinuate that a transported felon is only fit company for 'savages'? Depending on a colonial reader's social position, it could be read either way, creating a meaningful tension. We may reasonably surmise that the former was Brooks's view, the latter his patron-editor's.

Consider the opening of the narrative's final chapter: 'I had thought to finish. It is Saturday night. In front of the bark hut the place has been swept by Susey, and the fire burns brightly.'[85] This is not reporting an event but imagining a scene. Firelight, an image of flickering, transient life, is surrounded by night, an image of looming death.[86] We may suppose that the narrative voice, here patently neither that of Brooks nor Jack Bushman, symbolically 'thought to finish' more than an individual convict life; the entire 'convict stain' is implicitly encompassed. The valediction simultaneously embraces Susey, her people and their culture. The two great impediments to colonial 'progress', Aborigines and convicts, are yoked in doom. Nor is this conjunction unique in Australian writing of the period. In 1858, the Tasmanian historian Bonwick wrote, of the convicts:

> They will no more advance with progressive civilization than the blanketed Aborigine. Like the men of the woods they are rapidly dying off. A new and another race are elbowing them off the stage.[87]

Through such tropes, the worst of colonial crimes could be consigned to future oblivion in the 'Great Australian Silence'.[88]

Conclusions

Many other meaningful contradictions and contestations in this narrative might be explored in a longer study. Subversion, however, is always contained. The narrative's opening firmly states 'I am not about to paint myself an angel, or quarrel with the laws which drove me out from my country'. It closes 'if the life I have led has not taught me ought else, it has made me feel how sweet a thing is liberty ... people are foolish to risk its loss through dishonesty'. These carefully placed dykes surely reassured respectable *Courier* readers. As if threatened by the turbulent pressure in between them from horrific descriptions of brutal punishments, colonial respectability's defences are periodically reinforced. One instance concerns flogging at Moreton Bay: 'it was absolutely requisite for the proper observance of order, that there should be some severe ordeal, through which transgressors should pass; so that others might be taught the danger of disobedience'.[89] Here is patron-editor prose with a vengeance, the sentiment stiffling any 'convict voice'.

Nevertheless, this theme is quite soon followed by a powerful metaphor for liberty killed by cruel tyranny. A noble tree, now dead and its very stump gone, is recalled. On its trunk wretches were formerly flogged to the bone, the lashes also destroying the bark and killing the tree. That Pugh, or whoever, wrote this impassioned stuff to reproduce a convict's subversive agenda is wildly unlikely. Repackaging, however, is indicated by what immediately precedes it; 'the place was fast verging into a Pandemonium, when fortune sent a few free pioneers who cared for the observances of religion and morality, and these became the salt which prevented the putrefaction from extension'.[90] Here, the meaning of the word 'pioneers' is as earlier glossed and the infected penal past negatively defines the disinfected bourgeois future. A middle-class agenda rides the mark on Brooks's subversive resentments and it is noticeable that in this manoeuvre even the *Courier's* old feuds against the big pastoralists are forgotten.

Far from amplifying the 'convict voice', the narrative muffles it in an exercise of unequal power relations. Nevertheless, Evans and Thorpe do not hallucinate. Brooks's voice can be heard, if less distinctly and more intermittently than they suppose. Convict narratives can normally hardly offer more. We need not give thanks here for small mercies. *Passages* is contradictorily invaluable as both a telling instance of the anti-transportation agenda of the colonial middle class[91] and a cry of lived convict experience. The resulting tensions make it vivid. For historians of power relations, such understandings of convict narratives should enhance, rather than diminish, their importance. It is therefore hoped that this essay will serve to forward, if in a modified way, rather than to undermine the valuable work of Evans and Thorpe.[92]

Notes

1. See *Moreton Bay Courier*, 2, 9, 16, 23 and 30 April 1859.
2. e.g. in the ballad variously known as 'Moreton Bay', 'The Convict's Lament' and 'The Convict's Arrival'; see Bob Reece, 'Frank the Poet' in Bob Reece (ed.), *Exiles from Erin: Convict Lives in Ireland and Australia* (Basingstoke, Macmillan Academic and Professional Ltd, 1991), pp. 171–2.
3. See Tamsin O'Connor, 'Power and Punishment: The Limits of Resistance; The Moreton Bay Penal Settlement 1824–1842', BA (Hons) thesis, University of Queensland (1994), esp. ch. 1 and 'Conclusion', and her chapter in this volume, 'A Zone of Silence: Queensland's Convicts and the Historiography of Moreton Bay'. For the same process in Van Diemen's Land, see Henry Reynolds, '"That Hated Stain": The Aftermath of Transportation in Tasmania', *Historical Studies*, vol. 14, no. 53 (1969), pp. 19–31.
4. Even Lloyd Robson's influential *The Convict Settlers of Australia: An Enquiry into the Origin and Character of the Convicts Transported to New South Wales and Van Diemen's Land 1787–1852* (Carlton, Victoria, Melbourne University Press, 1965),

hostile as it is to the convicts, acknowledges 'the importance of the convicts to Australia's development' (p. 3), as implied by the title.

5. R. Evans and W. Thorpe, 'Power, Punishment and Penal Labour: *Convict Workers and Moreton Bay', Australian Historical Studies*, vol. 25, no. 98 (April 1992), pp. 90–111, esp. pp. 95, 98–100, 103 and 108.

6. *Passages*, ch. II, opening sentence, indicates the ship as the *G—*, embarking from Sheerness in 1818 with 262 convicts aboard. Evans and Thorpe, 'Power, Punishment and Penal Labour', p. 98, accepts that Brooks was 'sent to Australia in 1818'. However, no convict ship embarked from Sheerness bound for Sydney in 1818. Of the two convict ships whose name began with a 'G' which embarked from the United Kingdom for Sydney in 1818, the *Guildford* sailed from Cork while the *General Stewart* sailed from Portsmouth and had no convict aboard with a name remotely resembling Thomas Brooks; see Charles Bateson, *The Convict Ships, 1787–1868* (Glasgow, Brown, Son and Ferguson, 1959), pp. 342–3 and indents of the *General Stewart*, in Archives Office of New South Wales (henceforth AONSW), AO Fiche 640, Bound Indents 1818–1819, commencing p. 213. Two ships did embark from Sheerness for Sydney in 1819, but they were the *Surrey* and the *Lord Sidmouth*. Fortunately, a Thomas Brooke occurs in the indents of the *Grenada, 1819*; in later New South Wales records (see note 23 below), this man's name is given as Thomas Brooks. Brooke/Brooks is well within the common range of variation in recording convicts' names in New South Wales records. No Thomas Brooke (by whatever ship arriving in any year) occurs in either the NSW *General Muster 1822* or the *Census of New South Wales November 1828*, cited in note 23 below. We may, therefore, be reasonably confident that the Thomas Brooke aboard the *Grenada* in 1819 is the same man as Thomas Brooks, especially as so many other aspects of Thomas Brooks's verifiable career in New South Wales fit the narrative. *Passages*, however, is in error in stating that Brooks's convict ship carried 262 convicts: the *Grenada* embarked with 152 convicts, all of whom survived the voyage; see Bateson, *The Convict Ships*, p. 383. Neither Bateson nor the indents of the *Grenada* record its port of embarkation, a point on which it is safe to accept *Passages* as authoritative since it was a matter Brooks could hardly forget.

7. AONSW, Sydney, AO fiche 642, *Bound Indents 1818–1819*, entry for Thomas Brooke, *per Grenada* (1), arrived Sydney from England 21 October 1819, p. 409.

8. Fly-boats were specialist barges which provided (relatively) swifter transit of goods on inland waterways; the 'driver' managed the tow-horse.

9. Among works concerned with handloom weavers during the Industrial Revolution are: Duncan Bythell, *The Handloom Weavers: A Study of the English Cotton Industry* (London, Cambridge University Press, 1969); Edwin Hopgood, *A History of the Lancashire Cotton Industry and the Amalgamated Weavers' Association* (Manchester, Amalgamated Weavers' Association, 1969); R. Houston and K. Snell, 'Proto-industrialization? Cottage Industry, Social Change and Industrialization', *Historical Journal*, vol. 27 (1984), pp. 473–92; Norman Murray, *The Scottish Handloom Weavers, 1790–1850: A Social History* (Edinburgh, Donald, 1978).

10. e.g.: Robson, *The Convict Settlers of Australia*; A.G.L. Shaw, *Convicts and the Colonies: A Study of Penal Transportation from Great Britain and Ireland to Other Parts*

of the British Empire (London, Faber, 1966); C.M.H. Clark, 'The Origins of the Convicts Transported to Eastern Australia, 1787–1852', *Historical Studies*, vol. 7, nos 26 and 27 (1956), pp. 121–35 and 314–27; J.B. Hirst, *Convict Society and its Enemies: A History of Early New South Wales* (Sydney, George Allen and Unwin, 1983); Robert Hughes, *The Fatal Shore: A History of the Transportation of Convicts to Australia, 1787–1868* (London, Collins Harvill, 1987); Portia Robinson, *The Women of Botany Bay: A Reinterpretation of the Role of Women in the Origins of Australian Society* (North Ryde, Macquarie Library, 1988); Ralph Shlomowitz, 'Convict Workers: A Review Article', *Australian Economic History Review*, vol. 30, no. 2 (1990), pp. 67–88. The more recent studies listed here regard Robson, Shaw and Clark as indisputable on convict deviancy, mendacity and cunning.

11. For a negative portrayal of the regime at Newcastle, see Hughes, *The Fatal Shore*, pp. 433–8. However, Hamish Maxwell-Stewart, '*Convict Workers*, "Penal Labour" and Sarah Island: Life at Macquarie Harbour, 1822–1834' in this volume, reveals that ultra-harshness, although certainly a feature, was not the total reality of even the most notorious penal stations.

12. Stephen Nicholas (ed.), *Convict Workers: Reinterpreting Australia's Past* (Cambridge, Cambridge University Press, 1988), esp. Stephen Nicholas and Peter R. Shergold, ch. 5, 'Convicts as Workers'.

13. See A. Davidson, 'A Review of Convict Workers', *Australian Historical Studies*, vol. 24 (1989), pp. 480–1; J.B. Hirst, 'Convict Past Divides Historians', *The Age*, 21 Feb. 1989, p. 18 and 'Convicts and Crime', *Overland*, no. 113 (Dec. 1988), pp. 81–3; Stuart Macintyre, review article, *London Review of Books*, vol. 11, no. 18 (Sept. 1989), pp. 81–3; Portia Robinson, 'Getting a Nation's Record Straight?', *The Age – Arts and Books*, 21 Jan. 1989, p. 14; A.G.L. Shaw, 'Review of Convict Workers', *Victorian Historical Magazine*, no. 61 (May 1990), pp. 77–8; Ralph Shlomowitz, 'Convict Workers' (1990) and 'Convict Transportees: Casual or Professional Criminals?', *Australian Economic History Review*, vol. XXXI, no. 2 (Sept. 1991), pp. 106–8; F.B. Smith, 'Beyond the Uninviting Shore', *Times Literary Supplement*, 9–15 March 1990, pp. 261–2. N.G. Butlin, *Forming a Colonial Economy: Australia, 1810–1850* (Cambridge, Cambridge University Press, 1994), Part II, ch. 4, pp. 47–50, utilizes both Robson's and Nicholas's work on convicts' skills and work experience, but cautiously inclines to Nicholas whose sampling method he preferred.

14. e.g. J.M. Beattie, *Crime and the Courts in England, 1660–1800* (Oxford, Clarendon, 1986) and 'The Pattern of Crime in England 1600–1800', *Past and Present*, vol. 62 (1974), pp. 47–95; V.A.C. Gatrell, *Crime and the Law: The Social History of Crime in Europe Since 1500* (London, Europa 1980) and *The Hanging Tree: Execution and the English People, 1770–1868* (Oxford, Oxford University Press, 1994); D. Hay *et al.*, *Albion's Fatal Tree: Crime and Society in Eighteenth Century England* (London, Allen Lane, 1975); David Jones, *Crime, Protest, Community and Police in Nineteenth Century England* (London, Routledge and Kegan Paul, 1982); David Philips, *Crime and Authority in Victorian England: The Black Country, 1835–1860* (London, Croom Helm, 1977) and 'Crime, Law and Punishment in the Industrial Revolution' in Patrick O'Brien and Roland Quinault (eds), *The Industrial Revolution and British Society* (Cambridge, Cambridge University Press, 1993), pp. 156–82; Peter

Linebaugh, *The London Hanged: Crime and Civil Society in the Eighteenth Century* (London, Allen Lane, Penguin Press, 1991); George Rudé, *Criminal and Victim: Crime and Civil Society in Early Nineteenth Century England* (Oxford, Clarendon Press, 1985).

15. This point is extensively developed in Kirsty Reid, 'Work, Sexuality and Resistance; The Convict Women of Van Diemen's Land, 1820–1839', PhD thesis, University of Edinburgh (1995), chs 2 and 3.

16. Nicholas, *Convict Workers*, pp. 63–5 and 89. This is broadly supported by the studies cited in note 14 above, and by Reid, 'Work, Sexuality and Resistance' and Deborah Oxley, 'Convict Maids', PhD thesis, University of New South Wales (1991), also *Convict Maids: The Forced Migration of Women to Australia* (Cambridge, Cambridge University Press, 1996).

17. See Linebaugh, *The London Hanged*.

18. Widely discussed in Iain McCalman, *Radical Underworld: Prophets, Revolutionaries and Pornographers in London, 1795–1840* (Cambridge, Cambridge University Press, 1988).

19. See Eric Richards, 'Margins of the Industrial Revolution' and G.N. von Tunzelmann, 'Technological and Organizational Change During the Industrial Revolution' in O'Brien and Quinault (eds), *The Industrial Revolution and British Society* (1993), pp. 203–28 and 254–82.

20. Reid, 'Work, Sexuality and Resistance', ch. 6, identifies a similar change in Van Diemen's Land convict records from 1826, related to growing economic diversification and hence increasingly specialized labour demand.

21. Hyde Park Barracks, completed May 1819; see Hirst, *Convict Society and its Enemies*, pp. 41–4.

22. See John Ritchie, *Punishment and Profit: The Reports of Commissioner Bigge* (Carlton, Victoria, Melbourne University Press, 1970) and 'John Thomas Bigge and his Reports on New South Wales', *Royal Australian Historical Society Journal and Proceedings*, vol. 60, no. 1 (1974), pp. 12–27; Barrie Dyster, 'Public Employment and Assignment to Private Masters, 1788–1821' in Nicholas, *Convict Workers*, pp. 127–51.

23. See C.J. Baxter (ed.), *General Muster and Land and Stock Muster of New South Wales, 1822* (Sydney, ABGR in association with the Society of Australian Genealogists, 1988), p. 54, entry A 02229, Thomas Brooks. For Brooks at Port Macquarie, see depositions concerning the June 1825 convict outbreak there, AONSW, Clerk of the Peace, SC T131, 25/190; for Brooks at Moreton Bay, see M.R. Sainty and K.A. Johnstone (eds), *Census of New South Wales November 1828* (Sydney, Library of Australian History, 1985), p. 63, entry B 2453, Thomas Brooks.

24. Evans and Thorpe, 'Power, Punishment and Penal Labour', p. 100 and notes 24–5.

25. Evans and Thorpe, 'Power, Punishment and Penal Labour', p. 95.

26. Nicholas, *Convict Workers*, p. 3. The implication that 'retold' convict narratives are 'bad evidence' is banal. As for their dearth, the work of Evans and Thorpe, and Toni Johnson Woods, 'Virtual Reality' in this volume, should alert scholars to search for other forgotten narratives.

27. Nicholas, *Convict Workers*, pp. 3 and 45.

28. Hughes, *Fatal Shore*, pp. xiv–xv. For a critique of Hughes's claim, see Ian Duffield,

'Blockbusting Transportation', *Australian Studies*, no. 1 (June 1988), pp. 84–94, esp. pp. 86–7.

29. See J. M. Bennet, 'Feminism and History', *Gender and History*, vol. 1, no. 3 (Autumn 1989), pp. 251–72; L. Davidoff, 'Editorial: Why Gender and History?', *Gender and History*, vol. 1, no. 1 (Spring 1988), pp. 1–6; G. Block, 'Women's History and Gender History; Aspects of an International Debate', *Gender and History*, vol. 1, no. 1 (Spring 1988), pp. 7–30; M. Lake, 'Women, Gender and History', *Australian Feminist Studies*, 7 and 8 (Summer 1988), pp. 1–9.

30. Evans and Thorpe, 'Power, Punishment and Penal Labour', pp. 95–6. Important works by Michel Foucault on these matters are: *Discipline and Punish: The Birth of the Prison* (Harmondsworth, Penguin Books, 1982); *The Order of Things: An Archaeology of the Human Sciences* (London, Tavistock Publications, 1970); *The Archaeology of Knowledge* (London, Tavistock Publications, 1972); and *Power/Knowledge: Selected Interviews and Other Writings* (Brighton, Harvester Press, 1980). Evans and Thorpe cite the second and fourth of these.

31. e.g., the authors of *Convict Workers* do not ask why from 1827 indents recorded incoming convicts' prior occupations in more detail; see Reid, as cited in note 20 above, who does question why the same change in recording practice occurred in Van Diemen's Land in 1826.

32. '*Convict Workers* is arguably the most important book on convictism to emerge in recent times': Evans and Thorpe, p. 91.

33. Of course, coming to terms with Foucault clears the path for some informed contestation of his ideas; for an example, see the conclusion to Clare Anderson, 'The Genealogy of the Modern Subject: Indian Convicts in Mauritius' in this volume.

34. Evans and Thorpe, 'Power, Punishment and Penal Labour', p. 110.

35. Studies include: A. Conlon, '"Mine is a Sad Yet True Story": Convict Narratives 1818–1850', *Royal Australian Historical Society Journal*, vol. 55 (1969), pp. 43–7; A.W. Baker, *Death is a Good Solution: The Convict Experience in Early Australia* (St Lucia, University of Queensland Press, 1984); J.E. Hiener, 'Martin Cash: The Legend and the Man', *Tasmanian Historical Research Association – Journal and Proceedings*, vol. 14, no. 2 (1976), pp. 65–8; Ruan O'Donnell, 'General Joseph Holt' and Bob Reece, 'The True History of Bernard Reilly' in Bob Reece (ed.), *Exiles from Erin*, pp. 27–56 and 135–50; L. Hergenham, *Unnatural Lives: Studies in Australian Fiction about the Convicts from James Tucker to Patrick White* (St Lucia, University of Queensland Press, 1983) includes a study of *Ralph Rashleigh*, the transportation novel attributed to the convict James Tucker, a work which self-evidently blurs the lines between convict narrative and convict fiction.

36. See, for example: Linebaugh, *The London Hanged*, ch. 1, and Linebaugh, 'The Ordinary of Newgate and his *Account*' in J.S. Cockburn (ed.), *Crime in England 1550–1800* (London, Methuen, 1977), pp. 246–69; L. Faller, *Turned to Account: The Forms and Functions of Criminal Biography in Late Seventeenth and Early Eighteenth-Century England* (Cambridge, Cambridge University Press, 1987); and P. Rawlings, *Drunks, Whores and Idle Apprentices: Criminal Biographies of the Eighteenth Century* (London, Routledge, 1992).

37. Rawlings, *Drunks, Whores and Idle Apprentices*, general introduction, section on 'Writers and the Problems of Authenticity and Accuracy', pp. 4–9 and 16–24; for the words quoted in the main text, see p. 9.

38. Ibid., pp. 1–4.

39. Ibid., pp. 9–11 and 11–16.

40. Ibid., p. 12.

41. Male convict literacy is discussed in Nicholas, *Convict Workers*, pp. 75–8. Also see R.S. Schofield, 'Dimensions of Illiteracy, 1750–1850', *Explorations in Economic History*, vol. 20 (1973), pp. 437–54.

42. See Denis Cryle, *The Press in Colonial Queensland: A Social and Political History 1845–1875* (St Lucia, University of Queensland Press, 1989), p. 37.

43. Andrew Hassam, *Sailing to Australia: Shipboard Diaries by Nineteenth-Century British Emigrants* (Manchester, Manchester University Press, 1994), charts differences between middle and working-class emigrants' diaries. Were *Passages* not repackaged, its style should resemble the latter more than the former.

44. Rawlings, *Drunks, Whores and Idle Apprentices*, pp. 12 and 13.

45. Cryle, *The Press in Colonial Queensland*, ch. 2; for an account and analysis of the political economy of pro and anti-exile factions in the Northern Districts of New South Wales which were to separate as Queensland in 1859, see Jan Walker, *Jondaryan Station: The Relationship Between Pastoral Capital and Pastoral Labour 1840–1890* (St Lucia, University of Queensland Press, 1988), Part 1. Walker gives further rich detail on the pastoralists' recourse in these districts to ticket-of-leave criminal exile labour and bonded Aboriginal and Chinese labour in the 1840s and early 1850s, and the opposition to such practices from the mass of free immigrant settlers entering Moreton Bay.

46. Among the more important works are: William L. Andrews, *To Tell a Free Story: The First Century of Afro-American Autobiography* (Urbana and Chicago, University of Illinois Press, 1986); Houston A. Baker, *The Journey Back: Issues in Black Literature and Criticism* (Chicago and London, University of Chicago Press, 1980); Angelo Costanza, *Surprising Narrative: Olaudah Equiano and the Beginnings of Black Autobiography* (London and New York, Greenwood, 1987); P.D. Curtin, *Africa Remembered: Narratives of Africans from the Era of the Slave Trade* (Madison, Wisconsin University Press, 1967); C.T. Davis and H.L. Gates Jr (eds), *The Slave's Narrative: Texts and Contexts* (New York and Oxford, Oxford University Press, 1985); H.L. Gates Jr, *Black Literature and Literary Theory* (London, Methuen, 1984); H.L. Gates Jr, *The Signifying Monkey: Theory of Afro-American Literary Criticism* (New York and Oxford, Oxford University Press, 1989); H.L. Gates Jr (ed.), *The Classic Slave Narratives* (New York, Penguin, 1987); L.W. Levine, *Black Culture and Black Consciousness: Afro-American Folk Thought from Slavery to Freedom* (New York, Oxford University Press, 1977); P.C. Ripley *et al.* (eds), *Witness for Freedom: African American Voices on Race, Slavery and Emancipation* (Chapel Hill, NC, and London, University of North Carolina Press, 1993); Marion Wilson Starling, *The Slave Narrative: Its Place in American Literary History* (Washington, DC, Harvard University Press, 1988); J. Sekora and D.T. Turner (eds), *The Art of Slave Narrative: Original Essays in Criticism and Theory* (Macomb, IL, Western Illinois University

Press, 1982); R.B. Stepto, *From behind the Veil: A Study of Afro-American Literary History* (Urbana and Chicago, University of Illinois Press, 1979). Citation of the more important journal articles, essays in collective books and scholarly introductions to modern editions of slave narratives would prolong this footnote unduly. A complete scholarly bibliography would probably run to several thousand items.

47. Rawlings, *Drunks, Whores and Idle Apprentices*, p. 14; the Gramscian analysis continues pp. 14–16.

48. Exceptions are transported political offenders' narratives published for the USA, where damning British oppression, far from threatening, supported American power relations: e.g., William Gates, *Recollections of a Life in Van Diemen's Land* (Sydney, D.S. Ford, 1961; 1st edn, Lockport, NY, D.S. Crandall, printer, 1850); Linus Miller, *Notes of an Exile to Van Diemen's Land* (New York, Social Science Research Council of Canada *et al.*, 1968; facsimile reprint of Toronto, 1846 edn); John Mitchell, *Jail Journal, with an Introductory Narrative of Transactions in Ireland*, serialized in *The Citizen* (New York), 14 Jan. to 19 Aug. 1854 (reprinted London, Sphere, 1983). However, all these are as unsympathetic to ordinary transportees as Solzhenitsyn is to criminals in *The Gulag Archipelago*. Political offenders commonly regard being punished alongside ordinary criminals as the ultimate indignity.

49. Cryle, *The Press in Colonial Queensland*, pp. 30–34 and 36, sketches the rivalry between the two newspapers, from the founding of the *Free Press* by the pastoralist/pro-exile labour interest in 1850 to its collapse in early 1859.

50. Ibid., p. 36.

51. Proprietor 1846 to late 1859; see Cryle, *The Press in Colonial Queensland*, pp. 25 and 36–7.

52. For Lang's stormy career, see D.W.A. Baker, *Days of Wrath: A Life of John Dunmore Lang* (Carlton, Victoria, Melbourne University Press, 1985).

53. Cryle, *The Press in Colonial Queensland*, ch. 2.

54. Ibid., pp. 26–7.

55. Ibid., p. 36.

56. Based on J.V. Stalin's notorious toast 'To Science' at a banquet at the Soviet Academy of Sciences.

57. See Rawlings, *Drunks, Whores and Idle Apprentices*, pp. 22–3, 42–3, 81–3 and 113–17.

58. Miriam Dixson, *The Real Matilda: Women and Identity in Australia 1788 to the Present* (1st edn, Ringwood, Victoria, Penguin Books Australia, 1976; this edition, Ringwood, revised, 1984), p. 123.

59. Anne Summers, *Damned Whores and God's Police: The Colonization of Women in Australia* (Ringwood, Victoria, Penguin Books Australia, 1975), p. 270.

60. e.g. Reid, 'Work, Sexuality and Resistance', ch. 7, argues convincingly that Van Diemen's Land assigned convict women of the 1820s and 1930s exercised considerable workplace power. Robinson, *The Women of Botany Bay*, portrays ex-convict women as more often successful entrepreneurs than hitherto supposed and strongly engaged in family formation. Oxley, 'Representing Convict Women' in

this volume, also offers a strong critique of the 'ultra-degradation' school of representing convict women.

61. Leonore Davidoff and Catherine Hall, *Family Fortunes: Men and Women of the English Middle Class 1780–1850* (London, Hutchinson, 1987). Their views are used in Oxley, 'Convict Maids' and Reid, 'Work, Sexuality and Resistance', as a tool of interpretation.

62. Such representations must be distinguished from the reality of Victorian-era dominant class women's sexuality; see Penny Russell, '"For *better* and for *worse*": Love, Power and Sexuality in Upper Class Marriages in Melbourne, 1860–1880', *Australian Feminist Studies*, 7 and 8 (Summer 1988), pp. 11–28.

63. See article by Sturma, cited in note 64 below.

64. These points emerge from: Davidoff and Hall, *Family Fortunes*; Deborah Oxley, 'Female Convicts' in Nicholas, *Convict Workers*, pp. 85–97 and 'Convict Maids'; Marion Aveling, 'The Action of Gender in Early New South Wales Society', *Push from the Bush*, 24 (April 1987), pp. 31–40, and 'Imagining New South Wales as a Gendered Society, 1783–1821', *Australian Historical Studies*, vol. 25, no. 98 (1992), pp. 1–12; M. Sturma, 'Eye of the Beholder: The Stereotype of Women Convicts, 1788–1852', *Labour History*, 34 (1978), pp. 48–56.

65. See Alan Atkinson, 'Convicts and Courtship' in Patricia Grimshaw *et al.* (eds), *Families in Colonial Australia* (Sydney and London, Allen and Unwin, 1985), pp. 19–31. This fully accords with contemporary British working-class practices.

66. Henry Reynolds, *The Other Side of the Frontier: Aboriginal Resistance to the European Invasion of Australia* (Ringwood, Victoria, Penguin Books Australia, 1982), p. 84.

67. Raymond Evans, '"The Blood Dimmed Tide": Frontier Violence and Aboriginal Resistance' in R. Evans, K. Saunders and K. Cronin (eds), *Race Relations in Colonial Queensland: A History of Exclusion, Exploitation and Extermination* (St Lucia, Queensland University Press, 1975), p. 36.

68. For the violence and coercion suffered by Aboriginal women, see R. Evans, 'Harlots and Helots: Exploitation of the Aboriginal Remnant' in Evans *et al.*, *Race Relations in Colonial Queensland*, pp. 102–17; Mary Anne Jebb and Anna Haebich, 'Across the Great Divide: Gender Relations on Australian Frontiers' in K. Saunders and R. Evans (eds), *Gender Relations in Australia: Domination and Negotiation* (Sydney and London, Harcourt Brace Jovanovich, 1992), pp. 20–41; Ann McGrath, 'The White Man's Looking Glass: Aboriginal–Colonial Gender Relations at Port Jackson', *Australian Historical Studies*, vol. 24, no. 95 (Oct. 1990), pp. 189–206 and 'Born in the Cattle': *Aborigines in Cattle Country* (Sydney and London, Allen and Unwin, 1987), pp. 49–51.

69. See J. de Groot, '"Sex and Race": The Construction of Language and Image in the Nineteenth Century' in S. Mendus and J. Rendall, *Sexuality and Subordination: Interdisciplinary Studies of Gender in the Nineteenth Century* (London, Routledge, 1989); A. Stoler, 'Sexual Affronts and Racial Frontiers: European Identities and the Politics of Sexual Exclusivism in Colonial South-East Asia', *Comparative Studies in Society and History*, vol. 34, no. 3 (July 1992), pp. 514–51.

70. Paula Jane Byrne, *Criminal Law and Colonial Subject: New South Wales 1810–1830* (Cambridge, Cambridge University Press, 1993), ch. 5, pp. 141 and 146.

71. See Iaen McLachlan, *Place of Banishment: Port Macquarie 1818–1832* (Marickville, NSW, Hale and Iremonger, 1988), p. 85.

72. Eve Mumewa Fesl, *Conned!* (St Lucia, University of Queensland Press, 1993), pp. 43–4; Ross Fitzgerald, *From the Dreaming to 1915: A History of Queensland* (St Lucia, University of Queensland Press, 1982), p. 83.

73. e.g. The First Fleet repeated absconder, John Caesar, is said to have survived in the bush during one escape by menacing Aborigines with his musket, frightening them into flight and then taking their food. See William Bradley, *A Voyage to New South Wales 1786–1792* (Sydney, William Dixson Foundation Publication no. 11, 1969), p. 186.

74. Henry Gillman, Commandant Port Macquarie, to Frederick Goulburn, NSW Colonial Secretary, Sydney, 8 Feb. 1825, in AONSW, SC T21, No. 25/190.

75. This describes Goff as a 'half-caste lascar' – *Passages*, ch. II, in *Courier*, vol. XIII, no. 741, 9 April 1859. Though Goff was certainly black, no other source describes him as partly of lascar descent, nor is this probable in view of his name and origins; for these, see Ian Duffield, 'The Life and Death of "Black" John Goff: Aspects of the Black Convict Contribution to Resistance Patterns During the Convict Era in Eastern Australia', *Australian Journal of Politics and History*, vol. 33, no. 1 (1987), pp. 30–44, esp. pp. 31–2.

76. Contrast Duffield, 'Life and Death of "Black" John Goff', p. 33, with the account in *Passages*, ch. II, in *Courier*, 9 April 1859.

77. *Passages*, as cited in note 75 above.

78. See notes 70, 71 and 74 above. The convict settlement at Fort Dundas on Melville Island from 1824 to 1829 was not a penal station. Convicts were induced to volunteer to serve there by promised indulgences, not sentenced to serve there as a punishment. In many ways, however, Fort Dundas operated like a penal station. The constant hostility of the Tiwi people was a factor in the settlement's failure, although its military garrison attempted to protect convict work parties against Tiwi attacks and convicts were even permitted to bear arms for self-defence; see Hazel Marshall, 'Convict Pioneers and the Failure of the Management System on Melville Island, 1824–29', *Push from the Bush*, 29 (1991), pp. 43–4. This instance reveals how ineffectual the military could be in bush operations around a very remote settlement, when local Aborigines were uniformly hostile.

79. *Passages*, ch. II, in *Courier*, 9 April 1859.

80. *Passages*, chs. III and IV, in *Courier*, 16 and 23 April 1859.

81. *Passages* uses 'thug' here in the original sense of alleged Indian criminal devotees of Kali, strangling travellers for loot and as a sacrifice to the deity. The colonial invention of 'Thuggee' as a vast criminal conspiracy has been unmasked; see R. Singha, '"Providential Circumstances": The Thuggee campaign of the 1830s and Legal Innovation', *Modern Asian Studies*, vol. 27, no. 1 (1993), pp. 83–146.

82. *Passages*, ch. IV, in *Courier*, 23 April 1859.

83. See *Passages*, penultimate paragraph, ch. V, in *Courier*, 30 April 1859.

84. *Passages*, ch. V, in *Courier*, 30 April 1859.

85. *Passages*, ch. VI, in *Courier*, 30 April 1859.

86. The iconography here resembles those elegiac colonial Australian paintings of

small groups of peaceful Aborigines assembled by firelight at nightfall, images of the supposed 'dying race'. An example almost contemporary with *Passages* is Eugene von Guérard, *Stony Rises, Lake Corongamite* (Melbourne, 1857), now in the Art Gallery of South Australia.

87. Quoted in Tom Griffiths, 'Past Silences: Aborigines and Convicts in Our History Making', *Australian Cultural History*, vol. 6 (1987), p. 26.

88. See Henry Reynolds, 'The Breaking of the Great Australian Silence: Aborigines in Australian Historiography 1955–1983', Trevor Reese Memorial Lecture (University of London Institute of Commonwealth Studies, Australian Studies Centre, 1984). Reynolds, however, did not address the twentieth-century historiographical near silence that existed concerning the convicts until the 1950s. He could not therefore see this as, in some sense, linked to the silence concerning Aborigines. For a rich and wide ranging analysis of both silences as connected phenomena, see Tom Griffiths, 'Past Silences', pp. 18–32.

89. *Passages*, ch. V, in *Courier*, 30 April 1859.

90. Ibid.

91. For this agenda, see Hirst, *Convict Society and its Enemies*, ch. 4; Hughes, *The Fatal Shore*, chs 14–17; Jan Kociumbas, *The Oxford History of Australia*, vol. 2, *1770–1868: Possessions* (Melbourne and Oxford, Oxford University Press, 1992), chs 10 and 11; Reynolds, 'That Hated Stain'; Norma Townsend, '"The Clamour of … Inconsistent Persons": Attitudes to Transportation in New South Wales in the 1830s', *Australian Journal of Politics and History*, vol. 25, no. 3 (1979), pp. 345–57.

92. Despite interpretational differences with Raymond Evans and William Thorpe, I greatly admire their work, which both enabled and inspired this response. Raymond Evans, in a courteous private communication of 8 May 1995 to myself, discussed the possibility of a 'literary intercessor' in *Passages*, thus reducing the differences between us. My thanks also go to: Hamish Maxwell-Stewart and various of my Edinburgh students of Australian History for their critiques of an earlier draft of this chapter; Toni Johnson Woods for drawing my attention to Theophilus Pugh and to Cryle's *The Press in Colonial Queensland*; David Dabydeen, Polly Rewt and especially the late Paul Edwards for years of critically informed discussions of slave narratives. All remaining mistakes are my own.

CHAPTER TWO

Virtual Reality

Toni Johnson Woods

Introduction

Owen Suffolk arrived in Port Phillip on the *Joseph Somes* in 1847. He was a 17-year-old exile from Millbank, sentenced to seven years' transportation for fraud. Born in Finchley, Middlesex, in 1830 Suffolk lived a middle-class existence until his father's bankruptcy caused the break-up of the family. In an effort to relieve his family of a financial burden, Suffolk sailed to Rio de Janeiro as a cabin-boy. Unfortunately, upon his return his parents had moved and Suffolk failed to trace them. As a homeless child, he tried earning his keep in a variety of ways, including singing. Eventually he became a confidence trickster. He was arrested and convicted for forgery in March 1846. Twelve months after arriving as an exile in Australia he was convicted for horse-stealing. He spent the next 20 years in Pentridge, Melbourne Gaol, Cockatoo Island and the prison hulks *President*, *Success*, *Sacremento* and *Lysander*, for a variety of crimes, mainly horse-stealing and robbery-under-arms. He received convictions which totalled 27 years but served only 15 and held a ticket of leave three times. While in gaol, he bombarded the prison authorities with petitions and letters for his release and caught the ear of the then Secretary of Prisons, William a'Beckett. Finally in 1866 he was granted a free pardon. His unsigned autobiography appeared serially in the Melbourne *Australasian* (the weekly periodical from the offices of the *Argus*) from January to October in 1867.[1] By then, Suffolk had sailed for England (17 September 1866) on the *Norfolk*. How his life ends is still open to conjecture; all of the reports involve him in some crime though.[2]

'But in order to make you understand, to give you my life, I must tell you a story' writes Virginia Woolf in *The Waves*, adeptly describing the dual problem of autobiography: that of writers themselves writing it and that of readers reading writers' versions of their lives. The troubles inherent in self-fashioning have long been the concern of autobiography theorists. Writers may have power over their own narrative, perhaps even control over the evidence. So where is the reader placed? Reading the narrative offers the reader various positions between sceptic and believer. Perhaps none are more sceptical than readers of criminal autobiographies; a sub-genre not quite confessional and perhaps a little less honest than traditional autobiographies. An 'inevitability of fiction' occurs because writing is creative. Creativity interferes between the past recalled and the written word created. It is impossible for writers' perceptions to be impartial. Thus the writer's role is essentially that of interpreter and co-ordinator: in this process actual events become virtual.[3] Fiction, in other words, ensnares reality from the beginning. Roy Pascale suggests that 'we generally underestimate the importance in a man's life of his "life-illusion"' and posits that autobiographies somehow impress readers with their truth, though there are numerous ways in which they are not truthful.[4] Authors invite readers into their lives by establishing an intimacy. Autobiography offers seeming truth as its potent driving force.

Despite protestations of truth from convict autobiographers, their texts (like all narratives) are characterized by omission and selection. The criminal, nevertheless, has as much, if not more, to hide than the average autobiographer and thus omission often becomes a salient feature. Of course, this is not always the case. Foucault suggests that for pre-1789 French penal practice, scaffold speeches, embedded as they were in rites of purification, necessitated an absolute honesty.[5] Perhaps the moment before public execution did invoke such an honesty. The capitally condemned, however, by confessing their crimes immediately prior to death, may wittingly have played out their allotted 'theatrical' roles in a public ritual rather than recounting impartial truths about their offences. This process is further complicated in those convict autobiographies mediated through a third party before reaching the reader, due either to their authors' inadequate writing skills and/or their dependence on socially superior patron-editors to get their narratives published. Of course it is difficult to gauge the extent of such an outside influence. Ian Duffield has suggested editorial intrusion in Jack Bushman's story;[6] James Lester Burke ghosted Martin Cash's memoirs;[7] an 'over-zealous editor' stripped Jeffrey Mark of many misdemeanours;[8] and it is possible that Barron Field tampered with James Hardy Vaux's autobiography. James Hogan justified revising Jorgen Jorgenson's autobiography because it was 'written in a style that is both unfamiliar and unattractive to the ordinary reader ... retaining all its characteristic features, adhering strictly to recorded facts'.[9] Hogan seems unnecessarily intrusive – Jorgenson was literate enough to edit a newspaper in Tasmania. However, it has been claimed that the person who rendered at least one convict's oral account into literary form was no more than a faithful amanuensis:

it was taken down from his [William Derrincourt] lips, and that to attempt to tamper with it would be an injustice to the old gentleman, and, perhaps, annoying to the reader, as an instance of good material spoilt by incompetent hands.[10]

In the case of Owen Suffolk's *Days of Crime and Years of Suffering*, too, the editors of the *Australasian* claimed minimal editorial interference with his manuscript.[11] Nevertheless, approaching with scepticism a convict autobiography where authorship is known, proclaimed and verified is as essential as it is for those where the authorship is anonymous. No text is written in a vacuum, so Suffolk's tale is informed by generic, societal and literary constraints. As Paul Eakin writes in his introduction to Lejeune's *On Autobiography*: 'autobiography must be conceptualized not as some absolute literary essence but ... as historically variable, belonging as it does to constantly changing networks of social practice in which the life of the individual received articulation'.[12]

In the eighteenth century short criminal biographies abounded in Britain, as in the accounts by the Ordinaries of Newgate. In the nineteenth century, however, a new genre, the book-length convict biography, combined the sentimental with the adventurous and the didactic. In Britain before 1847 (the year of Suffolk's departure) only four convict biographies are known to have been published. In Australia, approximately six works had appeared.[13] Ten texts constitutes a small body of work. Therefore, it is no surprise that Suffolk's literary style mimics that of Dickens and Wilkie Collins — sensational, melodramatic and sentimental. Furthermore, it mirrors the journalistic style of both the time and the paper in which it appeared. Suffolk wrote within a romantic framework. His rhetorical mode is that of repentant criminal begging forgiveness of his audience for his evil ways while engaging their sympathy for crimes committed as a result of unfortunate circumstances — he is not of the criminal class. He had to fashion himself as a penitent criminal to ensure publication — the editors of the conservative *Australasian* would not have printed the story of an incorrigible malefactor. Thus Suffolk, like David Copperfield, constructed himself as the hero, albeit erring, of his own life. Yet in his self-fashioning, one can read a subtext which celebrates his misdeeds.

Examination of the three sources for Suffolk's story — his biography, the newspaper reports and colonial government documents — demonstrates the silence inherent in each. Collapsing the three, without privileging any, and writing in the gaps, constructs another 'virtual reality'. Suffolk was no ordinary convict (if such an animal existed). He rather debunks the myth of the convict as an undereducated, working-class pilferer of bread. His is a convict story replete with some of the emerging ideology of Australianness: hatred of the informer and authority figure; the myth of the romantic bushranger; and an admiration of physical prowess. Government documents reveal a brutally punitive system which, paradoxically, tried to treat Suffolk humanely. In the end, it is that which is left unsaid, the incidents glossed over or highlighted, which prove more illuminating than any explicit statement could have been.

Newspaper rhetoric: Victoria's convicticide

The threat of the reintroduction of transportation motivated the conservative *Argus* to maintain a rhetoric of terror. From its early days, it featured the latest criminal escapades in prominent positions, either in editorials or as second page stories (the first page was devoted to advertisements). Thus it made the public constantly aware (and scared) of the criminal problem. Victoria believed itself to be free of the convict 'stain'. Its attempts at 'convicticide' (killing its convict heritage) blinkered it to the truth. Howard Whittaker noted this blindness in his article 'Victoria's Convicts by Another Name' which calculated that 1727 convicted prisoners were transported to the Port Phillip area between 1844 and 1849.[14] Crime was perceived not as a local problem; rather it was imported, mainly from Tasmania. For example in March 1851, the *Argus* thundered:

> It will be seen by a case amongst our police intelligence of today, that some of the arrivals by the last trip of the *Shamrock* steamer [from Tasmania], have in the short space of a few hours after their arrival in Melbourne, made their debut at the police court charged with robbery. Is there not something radically bad in the system which sends to our shores almost daily such scoundrels as these? We do not get convicts direct, but our indirect imposts [*sic*] seems to be getting heavier every day.[15]

The *Argus* actually seemed to enjoy reporting crimes, which is exemplified by the following excerpt:

> It is almost gratifying that this second robbery has taken place, as it may prove the necessity of doing something immediately to stop the lawless career of the numerous criminals who are prowling through the country. It would not surprise me much if something be not done soon, to hear of some of the steamers or coasting vessels being carried off; in fact I would not be at all astonished to hear of the Banks in town being plundered some of these days.[16]

Aside from the sardonically gleeful tone, the writer utilizes personal intrusion (the use of 'me' and 'I') to create an intimacy which suggests that reader and writer are in accord. This much used rhetorical strategy creates an 'us' versus 'them' mentality and marginalizes and condemns the 'other'. Simultaneously, the reader associates the outsider with criminality.

Clearly, the newspaper reports were not entirely factual. Consideration must be given to the veracity of newspaper 'facts' in relation to the mood of the society at large and how it was produced and reproduced through journalism. The proprietor/editor of the *Argus*, Lauchlan Mackinnon, was known for his anti-transportation stance and thus his newspaper served as a vehicle for him to expound his ideas and influence his readers on this topic.

Despite the hue and cry over the dangers posed by the exiles, when Ian Wynd investigated this group in the 1980s, he uncovered only one convict who had turned bushranger – Owen Suffolk.[17] In 1851, the *Argus* kept suggesting that Suffolk was Codrington Revingston (whoever he was!), a 'notorious' bushranger terrorizing part of Victoria.[18] The *Argus*'s correspondent in Geelong aligned Suffolk with 'numerous criminals who are prowling through the country' in an attempt to paint him in the grimmest possible light.[19] But his own text disagrees with the newspaper reports. Both versions of events were embedded within their own rhetorical and narrational strategies: Suffolk's reivention as a romantic hero; and the editorial mood of moral panic over the activities of the notional 'criminal class'. Where the two strategies clash the most interesting sites for examination are formed. Mapping Suffolk's appearances in the *Argus* proves enlightening, especially as it published his prose, his poetry and his autobiography while vehemently denouncing what he represented.

Suffolk commanded what seems an inordinate amount of column space in the late 1840s and early 1850s. This coverage climaxed in 1851[20] with his bushranging escapades, subsequent trials and the printing of five poems.[21] It appears, when matched with his biography, that the majority of his court appearances were reported in the *Argus*. Upon his first arrest, it was written that the 'prisoner is a noted Pentonvillian and stands charged with several other crimes'.[22] One week later the newspaper added that 'there were other charges of horse stealing, and another of forgery'.[23] Court records document one charge of horse stealing – if he was charged for forgery it was mentioned neither in trial reports nor sentencing. The invocation 'Pentonvillian' is, itself, fraught with suggestion. Suffolk was actually from Millbank prison; nevertheless, the appellation 'Pentonvillian' had become common shorthand for the transported exile. Criminals thus labelled were represented as a public menace – they were young but deemed already wise in the wiles of the 'criminal class'. The word 'noted' conveys the meaning of a confirmed recidivist and infers a notoriety that Suffolk hardly warranted for his first Australian crime. In time, Suffolk's name became synonymous with bushranger.

Prison escapes were the epitome of convict transgression. The assumed violence of the escape and the potential threat to the public provided the ultimate danger. Naturally, the *Argus* reported these. Its favoured metaphor here was that of a zoo, a subtext which insinuates the irrational, treacherous nature of the convict by aligning criminal with animal. This can be seen in the description of the hulks moored in Hobson's Bay, which:

> held the worst desperadoes that can afflict society. Men hardened in iniquity, men whose whole career has been one succession of criminal atrocities, men almost sublime in infamy, men of brutal instincts, brutal habits, brutal feelings, brutal physiques and brutal passions. Men who add the cunning of the human intellect to the physical force and ferocity of the wild beast. Such men may be cowed and awed, but never reclaimed.[24]

Suffolk's escape in 1851 provided an ideal opportunity to illustrate how tenuous were the restraints that bound prisoners:

> One day this week ... the suspicions of Mr Ashley were excited by the unusual stillness amongst [the prisoners] at that hour; this induced him to search each ... on searching [Suffolk], Mr Ashley found some pieces of stone about eight inches long, neatly fitted, and bound together by a handkerchief, so as to form a compact mass; the ends of the handkerchief were artfully twisted into a convenient handle so as to form a very murderous weapon of attack in the hands of an expert ruffian; it was with a similar weapon, but less elaborately prepared, that the notorious David Haggart murdered the Dumfries gaoler in Scotland, some thirty years since. In reply to Mr Ashley's question, what he intended to do with this? Suffolk replied – 'To use it when I saw an opportunity'. As soon ... as Farrel, heard this [he] became quite outrageous, and would not submit to being searched but excited the other prisoners to resistance and violence. It required all the force in the prison, six or seven, to overpower and secure him.[25]

Note how Suffolk is aligned with a 30-year-old 'notorious' murder in Scotland. The fact that the paper could not invoke a more local (or more recent) murder suggests they were few and far between. Furthermore, on 28 March 1851, the *Argus* printed a paragraph on page 2 about twelve prisoners who were reported to have escaped from a Pentridge road gang two days earlier. Four or five of the 'greatest desperadoes' (favourite *Argus* term for convicts) rushed one foot guard, took his musket and threatened the mounted guard with it. Later the paper states that the captured Suffolk had 'avowed himself to be an absconder from the Pentridge Stockade'. No support for this occurs in Suffolk's court or prison records.[26]

Just in case the public forgot the human face of crime, the sufferings and injuries of victims were reported. The *Geelong Advertiser*, for example, ran updates on the failing health of a mail-cart driver who had been the victim of one of Suffolk's robberies.[27] Such stories, including this one, were naturally reprinted in the *Argus*. The emotive nature of this type of reporting reminded the general public of the consequences of crime, especially robbery-under-arms, and further inflamed its readers against the offenders.

After a while Suffolk's notoriety declined. His later criminal exploits barely rated a mention in the *Argus*. With an increasing population and growth in the press, he was downgraded to local newspapers, like the *Geelong Advertiser* and the *Ballarat Star*. Various factors could account for his eclipse in the *Argus's* columns. Firstly, his later offences were relatively unromantic (horse-stealing as compared with bushranging). Secondly, the growing population of Victoria generated more crimes to be reported and thus a metropolitan newspaper, like the *Argus*, had less space to devote to everyday country felons and felonies. Most important, perhaps, 'exile' transportation had ceased and the paper could now turn to other, more politically pressing, topics.

His-story: Suffolk as Lear, Count of Monte Cristo, Scarlet Pimpernel

From the first statement 'I am a convict', Suffolk tries to gain the sympathy of the reader. He positions himself outside society: both figuratively, as a criminal, and literally, as a loner. Furthermore, he writes that he sits in a confined area, imprisoned on a ship, exiled from his country, adrift on an ocean and thus alone and presumably unloved. But then he tries to establish a rapport by mentioning the books he has read, guiding readers to think 'this is no ordinary convict – he is educated'. Suffolk's rhetoric of intimacy persuades readers that they can read themselves into the text, so inducing a 'There but for the Grace of God' mentality. He then disarms with a confession that he writes for money, appealing to the conscience of potential philanthropists. He addresses readers in their 'happy home[s]' surrounded by 'loving hearts and fair faces'.[28] The reader is now in a powerful, comfortable position as pitying confidant.

Evoking a Lear mentality, Suffolk presents himself as more sinned against than sinning. He intimates, like many other convict narrators, that he would not have turned to crime if not for the bad hand fate had dealt him. His parents' desertion, the evil influence of other criminals, informers and his poverty are some of the expressly stated causes of his life of crime. His first crime committed on Australian soil, horse-stealing, was the result of working for a dishonest boss – Searle. Suffolk's description of Searle – as a crooked ex-policeman from Tasmania

– triply condemns the man. At this time, hatred of the gaoler's tyranny was collapsing into dislike for any authority figure, such as bosses or policemen. Members of the new police force were seen as little better than the criminals they were supposed to curb and catch. A corrupt policeman was, of course, the most despised. Echoing the *Argus*'s exhortations about Tasmanians, Suffolk manipulates Victorian xenophobia. His narrative alleges that he had to steal horses to escape the clutches of Searle and his unlawful actions.[29] Later Suffolk claims that his boss, while visiting him in gaol, tricked him into writing an admission of guilt, the result of which was a five-year sentence. The revelation of the confessional statement exhibits literary conflation of the highest order:

> To the hutkeeper at Mr Spring's Five-mile Station, – The horse which I left at your hut the other day, together with the saddle and bridle, is [*sic*] the property of Mr Scholes [i.e. Searle], from whose stable I stole them. You will therefore deliver them to him on his applying for them.[30]

According to Suffolk, the contents of the above note eventually provided the evidence which convicted him of horse-stealing. Fortunately the court file contains the original unsigned scrap of paper which reads 'I sold the horse of Mr Searle following description bay roan white saddle to Patrick Egan who resides in Ashby in a low roofed house whitewashed over. I received four pounds for it'.[31]

Comparing the two versions captures some of the tensions between real/remembered and real/constructed events. The most noticeable difference is the variation in style. The 'real' note is a bald statement devoid of literary pretence. Suffolk recrafted it into a more elegant and genteel version, in which the owner will 'apply' for his property which will be 'delivered' to him. The participants 'will' perform the recognized rituals of Victorian codified behaviour. Word choice gestures to a power hierarchy. Suffolk, in the recrafted version, instructs the hutkeeper 'you will' return the goods. The middle-class convict lords it over a working-class freeman (or possibly fellow-exile) and thus Suffolk asserts the authority of class. The original note does not state that he stole the horse, it merely admits to selling it without admission of theft. Overall, the revised note implies that Searle will regain his horse. Suffolk manages to construct himself in the most positive light possible.

Why did Suffolk bother reproducing the (reshaped) note at all? It was to provide a vehicle for reasserting the outside forces working against a man more sinned against than sinning. Although he repents his transgressions, when stripped of confessional rhetoric, it becomes obvious that Suffolk was drawn to crime by desire, not necessity. Even when, by his own admission, times were good and money plentiful, he could not resist a 'scam'. He was egalitarian in whom he stole from for he thieved from friend and foe alike. That he recounts these incidents says much for the audience: clearly he believed that they would forgive him if he were penitent enough.

Suffolk rewrote his bushranging episodes as moonlit escapades and fashioned himself as a hero of some dash and style. Consider the following description:

> At last came midnight. With it came the mail-coach, dashing rapidly along. Glanced the moonlight on the barrels of our pistols; mingled with the wind our sternly-spoken 'stand'; echoed to the wood a little scream; alighted from the mail five trembling passengers; cut were the traces; rifled were the bags; and thus, in a short half-hour, the mail was robbed ... The result of this nocturnal expedition turned out more amusing than profitable.[32]

His takings were lean, he was soon caught and the punishment was swift and harsh; however thrilling a midnight robbery might be, the highwaymen were not so smart, for the next day they could not cash their takings — the banks had been alerted. The subtext is that the reader is to forgive the robbers because they did not make a large profit. Night robbery is thus represented as more romantic than remunerative.

The *Argus*, however, tells a slightly different story:

> Between 9 and 10 o'clock, two men, well armed, and wearing masks, on foot, met the mail cart about half way between Cowie's Creek and the duck ponds, and called upon the driver to stop or they would fire at him. They then laid hold of the horses, compelled the driver to dismount, tied him with his own cravat, and led the horses off the road towards the beach, driving the mailman before them. Having tied the driver, spread eagle fashioned to the wheel, and also tied a female who was only a passenger to the shaft of the cart, they cut the harness: and took out the horses, then cut open the bags, emptied them out, and selected such letters and packets as they thought likely to contain money. They afterwards searched the mailman, and took from him his watch and a money order. Having mounted the mail horses without saddles they rode away in the direction of Geelong. Having extricated themselves, the mailman and the female passenger walked into Geelong, where they arrived at a quarter past one o'clock.[33]

The newspaper report is dry and pragmatic when compared with Suffolk's romantically narrated escapade. Midnight is replaced with the more mundane time of between 9 and 10 o'clock. Suffolk's inflation of the number of victims represents the robbers as the more courageous. How the two victims, on a dark lonely track late at night, must have felt, is not easily imagined outside such an experience. The driver, Mr Ross, suffered great mental anguish according to newspaper reports; only a few weeks previously, he had been shot during a similar robbery. The myth of the bush as a safe haven for women has been redressed by contemporary historians. So perhaps the soft-sounding 'little scream' from the female victim was more imaginative than realistic. The victims' long walk back to Geelong in the night reminds the reader that at the very least two people were greatly inconvenienced by the robbery. Of course, this may all have been exaggerated to inflame readers against Suffolk.

By romanticizing his criminal exploits, Suffolk places readers in the comfortable realm of adventure fiction. This device allows both female and male readers to admire him: the females for his romantic daring and the males for his physical prowess. As with robbery, this is particularly apparent in descriptions of his escapes which are written in a romantic, even humorous vein, designed perhaps to defuse the angst so easily aroused among respectable newspaper readers by accounts of escaped prisoners at large. Consider the following description:

> Police, Constables, there he is stealing the mare; quick — take him!' Very easy, said Mr Overseer; but the doing part of the business was not quite so facile a task. I was full of dare-devil, reckless spirit of the time and I sat my horse as statue-like as a dragoon on duty at the Horse-Guards, not attempting to move until the Constables had themselves mounted. Then, shouting out a defiance, I touched the mare's flanks with a spur and she bounded away with me at a speed which defied pursuit.[34]

It hardly 'defied pursuit': he was apprehended one mile later. The image of Owen allowing his pursuers time to mount and follow, insinuates what a fair bloke Suffolk was — then to thumb his nose at them reeks, in effect, of larrikinism.

Owen's escapes are thus retold in appropriately thrilling terms. He is resourceful too. In one police station, he 'went to work at my handcuffs. With some little pain and a great deal of perseverance I at last succeeded in getting them off'. Then he describes a comic scene as he flees wearing only his shirt, followed by bungling cops being bitten by their own tracker dogs:

> Now it so happened that Constable Morgan was bringing up the rear, and the 'good dog', acting upon the principle of the 'devil take the hindmost', made a spring at him, and brought him to the earth in a moment. The dog belonged to Johnson, and so Johnson had to turn back to bestow a few vigorous kicks upon poor Lion for the mistake he had made. All this gained me some little advantage, but my white shirt streaming in the moonlight

was very much against me. The constables kept shouting 'Stop him!' just as if they had been in London, but as the members of the vegetable kingdom 'have functional parts without possessing the power of voluntary motion', the trees didn't start off in pursuit. Still my fate was against me ... [35]

Suffolk is eventually subdued by three Aborigines. This carnivalesque description is a powerful rhetorical device which wins approval because it utilizes laughter to offset the criminal act of escaping. It also provides another opportunity for him to present a picture of fate working against him.

Elsewhere, too, he shows himself quick and resourceful, as when he flees from a court appearance:

> darted into the jury room, opened the window, jumped out, and made for the town but some non-official with a great zeal for justice mounted on [a horse], overtook me very quickly and ... ordered me to stop, giving me a cut with his whip to enforce the command ... I seized the fellow by the leg, and with a dextrous jerk threw him out of the saddle ... [in] a second I had seated myself in the saddle ... I reined sharp round, and made at full speed for the bush. [36]

In an anticlimactic outcome he is overtaken by a constable and 'quietly' surrenders. This bid for freedom is doubly thwarted: first by that reprehensible type, the zealous citizen, quick with the whip – a high condemnation in a cat-o'-nine-tails country; and second, the slowness of his horse. Scepticism of this account is, however, provoked when the newspaper account of the trial is examined: this spectacular run of events, which could hardly have gone unnoticed in court, did not even warrant a mention.

Significantly, the above escape accounts come in the middle of his story, a rhetorically important position because the narrative had begun to lag. Suffolk was evidently an acute enough writer to perceive this and inject some excitement accordingly. This technique is never employed for relating atrocious acts. Indeed, Owen clearly felt he had never committed any serious crimes. Thus, in an account of one robbery, by returning £5 to a passenger he had robbed of £2 only the night before, he recasts himself as a quasi-Robin Hood. [37] No verification for this philanthropy has been found, for the unidentified man failed to report the kindness. Whether he is a mere fictive device is impossible to know but doubts are aroused. Given the extent of press coverage which Owen received, the man would have had ample opportunity to reveal himself.

It was important that readers appreciated his hero status and thus Suffolk takes many opportunities to construct himself as a loyal mate to fellow robbers and prisoners. There is some corroboration of this trait. The *Argus* states that when in June 1851 he stood in the dock with Farrell for the Portland mail robbery, he 'boldly advocated the innocence of his companion'.[38] Exactly why he might do this is open to conjecture. Perhaps Farrell was relatively innocent and it was the third member of their gang, Harry Dowling, who was the active robber alongside Suffolk himself. According to the *Geelong Advertiser*, the judge remained unconvinced. In his summing up the paper reported that he ruled that Suffolk: 'solemnly declares that his fellow prisoner [Farrell] is innocent; but he has made no attempt to support it'.[39] Some passages in the narrative, too, serve to convey his devotion to the code of mateship, especially in hating 'dobbers' and refusing at all costs to 'dob in' mates. Instances include his fight in the compound at Cockatoo Island, when he battered another inmate because he had informed on a friend; and the infliction of 75 lashes on his back for refusing to reveal who had smuggled his letters out of gaol. Nevertheless, as will be seen below, Suffolk was, in fact, an informer himself when it suited him.

The pen is mightier than the sword

The Suffolk published canon is small: some poems[40] (unkind people may say poetastical verses); a few speeches (retold in his narrative); one letter (to the *People's Advocate*); and one autobiography.[41] This corpus, nevertheless, suffices to establish him as a significant literary figure among nineteenth-century Australian transported convicts, only a small minority of whom found their way into print. It was more than sufficient for Suffolk to consider and conduct himself as a writer. As Sturrock states, 'autobiographers write in order to proclaim their own ascendancy'. Owen Suffolk allows himself this privilege time and time again.[42] He often represents his courtroom speeches as gaining the admiration of those in court. In one instance he recreates at length what he claims to have spoken to London's Central Criminal Court. This, he proudly states, was reprinted at length in *The Times*. In reality, *The Times* reports that he remained doggedly silent throughout his court appearance.[43] These invented court speeches allow Suffolk to elaborate and embroider at length his beliefs. Far from being authentic reports, they are constructed self-representations.

Suffolk's education secured him a relatively easy life in prison. His penchant for petitioning, much to the vexation of some in the penal establishment's administration, extracted early releases. Certainly, it was his eloquence with the pen which earned him the favour of the then Governor of Prisons, William a'Beckett, who championed Suffolk's cause on account of the latter's literary skills. Suffolk even became known as the 'Convict Poet'. Sentenced to a cumulative total of 27 years, he served only 15 years 8 months. He was granted three tickets of leave, although two were revoked for misconduct. According to his own story he worked as prison librarian[44] and clerk. He evidently understood the power of the written word. For years he bombarded the authorities with petitions, memorials, letters of complaint and so forth. He divided the authorities into two camps: those who believed him worthy of the remissions he requested; and those who deemed his crimes too serious for his pleas to warrant special consideration. Finally, on 15 August 1866, almost as if the penal administrators were weary of his endless paper salvoes, C.H. Nicholson wrote:

> I would beg to recommend that he be permitted, at once to leave for England, on conditional pardon with the understanding that he is not again to return to this Colony, in which he is unlikely to be other than a most dangerous and undesirable member of society.[45]

This recommendation for, in effect, his deportation was implemented. It signally inverted the usual terms of conditional pardons granted to transported convicts, which stated that the beneficiary was forbidden, on pain of retransportation for life, to return to the United Kingdom, and must remain in the Australasian colonies. One can imagine the sigh of relief when the gaol authorities closed the Suffolk file.

Generally, Suffolk seems to have behaved himself in prison. Records show only three punishments at Cockatoo Island, all in 1850.[46] The first was 14 days' solitary confinement in the cells for neglect of work; next, the same punishment was earned for having a letter in his possession to send from the island; finally, he was sentenced to 21 days in the cells for fighting in the square. This does not, however, tally with Suffolk's reckonings. While on Cockatoo Island he claimed to have received 30 days' solitary confinement for fighting; seven days on bread and water and ten days' solitary for refusing to work; and, most seriously, 75 lashes for refusing to name the person who sent him a letter. As he tells it, each of the punishments results from his attempt to either shield or help fellow inmates – thus Suffolk writes his own part as a champion of the underdog. Refusal to work, it is true, would have been viewed by the prison authorities as evidence of stubborn criminal tendencies rather than the exercise of inherent political agency. The reluctance of prison authorities to record harsh punishments such as floggings is understandable but unlikely; and yet, significantly, no good convict yarn is complete without a flogging. The final entry for Cockatoo Island in March 1850 notes that Suffolk was due for a ticket of leave but had absconded with an illegal pass. He fails to mention the illegal pass.

Peter MacFie in his article 'Dobbers and Cobbers' gestures to the use of rewards to induce transported convicts to inform in Van Diemen's Land. Paula Jane Byrne has since found abundant evidence for a political economy of the informer in transportation-era New South Wales.[47] Suffolk's petitions thus expose him in the long tradition of convict-informer – a role written out of his text. Indeed, early in his narrative, he rails against the pressure to inform:

> I told them with real indignation, that criminal though I was, there were depths of baseness to which I could never descend, and that I could only regard such a proposal as the emanation of minds whose craven self-consciousness induced them to hold out to others what they would grasp at eagerly as a boon themselves. I will not court self-degradation by averting it in the villainous manner you would have me.[48]

These strong words would appeal to an audience – no one likes a snitch. He relates that while at Cockatoo Island, he befriended a man who confided his escape plan to another prisoner. During their escape, his friend was murdered. Suffolk, watching, concludes that the other escapee had informed the guards of the escape. Suffolk is so incensed that he hits the betrayer and murderer with a pickhandle.[49]

His petitions, however, belie his printed rhetoric. In them he freely admits to the treacherous actions against fellow prisoners which his autobiography omits. The truth is that Suffolk courted the prison authorities by spying on fellow prisoners – actions which he highlights in his petitions. Indeed he repeats *ad nauseam* how helpful he has been. For example he writes in one petition:

> a plan of a most cold blooded character was devised by a large number of prisoners [who] intended ... [to poison] the constables' tea, to enable [them] to escape from ... custody ... the petitioner appalled at [the plan] ... endeavoured to dissuade the concoctors ... but having failed deemed it his duty to thwart their intention [and] at once made a written statement.[50]

Furthermore, he boasts that he diligently scrutinized 'the whole body of prisoners' and often subjected their cells to 'rigid examination[s]'.[51] More than likely he was exaggerating his diligence to impress the authorities; yet these activities are barely hinted at in his autobiography. Thus, in a memorial, dated 11 July 1852, he states that during a rush by prisoners on their gaolers:

> your petitioner ... was desirous of rendering his assistance to the Gaol authorities but was directed [by] Mr Wintle to secure the door, leading from the gaol corridor into the front yard ... Mr Wintle considered the line of conduct your Petitioner was pursuing was of more service to the Government than any physical assistance your Petitioner could have rendered.[52]

Owen Suffolk both reveals and conceals himself in this instance. He claims to have helped the prison authorities but he also insinuates that he maintained faith of a sort with his fellow prisoners by adopting a passive stance. The statement implies an inactive role. He could perhaps claim to fellow inmates that he was merely following Wintle's orders under coercion.

Suffolk as sneak and informer directly contrasts with his written persona. An oblique reference occurs in his narrative to gaining a remission 'in consequence of some material assistance rendered by me to the gaol authorities on the occasion of a most desperate attack being made upon them'.[53] This suggests an awareness that these might be construed despicable actions best left cloaked in vagueness. Furthermore he claimed lofty altruism unmotivated by 'self-interest ... but by a desire of being deemed worthy of the kindness manifested towards him by gentlemen of high official position'.[54] Suffolk hoped to be rewarded and yet he claims in chapter 40 that 'I have violated no confidence. I have never betrayed the man who trusted me – I never shall'. This presents him in the most positive light possible. Evidently he constantly bore in mind the knowledge that informers are rarely admired – even by readers.

Suffolk's relationship with Wintle is murky. Wintle was his gaoler but they seem to have been intimate for all that. Several documents contain favourable comments in Wintle's hand about Suffolk. They appear to have colluded in altering some prisoners' records when Suffolk worked as a court clerk. Wintle was responsible for handling prisoners' money and money orders and he signed certain money transactions connected with the early release of inmates.[55] Though a subsequent official inquiry cleared Wintle of impropriety, its members were still 'at a loss to understand how he could let such large sums pass between the prisoners without having [his] suspicion excited'. Suffolk meanwhile applied and was granted remission. One clerk of the council refused to recommend Suffolk for remission.[56] On the other hand, William a'Beckett (then Secretary of Prisons) disagreed and believed Wintle's assertion that Suffolk was 'most useful and trustworthy' and should be granted a remission.[57] The Suffolk camp (including Wintle, the District Sheriff and a'Beckett) prevailed and a ticket of leave was secured for him. Either they believed Suffolk had reformed or there was some form of collusion. Not only was he granted a ticket of leave but, according to a sheriff's statement, given employment. He was later, however, charged with 'assisting' (altering fellow-inmates' sentences from four to two months), an offence carried out at the very time he was applying for remission! Ironically enough he was working in Castlemaine as a detective officer when arrested for this offence.[58]

Conclusion

Writing of the self is largely subtextual in Suffolk's narrative. One glimpses the real person when the text fails and gaps appear. At such times the text appears counterfeit, creating a 'state of legitimate mistrust'.[59] To paraphrase Lejeune, when the text appears authentic, giving all sorts of verifiable and likely particulars, ringing true, then Suffolk's story seems hollowest — he protests too much.[60] His rhetoric often reveals a delight in recounting his crimes. Thus examining Suffolk's story in the light of contemporaneous newspaper reports and prison records helps the reader to position the author. These other sources should not to be privileged, rather they help refashion Suffolk's literary self-construction. Newspaper reports and historical documents, on the one hand, rhetoricize the negative aspect of the convict; Suffolk, on the other, rhetoricizes the negative side of the penal system. Suffolk positions himself at the centre of the text and fashions himself as victim, hero and adventurer. His narrative is unusual in several ways. It is one of the few written by the convict himself and subject to minimal third-party intervention. In this respect it is in stark contrast to the 'Jack Bushman' narrative discussed by Ian Duffield — yet it remains as problematic as any biographical or autobiographical text.

Notes

1. His story has not been published in book form. Each chapter was published each week in the *Australasian* on pp. 7–8. Subsequent references will not, therefore, cite either the serial name or page number, merely a date and chapter number.
2. The printed sources utilized for this study of Suffolk and his autobiography are: the *Australian Dictionary of Biography*; Suffolk's autobiography, *Days of Crime and Years of Suffering* (henceforth *Days of Crime*), serialized in the *Australasian* (Melbourne, January–October 1867); the Melbourne *Argus* and the *Geelong Advertiser*. The following archive primary sources from the Victorian Public Record Office (henceforth VPRO), Melbourne, have also been utilized: Prison Register Males, vol. 1, no. 51, p. 53, and no. 107, p. 109, Series 515; Chief Secretary, In-Letters 1866/9027; Prisons box 302; Inspector General of Penal Establishments, Suffolk file, 57/1 to 57/1500, box 573.
3. Susanna Egan, *Patterns of Experience in Autobiography* (Chapel Hill, University of North Carolina Press, 1984), p. 14.
4. Roy Pascale, *Design and Truth in Autobiography* (London, Routledge and Kegan Paul, 1960), pp. vii and ix.
5. The whole question of scaffold confessions in *ancien régime* France is discussed at length in Michel Foucault, *Discipline and Punish: The Birth of the Prison* (New York, Vintage, 1979), ch. 2.

6. See Ian Duffield, 'Problematic Passages: "Jack Bushman's" Convict Narrative' in this volume.

7. And possibly Jeffrey Mark's autobiography. See W. and J.E. Hiener, 'Introduction' in Jeffrey Mark (ed. W. and J.E. Hiener), *A Burglar's Life* (Sydney, Angus and Robertson, 1968).

8. Ibid.

9. Jorgen Jorgenson, *The Convict King: Being the Life and Adventures of Jorgen Jorgenson retold by James Francis Hogan* (London, Ward and Downey, 1891), p. 3.

10. See Louis Becke, 'Introduction' in William Derrincourt, *Old Convict Days* (London, Fisher Unwin, 1899). Apparently a 'Mr Day' was the individual who transcribed William Derrincourt's oral account.

11. The authenticity of Suffolk's story was asserted by the editors in two separate instances. A note for *Days of Crime*, ch. 11, 9 March 1867, states that 'The quotation, of course, is incorrect; but we refrain from making any emendation whatever in the MS. Considering that the writer had no access to books, at least to play-books, his memory has served him tolerably well – Ed'. At the beginning of ch. 21, 11 May 1867, the editors further state: '[b]y narrating the events of his colonial career, the autobiographer ... has given full particulars of names, dates and places. For obvious reasons these have been suppressed ... The reader is therefore cautioned against making any attempt to exercise his ingenuity in connecting the scenes described in the narrative with actual occurrences in colonial history'. They had little imagination in their revisions. For example: Christopher Farrell becomes Christy and the 'Red Boot' becomes the 'Yellow Slipper'. Overall, the discernibly edited passages of the text mimic Suffolk's writing closely. If there was any further rewriting, it was extremely well done, as it is not apparent. It is usually prudent to be sceptical about editors' disclaimers of substantial interventions in a convict autobiographer's text, for to proclaim massive intervention would undermine 'authenticity' and thus the acceptance of readers. In this instance, and on balance, the printed text of *Days of Crime and Years of Suffering* is accepted as almost entirely the work of Owen Suffolk.

12. Paul John Eakin, 'Foreword' in Philippe Lejeune (ed. Paul John Eakin), *On Autobiography* (Minneapolis, University of Minnesota Press, 1989), p. xx.

13. Two of the six Australian texts are by Henry Savery, one by Jorgen Jorgenson, two by 'An Emigrant of 1821' and one by William Bland according to Anne Conlon, '"Mine is a Sad yet True Story": Convict Narratives 1818–1850', *Journal of the Royal Australian Historical Society*, vol. 55 (1969), pp. 43–82. Marcus Clarke's famed *For the Term of His Natural Life* was not serialized until 1870 (in the *Australian Journal* – a very popular monthly periodical).

14. Howard Whittaker, 'Victoria's Convicts by Another Name', *Royal Historical Society of Victoria*, vol. 55, no. 4 (1984), pp. 26–9; for Whittaker's numerical estimate see p. 26.

15. *Argus*, 26 March 1851, p. 2.

16. *Argus*, 21 May 1851, p. 2.

17. Ian Wynd, 'The Pentonvillians', *Victorian Historical Journal*, vol. 60 (Sept. 1989), pp. 37–46, esp. p. 43.

18. *Argus*, 22 May 1851, p. 3, and 23 May 1851, p. 2.

19. *Argus*, 21 May 1851, p. 2

20. In May 1851 he was in the *Argus* on five dates: 17, 19, 20, 24 and 31 May.

21. Unbeknownst to the editors; though his signature 'O.S.' is audacious, at this time he was being charged as George Mason and therefore was doubly assured of anonymity.

22. *Argus*, 12 Sept. 1848, p. 2.

23. *Argus*, 19 Sept. 1848, p. 2.

24. *Argus*, 23 April 1848, p. 2. The paper often resorted to animal metaphors like this one.

25. *Argus*, 21 June 1851, p. 2.

26. *Argus*, 23 May 1851, p. 2.

27. Quoted in the *Argus*, 20 May 1851, p. 2. The story is of Mr Ross, and is discussed in more detail below.

28. *Days of Crime*, ch. 56, 19 Oct. 1867.

29. Searle's motivation for framing Suffolk is never clarified. This gap in the text remains problematic. In the ensuing court case no other theft is mentioned; Suffolk is charged with horse-stealing only. Yet Suffolk writes of this incident which is clearly meant to justify his actions for horse-stealing. Again Suffolk rewrites himself as more sinned against than sinning.

30. *Days of Crime*, ch. 25, 1 June 1867.

31. Prison Register Males, vol. 1, no. 51, p. 53, and no. 107, p. 109, VPRO, Series 515.

32. *Days of Crime*, ch. 33, 20 July 1867.

33. *Geelong Advertiser*, reported in the *Argus*, 17 May, 1851, p. 2.

34. *Days of Crime*, ch. 24, 25 May 1867.

35. Ibid.

36. *Days of Crime*, ch. 25, 1 June 1867.

37. *Days of Crime*, ch. 34, 27 July 1867.

38. *Argus*, 23 June 1851, p. 2.

39. *Geelong Advertiser*, 23 June, 1851, p. 3.

40. He sent poetry to the *Argus*; he had the audacity to sign one poem with his real name and the others he signed as H. MANLY — a virile testament to his self-image.

41. Whoever chose the title, *Days of Crime and Years of Suffering*, understood the rhetoric of sentimentality. It merges the religious with the repentant. Days of crime suggests the ephemerality of the rewards of crime which are then followed by longer limbo years of suffering. It also suggests the inevitability of justice — that as the days will be followed by years, crime will be followed by suffering.

42. John Sturrock, *The Language of Autobiography: Studies in the First Person Singular* (Cambridge, Cambridge University Press, 1993).

43. London *The Times*, 4 March 1846, p. 4.

44. This is not verified in prison records.

45. VPRO, Box 235, series 3991.

46. VPRO, Prisons box 302.

47. Peter MacFie, 'Dobbers and Cobbers: Informers and Mateship Among Convicts, Officials and Settlers on the Grass Tree Hill Road, Tasmania 1830–1850',

Tasmanian Historical Research Association, vol. 35, no. 3 (Sept. 1988), pp. 112–27; Paula Jane Byrne, *Criminal Law and Colonial Subject: New South Wales 1810–1830* (Cambridge, Cambridge University Press, 1993), ch. 5.

48. *Days of Crime*, ch. 27, 15 June 1867.
49. *Days of Crime*, ch. 26, 8 June 1867. This is thought to refer to the fighting in the square incident noted in his prison records of 16 Aug. 1850.
50. Petition, 8 Aug. 1853, VPRO, Suffolk file, box 387.
51. Ibid.
52. Petition, 11 July 1852, VPRO, Suffolk file, box 387.
53. *Days of Crime*, ch. 39, 17 Aug. 1867.
54. Petition, 8 Aug. 1853, VPRO, Suffolk file, box 387.
55. In *Days of Crime*, ch. 40, 17 Aug. 1867. Suffolk avoids explicit denial: 'The warrants have evidently been altered. The man has evidently paid for the alteration. The order for the £40 is most certainly receipted by me. And so it is quite plain I have abused the gaoler's confidence, and violated the trust reposed in me.'
56. 27 July 1852, VPRO, Suffolk file, box 387.
57. William a'Beckett, 31 Dec. 1852, VPRO, Suffolk file, box 387.
58. District Sheriff's Office letter dated 9 Nov. 1853, VPRO, Suffolk file, box 387.
59. Lejeune, *On Autobiography*, p. 19.
60. Ibid.

CHAPTER THREE

Margaret Catchpole's First Ride?

Tina Picton Phillipps

'Oh! my mistress is dead! Oh! my mistress is dead!'[1] It is the last quarter of the eighteenth century. These words are shrieked by two female servants in the farmhouse kitchen of the possibly dead Mrs Denton. It is harvest time. Mr Denton and the farm labourers are all at work on a distant part of the farm. All action in the kitchen is restricted to a wringing of the hands, a stamping of the feet, and exclamations of 'Oh! my mistress is dead!' interspersed with shrieks. Imagine the scene: the two servants winding each other up into an ever greater state of hysteria; the men are in the fields far from the house. Is Mr Denton already a widower you may wonder? Fear not, reader, help is about to arrive; order about to be imposed upon the chaos; efficiency and capability are already at the kitchen door. The tension is broken with the words 'She is not dead'; a statement followed by 'Don't stand blubbering there, but get some cold water; lift up her head, untie her cap, loose her gown and raise her into the chair'. These words seem to evoke no immediate response from the servants since it is the newcomer who carries out the commands. Who has so fortuitously arrived and rescued from the jaws of death the ailing Mrs Denton? An angel in disguise? A fairy godmother of one of the servants? Is the life-saving of Mrs Denton now complete? Is there yet more to be accomplished? Yes indeed! More is required. Professional medical advice must be sought. So it is that the intrepid rescuer leaves the kitchen for the farm stables. Then, with neither saddle nor bridle, a 'fiery little Suffolk Punch' was up the high road to Ipswich with its rider to fetch Doctor Stebbin.[2]

So, who was this ageless, sexless individual? Allow me to introduce to you that rider: 'The Notorious Convict Margaret Catchpole'.[3] These words appear under a portrait by the Revd Richard Cobbold. This visual representation hangs in Christchurch Mansion Museum, Ipswich. Interest in Margaret Catchpole is not restricted to Suffolk where she was born. Australian historians of the early white period have made use of Catchpole's letters which are lodged in the Mitchell Library.[4] The introductory passage starting this chapter describes an early scene in *Margaret Catchpole: History of a Suffolk Girl* by the Revd Richard Cobbold, first published in 1845. The book and the portrait referred to above are not the only connections between author and subject.

Margaret Catchpole was sentenced to death at Bury Assizes in Suffolk on 9 August 1797 for her part in the theft of a 'roan coach gelding'.[5] Prior to the ending of the Assizes, she, along with two others, had her sentence commuted to transportation.[6] Thereupon she was incarcerated in Ipswich Gaol. While awaiting transportation she escaped, was recaptured and then transported in 1801.[7] The 'roan coach gelding' which she stole was the property of John Cobbold, brewer of Ipswich and father of Richard Cobbold. There was an additional connection between author and subject. For about 18 months Margaret had been employed by the Cobbold family 'as cook'.[8] In Cobbold's narrative this employment was extended to include Margaret's work with the Cobbold children.[9] This brought her into close proximity with Elizabeth Cobbold, Richard Cobbold's mother. Since Richard Cobbold was born in 1800 it is unlikely that he met Margaret Catchpole, let alone retained any direct memory of her. The accuracy of Cobbold's depiction of his subject is therefore open to question.

Indeed, the suffix to the 1858 edition of Cobbold's narrative indicates that his biographical integrity had been challenged.[10] Cobbold cited 'papers' on which his narrative had been based.[11] Gowring[12] and Shorter[13] were later both suspicious of the existence of these 'papers'. Shorter actually suggested that the narrative was based on orally-transmitted family stories.[14] Despite these early accusations, the *National Dictionary of Biography* entry for Margaret Catchpole is lifted uncritically from Cobbold's portrayal,[15] conferring on his narrative an authoritative 'gloss' of accuracy. By contrast with this British version of Catchpole's life, two Australian reference publications have recorded alternative dates of birth and death.[16] As a transported female convict Margaret Catchpole is surely unusual in having entries in these three works. It could indeed be argued that it is as a direct consequence of Cobbold's representation that these reference texts on Margaret Catchpole exist.

Subsequent commentators, whilst acknowledging Cobbold's 'economy with the truth', have testified to the narrative's popularity.[17] Indeed, the editions both prior and subsequent to Cobbold's death indicate that the narrative was a major publishing success.[18] Additionally, this narrative has been the source of subsequent representations of Margaret Catchpole.[19] By contrast with these fictional versions Harold Lingwood's biography of Margaret Catchpole remains unpublished.[20] So it would appear that Cobbold's fictitious representation has been more highly regarded than the 'facts' of Margaret Catchpole's life.

Clement Shorter first commented on the relationship between the author, his mother and Margaret Catchpole.[21] This chapter examines the relationship as described by Richard Cobbold. The argument is that the underlying object of Cobbold's text, despite its title, was to present a case exculpating his mother. His case removed any stigma which might be attached to Elizabeth through her connection with a transported convict. The nub of the argument is that Cobbold's narrative, to succeed in this task, required firstly to portray his subject as being deviant; secondly, to portray her in such a way as to indicate her potential for reform; and thirdly, to portray her reformation as only occurring when she came into contact with the reforming agency of Elizabeth. Textual analysis reveals that Cobbold's narrative owed more to the context of his own lifetime than it does to a historical reconstruction. This can be seen through his reinforcement of the contemporary social constructions of gender and class difference. Further, the narrative reveals the influence of the social theorists of the mid-nineteenth century through its subscription to the belief in the existence of a specific 'criminal class'.[22] Additionally, Cobbold's narrative contributes to the negative stereotyping of transported female convicts.[23]

To revert to the scene at the start of this paper, there are several puzzling and unexplained aspects. In that passage the 'intrepid rescuer' was Margaret Catchpole. The incident described took place prior to Margaret's fourteenth birthday. At no point in this scene did Cobbold deny Margaret's personal qualities of resourcefulness, initiative and ability to respond effectively to an emergency. Note also the reference to Margaret's equestrian skill in her four-mile bareback ride to Ipswich to fetch Doctor Stebbing. What purpose did this incident have in the context of the narrative? Should this episode with the unsaddled and unbridled 'fiery Suffolk Punch' be regarded as foreshadowing Margaret's subsequent criminal conviction for horse theft? One sentence suggests that this episode is more than a simple prophetic device. In describing Margaret's ride Cobbold commented: 'she did not stop even to tell her mother where she was going'.[24] Such a comment, under the circumstances, seems a strange inclusion. Was it a device to draw the reader's attention to Margaret's youthfulness? Did Cobbold suggest that Margaret was wayward in giving her ride to the doctor priority over her responsibilities to her mother? Or that Margaret was a naughty girl for failing to inform her mother of her destination? Given the manner in which the girl had been seen to cope with the emergency in the farmhouse kitchen, this sentence, with its undercurrent of admonition from Richard Cobbold, strikes the reader with no little force. It is therefore legitimate to question the previous events of the narrative. It is possible that by locating the text within the context of Cobbold's own lifetime the incident can be seen as the foundation upon which Cobbold establishes Margaret Catchpole's deviance. It is feasible that the decisively useful qualities which she displayed, and which Cobbold was at pains to impress on his readers, were inverted as indicators of her deviance.

Faber points out that during the 1840s 'social deference ... [was] ... a major theme of Victorian fiction'.[25] Margaret's independent actions in themselves can be seen as challenging the convention that actions by plebeians (particularly women) should be reactive, not proactive. In contrast to the household servants of the farm, Margaret took the initiative and acted.[26] She, aged 13, imperiously issued orders to the two servants. It was Margaret who was the dynamic agent of change in the emergency. Lerner points out that such fiction, as Cobbold's narrative surely was, is more likely to be prescriptive rather than descriptive.[27]

Cobbold indicated the inability of the female farm servants to function effectively in an emergency. This inability suggested that the plebeian class lacked initiative. The failure of the farm servants to respond effectively affirmed a specific code of social class. This code, while denying initiative to the plebeian class, assigned a leadership function to the dominant class. Additionally, such leadership was expected to come from a man. His Margaret challenged two assumptions of the prescribed social order. Her ability to act effectively contested the assumption that leadership must come from a member of the dominant class. Furthermore, being female, she defied the assumption that women were incapable of effective action. Moreover Cobbold isolated Margaret from members of her own class – she fails to fit into the prescriptive pigeon-holes in relation to class, sex or, indeed, age.

The mission to fetch Doctor Stebbing was successfully concluded and Margaret was regarded as a heroine. In the aftermath of the episode, however, Susan (Margaret's sister) 'perceived with satisfaction that Margaret, instead of being vain, and puffed up with the notice of the world, was quite the reverse'.[28] Susan was the guardian of the Catchpole household's morals.[29] Since Cobbold made no secret of his underlying evangelical Christian message,[30] it is certainly legitimate to extrapolate from this the moral precept that the approval of the world is worthless. There was, however, more to Margaret's withdrawal than a rejection of the world. Her action (of resourcefulness) and reaction (of withdrawal) must be seen within a broader context than that. Through Susan, Cobbold conveyed the contemporary middle-class disapproval of females whose behaviour or actions provoked comment, whether adverse or complimentary. This affirmed an agenda in which actions ceased to be gender-neutral but instead became morally and socially gender-predicated. Likewise, the view taken by the dominant class of an action was determined by the social class of the actor. A female whose actions lay beyond the domestic sphere was placing herself beyond control, supervision and chaperonage of parents, husband or employer.[31] Being 'in the world' as Margaret was on that early ride she was visible and, therefore, vulnerable. Her ability to maintain control of her circumstances therefore negated the assumption of female vulnerability. By being in the world and on horseback she was seen to confront the prescribed social order in which women were in need either of protection or control. The expectation that girls and women ought to remain within a domestic environment, be this the parental or marital home or that of an employer, was challenged by Margaret's bareback ride. Cobbold's admonition that 'she did not stop even to tell her mother where she was going' did not only draw attention to Margaret's age. It served as a reminder to his (middle-class) audience that girls go nowhere without firstly informing their mother − or at least, nowhere it was proper for them to go.[32] Cobbold had constructed Margaret as a negative role model in line with the social mores of his place and time.[33]

As well as retreating from the world, Margaret experienced feelings of shame. As indicated earlier, Cobbold's narrative contains many paradoxes and ambiguities. Although the argument set out above indicates the fruitfulness of exploring his narrative from within social constructions of class and gender, there is little in the incident he described to show why Margaret should feel 'shame'. In describing the events, at no point did Cobbold give any explicit cause for her 'shame'. Suppose, for the sake of argument, that this bareback ride was not a foreshadowing of Margaret's criminal conviction but was of some other significance. The ride was, indeed, the sole cause of her original notoriety. Cobbold's narrative even disclosed that Margaret accepted employment with a Mr Nathaniel Southgate to escape 'unpleasant observations'.[34] No immediate cause or reason is given, but the inference is that Margaret was sensitive to these. Obviously, then, this episode with the 'fiery Suffolk punch' is important − but in what way? What is the relevance of that bareback ride which took place before Margaret's fourteenth birthday?[35] Why does Cobbold deliberately describe the Suffolk punch as 'fiery'?[36] Is it possible that the answer can be found by linking this episode to another episode described in a subsequent passage? What happens if connections are drawn between this adolescent event and the romantic attachment Margaret formed with William Laud?

William Laud was to become a major influence upon Margaret. Two years had passed since the (in)famous ride. In advance of their first meeting, William was in conversation with his father. He expressed his interest in the young woman about whom he had heard so much. It transpired that William had first heard of Margaret in the local inn when he had been in the company of Captain Bargood. The very fact that he had heard of her is significant since it demonstrated that Margaret had acquired a 'reputation', the possession of which was, for Margaret as a female, tantamount to the loss of her 'good name'.[37] William's interest in Margaret also revealed something of the young man himself. To represent him as expressing an interest in a girl about whom he had merely heard was to hint that he was unsuitable. A further damning aspect was that he had been in the company of a smuggler − Captain Bargood.[38] Indeed, as the narrative unfolds, William Laud turns out to be a 'bad lot'.

The connection of these two episodes, Margaret's bareback ride to Ipswich with her subsequent notoriety, and her future lover's foreknowledge of her reputation based merely on that ride, leads to the following supposition. Margaret's sexuality and virginity were open to question and the word 'fiery' to describe the Suffolk Punch was used deliberately to hint at (sexual) excitement; that on her bareback ride to Ipswich Margaret experienced natural feelings of sexual arousal. Those 'unpleasant observations', which so upset her, possibly were suggestive comments relating female sexuality and horses. Is it therefore too extreme to suggest Margaret's loss of virginity was also inferred? The subsequent passage with the introduction of the smuggler, William Laud, and its subtext of 'reputation' and 'good name' is sufficient to damn Margaret in the eyes of a nineteenth-century audience as being precociously sexually deviant.[39]

Having demonstrated how Cobbold conveyed Margaret's deviance it is appropriate to indicate how her potential for reform is illustrated. In the earlier passage personal qualities were inverted to indicate her 'deviance' as a female plebeian. To explain how it was that she came to be introduced into the Cobbold household the narrative is now required to portray her in a more positive light.[40] It is therefore unsurprising that Margaret's potential for reform was to be found within a continuation of gender and class discourse revealed in Cobbold's narrative.

Through Margaret's romantic attachment to William Laud, Cobbold charted the moral and material disintegration of her immediate family.[41] By contrast with this, her own role was couched in terms of moral probity.[42] Cobbold's portrayal introduced her 'potential for reform' despite her attachment to William Laud.[43] Cobbold indicated the extent to which Margaret, in her attempts to reform Will, was aware of both the immorality and the criminality of smuggling.[44] Accordingly there is an ambiguous quality in this portrayal. Margaret's non-participation in Laud's criminal activities was not a neutral stance but was, according to Cobbold, based on her knowledge of both a moral and a social code. Such knowledge affirmed more than her 'potential for reform': it subscribed to the contemporary social construction of gender.[45] In this instance Margaret was portrayed by means of contrasting her behaviour and morality with those of her male relatives.[46] Although it was to her that the first consignment of smuggled goods was handed over, it was Margaret's father who negotiated their onward transmission.[47] Margaret was not tainted with crime by Cobbold despite her attachment to Laud, rather she was portrayed as a victim of her emotions.[48]

In contrast with the earlier episode when Margaret presented a challenge to the mid-nineteenth-century audience, she was now portrayed in such a light as to uphold the values of that society. Despite her direct emotional association with a smuggler and the involvement of her family in criminal activities, Margaret was shown in a more positive light through the focus on her moral integrity and emotional weakness. Such a portrayal affirmed the social construction of femininity within the mid-nineteenth-century context.[49]

Cobbold also illustrated Margaret's 'potential for reform' through his portrayal of her in her role as an employee. His narrative described a class division in which interpersonal relationships were very important indicators of social class. According to Cobbold, his subject received hostile comments from her fellow workers regarding her relationship with William Laud.[50] In contrast to these, her employers were described as being more sympathetic in their attitudes.[51] Thus the narrative subscribed to the paternalistic social order of Cobbold's lifetime. The serving class was portrayed as having 'the lying tongue of slander'.[52] The employing class was represented as more sensitive and merciful. Margaret's 'potential for reform' was indicated through Cobbold's description of her resultant appreciation: employers 'should be rewarded with more than usual exertions on her part'.[53] Cobbold distinguished the employing class and the employed class through their different reactions to Margaret. She was the vehicle through which Cobbold could promote a code of conduct for employers. Although no example is given in the narrative, Margaret, as portrayed by Cobbold, indicated her appreciation of her employers' attitudes. This appreciation could, according to Cobbold's discourse, result in material benefits as well as virtuous feelings for the employing class; the consequences of such benefits being beyond the formal exchange of labour for wages.

Cobbold reinforced Margaret's 'potential for reform' through a scene in which she is described as actively endorsing the hegemonic discourse of the patriarchal social order.[54] She had become a more biddable employee, anxious to please and conforming to her role within the employer/employee relationship. Her compliance with the rules of deference indicated her acceptance of her subordinate position. She had been transformed into a suitable employee for Mrs John Cobbold, despite her connection with the 'dangerous classes'.

Elizabeth Cobbold's influence upon Margaret Catchpole was initially within the domestic sphere. This lady's interest and questions were, however, directed at Margaret's personal life rather than her employment. Mrs Cobbold was the initiator of the first and subsequent dialogues between the two women.[55] There was no indication in the narrative that Margaret had ever sought advice from her about William Laud. Elizabeth Cobbold had, according to her son, the right to question Margaret about this relationship. The 'right' was assumed to be that Elizabeth knew what was good for her servant.[56] Cobbold described Margaret's resistance to these questions. Margaret was 'suspicious, distrustful, capricious' and she had 'a warped mind'.[57] Despite having been transformed into a suitable employee for his mother through an explicit affirmation of the patriarchal social order, Margaret's 'potential for reform' had not been fully realized.

Margaret's subsequent recognition of her mistress as a superior being took place after she had left the Cobbold household and had been accused of stealing John Cobbold's horse. Elizabeth Cobbold is described as fulfilling two distinct roles. On the one hand she is portrayed as having a major influence on her wayward servant. On the other hand Elizabeth was the unofficial bridge between the judicial process and Catchpole as the accused. The consequence of this influence was illustrated, in Cobbold's narrative, through Margaret's submission to her mistress. Moreover, Cobbold's description of the court procedures were such as to justify his mother's involvement with a tainted female felon.

Margaret is described as conceding her autonomy to her ex-employer – her persona becomes subordinate to the influence of Elizabeth Cobbold. The latter's influence over Margaret in this respect continued the earlier theme in the narrative whereby personal relationships were incorporated into Richard Cobbold's social class discourse. He describes his mother's visits to her ex-servant, both in London and in Ipswich gaols. Additionally Cobbold constructs a lengthy correspondence between the two women. This conveys homilies from his mother which are part of her purported influence on Margaret. One such is expressed in the following terms: 'a warning to all your sex, and especially to those in your situation of life, never to let passion get the upper hand of virtuous principle'.[58] This 'warning' is a further significant indication that Cobbold's narrative owes more to the context of his lifetime than a neutral historical reconstruction. Passion became an indicator of social class and was ascribed to the subordinate class.[59] Margaret's compliance with this injunction is demonstrated by the portrayal of her second court appearance when she was 'perfectly free from any of that emotion which she had formerly exhibited'.[60] The approval of those who were officially involved in her second trial is represented as a testimony to Elizabeth's interventions. Margaret's submission to such 'proper' moral and social authority is further reinforced by Cobbold's description of her life in Ipswich Gaol. She 'exercised a moral influence over those of her own sex who were inmates of the prison, such as no matron could hope to attain'.[61] Thus, Elizabeth Cobbold's influence was transferred, vicariously through Margaret, into Ipswich Gaol.

His mother's influence contributes to Cobbold's overall negative stereotyping of female convicts, conveyed through his illustrations of where Margaret differed from them. The impression given in the narrative is that Margaret's ascribed 'difference' was largely accountable to Elizabeth's influence. At Margaret's first court appearance in London, 'The judge ... [was] expecting to find a bold, athletic, female of a coarse and masculine appearance'.[62] The inference to be drawn from this is explicit. Female convicts were supposed to be instantly recognizable by their physical appearance.[63] In addition to their physique, Cobbold also used clothes as a means of their identification. Deference and respect were therefore indicated through the design and material of attire.[64]

Margaret wore 'a plain, blue cotton gown' at both court hearings.[65] The inference is clear – the typical female convict would challenge the ascribed right of the dominant class to their designs and materials by wearing similar clothes. Cobbold's Margaret is atypical in showing that she 'knew her place' by wearing a simple dress. He implicitly asserts the influence of his mother upon her servant in his description of the latter's behaviour in court. Margaret had 'a calmness of deportment without the least obduracy, and obtrusive boldness or reckless-ness'.[66] Margaret's ascribed difference is both how Richard Cobbold justifies his mother's actions and the means whereby Margaret is presented in a favourable light to his audience as one who has learned proper deference to her social superiors.

Margaret's reformation is firmly rooted within Cobbold's social class discourse. In contrast with Margaret's previous employers, he uses the words 'gentleman' and 'lady' of John and Elizabeth Cobbold. These terms demonstrate the contemporaneous recognition of the absence of homogeneity within the so-called 'middle classes'. Concern for Margaret's moral reform was, however, expressed by all of her employers.[67] The narrative draws upon the institutions of the state (the judicial and penal systems) and religion to justify Elizabeth Cobbold's interventions. Thus she is not only an agent of change in Margaret's life, but also represented as an agent of the state. The servant's acknow-ledgement of her mistress's superior moral and social status is expressed in a suitably deferential voice: 'Poor Margaret felt better ... with a heart much humbled'.[68]

The relationship between Margaret and her employer Elizabeth was originally located within the domestic or private sphere. The proposition that a sharp distinction can be drawn between 'private' and 'public' has been challenged as being an ideological construct.[69] Cobbold's narrative can be read as offering support to this challenge. The paradoxical nature of Margaret Catchpole's deviance and reformation, as described by Cobbold, is to be explained within the context of the dominant class's ideological construction of social class difference. This ideology was self-referential in relation to the subordinate class. Deference and compliance from the subordinate class confirmed the assumed need for leadership and authority from the dominant class. By contrast, failure by members of the subordinate class to give deference or to comply with the authority of the dominant class confirmed the ascribed essential difference between the social classes.[70]

The representation of Elizabeth Cobbold's influence over Margaret Catchpole was given an additional legitimacy within the text. A subliminal biblical metaphor is revealed when Elizabeth comes to see Margaret following the theft of John Cobbold's horse and prior to Margaret's first appearance at the Magistrates Court in London. Margaret is 'terrified beyond measure at the sight of her mistress'.[71] She already knows that there was a possibility of being sentenced to death. Richard Cobbold, however, implies that the prospect of the loss of her own life was less awesome to the thief than the appearance of her mistress. Here, it is possible that Genesis, chapter 3, is hinted at. Adam and Eve, having eaten the apple, were aware of their nakedness. But it was the presence of God which caused them to attempt to hide themselves. It was also God's presence, not the eating of the fruit itself, which gave rise to shame.[72] The metaphor is subsequently reinforced when Margaret indicates that the happiest hours of her life had been spent in the Cobbolds' garden.[73] Margaret's self-assessment, as described by Cobbold, implies a recognition of her own 'fall from the garden of paradise' as well as expressing his own deification of his mother.

Thus it is conveyed that prior to transportation Margaret Catchpole underwent her reformation. Despite the evidence of her emotional attachment to a smuggler, her family's involvement in both smuggling and poaching and her two crimes (horse theft and escape from gaol), Margaret is ultimately de-criminalized by Cobbold. His 'sainted' mother's interventions had wrought not only submissive deference but also reformation and repentance. These were therefore more than sufficient justification for Elizabeth Cobbold's contact with a tainted female, and are embedded in Cobbold's construction of social class difference and distance. His hegemonic discourse illustrates mid-nineteenth-century concern with plebeian deference to the dominant class. His narrative constructs a paradigm for contemporary power relations, based on his imaginary portrayal of Margaret Catchpole and her interactions with his mother.

Afterword: 'but I've no inclination to marry'[74]

This chapter has concentrated upon one fictional representation of a single female transportee, Margaret Catchpole. The influence of Richard Cobbold's narrative upon subsequent fictional portrayals of Margaret Catchpole is charted in note 19. These are likely to result in the ridiculous and indeed unanswerable demand that 'The Real Margaret Catchpole' appear. Such a demand is to open a veritable viper's nest and does, perhaps, illustrate a problematic at the heart of the papers collected here. Firstly, of course, there is the issue of whether or not such a nebulous character as 'The Real Anyone', let alone Margaret Catchpole, exists. Cobbold's representation of Margaret Catchpole is an obvious example of a constructed fictitious character. Could the historical record provide a less biased access to the historic actor? Margaret's letters have, indeed, been utilized by historians.[75] Of the letters, however, it is one extract which has almost become a cliché. This extract, 'i might a gon to Lived with maney of the saillrs that is to a Binn thear wife and might a Lived very well But i have no inklanashun', comes from a single letter written by Margaret to her Uncle and Aunt Howes.[76] This extract could almost be regarded as symbolic of the symmetry which exists between historians and writers of fiction.

Notes

1. R.S. Cobbold, *Margaret Catchpole: History of a Suffolk Girl* (London, Henry Colburn, 1845), in two volumes, vol. 1, p. 11.
2. All quotations in this paragraph were taken from ibid.
3. Christchurch Mansion Museum, *Ipswich: A Brief History and Guide* (Ipswich, Ipswich Museum Committee, 1964), p. 8.
4. A full citation of those historians who have used Margaret Catchpole's letters is beyond the scope of this chapter. The following is only a sample: M. Roe, 'Colonial Society in Embryo', *Historical Studies*, vol. 7, no. 26 (1956), pp. 149–59; P. Robinson, *The Hatch and Brood of Time* (Melbourne, Oxford University Press, 1985), p. 77, and *The Women of Botany Bay: A Reinterpretation of the Role of Women in the Origins of Australian Society* (North Ryde, Macquarie Library, 1988), p. 211; F. Clune, *Rascals, Ruffians and Rebels* (NSW, Angus and Robertson, 1987), chs 7 and 8, pp. 80–106.
5. From the original statement made by Margaret Catchpole. This is reprinted in Richard Barber, 'The Real Margaret Catchpole' in R.S. Cobbold, *Margaret Catchpole* (Ipswich, Boydell Press, 1979; reprint of 1971 facsimile of 5th edn of 1847), p. xi. Barber acknowledges as his source H. Lingwood's unpublished manuscript 'Homespun Heroine: Portrait of Margaret Catchpole'.
6. *Ipswich Journal*, no. 3376, 19 August 1797, back page, column 3.
7. There is a problem in ascertaining exactly which ship transported Margaret Catchpole. The indent, Archives Office of New South Wales, 4/3999, lists convicts for three transport ships – the *Nile*, *Minorca* and *Canada*.
8. R. Barber, 'The Real Margaret Catchpole', p. xii.
9. Ibid., p. xii.
10. R.S. Cobbold, *Margaret* (London, Simpkin Marshall, 1858), 'Suffix', p. 378.
11. Ibid., vol. 1, 'Preface', no page number.
12. R. Gowring, *Public Men of Ipswich and East Suffolk: A Series of Personal Sketches* (Ipswich, W.J. Scopes, 1875), ch. 25, pp. 170–5.
13. C. Shorter, 'Introduction' in R.S. Cobbold, *Margaret Catchpole* (London, Henry Frowde and Co., 1907), p. xii.
14. Ibid., p. vi.
15. Sir Leslie Stephen and Sir Sidney Lee (eds), *Dictionary of National Biography* (Oxford, Oxford University Press, 1959–60), vol. 3, p. 1187. In addition to citing erroneous dates of birth and death (in line with Cobbold's narrative) this entry also includes Catchpole's fictitious marriage. An additional comment is added: 'When later in life, trouble had subdued her undisciplined temper, genuine religious impressions and an unaffected desire to atone for the past became the dominant features of her character'.

16. A.G.L. Shaw and C.M.C. Clarke (eds), *Australian Dictionary of Biography* (Melbourne, Melbourne University Press, 1966), p. 215; and Walter James Jeffrey (ed.), *Illustrated Australian Encyclopaedia* (Sydney, Angus and Robertson, 1925), p. 242.

17. Clune, *Rascals*, p. 80, states Cobbold's narrative is 'a good yarn'; R. Blythe, 'Introduction' in Cobbold, *Margaret Catchpole* (Ipswich, 1979), p. ix, comments that the narrative has 'an enduring appeal'.

18. Prior to Cobbold's death (1877) eight separate editions of *Margaret Catchpole* appeared; thereafter there were three.

19. Alternative representations of Margaret Catchpole in works of drama, fiction and opera have appeared since 1852. In 1852 Edward Stirling, the prolific Victorian dramatist, wrote two versions (one, a three-act play; the other a one-act playlet). It is probable that the one-act playlet was written to avoid the contemporary theatre censorship laws. It could appear uncensored as part of a Music Hall programme – as one-act dramas often did. George Carter's novel, *Margaret Catchpole, The Girl from Wolfkettel* (London, Constable & Co., 1949), acknowledges the influence of Cobbold's narrative. There have been several children's books featuring Margaret Catchpole; the most recent of which, Sally Harris, *Smuggler's Girl* (Colchester, Anglia TV Books, 1991), also cites Cobbold's narrative. In 1981 an opera, *Worlds Apart*, was performed in Suffolk with a libretto by Ronald Fletcher acknowledging Cobbold's narrative as its source. It does not seem too extreme to suggest that Cobbold's narrative has been the foundation upon which a 'Margaret Catchpole Industry' has been built.

20. Copies of Harold Lingwood's unpublished manuscript, cited in note 5 above, are lodged in the Suffolk Record Office and the Battye Library, Perth, Australia.

21. Clement Shorter, 'Introduction', p. vi.

22. Jan Kociumbas, *The Oxford History of Australia*, vol. 2, *1770–1868: Possessions* (Melbourne and Oxford, Oxford University Press, 1992), pp. 282–3, states: 'concepts of phrenology, ethnology and … new science of criminology [were] being invented'; '"crime" … was caused by abnormal, physical, mental and social characteristics'; 'By the 1840s the new criminal anthropologists and sociologists had invented the term "the dangerous classes" to describe people … who were supposed to be pathologically different from the industrious working class'. In this connection Cobbold, *Margaret* (1845), vol. 1, pp. 49–51, describes John Luff as 'gruff and surly looking … a fellow who seemed formed of such materials as compose a cannon-ball … iron-hearted and iron fisted … a shaggy brow, and matted thick black hair … His eyebrows half-covered the sockets of his eyes … [His] dress might be taken for some honest ploughman, but whose countenance betrayed a very different expression – none of that open-ness and simplicity which good labourers and country-men wear'.

23. Phillip Tardif, *Notorious Strumpets and Dangerous Girls: Convict Women in Van Diemen's Land 1803–1829* (Sydney, Angus and Robertson, 1990) is perhaps the best collective description of such a stereotype, the title being a contemporary 'official' perception of those convict women. Tardif's work collates collected information from a variety of record classes.

24. Cobbold, *Margaret* (1845), vol. 1, p. 11.

25. Richard Faber, *Class in Victorian Fiction* (London, Faber and Faber, 1971), 'Introduction' and p. 146.

26. Cobbold, *Margaret* (1845), vol. 1, pp. 6–8.

27. G. Lerner, *The Majority Finds its Past: Placing Women in History* (Oxford, Oxford University Press, 1981), pp. 147–50. Lerner's argument is that fiction from the nineteenth century portrayed subordinated members of society, particularly women and the working class, as being deferential to the mores and dictates of the dominant class – such a framework thereby suggesting that fiction was disseminating a message of how society should or ought to be rather than portraying disaffection or resistance by members of the serving class.

28. Cobbold, *Margaret* (1845), vol. 1, p. 17.

29. It was not until after Susan's death that the Catchpole family became involved in 'crime' as receivers of smuggled goods, supplied by William Laud. The first consignment of these arrived as the Catchpole family returned from Susan's funeral. The inference here is that with the death of Susan the household had lost its moral centre. Furthermore Cobbold's portrayal of Susan conforms to the 'good angel' stereotype of femininity, discussed by Ian Duffield, 'Problematic Passages', in this volume.

30. Cobbold, *Margaret* (1845), vol. 1, 'Preface', no page number.

31. L. Davidoff, *The Best Circles* (London, Croom Helm, 1973), pp. 51–3. See also Mrs S. Ellis, *The Wives of England: Their Relative Duties, Domestic Influence and Social Obligations* (London, Fisher, Son and Co., c.1843), p. 307.

32. The assumption made is that Cobbold's readers were drawn from the (problematic) 'middle classes'. The bibliography regarding social class formation is so extensive as to preclude discussion within this chapter. The following have informed the argument: E.P. Thompson, 'Patrician Society, Plebeian Culture', *Journal of Social History*, vol. 7, no. 4 (1974), pp. 382–409; D. Newby, 'The Deferential Dialectic', *Comparative Studies in Society and History*, vol. 17 (1975), pp. 139–64; R.S. Neale, *Class in English History, 1680–1850* (Oxford, Blackwell, 1981) and 'Class and Class Consciousness: Three Classes or Five?', *Victorian Studies*, 12 (1968–69), pp. 4–32; L. Davidoff and C. Hall, *Family Fortunes: Men and Women of the English Middle Class, 1789–1850* (London, Century Hutchinson, 1987).

33. Davidoff, *Best Circles*, p. 51.

34. Cobbold, *Margaret* (1845), vol. 1, p. 14.

35. Ibid., vol. 1, p. 10.

36. In fact Suffolk Punches are renowned for their placid natures and gentle manners, which is in sharp contrast to Cobbold's description. See also Hannah More, cited in Davidoff and Hall, *Family Fortunes*, p. 123. In her novel, *Coelebs in Search of a Wife: Comprehending Observations of Domestic Habits and Manners, Religion and Morals*, More's negative portrayal of Miss Sparkes is linked to Miss Sparkes's knowledge of and ability with horses.

37. The importance of a girl maintaining her 'good name' (a euphemism for virginity) was a feature of nineteenth-century fiction. For example, see the contemporaneous novel by Anthony Trollope, *The Macdermotts of Ballycloran* (London, Penguin, 1993; facsimile of 1847 edition), which recounts the disasters which befell an Irish

girl who 'loses her good name'. Also see Mrs Ellis, *The Wives of England*, p. 309: 'For what has a poor girl but her character to depend upon?' To what extent the emphasis placed on 'a good name' was a feature of the dominant, rather than the plebeian class, is arguable. The point being made here is that Cobbold's narrative was addressed to an audience for whom this issue would have relevance.

38. Captain Bargood was the 'brains' behind a local 'Mafia' of organized crime which included both smuggling and poaching. It was through the Captain that William became involved in smuggling. Note also the implicit and explicit references to alcohol through Cobbold's name for the Captain – 'Bargood' – as well as through The Neptune, the inn where Laud had first heard of Margaret. Any contemporary reader involved in the temperance movement would have received an adverse impression from these references.

39. G. Lerner, *The Creation of Patriarchy* (New York, Oxford University Press, 1986), p. 216. Lerner describes how sexual deviancy was regarded as being sufficient to consign those so inclined 'to the lowest class status possible'.

40. Mrs Ellis, *The Wives of England*, p. 309: 'In the country it is comparatively easy to ascertain what is the general moral character of those around us'.

41. Cobbold, *Margaret* (1845), vol. 1, pp. 74–6, describes the moral decline of Margaret's brothers, Charles, Robert and John. This is as a direct consequence of the financial gains from the sale of the smuggled goods introduced into the Catchpole household. Charles stopped working and left home; Robert became an alcoholic and died; John became a poacher, was shot while poaching and, as a result of the gunshot, also died. John's deathbed speech was to blame his misfortunes on Margaret's relationship with William Laud. Margaret's father was dismissed from his employment with Mr Denton and therefore lost his tied cottage. From being in regular employment Mr Catchpole was forced to accept casual labouring work and was accommodated in a 'mean' cottage on the edge of the village.

42. Ibid., vol. 1, pp. 90–1, says 'she was far from ignorant of right and wrong. Her principles were good'.

43. Ibid., vol. 1, pp. 57–8 and p. 74 – Margaret was described as being 'never corrupted'; as having 'no covetous hankering'; and experiencing 'mortification'. These descriptions are all in relation to the smuggled goods which arrive, as gifts, from William Laud.

44. Cobbold, *Margaret* (1845), vol. 1, p. 57, described Margaret's motives thus: 'She would have given them [the smuggled goods] up to the government officers, but she saw that this would involve her lover'.

45. Ibid., vol. 1, p. 273: Margaret in speaking to Laud about the consequences of their relationship said 'much I have suffered on your account … but God has enabled me to bear all, with the hope that I should one day see you an altered man'. See also Davidoff and Hall, *Family Fortunes*, in which the ideology of femininity in the nineteenth century is discussed throughout. Whereas men were regarded as being morally weaker than women in relation to the vices of the world, the 'ideal' woman provided a moral standard to which men could aspire.

46. Mrs Ellis, *The Mothers of England: Their Influence and Responsibility* (London, Fisher, Son and Co., 1843), p. 313. Mrs Ellis draws the distinction between men and

women by questioning whether men 'reflect and calculate as women do upon the moral tendency of things'.

47. Cobbold, *Margaret* (1845), vol. 1, pp. 57–8.

48. Thus Cobbold, *Margaret* (1845), vol. 1, p. 153, said 'In the heart of Margaret … love was her life'.

49. Davidoff and Hall, *Family Fortunes* (see note 45 above). Cobbold was required to do no more than indicate Margaret's 'potential for reform'. Margaret's failure is an indication of where she still fell short of the 'ideal' woman. Such a failure was linked to her class status and her emotional weakness.

50. Cobbold, *Margaret* (1845), vol. 1, pp. 76 and 211.

51. Ibid., vol. 1, pp. 76–7, displayed this thus: 'It must not be supposed that Mrs Denton was unkind to Margaret, though her own servants took every opportunity to persuade her that she was a very worthless person'. See also vol. 1, p. 211: 'Her master and mistress were uniformly kind to her or she could not have borne her sufferings'.

52. This is in connection with the sailors who were seen to visit the Catchpole household. The full quotation is ibid., vol. 1, p. 76: 'the lying tongue of slander was sure to propagate some infamous story'. This could be regarded as an inference of prostitution.

53. Ibid., vol. 1, p. 209. This is quoted in the context of 'the indulgence of her kind master and mistress'. It should be noted that an 'indulgence' remains in the control of the donor and can be withdrawn at any time. Indulgences were to become incorporated within the relations of masters and assigned servants in both New South Wales and Van Diemen's Land during the convict period. See Kirsty Reid in this volume.

54. Catchpole, *Margaret* (1845), vol. 1, p. 176: 'Margaret rushed into the parlour, and fell at her master's feet imploring him to interfere'. This incident corroborated the power of the patriarch. Simpson, a fellow servant, had been teasing Margaret about her connection with Laud. Margaret's appeal to Mr Wake (her employer) choreographed her vulnerability, her need of protection and her willingness to accept that protection. This incident is in complete opposition to the earlier events described in this chapter in which Margaret challenged the assumption of female vulnerability. Lerner, *The Creation of Patriarchy*, pp. 212–29 and 234, argues that women accepted a subordinate role in exchange for male protection. This scene corroborates Lerner's model.

55. Cobbold, *Margaret* (1845), vol. 1, p. 321.

56. J. Donzelot, *The Policing of Families* (London, Hutchinson, 1980; 'Foreword' by Gilles Deleuze, trans. R. Hurley). This book traces the connections between the nineteenth-century philanthropic movement and the assumed right (by and of the dominant class) to intervene in the lives of the subordinate class.

57. Cobbold, *Margaret* (1845), vol. 1, p. 322.

58. Ibid., vol. 2, p. 191.

59. See Susan Mendus and Jane Rendall, *Sexuality and Subordination: Interdisciplinary Studies of Gender in the Nineteenth Century* (London, Routledge, 1989), p. 9: 'Despite the fact that the perfect Victorian lady was construed as passionless, the "low and

vulgar" Victorian woman was perceived as retaining the animal's sexual voraciousness'.

60. Cobbold, *Margaret* (1845), vol. 2, p. 193.
61. Ibid., vol. 2, p. 133.
62. Ibid., vol. 2, p. 113. See K. Reid, 'Work, Sexuality and Resistance: the Convict Women of Van Diemen's Land, 1820–1839', unpublished PhD thesis, University of Edinburgh (1995). Research on the female convicts transported to Van Diemen's Land indicates that they were for the most part under five feet tall. The description of Margaret Catchpole on the handbill issued after her escape from Ipswich Gaol states she was 'About 5 Feet 2 Inches high'.
63. The documents reproduced in Tardif, *Notorious Strumpets and Dangerous Girls*, reveal that the physical characteristics of the female convicts were recorded as a means of identification in the event of their absconding. A handbill (see note 62 above) described Catchpole as having a 'swarthy complexion ... very dark Eyes and Hair, – hard favoured'.
64. See Mrs Ellis, *The Wives of England*, p. 304: 'the little thoughtless girl [a nurserymaid] ... who never thinks herself, except how she shall manage to purchase a ribbon like that upon her mistress' cap'.
65. Cobbold, *Margaret* (1845), vol. 2, pp. 113 and 193.
66. Ibid., vol. 2, p. 193.
67. See Davidoff and Hall, *Family Fortunes*, p. 25: 'One of the strongest strands binding together urban and rural, nonconformist and Anglican, Whig, Tory and Radical, manufacturer, farmer and professional, wealthy and modest, was the commitment to an imperative moral code and reworking of their domestic world into a proper setting for its practice'.
68. Cobbold, *Margaret* (1845), vol. 2, p. 101.
69. See Davidoff and Hall, *Family Fortunes*, p. 33: 'Public was not really public and private was not really private despite the potent imagery of "separate spheres"'. See also Stephen Mintz, *A Prison of Expectations: The Family in Victorian Culture* (New York, New York University Press, 1985), p. 5: 'the Victorian home reflects the problem ... of a deferential, hierarchical, patronage society [and] the dynamics of the Victorian family and larger issues of authority, deference and discipline'.
70. A. Giddens, *Sociology* (Cambridge, Polity Press, 1990), pp. 117–55.
71. Cobbold, *Margaret* (1845), vol. 2, p. 98.
72. See ibid., vol. 2, p. 101: 'Mrs Cobbold ... placed before her mind the heinousness of her offence'.
73. Ibid.
74. Cited in Kay Daniels and Mary Murnane (eds), *Uphill All the Way: A Documentary History of Women in Australia* (St Lucia, Queensland University Press, 1980), p. 164. The sentiment underlying this statement is also recorded in Portia Robinson, *The Women of Botany Bay*, p. 211. In the latter work the quotation reads: 'There is a fine young man a-courting me, but I am not for marrying'.
75. See note 4 above.
76. See note 74 above: Daniels and Murnane, *Uphill All the Way*, reprints Margaret's letter.

CHAPTER FOUR

From Keneally to Wertenbaker: Sanitizing the System

Ruth Brown

Thomas Keneally has referred to the debt 'beyond estimation' that historical novelists owe to historians for having preshaped the past, and given it form and meaning. This is a conservative approach to history and the role of historians, suggesting that 'facts' about the past have already been unearthed and shaped by skilled professional historians. From this perspective, the role of the historical novelist might be the giving of imaginative life to facts already discovered and arranged in logical form: the novelist may, with artistic licence, add certain items and put a different gloss on others, but basically, historical knowledge is a given fact to be esteemed, not a process to be questioned.

I want to analyse Thomas Keneally's *The Playmaker* and Timberlake Wertenbaker's *Our Country's Good*[1] from a different perspective, that is, from Fredric Jameson's contention that our readings of the past are always vitally dependent upon our experience of the present.[2] I also hope to show how a subjective selection process can operate in apparently unproblematic conjunction with a confidence that history has been objectively formulated.

Keneally's novel *The Playmaker* is based on the events surrounding a convict production in 1789 of *The Recruiting Officer* by George Farquhar. There appears to be no record of who took part in or directed it, but Keneally assigns parts to names from historical record and this in itself lends an air of authenticity. He acknowledges sources, including: *The Journal and Letters of Lieutenant Ralph Clark*; David Collins's *Account of the English Colony in New South Wales*; and John Cobley's compilation *The Crimes of the First Fleet Convicts* and the same author's *Sydney Cove, 1788–1792*.[3] There is an evident fascination with 'facts' in the novel: details of crimes the convicts had been sentenced for, their slang, how food was rationed, how Sydney and Manly were so named and relations between the officers. The question, what evidence was employed in garnering these 'facts', might be less important than why they are likely to be accepted without question. Max Stafford-Clark, who commissioned *Our Country's Good*, the play based on Keneally's novel, writes: 'Keneally has emphasized how tangible and well documented was the animosity between Major Ross, who was the Senior Marine Officer, and Governor Phillip'.[4] It is not clear whether 'tangible' is Keneally's choice of adjective or Stafford-Clark's, but it conveys a sense of knowledge that is so sure it transcends the merely cerebral and mystifies any distinction between verifiable fact and received opinion. Stafford-Clark elaborates on the excitement of this sort of familiarity with the past:

> It's these facts about the convicts that are so gripping. Robert Sideway *did*
> found Australia's first professional theatre when he got his ticket of leave.
> Mary Brenham *did* have Ralph's child. Dabby Bryant *did* escape and Ralph
> Clark *did* have nightmares.[5]

The repeated emphasis – it *did* happen – indicates a need to touch the past amounting to a lust after understanding, and it is this urge, I think, that perpetuates a conception of history as fact and makes readers, even sophisticated ones, susceptible to the lure of an authoritatively shaped past.

Keneally is confident. His shape is of the First Fleet convicts as a race apart, with their own language and code of ethics, and their own deity called the Tawny Prince. A convict leader, Goose, is the embodiment of the malignant force: her murder by another convict as the play is about to be performed is presented as a triumph of good over evil, signalling that convicts are thenceforth redeemable into the orbit of established law. Most of the officers are decent men. Stafford-Clark says that Keneally told him of the respect with which the officers of the First Fleet are held by Australians: 'If Australian history does have captains and kings then Tench and Collins are among the captains'. Keneally went on to add that although the voyage of the First Fleet must have been horrific, 'it was also a triumph and I think it must have had an effect on convict morale. His Excellency made sure they got their vitamins'.[6] When Stafford-Clark and his cast had read Robert Hughes's *The Fatal Shore* they disagreed strongly that the voyage of the First Fleet was any kind of triumph, yet this does not seem to have diminished Keneally's authority in their eyes as an expert on convicts, on what Australians believe and on Aborigines. Stafford-Clark writes: 'He was, of course, particularly helpful on Arabanoo and the Aborigines'.[7] The 'of course' implies that the subject is a simple one, capable of only one interpretation which Keneally, as a well-known Australian, was bound to have got right. Keneally's authority is confirmed by an Englishman deferring to an Australian's superior knowledge, or possibly, shelving an awkward question of injustice as an entirely Australian responsibility.

Keneally's representation is, in the end, a celebration of a nation with the potential to live in harmony with itself. As the convicts present their play on the occasion of the King's birthday, the white population of Sydney is legitimized in its hierarchical form and dissent is contained. His Excellency the Governor sits in front with the Marine Officers, and his detractors Major Ross and Captain Campbell are there also, even though they distance themselves from the Governor as far as possible. Behind the line of officials sit the married Marines and their wives and children, and then less regular groupings of Marines and *Sirius* sailors and 'lags', male and female.[8] The position of the Aborigines is problematic because they are not there at the performance, and so are excluded from the triumphalist vision of a nation in a stage of incipient harmony. Arabanoo's death from smallpox is not permitted to detract from the triumph of the performance of the play. A note in the epilogue regrets that 'this flicker of a theatrical intent would consume in the end the different and serious theatre of the tribes of the hinterland'.[9] But it is just a note, peripheral to the central theme of the novel: the two strands of convicts and Aborigines are never reconciled, a failure perhaps acknowledged in the dedication 'to Arabanoo and his brethren — still dispossessed'. Regret is signalled, and compassion, but Aborigines are excluded from the nation-in-embryo. English culture, not Aboriginal, is celebrated: the unifying force is the civilizing power of art represented by the play most often performed on the English stage in the eighteenth century, and the romance that comes out of it between Ralph Clark, the officer who directs the play, and Mary Brenham, the convict who plays a leading role.

The shape that Keneally gives to the first convict settlement purports to be a tangible link with the past, an imaginative rendering of what actually happened. The circumstances of its production may have quite a lot to do with its perception of the Australian nation as potentially unified and self-regulating because it was published in time for the Bicentennial. And if the Bicentennial affected the production of *The Playmaker*, so too did Australian feminism and Keneally's response to it. As director of the convict play, Keneally's Ralph Clark is a hero, the facilitator of the harmony in the new community. This is very different from the Ralph Clark, who, in journals apparently intended for his wife to read, rails against 'damned bitches of convict women'.[10] Keneally seems to have felt that his memory deserves rehabilitating. Stafford-Clark writes: 'He told us that Australian feminists had had a field day at the expense of Ralph's journals, but Keneally thinks he "was just a poor narrow-minded neurotic — I wanted him to do the play because I so liked his dreams"'.[11]

It is not often, I think, that we are told so openly that the 'facts' of history are coloured by the personal enthusiasms of the recorder. There are many other ways in which the story of Ralph Clark could be told, and Stafford-Clark mentions one of them:

Ralph Clark's story can only be about the power of romance if you halt it (as Keneally does) at the point where he falls in love with Mary Brenham/ Silvia. The naming of their daughter Betsy Alicia after his wife, and his return to Plymouth abandoning his New World family turns the real history into a kind of Triumph of Pragmatism.[12]

Furthermore, making Clark the play's director reinforces class hierarchy: Hughes refers to plays performed on board convict transport ships[13] and this must have involved remarkable ingenuity, but, within the ideology of *The Playmaker*, only an officer is capable of redeeming convicts and introducing them into legitimate society through drama. The story would have taken on a different slant had Robert Sideway been made the director.

In his study of Keneally, Peter Quartermaine expresses reservations about him as a writer of historical fiction, suggesting that the apparently objective 'facts' which are the background to his imaginative reconstructions of the past, disguise a subjective and inevitably oversimplifying selection process. He says that this is the kind of history we have come to expect, as television drama has accustomed us to potted, easily assimilable versions of the past. The title *The Playmaker*, Quartermaine suggests, invites a perception of Keneally as skilled bookmaker, adroitly controlling his production from behind the scenes while appearing not to intervene at all as the 'facts' speak for themselves.[14] Quartermaine's worry that skilled surface performance might disguise a lack of depth echoes the concern of David English, who feels that Keneally's historical fiction relentlessly reduces a multifaceted past to an ever familiar and violent present.[15]

If, as Fredric Jameson has said, our readings of the past are always vitally dependent upon our experience of the present[16] we should not be too surprised, nor offended by the way Keneally appears to have given a simplified and personal version, understandable in the circumstances of its production, of a complex historical situation. What causes concern, I think, is that people are going to believe it: Keneally has authority, and there is, as I have suggested, an emotional preference for facts rather than representations. If the present is experienced as a time of confusion and rapid change, the urge to find conviction in the past is all the more imperative. This places historical scholarship in an awkward position: to say that 'truth' about the past is rhetoric dependent upon experience of the present might be seen as a logical deconstruction of the conservative view that historians assess the past objectively. But to go further and to propose that the notion of 'truth' has no existence at all outside the ways which we employ it, is to see ourselves as helpless victims in a shifting continuum where there are no entities like honesty, justice, fairness and so on, but only the exercise of power and language games where nothing can be proved, nothing believed. This is an untenable situation: Jean-François Lyotard

has suggested that the impossibility of proving that justice exists is matched by
an urgent need to behave as if it does, a conundrum which calls into question the
mind/body duality[17] and lends support to Keats's dictum that knowledge needs
to be proved 'upon the pulses'.[18] Accepting that understanding of the past is
dependent upon experience of the present does not eliminate the conviction, felt
upon the pulses, that the past is discoverable, and susceptible of moral
judgement. Another way of putting this would be to say that if 'facts' and
Platonic entities like justice and fairness cannot be accommodated within serious
historical scholarship, they are all the more likely to find a niche in popular
history.

If, in *The Playmaker*, an air of familiarity with a knowable past disguises a
subjective selection process, *Our Country's Good* is even more authoritative
about the past, yet at the same time it is deeply implicated in experience of the
present. We can deduce more than usual about the circumstances and processes
of its production because records were kept. In 1988, Max Stafford-Clark,
director of the Royal Court Theatre in London, asked Timberlake Wertenbaker
to write a play based on Keneally's novel. Stafford-Clark and the cast of the
Royal Court Theatre participated through a series of workshops in the evolution
of Wertenbaker's play and performed both it and *The Recruiting Officer*. Many
people, then, contributed to Wertenbaker's research: Stafford-Clark wrote a book
about the project and Wertenbaker and some of the actors have given
interviews.

The play that resulted from this collaboration tells basically the same story as
Keneally's with the same characters but a very different emphasis. The main
theme is the liberating power of the theatre: the founding of a new nation and
the plight of the Aborigines recede into the background. Phillip becomes a much
simpler character: the relationship with Arabanoo disappears and his main
function is to assert the redemptive power of drama. In one speech he says:

> The theatre is an expression of civilisation. We belong to a great country
> which has spawned great playwrights: Shakespeare, Marlowe, Jonson, and
> even in our own time, Sheridan. The convicts will be speaking a refined,
> literate language and expressing sentiments of a delicacy they are not used
> to. It will remind them that there is more to life than crime, punishment.
> And we, this colony of a few hundred will be watching this together, for a
> few hours we will no longer be despised prisoners and hated gaolers. We
> will laugh, we may be moved, we may even think a little.[19]

Major Ross and Captain Campbell, the two officers who oppose the
production, are demonized. They command one convict actress to drop to her
knees and bark like a dog, another to lift her skirts and display herself. The

convicts seem powerless to resist in the face of this brutalizing exercise of power, but they do resist through the medium of the play. Robert Sideway carries on rehearsing, finding through Farquhar the language to counteract brutality: 'What pleasures I shall meet abroad are indeed uncertain: but this I am sure of, I shall meet with less cruelty among the barbarous nations than I have found at home'.[20]

Wertenbaker introduces a new character, Liz Morden,[21] who is the most incorrigible of the women prisoners. She is condemned to death for stealing food: the evidence against her is flimsy, but she refuses to speak to defend herself until persuaded by Phillip that she must save herself, for the good of the play. She is persuaded, and when asked if she is good in her part she responds with a ringing affirmation of the ennobling power of drama: 'Your Excellency, I will endeavour to speak Mr Farquhar's lines with the elegance and clarity their own worth commands'.[22]

The end note of the play is a stage direction: 'And to the triumphant music of Beethoven's Fifth Symphony and the sound of applause and laughter from the First Fleet audience, the first Australian performance of *The Recruiting Officer* begins'.[23] Just how far should a representation stray from what is recorded about the past? Wertenbaker has never laid claim to historical accuracy, in fact she has made clear that her aim in writing the play was to show 'what it means to be brutalized – and how theater can be a humanizing force'.[24] The Australian penal system, then, is just a peg on which to hang themes of brutality and liberation. Nevertheless the production inherits an aura of authenticity from Keneally – characters' names, for example – and at least one critic is concerned about the effect this will have on understandings of the process of colonization.

In an article called '*Our Country's Good*: Theatre, Colony and Nation in Wertenbaker's Adaptation of *The Playmaker*', Ann Wilson notes that Aborigines are represented only by the periodic presence of a figure identified simply as The Aborigine, who comments on what he sees as if it were a bizarre dream. She finds the shift problematic 'inasmuch as it amounts to a denial of indigenous people because their voice is outside social discourse, relegated to the private idioms of dreamer'.[25] Wilson suggests furthermore that in asserting the civilizing power of English drama, Phillip is using a theatrical event to create homogeneity which will reinforce, not contradict, the ideology of English imperialism.[26] Thus not only the convict system but the whole imperialist project is sanitized, illustrating Benedict Anderson's point about imperialism making enormous progress in daintiness after the eighteenth century.[27]

This was not the effect intended, but a side product of the way research was conducted. In the two-week workshop in which the cast worked with Wertenbaker to provide her with material for her script, they talked to contemporary prisoners and military officers. Stafford-Clark reports that a high point for all of them was attending a play at Wormwood Scrubs Prison and talking with the cast afterwards. The prisoners said things like: 'Rehearsing is the only time you're not in prison' and 'It's the screws that make prison terrible'.[28] The more conventional research that they did – they all read Robert Hughes's *The Fatal Shore*, *English Society in the Eighteenth Century* by Roy Porter, and Mayhew's *History of the London Poor* – seems to have been evaluated in the light of their experience of contemporary prisoners. The way the past was understood in the light of the present is best illustrated in the research into the causes of criminality. Stafford-Clark explains that Wertenbaker needed detail about what turned a person into a professional criminal – the point at which stealing for a necessity changed to stealing as a matter of habit. Two of the cast talked to Rosie, who had been first in Holloway and then in Styal, and she explained that she first broke into big houses to have a look, then stole because she was hungry: Stafford-Clark comments 'We were all aware of the shocking and immediate parallels both to the women in *The Fatal Shore* and to the Mayhew accounts we had read'.[29] Rosie's story provides the basis for the explanation in *Our Country's Good* of how Liz Morden became a criminal.

The Royal Court Company's present experience was different from Keneally's, leading to a different reading of the past. For one thing their experience was English rather than Australian, based on contacts with contemporary prisoners which they found to be very moving. Ron Cook, the actor who played Phillip and Wisehammer, wrote of the visit to Wormwood Scrubs: 'You're getting information first hand, it's not any sort of intellectual exercise: you just observe the way people act, their atmosphere'.[30] Stafford-Clark refers to the 'enormous emotional power' generated by Liz Morden's speech to the Governor: Ann Wilson confessed to being deeply moved by it even though, as an academic, she was concerned about the contradictions inherent in the situation.

Another aspect of the present experience of the Royal Court Theatre that influenced the reading of the past in *Our Country's Good* was the state of drama in Britain at the time: pleas for the civilizing power of drama should be seen in the context of theatres feeling the pinch as funding for prisons was being cut. Stafford-Clark says that it is 'not the least of the play's achievements' that it stresses the power and enduring worth of theatre.[31] He was also concerned about increasing censorship in Britain at the time, and expressed amazement that Farquhar was allowed to write in 1706, and convicts to repeat in 1789, that in the army you learnt all about whoring, drinking, lying and bullying. In contemporary Britain, he said, that 'wouldn't even be allowed on Channel Four at three in the morning'.[32]

If contemporary censorship affects historical representations, so too do the personal enthusiasms of writers. Keneally was attracted to Ralph Clark's dreams:

Wertenbaker wanted to include a dream scene in which Ralph Clark's wife would cavort with one of the convicts. Stafford-Clark resisted because it was not a scene he felt able to stage: he was, however, interested in the vivid description in *The Fatal Shore* of an orgy which took place on the night after the arrival of the first fleet, as rum-maddened sailors slithered through the mud in pursuit of women convicts. Such a scene would have given a different slant to the play, but it had to be excluded, not on ideological grounds but because of the habits of actors. In the 1970s, Stafford-Clark reflected, the scene would have been fine, but in the 1980s, 'actors just won't take orgies seriously'.[33]

Does it matter that what goes into the shaping of history can be so arbitrarily decided? From my present experience, I think that it does. Keneally is popular, and *Our Country's Good* is possibly the best known representation of the Australian penal system in England today. Since 1993 it has been on the Associated Examining Board's A-level syllabus 660, an exam taken by over 20,000 students in 1994. There is no record of how many of them studied that particular text, but it is a popular choice at the schools near me: students find it accessible and they respond to its emotional power. In the current educational climate, a text which attracts customers and contributes to a good pass-rate is likely to be widely studied. I would see this as having the positive value that more people know something about convicts and about Aboriginal dispossession, and they might be tempted to explore further. And the play, like *The Playmaker*, draws attention to the concepts of individual worth, and of the brutalizing effects of brutal treatment.

Notes

1. Thomas Keneally, *The Playmaker* (London and Sydney, Hodder and Stoughton, 1987); Timberlake Wertenbaker, *Our Country's Good* (London, Methuen Drama, 1991).
2. Fredric Jameson, 'Marxism and Historicism' in Jameson, *The Ideologies of Theory: Essays, 1971–1986*, vol. 2, *Syntax of History* (London, Routledge, 1988), pp. 150–1.
3. See *The Playmaker*, author's note, no p. number. Also see: Ralph Clark (ed. Paul G. Fidlon and R.J. Ryan), *The Journal and Letters of Ralph Clark* (Sydney, Library of Australian History, 1981); David Collins, *An Account of the English Colony in New South Wales: With Remarks on the Dispositions, Customs, Manners etc of the Native Inhabitants of that Country*, vol. 1 (London, 1798; 2nd edn – with introduction by Brian H. Fletcher – Sydney, A.H. and W.A. Reed in association with the Royal Australian Historical Society, 1975); John Cobley (ed.), *The Crimes of the First Fleet Convicts* (Sydney, Angus and Robertson, 1970); John Cobley, *Sydney Cove, 1788–1792*, 3 vols (London, Angus and Robertson, 1980). Keneally's author's note also mentions Kenneth Gordon McIntyre, *The Rebello Transcripts: Governor Phillip's Portuguese Interlude* (London, Souvenir, 1984).

 4. Max Stafford-Clark, *Letters from George* (London, Nick Hern Books, 1989), p. 77.
 5. Ibid., p. 55.
 6. Ibid., p. 59.
 7. Ibid.
 8. Keneally, *The Playmaker*, pp. 289–90.
 9. Ibid., p. 305.
10. Quoted in Robert Hughes, *The Fatal Shore: A History of the Transportation of Convicts to Australia, 1787–1868* (London, Collins Harvill, 1987), p. 250. The words often attributed to Ralph Clark concerning the arrival of a female convict ship, 'not more of these damned whores', may be apocryphal but certainly seem to represent accurately enough his sentiments concerning convict women.
11. Stafford-Clark, *Letters from George*, p. 60.
12. Ibid.
13. Hughes, *The Fatal Shore*, p. 154.
14. Peter Quartermaine, *Thomas Keneally* (London, Edward Arnold, 1991), pp. 39 and 86.
15. David English, 'History and the Refuge of Art: Thomas Keneally's Sense of the Past', *Meridian*, vol. 6, no. 1 (Melbourne, 1987), pp. 23–9.
16. Jameson, 'Marxism and Historicism', pp. 150–1.
17. Jean-François Lyotard, *The Postmodern Condition: A Report on Knowledge* (Minneapolis, University of Minnesota Press, 1984), p. 77, and Lyotard, *The Differend: Phrases in Dispute* (Manchester, Manchester University Press, 1988), pp. 165–71.
18. John Keats, letter to J.H. Reynolds in Robert Gittings (ed.), *The Letters of John Keats: A New Selection* (London, Oxford University Press, 1970), p. 93.
19. Wertenbaker, *Our Country's Good*, p. 21.
20. Ibid., p. 65.
21. Morden is an imagined First Fleet convict. No convict of this name is listed in the most complete and up-to-date reference work on the personnel of the First Fleet; see Mollie Gillen, *The Founders of Australia: A Biographical Dictionary of the First Fleet* (Sydney, Library of Australian History, 1989).
22. Wertenbaker, *Our Country's Good*, p. 83.
23. Ibid., p. 91.
24. Ann Wilson, '*Our Country's Good*: Theatre, Colony and Nation in Wertenbaker's Adaptation of *The Playmaker*', *Modern Drama*, vol. 34, no. 1 (Toronto, March 1991), pp. 23–4.
25. Ibid., p. 30.
26. Ibid., p. 31.
27. Benedict Anderson, *Imagined Communities: Reflections on the Origin and Spread of Nationalism* (London, Verso, 1983), p. 91.
28. Stafford-Clark, *Letters from George*, p. 144.
29. Ibid., p. 115.
30. 'Dramatic Convictions: Dialogue between Playwright Timberlake Wertenbaker and Actor Ron Cook', *The Listener*, 30 Nov. 1989, pp. 38–9.
31. Stafford-Clark, *Letters from George*, p. 189.
32. Ibid., p. 39.
33. Ibid., p. 185.

Part 2

════════════

Questioning the 'Criminal Class'

CHAPTER FIVE

Representing Convict Women

Deborah Oxley

Lloyd Robson observed that 'the picture presented of the women convicted and transported to Australia is not an attractive one'.[1] On the same topic and in similar vein, A.G.L. Shaw commented that, even discounting for contemporary exaggeration, 'the picture they presented is a singularly unattractive one'.[2] Convict women were all refractory, drunken and immoral prostitutes, members of a professional criminal class with a severe disinclination to work, unskilled in all but vice and unfit to contribute to colonial economic development. None of this was true. Convict women were small-time sneak thieves and robbers whose human capital compared favourably with workers left behind in Ireland and England: many convict women were literate, numerate, skilled and semi-skilled workers in their most productive and reproductive years.[3] Robson's own quantitative evidence confirmed this. Yet it is exactly this gap between reality and representation that proves so fascinating. Self-consciously returning to the visual imagery of earlier writers, Michael Sturma argued that disparity arose because beauty lay in the eye of the beholder: subjective nineteenth-century accounts misled past historians.[4] Part 1 of this chapter explores this issue, further examining why contemporaries reached derogatory conclusions in the first place. Part 2 examines the way colonial rhetoric resonated with broader discourses on Britain's criminal women, again addressing issues of evidence and value systems. Part 3 concludes the chapter by arguing that through uncritically employing highly charged contemporary opinions as objective evidence, convicts have not only been misrepresented in the literature, but that the convict origins debate has been excessively politicized much to the detriment of Australia's economic history.

Part 1: Colonial estimations

A great quantity of the evidence amassed incriminating convict women has been anecdotal, a collection of vituperative remarks supplied by government officials and religious men attempting to impose authority on people little understood by them. These critics concluded that transported women were 'the most disgusting objects that ever disgraced the female form'; 'as bad as it is possible for human beings to be'; 'at times they are excessively ferocious ... all of them, with scarcely an exception, drunken and abandoned prostitutes'. The convicted woman's habits were 'loose, idle', 'her general character is immodesty, drunkenness and the most horrible language', she was 'bad beyond anything that you can fancy'.[5] Remarks were made by the women's gaolers, magistrates, men of the cloth with strict moral codes and by one other very significant group: employers.

Class relations between employer and employee played their part in this discourse on convict women. Colonial New South Wales was an arena where employer and employee battled to establish work relations – a negotiation hardly unique to Australia – but what was unique were the terms of warfare. Labourers were neither free nor slave, but criminals temporarily under the authority of the state. Nor were employers simply employers. Over a lengthy period, the state relinquished part of its authority over a significant number of transported felons through a process of 'assigning' convict workers to private employers. The latter assumed the task of managing these malefactors with the expectation of receiving productive labour along with state-subsidized food and clothing for their workforce. Convicts were thus the central element of a power matrix which constrained them both as workers and as criminals while simultaneously creating employers as both bosses and proxies for state authority. But relations were complex. Convict workers were constrained, but scarcity of labour gave them bargaining power. If mistreated, convicts had recourse to a number of colonial institutions such as the courts. And yet, failure to win their case entailed loss of privileges, even whipping.[6] Employers, on the other hand, faced an unusual problem: how to extract work effort from assigned convict servants. Coincidentally, as the major landowners, these employers also formed the local magistracy, enforcing a legal code which itself reflected these power relationships.

Working-class behaviour was criminalized through this code. Unlike Britain's labour force, Australia's workers faced a legal system which permitted incarceration for the worker who had a quick tongue, a sharp wit and a tendency to drink or who was rude with a proclivity to affront a 'superior'. Some contemporaries were conscious of this inequality. A Chief Justice of New South Wales observed:

In order to keep the convicts to their duty, they are subjected to a code of laws framed for such a purpose by the local legislature. These laws create a class of offences peculiar to the condition of the convicts — such as drunkenness, disobedience, neglect, absconding from service, abusive language, (to master or overseer) or other disorderly, (or dishonest) conduct — the breach of which is liable to be visited with summary, and in some cases, severe punishment.[7]

Sir George Arthur, Governor of Van Diemen's Land from 1824 to 1836, told the 1837 Select Committee on Transportation that:

the convict is subject to the caprice of the family to which he is assigned, and subject to the most summary laws. He is liable to be sent to a chain gang, or to be scourged for idleness, for insolent words, for insolent looks, or for anything betraying the insurgent spirit.[8]

In spite of the male pronoun, criticisms of this 'giant lottery' were just as applicable to female convicts, although for them getting pregnant also needs to be added to the list of offending actions. Such crimes might be dealt with through the courts, or by returning an assignee to the state. The outcome of this system was inevitable: colonial conviction rates were inflated and state residencies for convicts like the Female Factory at Parramatta were overused.[9]

Both these outcomes provided contemporaries with 'evidence' of convicts' poor characters, with the laws themselves endorsing value-judgements which condemned working-class resistance and indulgences such as drinking, swearing, smoking and skiving off work. It is from this perspective of coercive labour relations that we need to evaluate contemporary claims. James Macarthur, a large colonial landholder and employer, had found the convict women assigned to him as domestic servants to be 'most dissolute' and 'such very bad characters' because they were 'so very troublesome' and because 'there is no subject which occasions a greater amount of complaint to the different benches of magistrates than the conduct of the female convict servants'. James Mudie, master and magistrate famed for his unremitting lashing of workers who fell asleep on the job or were disobedient and insolent by his measure, vilified the women as 'exceedingly savage' for failing to comply to his standards, in terms of both work and sex. Based on his personal knowledge as a member of the employing class, Lieutenant Colonel Henry Breton believed the women to be shockingly dissolute and drunken. Breton illustrated his claim that the women were 'everything that is bad' with the case of a woman who wanted rum for her labour, else she was back off to the Female Factory.[10]

The Female Factory at Parramatta was a lying-in hospital, labour bureau, and place of secondary punishment. It may well have been perceived by some women as a place where refuge could be sought away from the dominant culture: a female enclave in a thoroughly male-dominated society. If women used this institution to escape from aggressive male employers, or men more generally, employers used the Factory as a method of labour control. The majority of women in residence had been returned for 'bad behaviour', such as drinking, swearing or otherwise showing disrespect for their employers. Inside they could also be found guilty of disorderly, insolent or disobedient conduct, fighting and quarrelling, idleness and neglect of work, foul language — activities that would incur a loss of privileges or other punishment. Working-class women found it remarkably easy to affront authority, and although they were not sent on chain gangs, in the Factory they too were subjected to often gruelling physical punishments such as the treadmill. These women were severely judged by harsh standards that in Britain could not easily be enforced but which in the colony were institutionalized in law. The Factory's Committee of Management observed, regretfully, 'how speedily a portion of the Female Convicts ... are returned to Government, and sent to the Factory at Parramatta ... in many cases, those persons have been returned for awkwardness or misbehaviour which, in free servants, would be noticed by a gentle reproof'.[11] For the Irish — the majority of convict women — issues were further complicated by their language. Complaints by employers that convict servants were obtuse and unresponsive to orders may have derived from simple misunderstandings as Gaelic speakers failed to grasp the meaning of commands. Employers were disgruntled at working-class morality, resistance and ineptitude, and many voiced their complaints to the 1837 Select Committee on Transportation which was decidedly keen on hearing them.

In the case of convict women the social dimensions of class, religion and ethnicity compacted with gender to exacerbate problems. Misunderstandings — and consequently misrepresentations — arose out of ignorance. The First Fleet provides one early example of this trend. Arthur Bowes Smyth was the surgeon on board the *Lady Penrhyn* and was thus responsible for the 109 women convicts that it carried. After favourably outlining the food and medical provisions that had been made for the convicts, his journal stated:

> I wish I cd. with truth add that the behaviour of the Convicts merited such extream indulgence — but I believe I may venture to say there was never a more abandon'd set of wretches ... The greater part of them are so totally abandoned & callous'd to all sense of shame & even of common decency that it frequently becomes indispensably necessary to inflict Corporal punishment upon them, and sorry I am to say that even this rigid mode of proceeding has not the desired Effect, since every day furnishes proofs of their being more harden'd in their Wickedness.

To what proofs does Bowes Smyth refer? To the women's 'matchless Hippocracy' unequalled:

> except by their base Ingratitude; many of them plundering the Sailors, (who have at every Port they arrived at spent almost the whole of the wages due to them in purchasing different Articles of wearing apparel & other things for their accommodation) of their necessary clothes & cutting them up for some purpose of their own.

Quite likely, the purpose was to stem the flow of menstrual blood. Most convicts were better nourished during the journey than at any earlier point in their lives, leading to regular bleeding in many women and accelerating menarche in others. It is somewhat surprising that a medical man like Bowes Smyth with a considerable experience of midwifery should have been so apparently unaware of other aspects of the female reproductive system. He considered provisions to be admirable in spite of the absence of any rags or such like for menstruating women, and then criticized these women – seemingly out of ignorance – when they attempted to find their own solution to the shortage. For this they were abused as being ingrates beyond redemption. Bowes Smyth despaired, 'nor do I conceive it possible in their present situation to adopt any plan to induce them to behave like rational or even human Beings'.[12]

Bowes Smyth was also upset by the women's use of 'oaths & imprecations'. Powerful contemporary observers had, as noted, demonized working-class cultural practices. In particular they were proscriptive of female behaviour, leaving convict women judged worse than convict men. Unbecoming behaviour was in some respects the women's quintessential crime. Immoral, licentious, drunken and uncouth, convict women were deemed more familiar with foul language than with decent womanly comportment, and their loose, immodest ways earned them disapprobation as 'damned whores' and 'abandon'd prostitutes'; it was not society that had abandoned the prostitute, but the prostitute who had abandoned social mores. As Marian Quartly has written, 'rather than their sexual morality it was the manners of the women – their demeanour, accent, language, and their deference, or lack thereof – which labelled them as good women or as whores in the eyes of the officers'.[13] In colonial New South Wales the title 'whore' was earned, not by selling sex, but by breaking rules. The oft quoted comment made by the colonist James Mudie is a very telling one. Mudie chose his words carefully when he described the women convicts as 'the lowest possible ... they all smoke, drink and in fact, to speak in plain language, I consider them all prostitutes'.[14] Some of them had even attended the theatre! Convict women were damned because they did not behave like ladies nor sober workers and because they failed to adhere to

Mudie's value-system. They got drunk, they smoked, they gazed back and they spoke in lewd ways their critics thought reserved for men.

Dissatisfaction with the women was expressed in sexual terminology: they were labelled whores, a metaphorical device distilling all the features that were the obverse of what became the Victorian feminine ideal; and disgracing their sex was a familiar reproach also levelled at other women. Free female immigrants to New South Wales fell victim to their masters' acerbic tongues. One Irish servant, for example, was considered a very bad sort. She was brought before the magistrate because she insisted on wearing 'patent leather pumps' when working at the washtub![15] I wonder if they were red? Quickly, immigrant women too were labelled whores. This commonality of experience between immigrants and convicts highlights what the real issues were: not criminal professionalism, but work relations, class, gender and ethnicity as well.[16] Women were damned for failing to work according to their masters' and mistresses' expectations. The cause of this name calling was a clash of gendered cultural values which left a yawning chasm of misunderstandings and interests between the two very different groups of observer and observed. On the one hand were young and often Irish Catholic women (many of whom were Gaelic speakers) from the labouring classes who found themselves living under coercive penal authority in a society where women were a scarce commodity; while, on the other hand, were placed the vocal English Protestant middle-class male employers of forced labour, who (perhaps guilt-ridden) engaged in sexual liaisons with the convict women but still judged their morality and found it wanting. In this highly charged atmosphere, only one side left enduring testimony.

Part 2: Bad women and criminal classes

Descriptions of female transportees resonated strongly with those applied to other criminal women held in British gaols. Both were considered 'worse' than their male counterparts, while both had their femininity questioned. Once more visual metaphors were rife with some racism thrown in for good measure. Again it was their 'immoral' behaviour more than their criminal activity which brought them into disrepute. Not all commentators held such opinions, but an influential minority did.[17] Arguably, had key Australian historians canvassed broader views they would have painted convict women quite differently — different palette, different picture. They themselves were, however, influenced not only by highly coloured colonial appraisals, but by select British criminological writings.[18]

Ostensibly, convict women were 'far worse and far more difficult of reformation than the man'.[19] Apparently, so were other female offenders more degenerate than their criminal brethren. 'It is a well-established fact in prison logistics that the women are far worse than the men', wrote Major Arthur Griffiths, an Inspector of Prisons and one time Deputy Governor of the women's prison at Millbank. 'When given to misconduct they are far more persistent in their evil ways, more outrageously violent, less amenable to reason or reproof.'[20] An anonymous contributor to *Cornhill Magazine* (revealed from accounts payable to be Mrs M.E. Owen) pursued the same line: 'Again, it is notorious that a bad man – we mean one whose evil training has led him into crime – is not so vile as a bad woman … there is more hope of influencing the former than the latter'.[21] Men were neither so vile nor as closed to the possibility of reform.

Nor was the manhood of male felons queried because they had offended. Women's experience was different: criminality put femininity on the line. Offending women lost their femininity and even their humanity. Bowes Smyth had bemoaned his inability to make convict women act 'like rational or even human beings'. Like transported convicts, other criminal women 'disgraced' their sex, leaving a hint of the wild beast. Mrs Owen continued. Criminal women were 'more uncivilized than the savage, more degraded than the slave, less true to all natural and womanly instincts than the untutored squaw of the North American Indian tribe'. While men and women were:

> equally criminal in one sense, in another sense there is a difference. The man's nature may be said to be hardened, the woman's destroyed. Women of this stamp are generally so bold and unblushing in crime, so indifferent to right and wrong, so lost to all sense of shame, so destitute of the instincts of womanhood, that they may be more justly compared to wild beasts than to women. To say the least, the honour of womanhood requires that a new appellation be invented for them.[22]

Similarly, the study of journalists Henry Mayhew and John Binny of London's prisons and prison life left them reeling from their encounter with women whom they found debased and without shame for the crimes they had perpetrated. Shocked, they concluded that such women were:

> utterly barbarized … without the faintest twinge of moral sense to restrain their wild animal passions and impulses; so that in them one sees the most hideous picture of all human weakness and depravity – a picture the more striking because exhibiting the coarsest and rudest moral features in connection with a being whom we are apt to regard as the most graceful and gentle form of humanity.[23]

According to Arthur Griffiths, the women's prison at Newgate was no more than 'a den of wild beasts, where only filth, disgusting odours, and all abominations reigned'. Crime was a slippery slope. 'No doubt when a woman is really bad, when all the safeguards, natural and artificial, with which they have been protected are removed, further deterioration is sure to be rapid when it once begins.'[24] This was the fall of woman – what 'abandonment' really meant.

What bad behaviour did the criminal women of Britain indulge in to lead to this characterization of utter degeneracy? For Mrs Owen the answer was difficult to localize:

> From the mass of evil habits that these women have accumulated, it is not easy to select illustrations that shall convey a vivid impression to the reader's mind. As a class they are guilty of lying, theft, unchastity, drunkenness, slovenliness. To finish the picture, it may be added, they are ignorant, so obtuse, that instruction might as well be given in an unknown tongue, so little do they understand it. Lying may be said to be their native language.[25]

Prison reformer Joseph John Gurney, the man who disparaged London's criminal women as filthy and disgusting 'scum', found the women incarcerated in Newgate prison 'ignorant to the greatest degree, not only of religious truth, but of the most familiar duty and business of life'.[26] Newgate was indeed 'a perfect sink of abomination'.[27] Three hundred women – tried, untried, felons and misdemeanants – plus their children, were crammed altogether into 190 square yards of space, without beds, cooking on the floor where they slept, many half-naked or in rags. But what really dismayed observers were not the conditions but the women's behaviour. American Quakers visiting Newgate in 1813 were 'shocked and sickened ... by the blaspheming, fighting, dram-drinking, half-naked women'.[28] It was clear what brought the women into disrepute. Griffiths complained how 'on all sides the ear was assailed by awful imprecations, begging, swearing, singing, fighting, dancing, dressing up in men's clothes'.[29] James Guthrie, one-time Ordinary of Newgate, also expounded upon 'the stupidity and hardness of these unthinking and miserable creatures' – the women and men in his cells – because they 'behaved very undecently, laughed and seemed to make a mock of everything that was serious and regular', by which he meant his sermons. One woman, Ann Mudd, 'used to sing obscene songs, and talked very indecently'. Another prisoner – a man – 'was a very profane, unthinking hearer, for he could not abstain from laughing' and yet another individual was reproved for having 'a smiling countenance'.[30]

Similarly, when Mayhew inquired about the 'incorrigibles' brought down from Brixton, the warder from Millbank responded that these 'were the very worst women in existence. I don't fancy their equal could be found anywhere'.

Why this assessment? Because these women were guilty of singing, dancing, whistling and using profane language, even in the punishment cells. The Matron was embarrassed: 'Their language to the minister is sometimes so horrible, that I am obliged to run away with disgust'. Not content with that, the women 'make songs themselves all about the officers of the prison. Oh! they'll have every one in the verses – the directors, the governor, and all of us'. Mayhew himself was confronted by the audacity of women who looked at him full in the face, and in the schoolroom too. 'As we glanced along the three rows of white caps, there was not one abashed face or averted tearful eye to be seen, whilst many grinned impudently on meeting our gaze.' Women failed to live up to expectations of polite and remorseful female behaviour, and the conclusion was reached about London's female prisoners that their 'most striking peculiarity ... is that of utter and imperturbable shamelessness'. Finally, the Matron remarked in somewhat astonished tones, 'some of our best-looking women are among the worst behaved of all the prisoners in the female ward'.[31]

Another reason for complaint was some women's destructive behaviour. Mayhew and Binny were taken on a tour:

> The matron now led us into a double cell, containing an iron bed and tressel. Here the windows were all broken, and many of the sashes shattered as well. This had been done by one of the women with a tin pot, we were informed. 'What is this, Miss Cosgrove?' asked the warder, pointing to a bundle of sticks like firewood in the corner. 'Oh, that's the remains of her table! And if we hadn't come in time, she would have broken up her bedstead as well, I dare say.'

Other women had torn their own clothes, and yet others took against themselves.[32] Mary McCarthy was 'a most artful, designing woman' because of her repeated attempts 'to destroy herself'. Repeated attempts at suicide, self-mutilation and starvation, along with the use of 'dreadful' language, led Ann Williams's demeanour to be described as showing 'strongly of artifice' for which the doctor recommended the punishment of a bread-and-water diet.[33]

Griffiths found that of all these 'very desperate characters' none was worse than Julia St Clair Newman. In Millbank Penitentiary Julia Newman's history was one of repeated offences. Initially these were her persistent attempts to gain writing materials and to pass letters on via other prisoners to her mother, gaoled along with Julia but held separately. Persistent punishment did not prevent these 'clandestine writings' and she further invited disaster with 'a long and critical examination of the young Queen, who had just come to the throne'. Additionally, Julia proved her depravity to the satisfaction of her gaolers through the destruction of property, by 'manifesting contempt of authority', through 'the frightful and horrible imprecations she uttered', and by singing, in particular, little ditties about the infirmary warder Mrs King: 'What a pity hell's gates are not kept by dame King / So surly a cur would let nobody in'. The primary reason for which the authorities were annoyed with Julia Newman changed over time as her crime altered from one of letter-writing to 'trying it on' or 'doing the barmy' – feigning lunacy. Evidence that she was pretending was weak. Attempted mutilation of herself (such as blackening her own eyes), violent tempers, refusal to eat, stating that she wished to be dead, attempting to hang herself on several occasions, and – most annoying to the authorities – indifference to punishment, all earned her repeated spells in the dark cell and in the strait-jacket. A comprehensive range of mechanical restraints fell victim to her amazing ability to dismantle and destroy them. Various punishments were inflicted; none succeeded in bringing her to her senses, or more aptly, to the sensibilities of her gaolers. Mr Nihil, who was in charge of Millbank, had only one fear regarding this case, that 'her own self-abandonment to violence may superinduce real madness, and then it will be said that our system at the Penitentiary had driven her out of her mind'. Neither Nihil nor Griffiths wanted to countenance the possibility that it *was* the severity of the prison system that drove one women to 'beat herself violently' and another to attempt 'to dash her brains out by striking her head violently against the wall'. Rather, this conduct merely confirmed their belief that these women were the 'dregs of society', 'England's social sewage' and that Julia Newman was simply a 'violent and obstinate girl'.[34] It would be interesting to know if male prisoners were assessed as bad by these same criteria.

Criminal women were judged badly because they failed to obey orders or to understand them, because they drank, sang, smiled, dressed up, flirted, showed no remorse, rebelled, destroyed, disobeyed, attempted suicide and, occasionally, because they broke the law. Such acts lost them their womanhood and even their human status. Reform aimed to replace 'drunkenness, ferocity, and abandoned licentiousness by sober decency of demeanour; loud ribaldry and oaths by silence or edifying talk; squalor and semi-nudity by cleanliness and sufficiency in attire', and to create 'a happy home of quiet and decorum'. But some, like Griffiths, thought reform of such women impossible. Achievements made by the prison reformer Mrs Elizabeth Fry and her associates from the Society for the Reformation of Female Prisoners were dismissed by Griffiths as transitory and she insisted that the women of the Ladies' Association had been 'duped' by the outward and 'most depraved and hypocritical' display of good behaviour put on by criminal women who momentarily hid their 'evil natures, which still rankled like hidden sores beneath'.[35] None, however, disputed that sobriety and silence were desirable.

Derogatory assessments of criminal women such as those made by Griffiths,

Mayhew, Binny, etc., formed part of a profoundly influential nineteenth-century discourse on what was called the 'criminal class', conceived as an organized group of professional prostitutes and outlaws choosing to live exclusively off immoral earnings. No such class existed, nor were systems of detection and prosecution sophisticated enough to even distinguish hardened offenders. Yet such a class was created at the level of myth. Douglas Hay identified the criminal law as an ideological system which 'contributed to the maintenance of order and deference'.[36] This feature of social control was no less true of criminal mythology. However, neither the law nor the mythology were solely restricted to *maintaining* order, but were used to promote a new order, particularly in urban centres. Crime and criminality provided an arena which allowed for the clear articulation of hegemonic values at a time of immense change. The old pre-industrial order was giving way to a new system of industrial production. Industrialization, urbanization and modernization transformed what was required of workers. Individuals were guided away from pre-industrial rural life-styles where work, leisure and family life were melded together and governed by the daily passage of the sun and marked in passing by seasonal events, and where welfare was a right. In place of the old order a new system of industrial labour arose which employed individuals according to fluctuating demands, determined from they knew not where, for regimented hours on unfamiliar machines, sometimes paid by the piece but nearly always required to satisfy their wants via the market place, with entitlements to welfare limited to those indisputably unable to work. Monumental transitions such as these brought conflict and tested employers' abilities to overcome entrenched social practices, such as the keeping of irregular hours, drinking and the absenteeism of 'St Monday'. It was within this context that the imperative emerged to label old practices associated with an earlier work orientation as dysfunctional and immoral, while sanctioning and celebrating the new. An imagined criminal class provided the opportunity.

Importantly, as noted by Clive Emsley, 'crime is not, and never was, confined to one social class, yet middle-class offenders were not included among the criminal class'.[37] Rhetoric was about workers, not criminals. Designed in the minds of 'moral entrepreneurs' like Henry Mayhew, the criminal class embodied all that was unacceptable in the industrial working classes.[38] Juxtaposed to the good worker was an evil criminal class created in contradistinction to capitalist production, its social organization and values. Consistency was maintained when it came to the gender order. Both men and women of this class were depicted as preferring the easy life. Both were irreligious, disrespectful of authority, contemptuous of laws and of the property rights of others. Both were untrained idlers unaccustomed to habits of work, who showed contempt for the honest society off which they parasitically lived. Both made poor parents. Both were threatening. Both behaved indecently. However, what constituted decency varied between men and women. A badly behaved working-class woman was someone who drank, sang raucous songs, swore, fought, acted in lewd ways, dressed boldly and was disobedient, disrespectful, cheeky, destructive and shameless; a woman who failed to behave according to a restrictive set of mores. This quintessential difference was expressed in the stratified nature of the mythical criminal class: the men were all professional criminals unwilling to work; while the women, rather than thieves and murderers, were professional prostitutes. Why? Because whoredom symbolized the failed and fallen woman.

There is a certain irony that criminal men were damned for failing to work, while criminal women were damned precisely for doing just that at the point where their labours entered the paid sector as prostitutes. It was an irony lost on the myth-makers. Protagonists in this debate did not consider prostitution work but a symbol for female degeneracy. Criminality and sexual impropriety, as it was deemed, became entwined with other labour market issues. Just as crime denied women femininity, so too did certain employments and lost femininity led inexorably to crime. Samuel Redgrave, Criminal Registrar in the Home Office, wrote 'the greatest proportion of female commitments has taken place in those counties where females are employed in the rudest and most unfeminine labours'.[39] In 1849 another social critic expressed this complementary view and causal explanation. Jelinger C. Symons believed 'that wherever women are much employed in masculine pursuits which tend to increase their power and opportunities of committing offences, the proportion of female to male offenders increases'.[40] Women engaged in what was becoming 'men's work' became criminal and licentious. When Subcommissioner Symons enquired into the state of the mining industry and found semi-naked women working long hours in harsh surrounds alongside non-familial men, he chose to liken the pits to a brothel.[41] Women engaged in 'inappropriate' work or any type of 'unwomanly' conduct were denied femininity and legitimacy. In this discourse they became the prostitute-criminal, the bad woman, the abandoned whore.

Part 3: History politicized

Criminal women had not been 'nice' – by definition they had broken at least one written law – and the criticisms they incurred were loud and clamorous. We have seen how such views were the products of a given historical moment, shaped by the biases of the time and of the individual observer concerned. Gender, ethnicity, class relationships, shifting labour markets and criminality *all* influenced the composition. Today we would not expect to share the same set of cultural assumptions underpinning past evaluations, but by uncritically employing these sources this is exactly what has occurred. Manning Clark dismissed his own quantitative evidence revealing high literacy rates, preferring to conclude on the basis of Mayhew's qualitative remarks that convicts suffered from 'mental imbecility', to give but one example.[42] Sadly, undiscriminating use of these politicized nineteenth-century texts – both colonial and criminological – has led to too many historians internalizing the values embedded in these selective historical records. Consequently, just as contemporaries sought to pass judgement on convict women's morals and behaviour, so it has become almost axiomatic that it is the historian's task to judge that nebulous object called convict 'character' as either good or bad, nice or nasty. Perceptively, Bernard Smith recognized that 'the very word "convict" concealed moral issues to which, in one sense, there were no purely historical answers, but a great potential to divide and separate out historians along an ethico-political spectrum'.[43]

On the other hand, for much of the twentieth century, *economic* historians were so preoccupied with rates of growth in Gross Domestic Product that convicts did not even rate a mention. Sometimes convicts were a lumpen proletariat beneath contempt, while at others they were simply irrelevant. When a team at the University of New South Wales finally turned attention on convicts as a labour input, they confounded the debate. *Convict Workers: Reinterpreting Australia's Past* sought to evaluate convicts as workers and the contributions they made to colonial economic development.[44] It remained resolutely unconcerned with the questions of convict morality and convict character that had for so long dogged the debate, sidetracking it down dead-end roads. In a series of conclusions this book found that 'the convicts transported to Australia were ordinary British and Irish working class men and women. They were not professional and habitual criminals, recruited from a distinct class and trained to crime from the cradle'; that the immigration of convicts was 'effective'; that the convicts brought useful skills to Australia; and that these were efficiently allocated through a labour market manipulated by the government.[45] Such findings represented a significant maturing of recent attitudes towards convicts and convict Australia which have, over the last two decades, fitted increasingly uneasily with the dominant explanation of convict origins which claimed that ancestry lay within a 'criminal class'.

Given the highly charged climate surrounding the convict origins debate, however, the absence of overt judgements on convict 'character' created a dangerous vacuum. Practitioners reading *Convict Workers* often either consciously or unconsciously sought moral statements, and when none were forthcoming they imputed them. My own chapter about female transportees in *Convict Workers* is a case in point. It elicited diametrically opposite criticisms because diametrically opposite values were read into it. Norma Townsend and David Kent have accused me of robbing convict women of their choices, diminishing their status as human beings, representing them as powerless 'victims of patriarchal, capitalist, middle and upper-class hegemony'.[46] On the other hand, Townsend's and Kent's colleague Miriam Dixson claims that my approaches 'effectively divorce these roles [as workers, wives and mothers] from the context of domination'.[47] Apparently, I deny women have power while simultaneously failing to recognize their powerlessness.

Neither contention is true, either of my work or of the convict women's positions. My quantitative investigations of a large database revealed that the women chose to act. They exercised their agency by investing in human capital (skills, literacy and numeracy), travelling around Ireland and Britain to maximize that investment (in search of jobs) and by choosing to commit crimes. Yet convict women exercised agency within a context of intensifying inequalities. Industrialization brought gains, but there were losses too. Women in late eighteenth to mid-nineteenth-century England faced a reality of declining overall economic opportunities (particularly in the countryside), increasing wage differentials between men and women, marginalization within the home, increasing unpaid work responsibilities and diminishing welfare supports. Perhaps prostitution was widespread because it was more profitable than most female employment, being located in one labour-market segment where women did not have to compete with men. Gender relations were being renegotiated, but in the countryside this meant a diminution of women's status and access to resources. Over time the heights women attained fell and their lives shortened. And yet, despite my work focusing upon material concerns, it is claimed by Dixson that I 'offer a picture of personality' suffering 'a dismaying one-dimensionality to convict subjectivity'.[48] In truth, 'personality' has nothing to do with my work at all.

Myopic nineteenth-century accounts have not only provided damning 'evidence' against convicts, they have also politicized the historical debate, creating a forum more concerned with judgement than illumination. Thwarted expectations led to condemnatory words that have repeatedly returned to haunt the convict women and to historians they seemingly confirmed expectations bred from the popular nineteenth-century theory of the 'criminal class'. But just as American plantation owners cannot be relied upon to give objective accounts of their slave workforce, neither can vexed Australian employers be trusted to give accurate assessments of their convict workers. When we look at the basis of their judgements we find much room to disagree. And what function does such evidence fulfil? Convict women may have been rude, brutish, lewd, but what does this tell us?

Misrepresenting convict women has had a debilitating outcome. Historians have been misled into constantly mistaking economic categories of poverty, prostitution and other forms of female labour for moral issues, and dismissing convict women as whores as if this alone defined their entirety and signalled their worthlessness. Misconceived as useless prostitutes, convict women have suffered badly from this stigma. Apart from its inaccuracy, such moral judgements have meant that prostitution was not considered work and nor have those labelled 'prostitutes' been conceived as working in any other capacity. Kay Daniels observed 'the woman who works as a prostitute is given no identity apart from this role and no location beyond the territory of her work place'. Deprived of any other life she appears, in this literature, as less than human, the archetypal 'bad woman' or sexual 'deviant'.[49] Judith Allen and Hilary Golder argued that prostitution (like wifery or motherhood) was work, but of a nature so intimate it involved the sale of something more than labour-power alone, making untenable the claim that in a patriarchal system female work and male work were essentially the same. Many found this realization so unpalatable that they readily perpetuated a mythical separation of work and sex that was too readily accepted by some mid-century historians.[50] But this *was* a myth, too often denied by the lives of working women in nineteenth-century Britain and Ireland familiar with sexual harassment, abuse and other less coercive sexual encounters. Twists of fate had left criminal women dispossessed: through crime they were robbed of their femininity; lost femininity was symbolized by the harlot; and the harlot was not a worker but an object of disgust.

This preference for passing judgement on morality and character has diverted analysis from the real issues of convict work and life. Consequently, convict women never emerged in the literature as potential workers, mothers, homemakers, partners, entrepreneurs, citizens and colonists; instead, they were misrepresented as bad mothers, undesirable marriage partners, as whores and a blight upon the colony. Only in recent times has the image begun to change as studies of colonial society revealed a more vibrant picture. Even so, the criminal class remains an underlying theme, and so too does judgement: some admirable women emerge as successful in the colony, reforming their hitherto criminal propensities, while others failed the reform test, remaining no-hopers unable to capitalize on new opportunities.[51] Precluded from analysis have been questions of the work histories these women brought with them, what training they possessed, whether they could read, write or count. There has been a failure to recognize the extent of apprenticed skills, informal training and of traditional homemaking trades brought by the convict women. These women offered a rich resource, and yet so little is known about how it was utilized.[52] Convict women's identities have been obfuscated and are only now being slowly excavated from the ruinous legacy of the convict origins debate. They are not the only ones to have suffered. Australia's economic history has been robbed of a vital dimension, leaving a tale only half told – and that half mistold.

Notes

1. L.L. Robson, 'The Origins of the Women Convicts Sent to Australia, 1787–1852', *Historical Studies, Australia and New Zealand*, vol. 11, no. 41 (1963), p. 53.

2. A.G.L. Shaw, *Convicts and the Colonies: A Study of Penal Transportation from Great Britain and Ireland to Australia and Other Parts of the Empire* (London, Faber and Faber, 1966; reprint Melbourne, Melbourne University Press, 1981), p. 164.

3. These issues are addressed in D. Oxley, 'Women Transported: Gendered Images and Realities', *Australian and New Zealand Journal of Criminology*, vol. 24, no. 2 (1991); Oxley, 'Packing Her (Economic) Bags: Convict Women Workers', *Australian Historical Studies*, vol. 26, no. 102 (April 1994), pp. 57–76; Oxley, *Convict Maids: The Forced Migration of Women to Australia* (Cambridge, Cambridge University Press, 1996).

4. See M. Sturma, 'Eye of the Beholder: The Stereotype of Women Convicts, 1788–1852', *Labour History*, 34 (May 1978). Other historians have also addressed this problem: Deidre Beddoe, *Welsh Convict Women: A Study of Women Transported from Wales to Australia, 1787–1852* (Wales, Stewart Williams, 1979); Marilyn Lake, 'Convict Women as Objects of Male Vision: An Historiographical Review', *Bulletin of the Centre for Tasmanian Historical Studies*, vol. 2, no. 1 (1988); Portia Robinson, 'The First Forty Years' in Judy Mackinolty and Heather Radi (eds), *In Pursuit of Justice: Australian Women and the Law 1788–1979* (Sydney, Hale and Iremonger, 1979); Anne Summers, *Damned Whores and God's Police: The Colonization of Women in Australia* (Ringwood, Victoria, Penguin Books Australia, 1975).

5. 'Report from the Select Committee on Transportation, together with Minutes of Evidence, Appendix and Index', *Parliamentary Papers* (PP), 1837 (518) XIX (Shannon, Irish University Press, *Crime and Punishment – Transportation* 2), pp. 96 and 148; 'Report from the Select Committee on Transportation, together with Minutes of Evidence, Appendix and Index' (Molesworth Report), PP, 1838 (669) XXII (Shannon, Irish University Press, *Crime and Punishment – Transportation* 3), p. ix. Thomas Potter MacQueen quoted in Summers, *Damned Whores*, pp. 272; Alick Osborne and Bishop William Ullathorne quoted in Miriam Dixson, *The Real Matilda: Woman and Identity in Australia 1788 to the Present* (Ringwood, Penguin Books Australia, 1976), p. 125.

6. P.J. Byrne, *Criminal Law and Colonial Subject: New South Wales 1810–1830* (Cambridge, Cambridge University Press, 1993); D. Neal, *The Rule of Law in a Penal Colony: Law and Power in New South Wales* (Cambridge, Cambridge University Press, 1991).

7. Quoted in W. Ullathorne, *The Horrors of Transportation* (Dublin, Richard Coyne, 1838), p. 8.

8. Ibid., pp. 17–18.

9. Michael Sturma, *Vice in a Vicious Society: Crime and Convicts in Mid-Nineteenth Century New South Wales* (St Lucia, Queensland University Press, 1983).

10. 'Select Committee on Transportation', 1837, pp. 96, 148 and 196.

11. *New South Wales Government Gazette*, no. 13, 30 May 1832, p. 111.

12. A. Bowes Smyth, *The Journal of Arthur Bowes Smyth* (Sydney, Library of Australian History, 1979; facsimile ed. P.G. Fidlon and R.J. Ryan), pp. 47–8.

13. M. Aveling (now Quartly), 'The Action of Gender in Early New South Wales Society', *Push from the Bush*, 24 (April 1987), p. 37.

14. 'Select Committee on Transportation', PP, 1837, p. 38.

15. Paula Hamilton, '"Tipperarifying the Moral Atmosphere"': Irish Catholic Immigration and the State 1840–1860' in Sydney Labour History Group, *What Rough Beast? The State and Social Order in Australian History* (Sydney, Allen and Unwin for the Australian Society for the Study of Labour History, 1982), p. 21.

16. D. Oxley and E. Richards, 'Convict Women and Assisted Female Immigrants Compared: 1841 – a Turning Point?' in Eric Richards (ed.), *Visible Women: Female Immigrants in Colonial Australia* (Canberra, Australian National University, 1995), pp. 1–58.

17. For alternative opinions see F.W. Robinson, *Female Life in Prison by a Prison Matron* (London, 1862); 'Report from the Select Committee on Secondary Punishments; together with the Minutes of Evidence, an Appendix, and Index', PP, 1831–2 (547) VII (Shannon, Irish Universities Press, *Crime and Punishment – Transportation* 1), pp. 11, 116–27.

18. For a more detailed account of how these texts have influenced historians see S. Garton, 'The Convict Origins Debate: Historians and the Problem of the "Criminal Class"', *Australian and New Zealand Journal of Criminology*, vol. 24, no. 2 (1991); Oxley, 'Women Transported'.

19. Quoted in Dixson, *Real Matilda*, p. 125. Also see 'Government and General Orders, 3 July 1799', *Historical Records of Australia*, vol. II, p. 586; 'Select Committee on Transportation', PP, 1837, p. 38.

20. A. Griffiths, *Memorials of Millbank and Chapters in Prison History* (London, Chapman and Hall, 1884), p. 198.

21. Anon., 'Criminal Women', *Cornhill Magazine*, vol. 14 (Aug. 1866), pp. 152–3. A Mrs Owen is recorded as receiving payment for this article in the magazine's accounts; Walter E. Houghton (ed.), *Wellesley Index to Victorian Periodicals*, vol. 1 (London, Routledge and Kegan Paul, 1966), p. 342.

22. Anon., 'Criminal Women', pp. 152–3.

23. H. Mayhew and J. Binny, *The Criminal Prisons of London and Scenes of Prison Life* (London, 1862), p. 466.

24. Griffiths, *Memorials of Millbank*, pp. 198 and 203.

25. Anon., 'Criminal Women', p. 153.

26. J.J. Gurney quoted in R.P. Dobash, R.E. Dobash and S. Gutteridge, *The Imprisonment of Women* (Oxford, Basil Blackwell, 1986), pp. 43–4.

27. Griffiths, *Memorials of Millbank*, p. 202.

28. Quoted in Dobash *et al.*, *Imprisonment*, p. 42.

29. Griffiths, *Memorials of Millbank*, p. 202.

30. Peter Linebaugh, 'The Ordinary of Newgate and his *Account*' in J.S. Cockburn (ed.), *Crime in England, 1550–1800* (London, Methuen, 1977), p. 252.

31. Mayhew and Binny, *Criminal Prisons*, pp. 271–3, 465–6 and 470.

32. Ibid., p. 272.

33. Griffiths, *Memorials of Millbank*, pp. 206, 208.

34. Ibid., pp. 205–8, 214–15, 217, 219, 222–3, 246, 258.

35. Ibid., pp. 203–4.

36. Hay quoted in A. Shubert, 'Private Initiative in Law Enforcement: Associations for the Prosecution of Felons, 1744–1856' in V. Bailey (ed.), *Police and Punishment in Nineteenth Century Britain* (London, Croom Helm, 1981), p. 37.

37. Clive Emsley, 'The Criminal Past: Crime in Nineteenth-Century Britain', *History Today*, vol. 38 (April 1988), p. 45.

38. David Philips, 'Moral Entrepreneurs and the Construction of a "Criminal Class" in England, c.1800–1840', unpublished paper presented to the Australian Historical Association Conference (University of Sydney, 1988).

39. Redgrave quoted in Mayhew and Binny, *Criminal Prisons*, p. 461.

40. Beddoe, *Welsh Convict Women*, p. 15.

41. *Leeds Mercury*, quoted in J. Humphries, '"The Most Free from Objection": The Sexual Division of Labor and Women's Work in Nineteenth-Century England', *Journal of Economic History*, vol. 47, no. 4 (1987), p. 939.

42. C.M.H. Clark, 'The Origins of the Convicts Transported to Eastern Australia, 1787–1852', *Historical Studies: Australia and New Zealand*, vol. 7, nos 26 and 27 (1956), pp. 121–35 and 314–27.

43. Bernard Smith, 'The Fatal Subject', *Scripsi*, vol. 4, no. 4 (1987), p. 59.

44. Stephen Nicholas (ed.), *Convict Workers: Reinterpreting Australia's Past* (Cambridge, Cambridge University Press, 1988).

45. Stephen Nicholas and Peter Shergold, 'Unshackling the Past' in Nicholas, *Convict Workers*, pp. 7–11.

46. David Kent and Norma Townsend, 'Deborah Oxley's "Female Convicts": An Accurate View of Working-Class Women?', *Labour History*, 65 (Nov. 1993), pp. 179–91.

47. In reply see D. Oxley, 'Exercising Agency', *Labour History*, 65 (Nov. 1993), pp. 192–9. Miriam Dixson, *The Real Matilda: Woman and Identity in Australia 1788 to the Present* (Ringwood, Victoria, Penguin Books Australia, revised 2nd edn, 1984), p. 276.

48. Dixson, *The Real Matilda*, p. 277.

49. Kay Daniels, 'Introduction' in Kay Daniels (ed.), *So Much Hard Work: Women and Prostitution in Australian History* (Sydney, Fontana, 1984), p. 1.

50. Allen and Golder quoted in Daniels, 'Introduction', p. 12.

51. Joy Damousi, '"Depravity and Disorder": The Sexuality of Convict Women', *Labour History*, 68 (May 1995), pp. 30–45.

52. Kirsty Reid's contribution to this book indicates that in the case of Van Diemen's Land the resources available for this task are extremely rich.

CHAPTER SIX

'Contumacious, Ungovernable and Incorrigible':[1] Convict Women and Workplace Resistance, Van Diemen's Land, 1820–1839

Kirsty Reid

Introduction: 'a continual warfare?'

Few historians would now support Manning Clark's proposition that 'not a single man or woman from the ranks of the convicts [rose] up and damn[ed] the system under which they suffered'.[2] In recent years, the received interpretation of convict protest as a 'sterile tragedy'[3] has been substantially challenged and revised. By systematically questioning a series of dominant assumptions regarding the convicts' social origins and the mechanisms of colonial class rule, and by reconsidering what constituted 'damning' the system, historians have begun to uncover a rich record of protest.[4]

Female convicts have, however, been present only around the fringes of these studies. Like their slave counterparts, convict women have been largely 'invisible' in many of the accounts of resistance.[5] This absence is all the more curious, for both groups were considered *more* troublesome and harder to control than their male counterparts.[6] Contemporaries were unanimous that female convicts were particularly difficult to control and discipline. The Van Diemen's Land press made repeated reference to this problem.[7] 'There is a class of servants in the Colony', *The Colonial Times* observed, 'the management of which produces more trouble ... than any other class.' 'We refer to the Female Prisoners of the Crown', the paper continued, 'whose tricks, manoeuvres and misconduct have baffled the exertions of every person appointed to control and correct them.'[8]

These opinions were partly shaped by the influence of contemporary gender ideologies which held that the criminal woman had 'fallen' further than her male counterpart. Even those who gave more measured opinions were, however, convinced that the women were exceptionally difficult to control. Lieutenant-

Governor Arthur, for example, informed the Molesworth Committee that female convicts were 'worse, in every respect to manage than male convicts'.[9] According to Principal Superintendent Spode, numerous difficulties had to be faced 'in bringing Prison discipline to bear' upon female convicts'.[10] 'They all feel that they are working under compulsion', Spode explained, 'which renders it almost a continual warfare between their employers and themselves.'[11]

Despite such contemporary opinion, the notion that female convicts substantially challenged the conditions under which they laboured has been all but absent from historical studies. Robinson and Perrott push all evidence of female 'misconduct' to the margins of their accounts, dismissing it as the recalcitrant behaviour of an irredeemably deviant minority.[12] Their work draws on a long tradition in which convict women have been perceived essentially as sexual actors and judged on 'moral' grounds. Robson, for example, turned a very different gaze upon the conduct records of male and female convicts in Van Diemen's Land. Where he perceived 'flashes of defiance and spirit' and evidence of individuals who 'refused to knuckle under' in the male records,[13] he found 'abandonment', 'immoral living' and 'indiscriminate love-making' in the female records.[14] A range of historical accounts have sexualized, and thereby peripheralized, female convict 'recalcitrance'.

Feminist scholars, on the other hand, have repeatedly reproduced the image of passive victim.[15] While this has faded in more recent accounts, the notion that the abuse of female convicts in assignment was rife still prevails. Alford argues, for example, that female convict servants were vulnerable to 'sexual abuse or enforced whoredom'; Daniels that 'convict servants seem to have been seen as women whose sexual services had been acquired along with their domestic labour'.[16] A series of revisionary feminist works have substantially modified the image of the convict woman as 'victim'. Most focus, however, on the ways in which the women were able to manipulate marital and familial relations to gain a degree of control over their lives.[17] The position of female convicts in assignment has, by contrast, received relatively little attention from feminist historians since Dixson and Summers published in the mid-1970s.

The persistent associations between female assignment and prostitution have sexualized historical understandings of the employer–female convict relationship. Consequently, historians have struggled to imagine convict women as rebellious workers. This has been further compounded by the assumption that their labour was systematically undervalued in the colonies. Convict women workers, it is argued, suffered an inordinate level of oppression and were thus largely unable to fight back.[18] Byrne's recent study reveals the way in which these dual notions concerning assignment continue to shape historical interpretations of female convict protest. According to Byrne, convict women were arraigned before the courts as the result of 'an area of tension different to that which produced the appearance of male servants: the identity of the female servant was bound up with incarceration ... and the value of sexuality'.[19]

The female convict servant, she concludes, 'was owned by the employer and could not bargain over her labour'.[20] This type of analysis is deeply flawed. It assumes that because domestic service tends to isolate and atomize workers, servants rarely protest. The workplace agency of servants varies, however, and depends crucially on local labour market conditions. Even in difficult labour markets domestic servants resisted employers. In early nineteenth-century Britain, for example, some servants, as the transportation records indeed reveal, used tactics such as theft and arson to hit back at employers.[21] In labour markets characterized by high levels of demand, the workplace power of servants was greatly increased. Thus, in late nineteenth-century Hamburg, servants expressed their dissatisfaction by repeatedly changing jobs – the result was servant 'turnover [on] unprecedented levels'.[22] Female convict servants in Van Diemen's Land, despite the constraints of assignment, exhibited a similar ability to up and leave employers.[23] Unlike free servants, the convict was not restrained by fear of unemployment. Moreover, the persistently high level of demand for female labour in Van Diemen's Land throughout this period created conditions conducive to this and other forms of workplace protest.[24] A volume of evidence from the police court records thus directly contradicts the historical consensus regarding the workplace oppression of assigned females.[25]

To 'influence their employer's quietude':[26] the tactics and aims of day-to-day resistance

Outright opposition to the system by female convict workers manifested itself relatively infrequently. Insubordination,[27] threatened and actual assault, and the wilful destruction of property account for just 2.5 per cent of charges laid (see Table 6.1). By contrast, relatively petty misconduct such as insolence, neglect, disobedience of orders and absence were well to the fore. This might be taken as support for the conventional image of female convicts as 'naughty' and 'refractory' children. Convict women have traditionally been 'portrayed as disobedient rather than rebellious'.[28] Such forms of behaviour are, however, common to workers in unfree societies and historians have increasingly recognized their importance as part of 'a dense pattern of day-to-day resistance'.[29]

Table 6.1 *Charges laid against 1344 female convicts brought before the VDL police courts, 1820–1839 (N = 1884)*

Offence	N	%
Absent without leave	323	17.0
Drunk/Drunk and disorderly	313	16.0
Insolence and impertinence	224	12.0
Absconding	139	7.3
Disobedience of orders	132	6.9
Neglect of duty	109	5.7
Disorderly conduct	82	4.3
Misconduct	56	2.9
Felony	73	3.8
Sexual misconduct	40	2.1
Refusing to work	26	1.4
Verbally abusing her employers	26	1.4
Out after hours	25	1.3
Assault	20	1.1
Refusing to return to her service	19	1.0
Returned to govt. pregnant	14	0.7
Dispute with fellow servants	12	0.6
Insubordination	11	0.6
Defamation of character	7	0.4
Immoral conduct	7	0.4
Overstaying her pass	7	0.4
Leaving/threatening to leave service	5	0.3
Wilful damage of property	5	0.3
Feigning of illness	4	0.2
Idleness	4	0.2
Threatening her employer	4	0.2
Violent and outrageous conduct	4	0.2
Refusing to go to her service	2	0.1
Arson	1	0.1
Other	10	0.5
Returned – No charge	171	8.9
N/A	9	0.5
Total number of charges	**1884**	**100**

Source: Archives Office of Tasmania, LC 53, 83, 247, 346, 362, 375; and Mitchell Library, TP 227, 262, 268, 270–273, 290, 291, 323, 325, 326, 334, 338

Day-to-day forms of resistance were particularly potent weapons when deployed by domestic workers who could constantly disrupt household routine. Domestic slaves, through a constant barrage of 'impudence, "uppityness" ... sauciness and subtle disrespect', were able, Fox-Genovese observes, to make 'the lives of privileged mistresses an unending war of nerves'.[30] Female convicts were similarly well positioned. Elizabeth Fenton wrote bitterly in her diary of the frustrations which assigned females inflicted upon her. Her experience began when, on arrival in Hobart, she sent two women on to prepare the family's Macquarie Street home. Upon checking, Fenton discovered that:

> though I had sent two servants every day for a week, who were supposed to be cleaning the house and furniture, it became very evident ... that their exertions had only extended to lighting fires to dress their dinners and keep them comfortable at their game of cards.[31]

Fenton's problems continued. Her diary complained of the 'direful necessity of having to lock everything up yourself' and the need to supervise even the 'smallest duty'.[32] Such complaints echo those made by employers in court. Peter Harrison, for example, was eventually forced to bring Margaret McDonald and Sarah Martin before a magistrate. 'Whenever I am from home', Harrison reported, 'I receive some complaint of their misconduct during my absence.'[33] Others spoke of how the female convict servant 'put the house completely in confusion'; was 'in the continual habit of absenting herself'; was 'very noisy and quarrelsome'; 'repeatedly insolent'; and would 'not do anything she was ordered to do'.[34] Many employers evidently had good reason to empathize with Fenton when she complained 'the perpetual encroachment of the servants upon my time is indescribable'.[35]

Day-to-day forms of resistance were expressions of resentment against the psychological conditions of assignment – a way of letting off steam. They were also intended to force employers to give ground on a range of substantive issues. They permitted the convict woman to challenge the deference implicit in household relations and to negotiate a range of material 'rights' relating to rations, workloads, control of the work process and the 'right' to independent leisure. Assigned females' convict resistance was primarily designed to set the conditions and define the limits of their *labour*.

The ration (provisions and clothing) functioned as the convict basic 'wage'.[36] Convicts were therefore concerned to assert their 'right' to that wage and to ensure that the provisions issued matched *their* interpretation of the regulations. Male convicts, for example, refused to accept kangaroo meat in lieu of the regulation mutton or beef.[37] Female convicts likewise regarded inadequate rations as legitimate grounds for protest. Sarah Jones refused to prepare supper because she was without shoes.[38] Mary Fearns warned her master that 'she would not stop if I did not allow her more than 2 ounces of tea per week'.[39] The ration was set according to the official regulations of the assignment system. These protests therefore reflected the willingness of convicts, male *and* female, to bargain 'for the restoration of their established rights'.[40]

The ration was central to the employer's ability to extract productive labour from the convict. Many 'bought' the co-operation of assigned workers by issuing extras. The prevalence of this practice was widely acknowledged.[41] Such indulgences had a dual function, serving both as an informal positive sanction and as a disciplinary sanction. By developing a notion of customary right, convicts, for their part, rapidly came to consider such supplements as an integral part of their ration. As they moved from assignment to assignment, convicts accumulated consciousness of a variety of such 'rights' which could be used to test the resolve of each new employer. Catherine Owen's first move in her new service was thus to inform her employers that she was *'accustomed* to smoke' and that 'unless she was allowed to smoke she would not stop'.[42]

To their dismay, many employers also found that extra rations were insufficient to secure obedience. Margaret Watson left work without permission, got drunk and proceeded to the Police Office to make a 'frivolous charge' against her master. All this, he reported, was despite the fact that she was 'not rationed but has as much as she wishes of good provisions'.[43] Despite extra rations, convict discontent often failed to evaporate. Indeed, in many cases, having secured their basic subsistence, convicts simply set their sights on other prizes. 'Adequate rations', as in the case of slaves, could have the 'reverse effect' from that desired by employers, for a 'reasonably fed workforce' was free to 'pay attention to the other necessities of life'.[44] One colonial newspaper thus complained bitterly that employers continued to be greatly annoyed by female convict servants even when they received good provisions and cash wages.[45]

Female convicts battled both to set the length of the working day and to limit workloads. Contrary to Byrne's belief that they were 'incarcerated' in employer's homes and at their constant beck and call, convict women exhibited well-developed notions of their own and their employer's time. Mary Ann Jubb refused to clean out a room because, she explained in court, her mistress had set her the task 'after my day's work was done'.[46] Other women were likewise motivated to act by the sense that customary 'rights' regarding the length of the working day were being infringed. When her master's child was sent to wake the servants early, Mary Ann Pitt threatened to 'box his ears if he called her' because, she declared, 'she would not get up for anyone sooner than her regular time'.[47]

Workloads were limited by convict women through surreptitious means such as feigning illness, shirking and going slow. Margaret Wood attempted to avoid work altogether by staying in bed under the pretext of illness – an attempt which failed when the doctor was called in.[48] Others sought to set the pace and determine the timing of their work. Elizabeth Wales informed her mistress that she would prepare the evening meal 'when she chose'.[49] Elizabeth Jones gradually performed fewer and fewer tasks. The day before she was brought to court, her master reported that 'all the prisoner did ... was to clean out one room and make a bed'.[50] Others bargained openly over workloads. Mary MacDonald threatened to withdraw her labour entirely if acceptable limits were not set. She absconded in order to complain at the police office that, despite being 'a hardworking woman', she was 'not able to do the work'. She was, she stated, only 'willing to go back if they keep the children away from me at night'.[51] Her bid was unsuccessful. As a general rule, however, the threatened withdrawal of labour did sway employers. Thus, when Martha Bellamy left her service because she felt the work was too heavy, her master persuaded her to return by promising to employ additional help.[52]

Convict women staked their 'right' to a degree of control and autonomy over their work in numerous ways. Some ignored or refused to accept orders unless they were issued by the actual individual to whom they had been assigned. Convicts were legally assigned either to the master *or* mistress of a house. Many women were clear as to who held the rights to their labour and sought to manipulate that knowledge. When George Lucas found Sarah Wilson, his wife's assigned servant, 'sitting idle in the kitchen' he ordered her to light a fire. Wilson refused, having just declared that she had 'nothing to do until *she* (her mistress) comes home'.[53] The general principle which inspired such conflicts was perhaps best expressed by Elizabeth Picket. 'If I am to remain here', Picket declared of her assigned service, 'I will not have as many mistresses and masters.'[54]

Attempts to supervise assigned females were often counter-productive. Convict women frequently retorted with verbal abuse and insolence. Captain Crear thus complained that whenever fault was found with Mary Redding's work 'she gives the most insolent answers ... [and] this language she repeats sometimes ten times in the week'.[55] Attempts at supervision or criticism could also produce a deterioration in the quality of the work performed. Thomas Archer, a wealthy and powerful colonist, criticized convict laundress Eleanor Wilson for putting insufficient starch on his shirts. Henceforth, he reported, she 'put so much starch on that the shirts are just like pasteboard and the sleeves are stuck together so tightly that I could not get my hands in'. 'No one on the Island', Wilson then informed Archer, 'should make her work.'[56]

Female convicts also limited workplace supervision by literally forcing employers to keep their distance. Some established proprietary 'rights' to certain rooms within the household, declaring them out of bounds to employers. The kitchen figured most frequently in such battles.[57] Maria Wright, for example, created such an atmosphere of intimidation that her mistress was 'afraid to go into the kitchen'.[58] Sidwell Sixspeach's 'great violence of temper and ... insolence' likewise so 'alarmed' her mistress, that Mrs Watson was fearful of being 'alone in the kitchen' with her. She had good cause for anxiety – Sixspeach threatened that 'if anyone provoked her she would throw a knife at them'.[59] Convict women who successfully contested the allocation of household space secured an important independent domain. This placed significant constraints on the employer's ability to oversee household work. In addition, women who controlled the kitchen greatly enhanced their opportunities for refreshment and leisure. Access to the pantry allowed household supplies to be easily raided. Regular contact with the outside world could also be maintained through the kitchen door, allowing both convicts and their visitors to come and go with relative ease. Convicts made ready use of these advantages. Mary Witherington, for example, courted convict Daniel Herbert in her master's kitchen and 'improperly made tea' for him. Several months later they applied for permission to marry.[60] Ann Willis and Francis Stanley used their employer's kitchen for a more intimate purpose and were consequently charged with 'indecently exposing their persons' after they were discovered together.[61] The importance of the kitchen as an independent space motivated some convicts to take resolute action to establish and maintain their control. When Elizabeth Walker was reprimanded for permitting a man to be in the kitchen she defiantly informed her mistress that 'she would not prevent it' and then refused to remain in her service.[62]

Many women made control of the work process a condition of service. Some therefore left their employment at the first sign of employer supervision or criticism. Rosina Sweeney had just arrived in her service when she informed her master that 'she would not work, that she would have stayed a few days but as I had reprimanded her she would not stop'.[63] Others, not quite so quick to leave, first attempted to negotiate for greater control over their work. Many bargained with their labour, offering a 'reasonable' level of service in return for a work environment relatively free of supervision. They therefore expressed a willingness to work *if* conditions were met. Significantly, some of those who subsequently left their service because these concessions were not forthcoming expressed a clear sense of grievance. Jane Fagerty, for example, was indignant that, despite her best efforts, 'she could give no satisfaction'.[64]

Female convict workers fought to ensure that 'free time' was allocated them, and also to assert their 'right' to determine their use of that time. They inflicted a range of penalties upon employers who resisted these demands. Many women simply took time when it was not granted and perceived this as their 'right'. Margaret Shaw thus pleaded guilty to absence but regarded the fact that her 'mistress would not give me leave' as sufficient justification.[65] Convict women regarded access to free time as a 'right' earned by labour. Eliza Murray assumed that her lengthy period of service gave her a legitimate claim for time off. 'She had been in the service of Captain Vicary fourteen months', she explained in court, 'and asked leave to go out for one hour which was refused.'[66] Rachel Leach and Elizabeth Winn informed their master that they would not work 'unless they had leave to go out'.[67]

Female convicts took advantage of almost every conceivable opportunity to secure their free time: Mary Ann Whitlock, sent on an errand that ought to have taken 15 minutes, returned some two hours later drunk and 'very insolent'; Elizabeth Winn was sent to church and stayed out overnight; and Rachel Leach was given leave 'to go out for a hour' but did not return for four days.[68] According to Constable Simmons, absent women were generally tracked down to 'public-houses, sly-grog shops and brothels'.[69] Alcohol and absenteeism were closely related: 44 per cent of the absentees returned drunk or were found drinking. Phoebe Allen and Sarah Wilkinson, discovered 'with liquor before them' in the skittle room of a Launceston public house, were typical.[70] Other sites of attraction included card games, dances, the races and 'disorderly houses': Elizabeth Hore was found at a dance; Margaret Peebles 'drinking ... fiddling and dancing' with several others in a dwelling-house; Mary Culley at Launceston racecourse; and Mary Keogan with a sailor in the bedroom of a 'very disorderly house'.[71]

'Disorderly houses' flourished throughout Van Diemen's Land. Their location was made known to female convicts through their own information networks. The women in the Houses of Correction were at the hub of these. According to Mary Haigh, for instance, women learned 'in the factory at what houses they can obtain liquor on the sly and those houses at which shelter is to be obtained when they abscond'.[72] Convict women made active use of this information – 'disorderly houses' were thus a popular destination for absentees. Although the going rate for prostitution varied, circumstantial evidence suggests it was, on the whole, relatively high – Rebecca Gentles claimed, for example, that she had been offered £2 sterling by an employer to allow him 'to be intimate with her'.[73] Rebecca Barton stated that she had, on at least one occasion, charged a fellow convict servant 10 shillings.[74] The frequency with which 'disorderly' houses attracted female absentees suggests that these relatively good rates were more widely available. Contrary to its conventional historical image, colonial prostitution therefore appears to have provided female convicts with significant material means. This enabled them to make the most of their absences from work and thus contributed to their ability to maintain independent leisure. In addition, women sent to be punished at the House of Correction for such absences fed their earnings from prostitution into the informal economy which flourished in such institutions – trading for privileges which substantially lessened the severity of their punishment.[75]

Sexual and romantic interests were powerful motives for absence. Numerous female absentees were apprehended in bed with men: Ann Powell, for example, had been missing several days when Constable Stewart found her in bed with Thomas Brown; and Esther Boulton was found in bed with Thomas Saunders in a hut on her master's farm.[76] Female absentees apprehended in bed with men were regularly discovered in 'disorderly houses'. Many of these houses had a dual function, operating both as brothels and as houses of assignation. Some of these absentees simply sought casual sexual liaisons, others were involved in longer-term arrangements, some of which culminated in marriage. Margaret Lowrie, for example, regularly absented herself in order to visit Charles Fitzhughes. Lowrie's master had barred the couple from meeting because he considered their relationship 'very improper'. Like other convicts in this situation, Lowrie was therefore only able to sustain her relationship through absenteeism. Such relationships were important not least because they raised the possibility of marriage and an early release from assignment. Motives were, however, far from solely instrumentalist. Lowrie thus continued to meet Fitzhughes for some 18 months after their petition to marry had been denied.[77] Couples often persisted in the face of harsh penalties, continuing to meet despite the risks. James Burton harboured Rosina Savilin from the constables at least three times in six weeks. Burton, a free man, accumulated fines of £90 sterling as a result. Savilin was sentenced to six months' imprisonment and had her sentence extended by twelve months.[78]

On rural properties the male workers' quarters were the most popular destination for female absentees. Many employers, despite close surveillance and threats of discipline, found it impossible to prevent this association. Sarah Elam's employer complained that, despite his best efforts, 'I cannot keep her from the men's hut'.[79] Mary Ann Pitt repeatedly defied her master by going into the workshop adjoining his house and informed him that 'no-one would prevent her' from doing so.[80] Wherever the men's quarters were situated they exerted a significant 'pull' on female convict workers. Together, convicts transformed sites such as huts, stables and barns into forums for their entertainment, allowing co-workers to come together to smoke, drink alcohol and tea, swap stories, play cards and have sex.[81] The persistence of these attempts by male and female convict workers to socialize together seriously calls into question Dixson's contention that they had antagonistic interests.[82]

Absenteeism caused considerable disruption to household routines. Many women left during the working day and without completing their tasks. Elizabeth Jones, for instance, defied her master's orders and visited the male workers' quarters twice in three days. She left 'her work undone' and her master reported that although he 'sent for her ... she did not come back'.[83] Others went just when they were most urgently needed. Ann Saunders and Ann Frances

Clifton deserted their master's premises when their mistress was due to give birth, leaving him to cope alone with 'six little children'.[84] With the minimum of effort, an absent convict could substantially inconvenience her employer.

Convict women denied free time also retaliated by socializing on their employer's premises. This disrupted the household and caused employers considerable concern. Female convicts who became drunk on the premises, for instance, commonly did so in their employer's time and at their expense. Drunken servants were not only incapable of work but also commonly insolent and disruptive. When Mary James got drunk she refused to obey orders and 'used very abusive language', calling her mistress a 'drunken Irish bitch'.[85] The deferential relationship which employers fostered with convict servants was undermined when a drunken servant spoke her mind in this way, particularly if she did so publicly. Incidents of this type also had the potential to escalate, thus entirely undermining household order. Many women, not content to drink alone, supplied co-workers with alcohol. Elizabeth Doyle's actions were characteristic: she stole her employer's gin and distributed it between the other servants, encouraging them to get drunk with her.[86]

Convict women also sought freedom of association – the 'right' to spend time with companions of their own choosing. Employers struggled to prevent this. Some sought to cut all lines of communication between convict servants and the world beyond the household. Dr Brock was thus extremely anxious to prevent Ann Heath from standing outside his house talking to a man, and threatened to call a constable if he found her 'out again'.[87] Mr Walker intercepted Jane Jones's letters. Jones was consequently charged with 'disorderly conduct' because she had been 'writing ... to other person's men servants in order to induce them to come to the farm for improper purposes'.[88] Other employers took steps to break up relationships they considered 'improper'. George Thompson 'tried to stop the improper connection' between Mary Ann Woodcock and John Beckett, both convicts assigned to his service. When his own efforts failed, he arraigned them before a magistrate who re-assigned Beckett 'to the extreme north of the Island'.[89]

Absenteeism provided one method of securing independent leisure time: out of sight of employers, convicts were also, temporarily, out of their control. Convict women also maintained relationships by smuggling companions into their employer's house. Sarah Lawrence, for example, secretly admitted Charles Bayley into her master's house at three o'clock in the morning.[90] Others let friends and partners enter through windows after dark, or concealed them in hideaways throughout the household until a convenient time to meet arose: Hannah Wilson smuggled fellow convict worker Miles Flinn under her bed; Barbara Kerr hid Samuel Turner up her bedroom chimney.[91] Some women openly rejected employer attempts to control their personal lives. Thus, Ann

Clifford defiantly informed her master that she 'would speak to anyone she chose'.[92] Jane Hendon made the continued availability of her labour dependent on employer concessions in this area. She refused to remain in his service, her master reported, 'on account of my having refused to allow a man of the name of Sutton to visit her'.[93]

The numerous penalties which convicts imposed upon employers who failed to respond to their demands for independent leisure time encouraged compromise. In return for work, some therefore issued convict servants with passes, allowing them to go out without police interference.[94] Others simply turned a blind eye to absenteeism. Mary Haigh thus recalled an assignment where she had been able to 'do as I liked. I was allowed to drink, go to the Public House and might remain out all night if I pleased'.[95] The result of this compromise was, as Bridget Monaghan explained, that 'there are a good many places ... [where] women ... can go in and out when they like and have men to see them'.[96] The authorities were well aware of this. As Constable Brice noted, 'there are persons who do not care what their servants do if they have done a little work for them'.[97]

Of such importance was the 'right' to free time and independent leisure that female convicts regarded it as the central test of whether a service was 'good' or 'bad'. According to Mary Haigh 'services where women are well kept and clothed but overseen are considered bad situations, and those in which women are allowed to do as they please are held to be good ones'.[98] Convict department officials made similar claims. John Hutchison, Superintendent of the Hobart Female House of Correction, claimed, for example, that convict women considered certain services to be good 'merely because of the licence they allow to their servants'.[99] Women resisted assignment to 'bad' services by committing offences in order to be returned to the House of Correction. 'I have run away from various causes', one woman explained, '[but] I generally absconded because I was refused leave out.'[100] 'They would sooner be in the Factory', Bridget Monaghan stated of her fellow female convicts, 'unless they can get to a place where they have plenty of liberty.'[101]

Assigned female convicts in Van Diemen's Land took action to shape the conditions of their *labour*. They brought their employers to the negotiating table over a range of workplace issues. These negotiations were so important that convict women made their continued access to them a fundamental condition of their labour. It was then, above all, their 'right' to workplace negotiations which female convicts sought to establish and defend. Employers who threatened, or resorted to, the power of the magistrates were regarded by convict women to have crossed the rubicon of household negotiations. Many women responded by permanently withdrawing their labour. Ruth Beckerdike's conduct speaks volumes. She refused to enter her master's house on her return from the punishment cells. Instead, she stood outside the front door, demanding that her master come out. When he appeared, Beckerdike declared that she would 'never work another hour' in his service because he had had her punished.[102] Convict women had little interest in remaining in services where their attempts to negotiate improved conditions of labour failed. Employers unwilling to settle workplace disputes internally therefore commonly paid for this inflexibility by the loss of their servants' labour.

Conclusion: accommodation and resistance

The importance of day-to-day forms of resistance has been much debated by historians of unfree labour.[103] Some have found its methods wanting on the grounds that, in order to bargain with the system, the worker was first required to acknowledge it. While this debate has mainly focused on New World slavery, its influence has been discernible in the historiography of convict resistance.[104] Thus, Maxwell-Stewart concludes that convict worker resistance, while important, should not be overestimated, because 'ultimately [it] served to strengthen those invisible ideological shackles which bound the prisoner within a system of naked exploitation'.[105]

Everyday forms of resistance were, however, favoured by convict women workers because they were effective. Unlike methods of outright opposition to the system, such as arson or assault, these tactics were expressions of the workplace power of assigned female workers in Van Diemen's Land. Those who resorted to outright rejections of the system were, by contrast, displaying their relative powerlessness. They were commonly women for whom other, more subtle, channels of resistance had been closed off. They made their 'declarations of open war' only after 'a protracted struggle on different terrain'.[106] Many were clearly driven to these extremes. Explosions of anger left the convict open to state retribution and produced few discernible long-term benefits.

Convict women rarely rejected the assignment system outright. If this was a 'concession' to the power of the colonial state, it was one which brought them innumerable tactical benefits. Recognition that their power was workplace-based allowed the women to manoeuvre within the system and thus to subvert its meaning at every turn. Female convict workers transformed the assignment system in Van Diemen's Land by substantially constraining its coercive element. Far from strengthening their 'ideological shackles', convict women were able to undermine the entire premiss of the system. They exercised their 'right' to choice, whether it be over the employer they worked for or the food they ate, and were able to establish that 'right' as a fundamental condition of their labour. Like New World slaves, convict women therefore 'accepted what could not be avoided', but 'simultaneously fought for ... [their] moral and physical survival'. 'Accommodation and resistance', as Genovese observes of slave workers, 'developed as two forms of a single process.'[107]

Notes

1. Description of female convict servants, *Launceston Advertiser*, 26 June 1832.
2. C.M.H. Clark, 'The Origins of the Convicts Transported to Eastern Australia, 1787–1852', *Historical Studies, Australia and New Zealand*, vol. 7, no. 27 (1956), p. 327.
3. R.W. Connell and T.H. Irving, *Class Structure in Australian History: Documents, Narrative and Argument* (Melbourne, Longman Cheshire, 1980), p. 50.
4. See: Alan Atkinson, 'Four Patterns of Convict Protest', *Labour History*, vol. 37 (1979), pp. 28–51; Paula Jane Byrne, *Criminal Law and Colonial Subject: New South Wales, 1810–1830* (Cambridge, Cambridge University Press, 1993), pp. 19–72; David Kent, 'Customary Behaviour Transported: A Note on the Parramatta Female Factory Riot of 1827', *Journal of Australian Studies*, vol. 40 (1994), pp. 75–9; Hamish Maxwell-Stewart, 'The Bushrangers and the Convict System of Van Diemen's Land', PhD thesis, University of Edinburgh (1990), pp. 94–151 and 193–233; W. Nichol, 'Malingering and Convict Protest', *Labour History*, vol. 47 (1984), pp. 18–27 and 'Ideology and the Convict System in New South Wales, 1788–1820', *Historical Studies, Australia and New Zealand*, vol. 22, no. 86 (1986), pp. 1–20; Tamsin O'Connor, 'Power and Punishment: The Limits of Resistance; The Moreton Bay Penal Settlement, 1824–1842', BA (Hons) thesis, University of Queensland (1994), pp. 57–138; Kirsty Reid, 'Work, Sexuality and Resistance: The Convict Women of Van Diemen's Land, 1820–1839', PhD thesis, University of Edinburgh (1995), pp. 233–73.
5. On the historiography of female slave resistance see Bridget Brereton, 'Searching for the Invisible Woman', *Slavery & Abolition*, vol. 13, no. 2 (1992), pp. 86–96.
6. Concerning slaves, see Barbara Bush, *Slave Women in Caribbean Society 1650–1838* (London, James Currey, 1990), pp. 53–5.
7. See, for example: *Launceston Advertiser*, 25 Jan. 1832; *Tasmanian*, 23 Aug. 1833; *Bent's News*, 19 March 1836; *Tasmanian*, 19 July 1839.
8. *Colonial Times*, 18 Feb. 1840.
9. George Arthur, 'Minutes of Evidence taken before the Select Committee on Transportation', *Parliamentary Papers*, vol. 19 (1837), p. 312.
10. Josiah Spode, 30 Aug. 1837, Archives Office of Tasmania (henceforth AOT), CSO 5/134/3210, p. 254.
11. Ibid., p. 255.
12. Monica Perrott, *A Tolerable Good Success: Economic Opportunities for Women in New South Wales 1788–1830* (Sydney, Hale and Ironmonger, 1983), p. 40; Portia Robinson, 'The First Forty Years' in Judy Mackinolty and Heather Radi (eds), *In Pursuit of Justice: Australian Women and the Law, 1788–1979* (Sydney, Hale and

Ironmonger, 1979), p. 5; Portia Robinson, *The Hatch and Brood of Time: A Study of the First Generation of Native-Born White Australians* (Melbourne, Oxford University Press, 1985), p. 94.

13. Lloyd Robson, *The Convict Settlers of Australia: An Enquiry into the Origin and Character of the Convicts Transported to New South Wales and Van Diemen's Land 1787–1852* (Carlton, Victoria, Melbourne University Press, 1965), pp. 97 and 105.

14. Ibid., pp. 134–5 and 145.

15. Miriam Dixson, *The Real Matilda: Woman and Identity in Australia, 1788–1975* (Ringwood, Victoria, Penguin, 1976), pp. 115–53; Anne Summers, *Damned Whores and God's Police: The Colonization of Women in Australia* (Ringwood, Victoria, Penguin Australia, 1975; reprint 1990), pp. 267–89; Anne Summers, 'Hidden from History: Women Victims of Crime' in Satyanshu Mukherjee and Jocelynne Scutt (eds), *Women and Crime* (Sydney, George Allen and Unwin, 1981), pp. 22–30.

16. Katrina Alford, *Production or Reproduction? An Economic History of Women in Australia, 1788–1850* (Melbourne, Oxford University Press, 1984), p. 168 and Kay Daniels, *So Much Hard Work: Women and Prostitution in Australian History* (Sydney, Fontana/Collins, 1984), p. 38.

17. See: Marion Aveling, 'She Only Married to be Free: or Cleopatra Vindicated' in Norma Grieve and Patricia Grimshaw (eds), *Australian Women: Feminist Perspectives* (Melbourne, Oxford University Press, 1981), pp. 119–33; Marion Aveling, 'Bending the Bars: Convict Women and the State' in Kay Saunders and Raymond Evans (eds), *Gender Relations in Australia: Domination and Negotiation* (Sydney, Harcourt Brace Jovanovich, 1992), pp. 144–57; Patricia Grimshaw, 'Women and the Family in Australian History – A Reply to *The Real Matilda*', *Historical Studies, Australia and New Zealand*, vol. 18 (1978–79), pp. 412–21.

18. See, for example, Connell and Irving, *Class Structure*, pp. 56–7; and Alford, *Production or Reproduction?*, pp. 161–2.

19. Byrne, *Criminal Law*, p. 51.

20. Ibid., pp. 50–1.

21. See Theresa McBride, *The Domestic Revolution: The Modernisation of Household Service in England and France, 1820–1920* (London, Croom Helm, 1976), pp. 99–108. Domestic servants in Atlanta organized and took strike action in the early 1880s – see David Katzman, *Seven Days a Week: Women and Domestic Service in Industrializing America* (New York, Oxford University Press, 1978), pp. 195–7.

22. Katharina Schlegel, 'Mistress and Servant in Nineteenth-Century Hamburg: Employer/Employee Relationships in Domestic Service, 1880–1914', *History Workshop Journal*, vol. 15 (1983), p. 75.

23. Kirsty Reid, 'Work, Sexuality and Resistance', pp. 260–8.

24. Ibid., pp. 144–88.

25. This chapter draws upon material from the VDL police court records. While a substantial body of these records survive, they are not intact. The 1344 assigned convict women studied here were therefore not the only assigned females arraigned before the police magistrates in this period, but only those for whom relevant records survive. No attempt is therefore made to estimate the frequency with which female convicts appeared before the colonial courts.

26. *Bent's News*, 19 March 1836.
27. Insubordination was a separate category of offence from charges such as disobedience of orders or insolence, although they involved insubordinate behaviour. The charge of insubordination covered the most serious offences of this type.
28. Kay Daniels, 'The Flash Mob: Rebellion, Rough Culture and Sexuality in the Female Factories of Van Diemen's Land', *Australian Feminist Studies*, vol. 18 (1993), p. 134.
29. See, for example, Elizabeth Fox-Genovese, *Within the Plantation Household: Black and White Women of the Old South* (Chapel Hill, University of North Carolina Press, 1988), p. 315.
30. Ibid., p. 309.
31. Elizabeth Fenton, *The Journal of Mrs Fenton: A Narrative of her life in India, the Isle of France, and Tasmania during the years 1826–1830* (London, Edward Arnold, 1901), p. 355.
32. Ibid., pp. 356 and 371.
33. 136D Margaret McDonald per *Mary* and 188M Sarah Martin per *William Bryan*: 6 April 1836, Mitchell Library (henceforth ML), TP 290.
34. 154G Mary McGoverin per *New Grove*, 31 Oct. 1837, AOT, LC 83/2; 139M Ellen Murphy per *America*, 7 Jan. 1834, ML, TP 227; 223S Anne Smith per *Hydery*, 6 Feb. 1834, ML, TP 227; 110 Mary Ann Ody per *America*, 24 March 1834, ML, TP 227; 177L Maria McLean per *Atwick*, 4 March 1839, ML, TP 326.
35. *The Journal of Mrs Fenton*, p. 356.
36. Maxwell-Stewart, 'The Bushrangers', p. 119.
37. Ibid.
38. 106J Sarah Jones per *William Bryan*, 3 May 1834, ML, TP 254.
39. 116F Mary Fearns per *Edward*, 25 Oct. 1836, AOT, LC 362/3.
40. Atkinson, 'Four Patterns of Convict Protest', p. 39.
41. See, for example, George Arthur, 'Minutes of Evidence taken before the Select Committee on Transportation', *Parliamentary Papers*, vol. XIX (1837), p. 284.
42. 80 Catherine Owen per *Lady of the Lake*, 11 Oct. 1837, AOT, LC 83/2 (emphasis added).
43. 286W Margaret Watson per *Hector*, 11 March 1837, ML, TP 290.
44. Mary Turner, 'Slave Workers, Subsistence and Labour Bargaining: Amity Hall, Jamaica, 1805–1832', *Slavery & Abolition*, vol. 12, no. 1 (1991), pp. 92–106.
45. *Bent's News*, 15 Oct. 1836.
46. 123J Mary Ann Jubb per *New Grove*, 19 March 1836, ML, TP 338.
47. 143P Mary Ann Pitt per *Arab*, 11 Sept. 1838, ML, TP 326.
48. 239W Margaret Wood per *William Bryan*, 17 Dec. 1833, ML, TP 326.
49. 306W Elizabeth Wales per *Westmoreland*, 1 Aug. 1837, AOT, LC 83/2.
50. 116J Elizabeth Jones per *Siren*, 2 Feb. 1839, ML, TP 334.
51. 91D Mary MacDonald per *Harmony*, 17 May 1832, ML, TP 323.
52. 121B Martha Bellamy per *Sovereign*; Phillip Tardif, *Notorious Strumpets and Dangerous Girls: Convict Women in Van Diemen's Land, 1803–1829* (henceforth NSDG) (Sydney, Angus and Robertson, 1990), ref. 1240.

53. 295W Sarah Wilson per *Arab*, 26 Jan. 1837, AOT, LC 362/3 (emphasis in original).
54. 90P Elizabeth Picket per *Hydery*, 22 July 1833, ML, TP 325.
55. 128R Mary Redding per *Jane*, 13 June 1834, ML, TP 254.
56. 208W Eleanor Wilson per *Hydery*, 7 Nov. 1836, AOT, LC 362/3.
57. Female convicts also contested their 'right' to do as they chose in their sleeping quarters. Twice in two days, for example, Janet Alexander barricaded herself in her bedroom while allowing 'a man named Burton' to come and go via her window. 111A Janet Alexander per *Nautilus*, 8 June 1839, ML, TP 334.
58. 227W Maria Wright per *Jane*, 21 Feb. 1837, AOT, LC 362/3.
59. 260S Sidwell Sixspeach per *Edward*, 13 Feb. 1837, ML, TP 338.
60. 126W Mary Witherington per *Harmony*; 810H Daniel Herbert per *Asia* (3), NSDG, ref. 1588.
61. 266W Ann Willis per *New Grove* and 1988S Francis Stanley per *Waterloo*: 1 July 1836, AOT, LC 362/3.
62. 165W Elizabeth Walker per *America*, 29 Feb. 1836, AOT, LC 362/3.
63. 351S Rosina Sweeney per *Nautilus*, 1 May 1839, ML, TP 326. Sweeney was sentenced to seven days solitary but ordered to be returned to her service. Her master's 'victory' was, however, short-lived. The day after she returned from punishment he was forced to bring her before the magistrate again, this time for drunkenness. Sweeney was returned to government for reassignment as she desired: 9 May 1839, ML, TP 326.
64. 79F Jane Fagerty per *Mellish*, 8 Aug. 1833, ML, TP 325.
65. 182S Margaret Shaw per *America*, 24 June 1834, ML, TP 227.
66. 181M Eliza Murray per *William Bryan*, 11 June 1838, ML, TP 334.
67. 125L Rachel Leach per *Jane*, and 32W Elizabeth Winn per *Lord Wellington*: 3 March 1834, ML, TP 227.
68. 205W Mary Ann Whitlock per *Hydery*, 1 Feb. 1834, ML, TP 227; 32W Elizabeth Winn per *Lord Wellington*, 22 April 1834, ML, TP 227; 125L Rachel Leach per *Jane*, 1 April 1834, ML, TP 227.
69. Constable Simmons, 20 Dec. 1841, AOT, CSO 22/50, pp. 213–14.
70. 43A Phoebe Allen per *Persian* and 95W Sarah Wilkinson per *Persian*: 16 Dec. 1833, ML, TP 227.
71. 235H Elizabeth Hore per *New Grove*, 29 Dec. 1838, AOT, LC 375/2. 93P Margaret Peebles per *Hydery*, 5 Jan. 1838, AOT, LC 347. 158C Mary Culley per *America*, 26 Sept. 1839, AOT, LC 347. 83K Mary Keogan per *Frances Charlotte*, 21 Oct. 1837, AOT, LC 347.
72. 269H Mary Haigh per *Arab*, Jan. 1842, AOT, CSO 22/50, pp. 313–14.
73. 164G Rebecca Gentles per *Hector*, 16 Feb. 1839, AOT, LC 347.
74. 61B Rebecca Barton per *Northampton*, 29 Dec. 1826, AOT, LC 347.
75. AOT, CSO 22/50.
76. 28P Ann Powell per *Brothers*, 21 July 1830, AOT, LC 347. 227B Esther Boulton per *Hydery*, 27 Sept. 1836, AOT, LC 362/3. For other examples, see: 47G Jane Griffith per *Henry*, 26 Dec. 1827, AOT, LC 347; 38P Maria Price per *Henry*, 23 May 1826, AOT, LC 347; and 108W Margaret Wall per *Mermaid*, 16 Dec. 1829, AOT, LC 347.

77. 62L Margaret Lowrie per *Sovereign*, 25 June 1833, ML, TP 325, *NSDG*, ref. 1276.

78. 213S Rosina Savilin per *Frances Charlotte*, 10 Oct. 1834, AOT, LC 347.

79. 39E Sarah Elam per *Jane*, 12 July 1836, ML, TP 290.

80. 143P Mary Ann Pitt per *Arab*, 31 Oct. 1838, ML, TP 326.

81. Elizabeth Winterflood's master, for example, twice 'discovered [her] in the barn with one of my prisoner servants'. 299W Elizabeth Winterflood per *Arab*, 26 Dec. 1837, AOT, LC 83/2.

82. Dixson, *The Real Matilda*, p. 123.

83. 116J Elizabeth Jones per *Siren*, 11 Nov. 1836, AOT, LC 362/3.

84. 157S Anne Saunders per *Eliza* and 112C Ann Frances Clifton per *Mermaid*: 19 April 1833, ML, TP 253.

85. 10J Mary James per *Morley*, 23 Dec. 1833, ML, TP 227.

86. 61D Elizabeth Doyle per *Providence*, 16 Jan. 1837, AOT, LC 362/3.

87. 313H Ann Heath per *Nautilus*, 8 June 1839, ML, TP 326.

88. 105J Jane Jones per *William Bryan*, 27 Sept. 1836, AOT, LC 362/3.

89. 190W Mary Ann Woodcock per *Mary* and 911B John Beckett per *Earl St Vincent*: 26 Aug. 1835, AOT, LC 83/1.

90. 144L Sarah Lawrence per *New Grove*, 3 Jan. 1838, AOT, LC 83/2.

91. 31W Hannah Wilson per *Morley*, 5 Sept. 1835, ML, TP 290. 53K Barbara Kerr per *Borneo*, 31 Dec. 1830, AOT, LC 347.

92. 127C Ann Clifford per *Harmony*, 2 Jan. 1834, ML, TP 227.

93. 247H Jane Hendon per *New Grove*, 23 June 1838, ML, TP 326.

94. Although this decreased the incidence of unexpected absences, it was far from trouble-free. Many convicts simply overstayed their pass.

95. 269H Mary Haigh per *Arab*, Jan. 1842, AOT, CSO, 22/50, p. 309.

96. 66M Bridget Monaghan per *Sovereign*, Jan. 1842, ibid., p. 299.

97. Constable Henry Brice, 20 Dec. 1841, ibid., p. 217.

98. 269H Mary Haigh per *Arab*, Jan. 1842, ibid., p. 313.

99. John Hutchison, 11 Dec. 1841, ibid., p. 117.

100. 305H Grace Heinbury per *Atwick*, Jan. 1842, ibid., p. 267.

101. 66M Bridget Monaghan per *Sovereign*, Jan. 1842, ibid., p. 299.

102. 241B Ruth Beckerdike per *Frances Charlotte*, 24 Nov. 1834, ML, TP 254.

103. See, for example: Eugene Genovese, *Roll Jordan, Roll: The World the Slaves Made* (New York, Pantheon Books, 1974), pp. 597–8, 621 and 658–9; and Robert Paquette, 'Slave Resistance and Social History', *Journal of Social History*, vol. 24, no. 3 (1991), pp. 681–5.

104. O'Connor has criticized Atkinson on this point. See O'Connor, 'Power and Punishment', pp. 15–18.

105. Maxwell-Stewart, 'The Bushrangers', p. 231.

106. James C. Scott, *Weapons of the Weak: Everyday Forms of Peasant Resistance* (New Haven, CT, Yale University Press, 1985), p. 37.

107. Eugene Genovese, *Roll Jordan, Roll*, p. 658.

CHAPTER SEVEN

A Zone of Silence: Queensland's Convicts and the Historiography of Moreton Bay

Tamsin O'Connor

The modern city of Brisbane is the capital of Queensland, the sunshine state, and exudes considerable municipal pride as the nation's 'most liveable city'. Few of its inhabitants are aware that once a life sentence to Norfolk Island was considered preferable to life in Brisbane Town.[1] Brisbane, nevertheless, was the administrative centre of the penal station of Moreton Bay, where over 2000 men and almost 150 women served colonial sentences of between three years and life. The penal station opened in 1824 and for 18 years successive military detachments and a handful of civilian administrators extracted labour from unwilling convict bodies. In 1842 the district was thrown open to meet the pastoral invasion and 17 years later, in 1859, the colony of Queensland was declared. By then the process of dismantling the convict past was well under way.

The first free migrants had immediately and deliberately distanced themselves, physically and psychologically, from a past to which only a sense of disgrace seemed to attach.[2] The reputation of the developing district was threatened on two fronts – by the status of the first European arrivals as 'twice and thrice convicted felons' and by the brutality of the system that punished them. Regardless of how the blame was apportioned the colonists were unanimous in their desire to expunge memories of a 'hateful and burdensome past'.[3] Thus, with each passing generation the zone of silence around the experience of Moreton Bay was reinforced. Only two stone buildings, far away enough from the central business district and sufficiently neutral in appearance, have survived.[4] Elsewhere memories of the system were less easy to contain and suppress, but in Queensland specific historical and geographical factors aided the 'forgetting' process. No one had been permitted within 50 miles of the penal settlement. It had therefore existed in total isolation, defined only by its punitive function. Thus, when the remaining convicts were dispatched southward in 1842, the free settlers were filling a seemingly empty vessel. Yet even the most determined efforts cannot obliterate 18 years of history. Accordingly as the physical relics of the convict era were dismantled or left to crumble, historians applied themselves to the task of reconstructing a past Queenslanders could live with. Thus, by 1959, when the state celebrated a century of responsible government with the publication of *Queensland Daughter of the Sun*, the penal settlement was officially banished from the past with one terse reference: 'The period of convict settlement was brief and its impact on the subsequent social and economic history of Queensland negligible'.[5] Over 30 years later this closure around the lives of the men and women whose coerced labour built Brisbane Town remains almost as firm.

To be sure the number of convicts sentenced to Moreton Bay was relatively small and the duration of the settlement's history relatively short. However the cliometric insignificance of Moreton Bay obscures its real importance. The American Scholar James C. Scott reminds us that domination 'does not persist of its own momentum ... [it] can be sustained only by continuous efforts at reinforcement, maintenance and adjustment'.[6] The establishment of Moreton Bay was not peripheral to transportation but crucial to its reinforcement. In the years between 1819 and 1821, Commissioner J.T. Bigge had cast a jaundiced eye over the disciplinary operations of New South Wales and found the elements of deterrence, terror and reformation lacking. Ironically his suggested remedy for an ailing transportation system was further transportation.[7] Accordingly Moreton Bay and Norfolk Island (1825) were opened to support the existing settlement of Port Macquarie (1821), forming a network of draconian secondary punishment centres on the distant boundaries of New South Wales. In Van Diemen's Land the pattern was reproduced with Macquarie Harbour (1822), Maria Island (1825) and Port Arthur (1832). Far more was at stake than the utilization of a valuable state asset or the punishment of individual offenders. As Raymond Evans and William Thorpe stress: 'the secondary punishment centres ... were to become virtually the *sine qua non* of the official pattern of social control considered necessary to make assigned, coerced labour obedient, productive and profitable'.[8] Moreton Bay, like all penal stations, had a broad remit; to punish the convicts it contained and to 'impress' the free and bond of Britain and the colonies. Its history represents a logical progression in an emergent class struggle in which the state mobilized all its forces to discipline its most valuable but potentially threatening resource – labour. In this way, the convict experience of Moreton Bay was not just an intensely punitive physical and psychological ordeal, it was also an ideological construct that served a crucial role in the broader discourse of social discipline.[9] Moreover, a close analysis of the settlement's history offers insights not merely into the nature and function of punishment, but also issues of class, gender and race. In short, it was a potent concentration of all the ingredients of colonial power relations.

Yet, the history of Moreton Bay has remained a matter of mainly local concern, to be viewed in isolation from the wider transportation system and reluctantly accommodated in the history of Queensland. In this parochial context it has been treated merely as an unfortunate backdrop to the 'real' business of the state's history — exploration and economic and political development. The men and women who started it all have been left buried in the historical record. They necessarily make regular 'walk on' appearances as 'the convicts', but they remain a passive amorphous group who exist only in relation to the free men who controlled their lives.

Any survey of Queensland historiography must begin with its earliest contributors.[10] They are crucial for they launched certain precedents that have enjoyed great resilience. Each in varying degrees demonstrates an aversion to the convict taint that would remain the principal popular response for years to come. William Traill, writing in 1886, is representative of an historical tradition which skirts over the first 18 years of European settlement eager to reach 1842, the 'destined hour' when the 'kiss of free colonisation aroused the territory from the long lethargy imposed by the restrictions of penal settlement'.[11] The authors of a 1900 publication are more forthright in their rejection of Queensland's convict past:

> Shall we pass it over? We think so. Queensland's infantile days were broad arrowed with crime ... the curse of the whippers and the prayers of the whipped, was the doleful music played at its birth. Convictism hung like a pall over Moreton Bay.[12]

The convict period is dismissed, perhaps even justified, as a product of 'infantile days', and by implication maturity was bestowed by the onset of free settlement. Fredrick Morrison's 1888 contribution adopts a similar format:

> It is needless to say much in regard to the penal era, other than so far as to place on record some of the more salient points to which future generations may with profit refer ... The type of serfdom that existed ... was of a kind most repulsive to all such as are actuated by humanitarian sentiments.[13]

The message is clear — 'least said soonest mended'. Yet this open rejection of the convict past is in itself less significant than the way in which Queensland's first historians tailored their response to create the basis of an historical tradition. Their self-appointed task was to make the demoralizing consequences of a painful past disappear with the magic of inevitable progress. Morrison's reassuring tones are typical: 'We are scarcely qualified, by our superior advantages and education, to judge of the roughness characteristic of those masters who were placed over the penal population of Moreton Bay'.[14] In summoning notions of enlightened progress historians were attempting to make the recent convict past appear as alien to life in late colonial Queensland as the European 'dark ages'. By 1925 the temporal and psychological gulf was sufficiently wide for W.W. Craig to state that: 'the convict colony ... and the city which Brisbane ultimately became, are in every important particular, cut off from one another'.[15]

Ironically early historians were able to make the worst aspects of this dubious past work in their favour. The brutality of the settlement invariably, albeit briefly, comes to the fore – almost as if the writers cannot resist the opportunity to showcase some evocative metaphors. Yet the often flamboyant prose serves a very real purpose, conjuring up tantalizing scenes of extreme behaviour that could only help to emphasize the carefully constructed distance between the penal era and free settlement. This device of disassociation is typically heightened by sensationalizing the regime of the notorious Commandant Patrick Logan.[16] Like Traill and Morrison, John J. Knight and William Coote consider the system only to dwell upon the 'most cruel and tyrannical period of [Moreton Bay's] history'.[17] In so doing they established a false relationship of cause and effect between Logan's personal command and the undeniable severity of the settlement.

This has had significant historiographical repercussions. First it launched a preoccupation with the nature of the commandants and their officers, rather than the system they operated. Secondly, it has encouraged historians to level their critique at one personal regime of many, creating the impression that before and after Logan the convict's lot was immeasurably better. Thus, the focus for study became the individual oppressor rather than an oppressive system. Moreover, as Ross Fitzgerald points out, the implication that the evils of convictism were attributable to a single man denies 'the connection of that period to subsequent events', sparing Queenslanders the task of painful self-examination.[18] More importantly, if the severity of the system is rendered an aberration of character, the convicts are denied a right of reply. Historians have exerted all their explanatory energy upon Logan, making no attempt to examine critically either the complex structures of domination at the settlement or the significance of the convict response. Indeed these strategies of avoidance have proved so effective that they provoked a concerted effort in recent years to 'rehabilitate' Logan and so definitively bleach the stubbornest of Queensland's 'hated stains'.[19]

What then of the convicts? Queensland's first historians were perched precariously on the fence as they struggled to reconcile the 'frightful scene' of Brisbane's birth with the 'honour and glory of [their] present civilisation'.[20] The crimes of the convicts and the brutality of their punishment further confounded the equation. Knight was exceptional in his sympathetic use of convict testimony. However, given the power of the convict taint, his sources are unnamed and their memories are predominantly used to measure Logan's tyranny. Coote is disinclined to consider 'all the prisoners as the refuse of mankind'.[21] Morrison goes further and acknowledges 'those unfortunates who many years ago sowed the seed from which we are deriving a beautiful harvest'.[22] Craig is less generous, though more typical, dismissing the convicts as of the 'worst and most desperate class' and their contribution as 'inefficient and ineffective'.[23] Regardless of the role the convicts are accorded, a rigid framework of analysis based exclusively upon issues of local development was established, leaving significant convict lives to be swept along in an historical continuum with no meaning beyond the founding of a 'respectable' and 'progressive' state – a state which had, after all, proclaimed itself a land fit for the Queen.[24]

This parochialism was in part exacerbated by a long academic silence. The early historians had set in motion yet another enduring precedent – Queensland's past was established as the preserve of the 'interested amateur'.[25] Throughout the 1960s, when academics in the south-eastern states began a serious historical assault on the convict past, the University of Queensland remained detached. The first academic contribution to the history of the Moreton Bay penal settlement did not appear until 1982.[26] This did not reflect a bias against convicts in particular, but rather Queensland's history in general. Although the conservative social historian, Allen Morrison, and a number of young graduates were beginning to investigate local issues, the History Department exerted its academic energy on the centres of power to the south and, of course, the history of the 'old country'. Even today there are relatively few Australianists, although Asia and America have replaced Britain as the principal areas of study. Consequently the further exploration of the history of the penal settlement was left to the Royal Historical Society of Queensland. Taking their lead from Raphael Cilento and Clem Lack, they constructed a history that could be accommodated into their vision of statehood by virtually excluding convicts and women, while portraying the destruction of Aboriginal society as the (free) white man's 'triumph'.[27]

With the accumulated confidence of over a century of statehood the new guardians of the past were apparently ready to face the first 18 years. However, the convicts recede further into the zone of silence as only limited features are deemed worthy of consideration. There is a tendency to dwell on correspondence between Governor Brisbane and the British Colonial Secretary suggesting that Moreton Bay was more suitable for free settlement. This, of course, would have saved Queensland from the stain of convictism. A typical example of this is seen in the work of Douglas Fraser which, with no hint of irony, transforms the penal era into the pioneering days of 'Early Public Service in Queensland'. He defended his subject matter before the stalwarts of the society by summoning a wistful historical might-have-been:

> Some Queenslanders are reluctant to have the origins of the state as a penal settlement discussed ... for those who feel ashamed ... let them be consoled by the fact that the British Government rescinded the order to commence Moreton Bay as a penal settlement ... feeling it was more suited for general colonisation.[28]

Closely linked is a preoccupation with issues of location, catering to Queenslanders' desire to define themselves geographically. Almost every history of Moreton Bay gives disproportionate weight to the circumstances surrounding the transfer of the settlement from Redcliffe to Brisbane. Similarly the expeditions conducted by transitory visitors like John Oxley and Allan Cunningham are exhaustively detailed: the charting and taming of the wilderness represented as an essential prerequisite to the white man's 'triumph'.[29]

Consideration of the settlement itself centres upon the administrative and pioneering qualities of the commandants. In 1963 Louis Cranfield noted that 'for many years historians ... contended that the unsavoury aspects of the early settlement were best forgotten'.[30] He was determined to bring the penal settlement back into the historical fold, but minus the convicts it contained. He assesses each of the eight commandants and, despite some reservations about Logan, he is satisfied that they held up the traditions of the British army 'honourably and well'. He then asserts without further preamble that 'The Moreton Bay Penal Settlement did much towards hastening the development, not only of the state of Queensland, but also the greater part of New South Wales'.[31]

A 1963 article by Douglas Gordon, the then professor of social and preventive medicine at the University of Queensland, proves an important exception to the local rule of concealment.[32] His study of sickness and death at the settlement reveals an unprecedented degree of archival research and critical interpretation. Struck by the incredibly high rates of mortality and morbidity among the local convict population, Gordon makes a statistical and qualitative study of the prevailing social and environmental conditions.[33] There is no attempt to prevaricate or justify, nor any hint of an ultimate 'triumph' or of 'progress'. He examines the penal settlement without recourse to heroic tales of exploration – instead his task is one of academic inquiry into the 'tragedy of Moreton Bay'.[34]

Gordon's article was, however, something of an aberrant interlude and more recently Hector Holthouse demonstrates how thoroughly the convict experience of Moreton Bay has been submerged under the tide of 'progress'. The relevant chapters in his 1975 history of Queensland are devoted almost entirely to exploration, while examination of the penal settlement is restricted to an account of building operations and matters of topographical interest. Significantly the convicts are no longer 'unfortunates' who deserve a share of the 'honour and glory', instead they appear only as an unworthy labour force for the free officials who energetically tackled 'the colossal task ahead'.[35]

Thus, while the convicts are unwelcome protagonists in the genesis of Queensland, their gaolers attain pioneering status. This invariably leads to a defence or indictment of Patrick Logan. His misdeeds and violent death presented a challenge even to the sanitizing abilities of local historians. The apologists were, however, undaunted.[36] Early historians, though discomfited by Logan's 'despotic authority', exonerated him as an 'explorer and founder'.[37] More recently, tales of his brutality are dismissed as 'the spirit of denunciation' and he has been fully rehabilitated as a 'conscientious, vigorous, driving man'.[38] His skills as an administrator and explorer are emphasized, allowing him to be eased into a Whiggish history of linear progress. Indeed his name is forever immortalized in one of Brisbane's greatest monuments to sanitized 'progress' — the Logan City Hyperdome. The convicts meanwhile remain peripheral, at best serving as a reminder that 'a nation's greatness is measured by the distance it has travelled'.[39]

Clearly then, an *a priori* historical agenda has created an identifiable historiographical tradition with a self-serving teleology. However, the problem is methodological as well as conceptual. Access to the past is predominantly gained through what James C. Scott calls the 'official transcript' of the dominant elite.[40] This is particularly apparent in the study of convictism, for its history is retrieved from the mass of indents, punishment records, court depositions and official correspondence devoted to the processes of domination. Thus, the convicts' voices are predominantly mediated by the authorities and their actions interpreted in the light of the ideology of power.[41] This is particularly problematic in the context of Moreton Bay, as a common feature of the writings of Queensland historians is their uncritical acceptance of the views expounded in official documents. Reading the historical record against the grain and interpreting the past from 'the bottom up' has not appealed to 'triumphant' Queenslanders. The influence of social history has barely touched the historiography of Queensland's convict past. Indeed, the most striking thing about the historical literature of this period is the remarkable longevity of a theoretically impoverished, parochial and blinkered empiricism. The 'official transcript' of Moreton Bay persists as the only 'true-script' leaving the experiential meaning of penal servitude unexplored.

The wider implications of the convict experience have been submerged not merely by a preoccupation with issues of growth and development, but also by the presumption that the Moreton Bay penal settlement was a discrete, self-evident manifestation of legal retribution. Accordingly, while the extreme nature of the disciplinary function of Moreton Bay is deplored or excused the criminality of the convicts is never questioned. Historians typically litter their prose with colourful descriptions emphasizing the 'deplorable character' and moral turpitude of Queensland's convicts.[42] However, this easy assumption of criminality as an objective category is by no means exclusive to the historiography of Moreton Bay. For, while Queenslanders were anxious to establish their state's credentials, historians of the wider convict system were engaged in a similar task. Like so many Australian historians they were compelled by a search for the 'holy grail' of national identity. Consequently, while the convict system's brutality is prominent in most traditional accounts, our understanding of the motives behind the mechanisms of power has been skewed by a retrospective preoccupation with the convicts' moral credentials and a ready willingness to reiterate historic definitions of criminality. In 1956 Manning Clark launched his professional criminals and prostitutes onto the historical stage and there they have remained, if no longer unassailed by differing interpretations.[43] As the influence of *Convict Workers* spreads and the feminist challenge gathers pace this is becoming a well-charted but also strongly contested historiographical territory.[44] However, beyond the increasingly rigorous revisionist critique, there is an additional point to be made.

The idea of an unprepossessing class of professional criminals and prostitutes has important ramifications for the study of Moreton Bay. Once the 'dangerous classes' are identified, and nineteenth-century representations of criminality embraced, then those convicts who committed further crimes in the colony, or fell foul of the regulations, are, by definition, the most dangerous of all. Consequently their resistance is negated into intrinsic deviance and irreformability.[45] Equally, many historians have assumed that the severity of penal station life is merely an official, albeit unenlightened, response to recidivism. As a result the prevailing historical interpretation of settlements of further punishment can be summarized as desperate measures to counter 'desperate characters'. Thus, the notion of criminality has become a convenient explanatory refuge, sparing historians the task of examining closely and critically the role of centres of secondary punishment. Moreton Bay makes only the briefest of appearances in the scholarly literature devoted to the Australian transportation system. At best it merits a few short paragraphs, at worst it fails to warrant even a footnote.[46] This general scholarly indifference tacitly supports Craig's belief that: 'the penal station remained a mere excrescence on the country's history, and never formed any ... part of national life'[47] – a view local academics have done little to challenge.

The first substantial publication devoted entirely to the penal settlement did not appear until 1975, and even then it was only a collection of documents.[48] J.G. Steele's *Brisbane Town in Convict Days* has become a principal reference work for any student of the period. However, given the limitations of the existing historiography, it is a disappointing beginning. It neatly consolidates past themes, maintaining the closure against the convict voice by categorizing convict testimony as 'convict tales' and convict action as 'convict cunning'.[49]

All was quiet again until the 1980s when a number of significant academic works finally appeared. First into the field was Ross Fitzgerald with his sweeping revision of Queensland's past. His treatment of the convict period points to many of the historiographical limitations outlined here. Nevertheless, after scolding the undue focus on Logan's tyranny, he promptly weighs the merits of his regime.[50] He draws his survey to a conclusion by stating that: '[Commandant Clunie] shared with Logan the dubious honour of being the longest serving commandant at Moreton Bay. However, his reign was relatively uneventful'.[51] Critical or otherwise, this keeps the focus firmly levelled upon commandants and Logan in particular, while begging the question: 'what constitutes eventful?' Under Clunie's administration European numbers peaked at penal Moreton Bay and the settlement reached its greatest geographical spread. During this time deteriorating race relations culminated in full-scale military assaults upon the Aborigine population of Stradbroke Island.[52] Things were no less uneventful for the convict population. Harsh punishment and the resistance that provoked it was not exclusive to Logan's regime. Indeed Clunie conducted the first execution on what was to be Queensland soil, and the whippings continued unabated. Moreover, female convicts began to arrive in increasing numbers, providing yet more scope for conflict as the history of white Queensland's gender relations began.[53] In assuming all fell quiet with the demise of Logan, Fitzgerald unwittingly highlights the pitfalls inherent in any attempt to write a revisionist history based almost entirely upon secondary source material.

The first academic attempt to provide an empirical and interpretive study of the whole period came from Ross Johnston in *Call of the Land* (1984) and *Brisbane: The First Thirty Years* (1988). The chauvinist and simplistic explanations of the Royal Historical Society of Queensland school are replaced by scholarly analysis, but the penal settlement remains an historical preface to the development of Queensland and the City of Brisbane. In *Call of the Land* the period of convict settlement is characterized as 'marking time' and the convicts themselves appear only as fodder for 'Logan's stern efforts' and the 'brawn essential for success'.[54] Even in his later, more detailed study, the convict experience remains subordinate to the themes of growth and development. In the chapter entitled 'People and Plans', one might expect some consideration of the convicts and their desires, but the lion's share of the account goes to the plans and projects of free men. The only convicts named are Pamphlett, Finnegan and Parsons, who were not even under sentence to Moreton Bay.[55]

This leads to the absorption of convicts into the mainstream account. Certain male convicts associated with Moreton Bay are relatively well known. The three accidental explorers have been permitted recognition precisely because they can be accommodated beyond the context of convictism.[56] Accordingly, the only two detailed convict biographies centre on two individuals already located in the 'authorized' historiography. Christopher Pearce has shifted the non-academic agenda by writing on Thomas Pamphlett's experience of transportation.[57] Similarly the academic historian, D.J. Mulvaney, has made a case study of John Graham.[58] Such contributions are important but there is still a quibble. These men were singled out because exceptional circumstances drew them into stories of exploration and chivalrous rescue. When Pamphlett was picked up by Oxley in 1823 and led his party to the Brisbane river and when Graham rescued Eliza Fraser, they transcended their convict status and the door of historical posterity was thrown open.[59]

Mamie O'Keefe highlights aspects of the convict experience in a more general way. She is harder to categorize: as a professional archivist she falls between the academic and non-academic traditions. In addition to her *Brief Account of the Penal Settlement of Moreton Bay*, two important articles bring convict action to centre stage.[60] Although O'Keefe's subject matter potentially provides valuable insights into the nature of convict resistance at the settlement, her work is essentially an exercise in retrieval rather than interpretation and the prevailing empirical bias is all too evident. Her article on runaways is presented, not in the light of convict agency, but as a problem for the authorities.[61]

The first hint of a conceptual interpretation of the convict experience is the work of Kay Saunders. She identifies the extraction of labour from a convict workforce as the first phase in a sustained exploitation of unfree labour, persisting throughout the colonial period and beyond.[62] This is an important step, but the penal settlement is not under the microscope – it remains a mere precursor to later events. This is also partly true of Libby Connors's contribution.[63] Her PhD thesis examines the operation and nature of the colonial criminal justice system in Queensland and her introductory chapter on the Moreton Bay settlement is one of the most important studies to date. Connors challenges the 'simple account' by placing the history of the settlement in an analytical framework informed by the issues of power and authority. Drawing on the arguments of British social historians and the theoretical insights of Foucault, she does indeed provide 'a fresh perspective on the internal functioning of the penal settlement'.[64] Yet a qualification is necessary –

Connors's analysis is, in many respects, limited by the broader arguments of her thesis. In challenging earlier accounts of the colonial judicial system she reduces Moreton Bay to a mere device against which to measure the development of later draconian penal sanctions. In attempting to apply Foucault, and so demonstrate that 'progress' is a dubious notion, Connors overstates her case, arguing that the Moreton Bay penal settlement compared favourably to subsequent systems of total incarceration. Thus, while the emphasis is on increasing severity rather than enlightened progress, her argument is ultimately no less linear than those she seeks to rebut.

There is recent work which levels its gaze on the settlement without treating it as a preface or adjunct to other fields of investigation. Jennifer Harrison has extensively researched the Irish origins of the settlement's female prisoners and military personnel, uncovering valuable new material.[65] Nevertheless, she tends to take the official record at face value. Although she challenges the idea that the convicts were 'desperate characters', she is certain of their criminality, describing the female convicts as 'common thieves', 'miscreants' and 'recidivists'.[66] There is no exploration of the economic and political meanings behind such designations. Her response to the issue of severity is one of denial. Perhaps influenced by the efforts of Logan's apologists, and recent developments in the broader historiography of convictism, she dismisses the evidence of officially sanctioned brutality in favour of the dubious notion of official fair play: 'Investigations have shown that if the convicts behaved and conformed, the authorities treated them quite fairly'.[67] This tendency to summon the benign face of the system is also apparent in a contribution from Francis O'Donoghue. With an uncritical eye he examines the historical records of 1838 from the point of view of Commandant Cotton and his officers. Uncovering a hint of paternalism, he dubiously assumes all was well for the convict in 1838.[68] Although O'Donoghue and Harrison innovate in subject matter, there is a strong ideological and methodological continuity with traditional accounts. Their focus is from above; the convict experience is refracted through their gaolers' eyes.

Harrison and O'Donoghue's perception of power relations at Moreton Bay places them on a benign bandwagon set in motion by recent revisionist historians of the transportation system. To clarify, the traditional account of the transportation system hinges on the intrinsic criminality of the convicts and the severity of the system. Historically these factors converge on the then contemporary notion of 'just denigration'. This single phrase encapsulates the two central themes of the revisionist challenge. A new generation of historians, while emphasizing the extent of imposed denigration, question whether it can be accepted as 'just'. Accordingly, they refute the existence of the criminal class and examine the role of punishment in a social context beyond the merely teleological.[69] Further, there is a move towards a consensual rejection of what

Stephen Nicholas characterizes as 'the peculiar insularity of much Australian history which treats transportation and convictism as peculiarly Australian'.[70]

This appears to create an historiographical environment in which the closure around the experience and meaning of Moreton Bay can be prised open. However, there is a second, less liberating, revisionist agenda. J.B. Hirst, unable to disengage from the notion of the criminal class, preferred to rewrite the past by challenging the issue of 'denigration'. He accommodates Clark's dangerous classes in a revisionist context, which muffles the lash and refutes tales of brutality, in order to display relative material comfort and opportunity.[71] He finds support from a seemingly unlikely quarter. *Convict Workers* purports to be a history written from the 'bottom up',[72] yet the authors have constructed a neat formula in which punishment is rendered incidental, thus unintentionally reinforcing Hirst's benign image of the system.

Clearly, in whatever way the convicts themselves are represented, a new historiographical trend seeks to minimize pain and punishment in the convict experience. The Moreton Bay convicts, were they able to read Hirst and *Convict Workers*, would have been astonished to learn of the 'judicious' use of the lash.[73] Moreover, if the material conditions of the Australian convicts were less severe than has been supposed, then the experience of Moreton Bay is reduced to a peripheral exception to the rule of economic rationalism. Indeed, this breed of historical accountants has chosen to discard penal stations from its calculations, dismissing them as 'being statistically of minor importance' and as a vision of the popular imagination.[74]

As we saw above, Jennifer Harrison hints that the system was not driven exclusively by the negative incentive of painful punishment. Quite properly she recognizes, albeit implicitly, that labour and compliance were also extracted through the operation of positive incentives in the form of indulgences and material rewards. This underpins the revisionist rejection of traditional assessments of the system as punishment-driven.[75] However, positive incentives were defined by and effected through the very existence of their 'negative alter ego', variously represented by the treadmill, the cells, the ironed gangs, extended sentences and the penal stations themselves. Moreover, the operation of positive incentives at Moreton Bay enhanced the relentless regime of domination, given that they were linked inextricably to the convict policing system. We will only achieve a full understanding of the convict experience if we expose domination in all its guises. It is not merely a question of pain versus perks, nor can the use of incentives be held up as evidence of a benign or economically rational state; what the state 'giveth' the state 'taketh' away. Carrot was always proffered under the shadow of the stick.[76] Clearer understanding of the nature and function of domination will reveal Moreton Bay's strategic significance as a weapon of the powerful and as a testing ground for the weapons of the weak, placing it in the crucially important discourse of domination and resistance.

This brings us to Raymond Evans and William Thorpe's recent article in _Australian Historical Studies_.[77] They challenge some of the less sustainable premisses of the cliometrics of _Convict Workers_ and the detail of their argument requires no repetition here. However, it is crucial to emphasize that their work represents the first attempt to breach an hitherto impregnable zone of silence around the convict lives of Moreton Bay. First they break 'State' boundaries, thus creating a more sophisticated framework for reassessing Queensland's convict past by placing penal settlements firmly in the wider context of convict society and exploitative power relations. By engaging in debate with the literature of the system at large, Evans and Thorpe shift the focus away from the relative merits of the commandants and optimistic or pessimistic teleologies of punishment. Instead they focus on the relationship between convicts and gaolers; between subordinates and superordinates. In doing so they contribute 'new understandings of the convict system'.[78] Thus, not only do they release Moreton Bay from its parochial moorings, but they also demonstrate that no history of the convict system can claim to have revealed its true nature if secondary punishment centres like Moreton Bay remain out of the account. Underpinning their arguments is a more general concern. They aim to give credence to otherwise mute convict voices, by pointing to the value of convict testimony and the importance of low-level resistance. To be sure, as Ian Duffield argues in his discussion of Jack Bushman's 'Problematic Passages', there is delicate methodological ground to be negotiated – by all social historians – to prevent credence collapsing into the credulity of theoretical innocence. Evans and Thorpe do not intend to 'counter-privilege' the convict voice, but rather they seek to redress a radical imbalance by breaking a long silence. They show that the disenfranchised voices of history can speak beyond 'the dried dust of statistics', and with an authority beyond the merely apocryphal.[79]

Evans and Thorpe succeed in launching an effective challenge to the closure in local and general convict historiography by beginning to reveal the centrality of the disciplinary role of penal stations in convict society.[80] Moreover, they also find new meanings behind the convict responses to their lived experience of Moreton Bay. The mould has shown its first crack, although their fellow Queenslanders have yet to notice, let alone acknowledge it. In 1898 Knight lamented that 'It will ... take more years than have yet rolled by to blot out from the history of Moreton Bay such scenes as those which formed the routine of its earliest days'.[81] His pessimism was unwarranted – he had underestimated the sanitizing power of the historian's pen. The strength and longevity of the closure around Moreton Bay can be explained partly in terms of a deeply ingrained political conservatism, personified in later years by the former premier, Joh

Bjelke-Petersen. Queensland's convict beginnings, the compulsion to silence, and the state's reactionary reputation are not unrelated factors. Nevertheless, the Moreton Bay records are available in the Sydney Archives and they are not stamped 'for Queenslanders' eyes only'. To perceive Moreton Bay as an exclusively local issue requiring only local resolution is to misrepresent salient convict lives and the significance of the system which overwhelmed them.

Notes

1. Many convicts attempted to escape Moreton Bay in the hope that on recapture they would be sentenced to Norfolk Island, where they believed conditions to be less arduous; Tamsin O'Connor, 'Power and Punishment: The Limits of Resistance. The Moreton Bay Penal Settlement, 1824–1842', BA (Hons) thesis, University of Queensland (1994), pp. 86–7. This chapter is based on the introduction to this thesis. Also see D. Gordon, 'Sickness and Death at the Moreton Bay Convict Settlement', *The Medical Journal of Australia*, vol. 11, no. 12 (1963), pp. 473–80.

2. Many thanks to Raymond Evans for allowing me to read the unpublished manuscript of his forthcoming and as yet untitled book on the social history of Queensland, which details some of the early colonists' practical attempts to distance themselves from 'something still so demonstrably in their midst'.

3. Evans, 'Moreton Bay', introduction to his unpublished manuscript on the social history of Queensland, p. 3.

4. Namely the Windmill high on Wickham Terrace and the Commissariat (now Colonial) Stores on the flood-prone low ground close to the river.

5. Clem Lack (ed.), *Queensland, Daughter of the Sun: A Record of a Century of Responsible Government* (Brisbane, Jacaranda, 1987), p. 54.

6. J.C. Scott, *Domination and the Arts of Resistance: Hidden Transcripts* (New Haven, CT, Yale University Press, 1990), p. 45.

7. [J.T. Biggel, 'Report of the Commissioner of Inquiry on the Colony of New South Wales, 6 May 1822', *Parliamentary Papers*, vol. 1.

8. R. Evans and W. Thorpe, 'Power, Punishment and Penal Labour: *Convict Workers* and Moreton Bay', *Australian Historical Studies*, vol. 25, no. 98 (April 1992), p. 100.

9. For a detailed empirical and conceptual analysis see O'Connor, 'Power and Punishment', ch. 2 and the conclusion. For an examination of the severity of settlement life see chs 2–4.

10. For an effective summary of the nature and concerns of early Australian histories see R. Evans, 'Australian Historiography' in D.R. Woolf (ed.), *Making History* (New York, Garland, forthcoming 1997); this volume is an encyclopedia of historiography.

11. W.H. Traill, 'Historical Sketch of Queensland' in Andrew Garran (ed.), *Picturesque Atlas of Australia* (Sydney, Lansdowne Press, 1974; facsimile of Sydney, 1886 edition), p. 20.

12. 'Queensland 1900', *A Narrative of her Past, Together with Biographies of her Leading Men* (Brisbane, Alcazar Press, 1900).

13. W.F. Morrison, *The Aldine History of Queensland* (Sydney, Aldine Company, 1888), p. 145.

14. Ibid.

15. W.W. Craig, *Moreton Bay Settlement, or Queensland before Separation 1770–1859* (Brisbane, Watson, Ferguson, 1925), p. 57; also see W. Coote, *History of the Colony of Queensland* (Brisbane, William Thorne, 1882), p. 17.

16. Patrick Logan was commandant from 1826 until his murder in 1830 and has even inspired a biography, C. Bateson, *Patrick Logan* (Sydney, Ure Smith, 1966).

17. J.J. Knight, *In the Early Days: History and Incident in Pioneer Queensland* (Brisbane, Sapsford, 1898), p. 25; Coote, *History of the Colony*, p. 18.

18. R. Fitzgerald, *From the Dreaming to 1915: A History of Queensland* (St Lucia, University of Queensland Press, 1982), p. 71.

19. H. Reynolds, '"That Hated Stain": The Aftermath of Transportation in Tasmania', *Historical Studies, Australia and New Zealand*, vol. 14, no. 53 (1969), provides the metaphor here.

20. Morrison, *Aldine History*, p. 144.

21. Coote, *History of the Colony*, p. 16.

22. As note 20. Another writer who shows sympathy is Archibald Meston, *A Geographic History of Queensland* (Brisbane, Government Printer, 1995), p. 11.

23. Craig, *Moreton Bay*, p. 57.

24. There had been some debate about naming the state after John Dunmore Lang, who had done so much to encourage free settlement at Moreton Bay. The idea was quickly quashed as 'Langsland' was horribly close to 'Lagsland'.

25. This is not to suggest that history should be the preserve of academics nor to imply that non-academic history is somehow less legitimate. In 1960s Queensland, however, the interest of the amateurs was more vested than curious.

26. W.R. Johnston, *Call of the Land: A History of Queensland to the Present Day* (Brisbane, Jacaranda Press, 1982); a short BA (Hons) thesis by Alison Goleby, written in 1949, on the 'General Character of the Penal Settlement' seems to have gone astray and was unavailable to the writer.

27. R. Cilento and C. Lack, *Triumph in the Tropics: An Historical Sketch of Queensland* (Brisbane, Smith and Paterson, 1959).

28. D.W. Fraser, 'Early Public Service in Queensland', *Royal Historical Society of Queensland Journal* (hereafter *RHSQJ*), vol. 7, no. 2 (1962–63), pp. 53–4.

29. Among the old histories see: Knight, *The Early Days*; Morrison, *Aldine History*; Traill, 'An Historical Sketch'; Coote, *History of the Colony*; Craig, *Moreton Bay*. For modern examples see Cilento and Lack, *Triumph*; Lack (ed.), *Queensland, Daughter of the Sun*; W.R. Johnston, *Call of the Land* and *The First Thirty Years* (Brisbane, Boolarong, 1988); H. Holthouse, *An Illustrated History of Queensland* (Adelaide, Rigby, 1978); and R. Fitzgerald, *From the Dreaming*.

30. L. Cranfield, 'Early Commandants of Moreton Bay', *RHSQJ*, vol. 7, no. 2 (1963–64), p. 397.

31. Ibid., pp. 59–60.

32. D. Gordon, 'Sickness and Death at the Moreton Bay Convict Settlement', pp. 473–80.

33. Gordon discovered a death rate of 1 in 10, not including death by violence or absconders who were never traced: ibid., p. 475.
34. Ibid., p. 480.
35. Holthouse, *Illustrated History*, p. 27.
36. Holthouse, *Illustrated History*, pp. 27–8; W.R. Johnston, 'A Study of the Relationship between Law and the Community in Colonial Queensland', MA thesis, University of Queensland (1964), pp. 3–5. The most astonishing defence of the Logan regime is D.W. Fraser's 'Settlement in the Logan Period', *RHSQJ*, vol. 7, no. 3 (1962–63), pp. 451–3.
37. Traill, 'An Historical Sketch', pp. 14–15; Morrison, *Aldine History*, p. 149; and Coote, *History of the Colony*, p. 21. Also see Meston, *Geographic History*, pp. 11–12.
38. Johnston, *Call of the Land*, p. 21; Holthouse, *Illustrated History*, p. 27.
39. Fraser, 'Early Public Service', pp. 53–4.
40. This term is coined by Scott, *Domination*, pp. x–xi.
41. Ibid., p. 87. This point is effectively made by Evans and Thorpe, 'Power, Punishment and Penal Labour', p. 95.
42. There is a strong continuity of meaning between Traill's use of the phrase 'frantic ruffians' in 'Historic Sketch', p. 14, and Jennifer Harrison's recent use of 'wrong doers' and 'miscreants' in her article '"The Very Worst Class": Irish Women Convicts at Moreton Bay' in B. Reece (ed.), *Irish Convict Lives* (Sydney, Crossing Press, 1990), p. 184.
43. C.M.H. Clark, 'The Origins of the Convicts Transported to Eastern Australia, 1787–1852', *Historical Studies, Australia and New Zealand*, vol. 7, no. 26 (1956), pp. 121–2. For a recent and comprehensive survey of the relevant literature see S. Garton, 'The Convict Origins Debate: Historians and the Problem of the Criminal Class', *Australian and New Zealand Journal of Criminology*, vol. 24, no. 2 (1991), pp. 66–82. *Representing Convicts* adds its weight, explicitly and implicitly, to the gathering critique of the views of Clark and his school.
44. An example of both trends is Deborah Oxley's 'Representing Convict Women' in this volume. Also see Oxley, 'Female Convicts' in S. Nicholas (ed.), *Convict Workers: Reinterpreting Australia's Past* (Cambridge, Cambridge University Press, 1988), and her 'Convict Maids', PhD thesis, University of New South Wales (1991).
45. A.G.L. Shaw, *Convicts and the Colonies: A Study of Penal Transportation from Great Britain and Ireland to Australia and Other Parts of the Empire* (London, Faber, 1966), p. 164. This has been taken on board by Queensland's academic historians; see, for example, Johnston, *Call of the Land*, p. 21; Harrison, '"The Very Worst Class"', pp. 179–94.
46. A marked exception to this cursory treatment is Robert Hughes, *The Fatal Shore: A History of the Transportation of Convicts to Australia, 1787–1868* (London, Collins Harvill, 1987), pp. 441–55.
47. Craig, *Moreton Bay*, p. 57.
48. J.G. Steele, *Brisbane Town in Convict Days, 1824–1842* (Brisbane, University of Queensland Press, 1975).
49. Steele is a scientist, not an historian. His intention was to bring to notice the documents themselves and he did not intend his accompanying commentary to be

the definitive word on Moreton Bay. It is the perception of others that presents the problem.

50. Fitzgerald, *From the Dreaming*, pp. 71–84.

51. Ibid., p. 85.

52. For a detailed analysis of race relations at the Moreton Bay Penal Settlement – yet another traditional zone of silence in Queensland History – see R. Evans, 'The Mogwi Take Mi-An-Jin. Race Relations at the Moreton Bay Penal Settlement: 1824–1842' in R. Fisher (ed.), *Brisbane: The Aboriginal Presence 1824–1860, Brisbane History Group Papers*, no. 11 (1992), pp. 6–30, and '"What Do You Want? Do You Wish to Kill Me?" Early Racial Contact and Conflict on Stradbroke Island' in Regina Ganter (ed.), *Whose Island? The Past and Future of North Stradbroke* (Griffith University, Queensland Study Centre, 1992), pp. 23–36.

53. See O'Connor, 'Power and Punishment', pp. 50–5, 114–15, 154 and 156–8.

54. Johnston, *Call of the Land*, pp. 22 and 25.

55. Johnston, *Brisbane*, pp. 54–68.

56. Pamphlett, Parsons and Finnegan were all castaways picked up by Oxley's 1823 surveying party. Pamphlett was unlucky enough to return to Moreton Bay as a colonial prisoner. Both early and modern histories relate their tale. Even Cranfield admits these men, who discovered the Brisbane, Macleay and Clarence rivers, into his account: 'Early Commandants', p. 387. The editors of *Queensland, Daughter of the Sun* also mention these men, but never even hint at their convict status. Instead they euphemistically refer to them as 'shipwrecked timber getters', p. 54.

57. C. Pearce, *Through the Eyes of Thomas Pamphlett, Convict and Castaway* (Brisbane, Boolarong, 1993).

58. D.J. Mulvaney, 'John Graham: The Convict as Aboriginal' in Reece (ed.), *Irish Convict Lives*, pp. 108–47.

59. Eliza Fraser was the wife of the Captain of the *Stirling Castle*, which was wrecked to the north of Brisbane with few survivors. Eliza's plight was intensified on being captured by the Aborigines. Her rescue by Graham has inspired works by both Sidney Nolan and Patrick White, and her story was even made into a feature film.

60. M. O'Keefe, *A Brief Account of the Moreton Bay Penal Settlement* (Brisbane, John Oxley Library, 1974); 'The Runaway Convicts of Moreton Bay', *RHSQJ*, vol. 10, no. 1 (1975–76), pp. 52–71; and 'A Report of Missing Tools and Other Items – Moreton Bay Penal Settlement, 1928', *Queensland Heritage*, vol. 3, no. 2 (May 1975), pp. 7–11.

61. O'Keefe, 'The Runaway Convicts of Moreton Bay', p. 52.

62. K. Saunders, *Workers in Bondage: The Origins and Bases of Unfree Labour in Queensland 1824–1916* (Brisbane, University of Queensland Press, 1982).

63. L. Connors, 'The Birth of the Prison and the Death of Convictism: The Operation of Law in Pre-Separation Queensland, 1839–1859', unpublished PhD thesis, University of Queensland (1990).

64. Ibid., p. 23.

65. J. Harrison, '"The Very Worst Class"' and 'Governors, Gaolers and Guards: The Irish Soldiers in the British Army at Moreton Bay, 1842–42', unpublished paper, University of Queensland (1994).

66. Harrison, '"The Very Worst Class"', p. 179.

67. Harrison, 'Governors, Gaolers and Guards', p. 6.

68. F. O'Donoghue, 'Winding Down the Convict Machine: Brisbane 1838', *Push from the Bush*, 13 (Nov. 1982), pp. 25–6.

69. D. Neal, *The Rule of Law in a Penal Colony: Law and Power in Early New South Wales* (Cambridge, Cambridge University Press, 1991), pp. 46–7; M. Sturma, 'Eye of the Beholder: The Stereotype of Women Convicts, 1788–1850', *Labour History*, vol. 34 (May 1978), pp. 3–10; M. Lake, 'Convict Women as Objects of Male Vision: An Historiographical Review', *Bulletin of the Centre for Tasmanian Studies*, vol. 2, no. 1 (1988), pp. 40–8.

70. Nicholas, *Convict Workers*, p. 4; Neal, *The Rule of Law*, p. xii; Evans and Thorpe, 'Power, Punishment and Penal Labour', p. 92; H. Maxwell-Stewart, 'The Bushrangers and the Convict System of Van Diemen's Land, 1803–1846', unpublished PhD thesis, University of Edinburgh (1990), pp. 53–60.

71. J.B. Hirst, *Convict Society and its Enemies: A History of Early New South Wales* (Sydney, George Allen and Unwin Australia, 1983), p. 92.

72. Nicholas, *Convict Workers*, p. 4.

73. Ibid., p. 181; Hirst, *Convict Society*, p. 57–69.

74. This is one of Evans's and Thorpe's criticisms, 'Power, Punishment and Penal Labour', p. 100.

75. See Hirst, *Convict Society*, pp. 50–3 and 83–6; and, Nicholas, *Convict Workers*, pp. 6 and 152–66.

76. S. Fenoaltea, 'Slavery and Supervision in Comparative Perspective: A Model', *Journal of Economic History*, vol. 44, no. 3 (1984) pp. 57 and 61–70; and O'Connor, 'Power and Punishment', pp. 62–8.

77. Evans and Thorpe, 'Power, Punishment and Penal Labour', pp. 90–111.

78. Ian Duffield, 'Problematic Passages: "Jack Bushman's" Convict Narrative' in this volume, p. 23.

79. Nicholas (ed.), *Convict Workers*, p. 45. The authors claim there is no convict voice beyond that which can be gleaned from statistics.

80. Their project continues to evolve theoretically and empirically with 'Freedom and Unfreedom at Moreton Bay: The Structures and Relations of Secondary Punishment', presented at the conference 'Beyond *Convict Workers*', University of New South Wales (Oct. 1995). This event may indicate a future convergence between the *Convict Workers* approach and that of Evans, Thorpe and myself. The conference was organized by Deborah Oxley and Barrie Dyster, two of the *Convict Workers* authors, and other *Convict Workers* authors also presented papers.

81. Knight, *The Early Days*, p. 25.

CHAPTER EIGHT

Convict Workers, 'Penal Labour' and Sarah Island: Life at Macquarie Harbour, 1822–1834

Hamish Maxwell-Stewart

In an innovative article, 'Power, Punishment and Penal Labour', Ray Evans and William Thorpe attacked a series of claims made by the contributors to *Convict Workers*.[1] Much of their fire was directed at the failure of Stephen Nicholas *et al.* to take an holistic view of convict society. The charge was that, by focusing on assigned and skilled government labour, *Convict Workers* had ignored other important aspects of the convict experience. This, combined with an uncritical use of official data, had produced a sanitized and myopic vision of convict society. In support of their argument Evans and Thorpe produced qualitative evidence, drawn primarily from Moreton Bay convict narratives, which was at odds with much of the substance of *Convict Workers*. To quote a key passage:

> Places of secondary punishment like Moreton Bay, Port Macquarie and Norfolk Island receive scant attention in *Convict Workers*. There is no serious attention given to the question of how the inclusion of such places into the analysis might alter its perceptual framework; or whether such a framework could indeed incorporate them; or how secondary punishment regimes varied in degrees and in kind from that of government employment and private assignment.[2]

While this attack is germane, it is arguable that Evans and Thorpe's alternative account lacks depth. To be sure, 'Power, Punishment and Penal Labour' provides many graphic illustrations of the 'nasty, short and brutish' lives of ganged convicts at Moreton Bay.[3] Yet, beyond the brief statement that penal stations were 'necessary to make assigned, coerced labour obedient, productive and profitable' little is offered to connect the 'body' of the convict system to its 'lower digestive' tract.[4] The purpose of this chapter is to explore the functioning of one particular penal settlement, Sarah Island, Macquarie Harbour, Tasmania, in relation to the operation of 'convict society' on a wider level. Such an analysis will shed light on some of the intriguing questions posed by Evans and Thorpe.

Before embarking on this micro/macro approach it is necessary to understand the nature of convictism. What does it mean to be a convict? Much of Evans and Thorpe's attack centres on the extent to which *Convict Workers* underplayed the use of punishment. This is an important part of their argument, as the nature of Australian punishment regimes is used to distinguish convicts from wage workers and slaves. They claim that, unlike slaves, convicts were not driven at work to maximize output. Instead the work was organized so as to be as painful as was consistent with the delivery of punishment. This perspective has merit but it is not without its problems. The most obvious of these are that the kind of conditions that Evans and Thorpe describe do not apply to all convicts. It would appear that Evans and Thorpe are particularly concerned with the levels of pain inflicted on convicts in penal stations. Yet only 2259 male convicts and 148 female ever experienced life at Moreton Bay. The equivalent figures for Macquarie Harbour are 1153 male convicts and an unknown but very small number of women.[5] Thus, their definition of 'penal labour' can only be applied to a minority of convicts.

The lash, ironings, headshaving of women and solitary confinement are all central to any reading of the experience of transportation. All of these instruments were used to hurt, degrade and humiliate convicts. Yet those convicts remained convicts irrespective of whether they were beaten, chained, shaved or confined. The same argument can be applied to the 'benign treatment' thesis. That some assignees happened to be as well or better treated than free workers does not render convictism an irrelevant condition – a mistake that Hirst makes in his discussion of assignment in New South Wales.[6] Instead we have to turn to John West, a contemporary anti-transportationist, for a definition of convictism:

> True, he [the convict] was well fed, while many in England laboured hard,
> and yet went hungry and poor; but nothing reconciled the prisoner to his
> bondage: he compared his condition not with the British pauper, but those
> who, though working in the same field, were masters of their own labour.[7]

As West recognized, it is the sentence which distinguishes transportees from other workers. This was a contract imposed on the convict by a British civil or military court. A sentence *per se* did not condemn the transported convict to a life of unremitting toil and physical abuse, rather the penalty extracted was the expropriation of the prisoners' right to exchange their labour power for a wage.[8] The transportee was in effect constructed as an object: catalogued; described;

dispatched; and provided with a number. The job of convict administrators was to manage their human resources in a manner consistent with the production of goods and utilities which could be offset against the costs of British penal policy while fostering colonial economic development in a manner consistent with metropolitan interests. The substitution of a ration for a wage underwrote this process: a ration is not an income because it is not earned. Just as machines have to be maintained in order to remain productive, convicts had to be fed, clothed and housed.[9]

The convict system was not, however, this simple. As convicts were not machines some additional mechanism was required to turn their latent labour power into a productive force. Two options were open to the managers of convict labour. Their unfree workforce had either to be induced or forced to participate in the work process. Despite the emphasis by Nicholas *et al.* on the use of incentives, both strategies were employed. This is best illustrated through the use of examples. Consider the case of a shepherd. Here a number of factors preclude the use of overt force. In order to punish workers for non-participation it is necessary to catch them shirking. It would be ludicrous, however, to hire a monitor to check up on a single individual. In any event, once the shirker has been caught what options are open? The use of force will only increase levels of workforce resentment and where livestock is concerned the costs of employing a resentful workforce can be considerable.[10] To be sure convict managers could punish a shepherd who 'lost' his flock. For example, Nathaniel Hartley, one of A.W.H. Humphrey's assignees, was given 50 lashes and transported to Macquarie Harbour for having '120 sheep and two merino rams deficient from his Master's flock'.[11] This may have served as a warning to others, but did not recover Humphrey's investment.

For tasks involving a small number of skilled individuals, and substantial investments in fixed capital, the lash is likely to prove an inefficient management tool.[12] Instead it lies in the manager's interests to encourage his convict labour force to identify their own best interests with the accomplishment of the task in hand. To quote the Superintendent of the Van Diemen's Land Company, 'it is not in the interests of the master to make his (the convict's) service a punishment, but rather to make the condition of the convict as comfortable as is consistent with economy'.[13] This view of the convict system is consistent with the Nicholas 'benign treatment' thesis. The contributors to *Convict Workers* get it wrong, however, in their failure to recognize that there was much more to the convict labour experience than incentive-based management schemes.

Coercion was employed in Eastern Australia. The device which enabled the use of force was the labour gang. While the work undertaken by gangs varied, all were characterized by the performance of repetitive tasks which could be undertaken without recourse to expensive machinery. Examples included manning capstans, wheeling coal carts, crushing aggregate, navigating easements and carrying timber. These tasks can be more efficiently accomplished by a team of workers than an individual. There are other advantages, however, to be obtained from gang organization. Labour was ganged in Eastern Australia to allow it to be monitored. The task of the overseer was to detect shirkers so that they could be punished. Many gang workers were beaten in front of their work mates in a system calculated to produce high levels of workforce participation through the use of violence; this is strongly parallel to the flogging of ganged slave labour.[14]

The post-Bigge Report reorganization of the Vandemonian convict system was designed to locate both coercion and incentive-based management strategies within a hierarchical structure. Each convict was allocated to one of six labour categories. The top category, reserved in theory for the 'best behaved', contained ticket-of-leave holders. The second included both convicts assigned to settlers and government 'mechanics'. The third consisted of public works convicts confined at night in the prison barracks. The fourth and fifth categories were reserved for convicts detailed to road and ironed gangs respectively. Finally, the bottom level was occupied by those who had been retransported to penal settlements. The principle was that management strategies in the top half of the system were incentive-based while work undertaken in the bottom three tiers was organized around the gang, triangle and lash.

What made this organization a particularly effective management tool was its ideological trappings. The language employed by managers to describe the provision of incentives is particularly important. Incentives were dressed up as largesse bestowed out of the kindness of the managers' hearts.[15] By accepting these indulgences convicts acquiesced in a deferential relationship between the unfree and their managers, a relationship further underscored by their dependence on managers for favourable memorials which could secure permission to marry and tickets of leave.[16]

The convicts' best defence was to attempt to impose their own set of values. A good example of this is the refusal to consume kangaroo in lieu of the normal beef or mutton ration. Masters saw no difference between the two, as both were bestowed as an 'indulgence' in greater quantities than the government ration. Convicts, however, were reluctant to accept anything which in their eyes cost their 'employer' little or nothing.[17] By attempting to convert an indulgence into a payment, convicts threatened to destroy the dynamic of paternalistic control. Yet there were limits. When one assigned servant told his master 'he well earned all he ate', his master appeared startled and 'rebuked him sharply for his base ingratitude'.[18] Ultimately the labour gang beckoned for those who refused to play the dutiful servant.

In this sense labour gangs were more than an efficient means of forcing convicts to perform repetitive manual tasks. The risk of demotion was important in preventing what might be termed 'incentive inflation'. Without the road gangs, ironed parties or chain gangs in convict Eastern Australia, master–servant relations might have been more like those described by Hirst.[19] Thus labour gangs functioned in a similar way to 'nigger breakers' in the *ante-bellum* South: typically poor white farmers who rented labour at minimal rates from planters who wanted their slaves cured of 'impudence'.[20] Nevertheless, the notion of the road gang as punishment squad clashes with Nicholas's conception of the efficient deployment of labour. While the heavy use of negative sanctions was suited to this type of work organization, the choice of labour was less efficient. As West reported:

> It did not infrequently happen that a tailor or other sedentary craftsman was sentenced to the roads, but in breaking stones there is an art and while the dextrous could make every blow effective, the utmost toil of the novice left a deficiency in the task. To admit excuse would have disturbed the calculations of labour, and the defaulter was delivered at once to the flogger.[21]

There is some evidence that the convict administration attempted to minimize the dislocation caused by the need to punish. First, it is unlikely that magistrates' benches were as impartial as is made out by the protagonists of transportation. On the one hand, masters could use the bench as a vehicle for giving valued workers a rap over the knuckles and, on the other, as a firing mechanism for the useless. The point is that if a master lost a convict through a bench ruling the state was obliged to supply another. It is not difficult to see that there might be a temptation for settler agriculturists to dispose of weavers, for example, in the expectation of having them replaced with agricultural workers. Indeed the Quakers, Backhouse and Walker, made precisely this accusation.[22] As a result, convicts sentenced to labour gangs were disproportionately composed of men whose skills were not required by either private or public-sector managers. In colonial terms, the principal asset possessed by these convicts was their muscle power: they were just those kind of individuals that it made economic sense to beat, push and cajole.

Robson and Moore unwittingly measured the effects of these factors. Both concluded that young unskilled workers were more likely to reoffend than older skilled transportees.[23] While it may be tempting to interpret these findings as evidence of the recidivist tendencies of nineteenth-century street urchins (*à la* Dickens) the findings are open to other constructions. Because of the way that incentive and coercion-based management strategies were structured within the

Vandemonian convict system, there was a tendency for a cream of skilled convicts to rise while the unskilled sank. As sinking meant encountering increasing measures of coercion, the probability of further damning entries being added to a convict's conduct sheet increased, lessening the probability of early release. The structure of the labour market and the role that magistrates' benches played as an adjunct to labour discipline accelerated this process. Like the unskilled, younger convicts were victimized through their masters' reluctance to bear training costs for workers whose long-term services could not be guaranteed. Thus, the Molesworth Committee's charge which hit the system the hardest was that it was a giant lottery.[24] This is perfectly true – how a convict fared had little to do with the crime for which he or she was transported and everything to do with their potential (or lack of it) as human capital. Thus twenty-, thirty- and forty-something blacksmiths, clerks and ploughmen were, on the whole, well treated while teenage weavers and labourers were disproportionately exposed to the rigours of gang management.

The work reserved for punishment labour did not, however, just consist of crushing aggregate and navigating easements. Each road gang required masons, carpenters, bricklayers, blacksmiths, sawyers, timber fellers, carters, cooks and a clerk. Amongst the supplies dispatched by the magistrates some men possessed skills suited to the performance of these specialized tasks. Indeed, it is not uncommon to find the words 'but to be kept at his trade' entered after a road gang sentence. The remaining positions were filled by 'deserving' convicts plucked from the road gang by the omnipotent station superintendent. Two factors were at work here. The loss of productivity occasioned by the demotion of small numbers of skilled convicts could be kept to a minimum by allocating those prisoners to ancillary positions where their skills could be utilized. Second, some positions could be kept open for unskilled convicts promoted from the gang. While this was consistent with a wider convict-management strategy based on promotion and demotion, it also supplied the administration with a retraining facility.

Can penal stations be included in this model of the convict system? Despite the historiographical emphasis on the lash, cannibalism and brutal murders, it is apparent that Macquarie Harbour was much more than a breaker's yard for irreclaimable convicts.[25] A principal function of the Sarah Island settlement was to exploit the natural resources of the harbour, particularly Huon pine. Although a steady supply of planks were shipped to Hobart, much of the timber cut by convict felling gangs was processed into finished articles. While furniture was manufactured at the settlement the most important export commodities were boats and ships.

A shipyard might appear incompatible with the performance of punishment labour. This was not, however, the view of Captain Butler, Commandant at

Macquarie Harbour in the mid-1820s. In a report to Lieutenant-Governor Arthur, Butler stressed the importance of the settlement as a retraining facility. In his words, there are those 'such as weavers, tailors, cotton spinners and other sedentary trades, who are unfit for and disinclined to outdoor labour; and I should conceive a very troublesome and useless set for settlers'. As Commandant, Butler was in a good position to make this assessment. The human cargoes disgorged on the shores of Sarah Island did indeed contain a disproportionate number of textile workers.[26] The useless, however, could be redeemed. As raw materials the newcomers were first supplied to the timber-rolling, dragging and carrying gangs. From there they could graduate to timber rafting. Promotion might follow to an out-felling gang with an introduction to the use of the axe and cross-saw. Those who mastered these techniques could expect further elevation, first to a position as sawyer or fencer, then to assistant carpenter and finally to shipwright's attendant. According to Butler the system had several advantages. The returned Macquarie Harbour convict would work hard and without complaint: virtues that his tales of life in a timber hauling gang were likely to inculcate in other convicts. At the least he would be more expert in clearing, breaking and fencing land. Many, however, would return to the bosom of the system with superior skills. In Butler's words, these were consequences 'which, independent of the reformation effected in their habits, cannot, I should consider, be otherwise than beneficial to a community where such high wages are demanded by mechanics'.[27]

Much has been written about the 'unremitting' nature of work carried out by penal station convicts.[28] Yet, it is apparent that, as the nature of the tasks undertaken varied, there was a wide disparity in the day-to-day conditions experienced by convicts under sentence of retransportation. In essence, Macquarie Harbour was the convict system in miniature. It consisted of four labour tiers and an attendant group of convict wardens. Shipwrights, carpenters, coopers, anchor and chain forgers, blacksmiths, tanners, masons, bricklayers, clerks and seamen formed an élite. An indication of the scale of the work undertaken by these construction crews can be gleaned from the output of the shipyard. In just 13 years Macquarie Harbour produced: one 200-ton barque; five brigs averaging 130 tons; three cutters of 50 tons; seven schooners of 25 tons; at least 24 sloops, lighters and launches; and in excess of 46 smaller craft.[29] Labour was coerced from these skilled production teams by the use of a variety of incentives. The superintendent, overseers and clerks were salaried.[30] The boat crews, shipwrights, carpenters and blacksmiths were given a weekly top-up allowance of seven pounds of flour or three of flour and seven pounds of potatoes.[31] Spirits and tobacco were also made available and separate living quarters provided.[32] If adequate levels of incentive had not been supplied, leaking ships and high rates of industrial sabotage would have ensued. There is little evidence that Macquarie Harbour vessels were substandard and amongst 1570 offences analysed for this study only two could be found which might be construed as sabotage.[33]

The second tier consisted of an intermediate group of prisoners who worked in teams forging nails, sawing and felling timber. This was largely composed of prisoners elevated from the punishment gangs. Although they were provided with fewer incentives than mechanics, the management of their work was nevertheless characterized by performance deals. Traditionally sawyers, treenail mooters and nailers were paid on piece rates. A similar system seems to have been employed at Macquarie Harbour.[34] As an incentive, teams earned the right to spend Saturday fishing if the weekly task was completed by the Friday. Another scheme allowed convicts to dispatch one team member to the mainland to construct kangaroo pits. His task would be completed by the remaining convicts who would then share the proceeds of the hunt.[35]

The bottom two tiers of the system consisted of gangs (a home gang and two out gangs). It is this group of prisoners upon whom the brunt of the punishment fell. All tasks undertaken by the home and out gangs were supervised by overseers. The labour performed required team work, but few skills other than the input of co-ordinated muscle power. Few tools were required beyond hand spikes and cant hooks. In short, this was the type of labour ideally suited to the use of coercive management strategies. The home gang occupied the bottom rung and was composed of convicts who had been sentenced by the Commandant to a stint of hard labour. Four types of work appear to have been undertaken: capstan manning, particularly in the mill where the settlement's flour was produced; work in the lumber yard, which consisted of moving Huon pine logs (weighing up to twelve tons a piece) to the saw-pits and planks to the shipyard; the disassembly of rafts of logs towed from the mainland; finally, rock dredging and slipway construction around the shoreline. Home gang convicts completed these tasks (except, presumably, diving for stones) while wearing leg irons. Irons were employed to make the work hurt (leg irons were also known as punishment irons) and as a deterrent to escape. It is this second reason which helps to explain why the convicts in the bottom tier of the system were stationed on Sarah Island. The home gang was composed largely of convicts who had been involved in escape attempts. The standard punishment for Macquarie Harbour absconders was 100 lashes and six months in irons. Irons made it impossible to contemplate swimming. Their use turned Sarah Island into the Macquarie Harbour maximum security wing.

The out gangs were ferried to their work stations on the mainland each morning. Four different types of task were undertaken by convicts in this labour category. First, roadways were cut through the temperate rain forest which surrounded the upper reaches of the harbour. These access routes, which were paved with inferior logs and the debris of the felling operations, were used by hauling gangs to remove felled timber to the shoreline. Once at the water's edge, the logs were rafted together by a team of convicts working up to their chests in water. These rafts were then towed to Sarah Island. There appear to have been two out gangs, one detailed to clearing roadways and dragging, the other to rafting and towing.

Based on the recollections of the commissariat officer, Thomas Lempriere, and data gleaned from offence registers, a reconstruction of Macquarie Harbour is now possible. Between 36 and 38 men were occupied in the shipyard. Three boat crews account for a further 18 convicts. To this must be added smiths, farriers, founders, tanners, masons, bricklayers, bakers and cooks, gardeners and clerks, estimated at 22 individuals.[36] Convict NCOs form an analogous group of about 18 promoted prisoners.[37] A middle tier of about 56 convicts was composed of sawyers, treenail mooters, nailers, officers' servants, storemen, hospital orderlies, firewood cutters, water carriers, tree fellers and charcoal burners.[38] The mean Macquarie Harbour population can also be calculated at about 260 prisoners.[39] Based on these figures, 7 per cent of prisoners were NCOs; 36 per cent mechanics, boatmen, cooks, gardeners and clerks; and 22 per cent intermediate convicts (sawyers, nailers, timber fellers, etc.).[40] Thus just 35 per cent, or approximately 90 men, were employed in the gangs at any one time. It must be appreciated, however, that due to turnover (the result of promotion and demotion), the experience of gang labour was more widespread than implied by a casual glance at these estimates. It seems likely that the majority of penal station convicts experienced gang life at some time.

Was the division of labour at Sarah Island exceptional? The evidence is that, in Vandemonian terms, it was not. Port Arthur inherited the Sarah Island shipyard work. The settlement also contained shops for painters, carpenters, wheelwrights, coopers, tailors, shoemakers, tinmen and blacksmiths.[41] Maria Island possessed a pottery, brickfield, cloth manufactory, mechanized felling house (complete with reservoir and race), tannery and shoemakers' and blacksmiths' shop, in addition to the regular array of support workers. Indeed, Lempriere considered that convicts were allowed 'great latitude' at this settlement, particularly in the allocation of garden plots as an incentive.[42]

The remainder of this chapter will explore some of the implications of this division of labour through an examination of: the distribution of punishment; the operation of penal station black economies; the calorific content of the gang diet; and the relations between retransportees and their convict overseers and constables. While all of these themes are deserving of greater attention, it is hoped that this preliminary survey will help to contextualize some of the complexities inherent in the organization and operation of Macquarie Harbour and other Eastern Australian penal stations.

An analysis of offence registers confirms that, as with other levels of the convict system, skill mattered at Macquarie Harbour. The fate of agricultural workers illustrates this. A theme of the pre-*Convict Workers* historiography is the contrast between the behaviour of urban 'ne'er-do-wells' and rural convicts.[43] An alternative explanation is that the treatment awarded to convicts was largely dependent on the demand for the skills possessed by each transportee.[44] Those with valued skills, for example agricultural workers, were disproportionately employed in situations characterized by the use of incentive-based management schemes. Thus it is not surprising that this category of workers is underrepresented at Macquarie Harbour.[45] Yet, once landed on the shores of Sarah Island, the ploughman's prospects were bleak. In an economy where agricultural skills were greatly oversupplied the once prized rural worker was converted to gang fodder. The effects of this are illustrated in Figure 8.1.

The range of conditions experienced by convicts at Macquarie Harbour differed in other ways. Black economies are important to the unfree. For convicts, the substitution of a ration for a wage was a day-to-day reminder of their servile status. Thus, while the 'small luxuries' obtained through trafficking relieved the monotony of life on the ration, they had a deeper significance. The convict black economy was liberational in the sense that to engage in economic transactions is to challenge the concept of labour unfreedom.[46] Through the production and exchange of goods and services convicts were able to redefine themselves as something other than an object. It was thus important to the administrators of convict labour that trafficking within penal settlements should be strictly controlled. Given the isolated location of Macquarie Harbour, and the means of physical restraint available, this would appear to have been a realistic objective there, if anywhere. One of the advantages of sea-borne communication was that it was easier to regulate than terrestrial access. By placing a military detachment on convict supply vessels the sole line of communication between penal and parent settlement could be patrolled. Everything which came in and out of the settlement could be kept within the range of a Brown Bess. Internal controls were enforced through a mixture of military sentries, a convict constabulary, night-watchmen, searches and security fences. Despite these measures, clandestine economic activity was a daily feature of life at Macquarie Harbour.

Trade thrived between the military and skilled production crews. Tobacco and alcohol went in one direction and boards, brooms and cabinet furniture in the other (presumably for sale in Hobart).[47] The trade in manufactured articles was supplemented with natural products. Most of these were smuggled into Sarah Island by returning timber fellers and charcoal burners.[48] Many of these commodities were manufactured (or expropriated) in government hours, employing government tools and resources. On the one hand, the prevalence

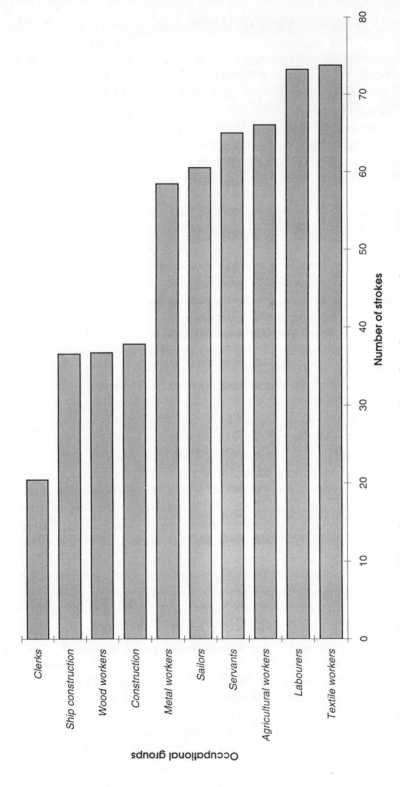

Figure 8.1 Lash count per occupational category (mean number of strokes received per convict)

Source: Based on 505 Macquarie Harbour convict descriptions and corresponding offence records: Archives Office of New South Wales, Convicts Indents and Muster papers re convict ships; Archives Office of Tasmania, Con 23 and Con 31

of trafficking underscores the opportunities available to Sarah Island production teams. On the other, it provides evidence of the gap between the world of ganged convicts and those in incentive-based management schemes. The tobacco and spirits bartered from the military were recirculated amongst the convict population in return for items of slop clothing and food.

This elicit trade had a detrimental effect on gang rations. As Martin Cash reported of Port Arthur, 'three parts of the flour is purchased from the cook by the overseers ... and a modicum of the remaining proportion is absorbed in ... cakes to be distributed in the shape of bribes to the sub-overseers and watchmen who may be privy to their mode of traffic'.[49] Penal station black economies accentuated the gulf between the experience of ganged and non-ganged convicts. Even assuming the gang ration was always supplied, it would have yielded approximately 3000 calories a day. This is about 1000 calories less than that provided to assignees but is in excess of the recommended minimum for adult males cited by Nicholas.[50] As Evans and Thorpe point out, however, these figures cease to appear generous when the nature of the work undertaken is considered.[51] The punishment gang at Macquarie Harbour worked a 57-hour week on a maximum of 21,000 calories. Employing the data supplied by Sutch, the remaining 111 hours of sleep, rest and light work would have consumed about 9300 calories at 1.4 a minute, thus leaving 11,700 calories a week for gang labour. This is enough for only 19½ hours very heavy labour (calculated at 10 calories a minute).[52] Indeed actual calorie consumption was probably higher than this as convicts worked for much of the time in damp or wet clothing in low temperatures which were exaggerated by wind chill. Thus, even disregarding climatic conditions and probable ration shortfalls, the gang diet is patently insufficient for the accomplishment of 'constant, active, unremitting employment ... in very hard labour'.[53] Clearly something had to give: either Macquarie Harbour had morbidity and mortality rates resembling a Japanese prisoner-of-war camp; or the nature of the work undertaken was not as severe as hitherto supposed.

If official reports are to be believed, the latter explanation is the more likely. According to the evidence supplied by the Quakers Backhouse and Walker, the Macquarie Harbour annual death rate was 28.5 per 1000.[54] This is high for an adult male population. It compares, for instance, to a death rate of 14 per 1000 for troops stationed in the British Isles in the 1830s.[55] It is much lower, however, than those reported for Japanese-run POW camps. Niigata camp, for example, had a death rate of 144 per 1000 in 1944.[56] The morbidity evidence is conflicting. Backhouse and Walker reported that there were seldom more than three convicts in the hospital at a time. Yet they also cite the surgeon who claimed that prisoners were slow to recover from illness due to the poor nature of the diet.[57] Another surgeon, John Barnes, reported that rheumatism, scurvy and dysentery were 'common diseases' during the 18 months he was stationed at Macquarie Harbour, 'but that these ... were generally mild in their nature'.[58] Thomas Lempriere thought that the general state of convict health was low. While he stressed that few lives were lost to natural causes, he blamed chronic morbidity rates on the climate, salt rations and the proportion of work undertaken in water.[59]

As at Moreton Bay, further evidence of the insufficiency of penal station rations can be found from a perusal of conduct records. Charges of stealing articles of food are commonplace.[60] In the months of March and April 1828, for example, 21 convicts received punishments of between 12 and 100 lashes for stealing potatoes and other provisions. The clustering of theft of food charges supports contemporary accounts of periodic supply shortages occasioned by bad weather impeding shipping movements.[61] The implications are that the diet supplied to Macquarie Harbour labour gangs was nutritionally deficient but that convicts were not pushed at work until they dropped. A more realistic view is that bouts of very heavy labour, such as dragging and landing logs, were interspersed with periods of rest and lighter work.

These findings should be kept in perspective. There is plenty of evidence that life in a penal station labour gang was physically and psychologically demanding. Charges of malingering abound in the records.[62] Other convicts tried more elaborate stratagems. John Salmon was given 50 lashes for 'falsely stating he would point out the body of a man he had murdered near Pittwater'.[63] It is unclear whether Salmon succeeded in obtaining a 'slant' to Pittwater. When James Mason cut off two of his fingers 'in order to deprive the Gov^t of his labour', he too was given 50 lashes.[64] Yet the single greatest testimony to the horrors of life in a penal gang are the rates of absconding. In all, 11 per cent of all Macquarie Harbour arraignments involved escape attempts. These accounted for 30 per cent of all strokes administered at an average of 77 'stripes' per would-be escapee.

The role played by convict NCOs is central to an exploration of the dynamics of penal gangs. In general, overseers must walk a tightrope between management and workforce. As Genovese wrote of *ante-bellum* slave society:

> The overseers ... knew that they would not keep their jobs without some degree of support in the quarters, and accordingly, they tried to curry favour. No sensible slaveholder wanted a man who could not maintain a certain level of morale among the slaves.[65]

Macquarie Harbour punishment gangs were different. When Joseph Armstrong, a constable stationed with the Gordon River Gang, permitted two of his charges to go fishing at Birch's River, he was sentenced to three days' solitary confinement on bread and water and dismissed as a constable.[66] The importance of this is that productivity deals involving the right to fish and hunt were struck with Sarah Island production teams. The refusal to allow gang constables and overseers the latitude to negotiate similar arrangements provides a graphic illustration of the nature of the work process. Clearly the maximization of output was not the overriding objective.

Despite the small number of individuals concerned, penal station punishment regimes had an important influence on the dynamics of convict society. This can be illustrated in the treatment meted out to Macquarie Harbour overseers and constables. Deprived of the ability to play the role of intermediate managers, penal settlement NCOs were invariably perceived as statist tyrants. Attacks on them were not infrequent. James Crawford first refused to work for his overseer and then stuck him with a knife, stabbing him in the head and neck. Joshua Seaburn struck his gang constable with a maul (a hammer used for driving piles).[67] Other Macquarie Harbour NCOs did not survive the attentions of their charges. Constable Craggs was killed by Thomas Peacock who declared 'that he should now die happy since he had caused his death'.[68] Another constable, George Rex, was drowned by nine convicts who held his head under the water. Subsequently, James Dalway was given 50 lashes for 'contemptuous and jeering conduct' when Rex's body was being carried to the grave. Shortly afterwards two other convicts, both of whom had appeared as witnesses at the murder trial, were also killed.[69]

This animosity was not restricted to the confines of Macquarie Harbour. When William Hopper, an ex-Sarah Island prisoner, was transferred to the Hobart Prison Barracks he renewed an old (and unwelcome) acquaintance with John Flynn. Hopper lunged at Flynn, urging the other prisoners to do likewise, while shouting 'he used to cut the men's flesh at Macquarie Harbour'.[70] Another ex-Macquarie Harbour man, John Smith, absconded from the St Peter's Pass chain gang. Smith headed for the Superintendent of Convicts' Office, Hobart, where he turned himself in. He explained that the cause of his absconding was 'the ill usage he received from the men in consequence of his having been an overseer at Macquarie Harbour'.[71]

Macquarie Harbour labour gangs were, in the eyes of convicts, somewhere apart and removed from ordinary experience. In short they were the unacceptable face of convict management rather than a receptacle for unacceptable convicts. This was the gist of Henry Jones Batchelor's confiscated history. Batchelor, an attorney's clerk from Bath, was sent to Macquarie Harbour after he was caught altering the police office registers.[72] Despite a recommendation that he should not be employed at his trade, Batchelor was appointed clerk to the Commandant. This gave him access to the penal station records. On 7 September 1829 Batchelor gave the only rendition of his history.

In front of 'several of the prisoners' he read from a paper written in his hand 'a false & malicious statement relative to the punishments inflicted by former Commd[ts] at this Settlement'. He was charged with subversive conduct, sentenced to three weeks' solitary confinement and cast into the lumber gang.[73]

Evans and Thorpe's categorization of retransported convicts as 'penal labourers' is apt.[74] Unlike slaves, the work undertaken by ganged re-transportees was constructed to be a punishment in its own right, hence the prohibition of performance deals, the resort to frequent beatings and chainings and the observance of strict ration controls. These were not (at least in the direct sense) productivity measures. However, these conditions were exceptional. Sarah Island NCOs were regarded by the convict population as objects of aversion, not because they had been overseers or constables, but because they had occupied those positions at Macquarie Harbour. Outside the Sarah Island gangs, 'penal labour' touched upon the lives of convicts, but cannot be used to describe working conditions. The majority of prisoners were 'convict workers', deprived of property rights in their labour and managed through the balancing of positive and negative incentives at the margin. The experience of 'penal labour' was created to inform the dialogue between convicts and managers. Put simply, the image of the penal settlemant hauling gang was employed to curb incentive inflation. Yet on its own, this explanation cannot account for the complexity of Sarah Island. To compensate for the effects of extracting labour from most prisoners through a mixture of incentives and coercion, the convict system developed a complex hierarchy of gangs and associated production teams. While the gangs were the descent mechanism, the production teams were the up elevator. Through these ancillary units, a colon for the discharge of waste was converted to a labour recycling pump. The job of the production team was two-fold: to filter out the skilled and put them back to productive use; and to retrain the unskilled. Thus the functioning of the convict system depended upon the oversupply of skill to drive colonial growth rates.[75]

Production teams have a further importance in that they aid an understanding of how 'penal labour' was enmeshed within a wider scheme of convict management. A promotional framework balanced the repressive mechanism which dropped convicts into the abyss, for it was only through the grateful acceptance of the hand of paternalism that the deferential convict could be plucked from his 'former sufferings'. If an understanding of the functioning of Sarah Island helps to locate 'Power, Punishment and Penal Labour' within a wider political economy, the same is true of *Convict Workers*. While many of the claims made by Nicholas *et al.* require modification, their arguments are not fatally undermined by the intrusion of penal economies. Indeed the opposite is true. Without the economic models developed in *Convict Workers* it would be difficult to locate Sarah Island, as a colonial shipyard, within a wider framework.

Armed with this understanding, the importance of the 'variations in degrees and kind' between the organization of assigned service and penal stations can be perceived. Macquarie Harbour was more than an annexe in the west, geographically remote and of little significance to the system as a whole. In economic and ideological terms it can be located at the heart of the transportation system. In this sense, penal stations were organic pumps necessary for the regulation of a complex political economy. Once this is understood the dichotomy inherent in the literature disappears. Within the confines of Sarah Island, both historically and historiographically, *Convict Workers* and 'penal labour' worked (and work) side by side.

Notes

1. Stephen Nicholas (ed.), *Convict Workers: Reinterpreting Australia's Past* (Cambridge, Cambridge University Press, 1988).
2. R. Evans and W. Thorpe, 'Power, Punishment and Penal Labour: *Convict Workers* and Moreton Bay', *Australian Historical Studies*, vol. 25, no. 98 (1992), p. 100.
3. The Evans and Thorpe versus *Convict Workers* dichotomy is reminiscent of Michael Craton's article, 'Hobbesian or Panglossian? The Two Extremes of Slave Conditions in the British Caribbean, 1783–1834', *William & Mary Quarterly*, 3rd ser., vol. 35 (1978), pp. 324–56.
4. Evans and Thorpe, 'Power, Punishment and Penal Labour', p. 101.
5. Evans and Thorpe, 'Power, Punishment and Penal Labour', p. 107. Figures for Macquarie Harbour from A.G.L. Shaw, *Convicts and the Colonies: A Study of Penal Transportation from Great Britain and Ireland to Australia and Other Parts of the Empire* (London, Faber, 1966), p. 210.
6. J.B. Hirst, *Convict Society and its Enemies: A History of Early New South Wales* (Sydney, Allen and Unwin, 1983), p. 26.
7. J. West, *The History of Tasmania*, vol. 2 (Launceston, Dowling, 1852), p. 231.
8. S. Nicholas, 'The Convict Labour Market', *Convict Workers*, pp. 113–14.
9. S. Nicholas, 'The Organisation of Public Work', *Convict Workers*, p. 125; S. Engerman, 'Some Considerations Relating to Property Rights in Man', *Journal of Economic History*, vol. 33 (1973), pp. 45 and 61; and G. Canarella and J. A. Tomaske, 'The Optimal Utilization of Slaves', *Journal of Economic History*, vol. 35 (1975), p. 622.
10. Thus, when asked by the Molesworth Committee if it was common for assigned servants to injure their master's cattle, Peter Murdoch replied 'I think it very much depends on how the men are fed and treated': PP, XXII (1837–38), Minutes of Evidence; P. Murdoch, p. 123.
11. 227H Nathaniel Hartley per *Caledonia*, Archives Office of Tasmania (henceforth AOT), Con 31, Offence Registers, 29 November 1821 – all subsequent references to material from the Con 31 series will be cited thus: police number; name; and ship. Also see *Hobart Town Gazette*, 1 Dec. 1821.

12. S. Fenoaltea, 'Slavery and Supervision in Comparative Perspective: A Model', *Journal of Economic History*, vol. 44, no. 3 (1984), pp. 637–43 and S. Fenoaltea, 'The Slave Debate: A Note from the Sidelines', *Explorations in Economic History*, vol. 18, no. 3 (1981), pp. 304–8.

13. Shaw, *Convicts and the Colonies*, p. 220.

14. Fenoaltea, 'Slavery and Supervision', pp. 637–43; R. Findlay, 'Slavery, Incentives, and Manumission: A Theoretical Model', *Journal of Political Economy*, vol. 83 (1975), p. 924.

15. See for examples Shaw, *Convicts and Colonies*, p. 220.

16. For a wider theoretical perspective see H. Newby, 'The Deferential Dialectic', *Comparative Studies in Society and History*, vol. 17 (1975), pp. 151–3.

17. PP, XLII (1837–38), Copy of Despatch from Lieutenant-Governor Sir John Franklin to Lord Glenelg, Note (G), Testimonials by Messrs Backhouse and Walker, p. 32.

18. Diary of James Cubbiston Sutherland, 23 Oct. 1824, AOT, N61/1.

19. Hirst, *Convict Society*.

20. E.D. Genovese, *Roll Jordan Roll: The World the Slaves Made* (New York, Pantheon, 1974), p. 22.

21. Department of Main Roads, Tasmania, *Convicts and Carriageways: Tasmanian Road Development until 1830* (Hobart, Department of Main Roads, 1988), p. 133.

22. PP, XLII (1837–38), Backhouse and Walker, p. 25.

23. J. Moore, *The Convicts of Van Diemen's Land, 1840–1853* (Hobart, Cat and Fiddle, 1976), pp. 72–90, 93 and 102. L.L. Robson, *The Convict Settlers of Australia: An Enquiry into the Origin and Character of the Convicts Transported to New South Wales and Van Diemen's Land 1787–1852* (Carlton, Victoria, Melbourne University Press, 1976), pp. 92–3 and 157–8.

24. N. Townsend, 'A "Mere Lottery": The Convict System in New South Wales through the Eyes of the Molesworth Committee', *Push from the Bush*, 21 (1985), p. 75.

25. For an account of Alexander Pearce the cannibal see R. Hughes, *The Fatal Shore: A History of the Transportation of Convicts to Australia, 1787–1868* (London, Pan, 1987), pp. 218–26.

26. Compared to a comparative sample of convicts arriving in Australia in the early 1820s, weavers were overrepresented at Macquarie Harbour: an observed occurrence of 10 per cent compared to an expected of 4 per cent. Comparison of the occupations of 505 Macquarie Harbour convicts with 735 convicts arriving on six transports in New South Wales in 1821, in B. Dyster, 'Public Employment and Assignment to Private Masters, 1788–1821', *Convict Workers*, p. 140 (note most Macquarie Harbour convicts arrived in Australia between 1817 and 1825, many on the same transports as those employed in the Dyster analysis); Archives Office of New South Wales (henceforth AONSW), Convicts Indents; AONSW, Musters and other papers re Convict Ships; Public Record Office London (henceforth PRO), HO 10/10/43, 'Register of Convicts arriving in Van Diemen's Land 1817–1821'; HO 10/10/44, 'Muster of Convicts (Van Diemen's Land), 1823'; HO 10/10/45, ditto, 1825; HO 10/10/46, ditto, 1830; and HO 10/10/47, ditto, 1832.

27. PP, XII (1837–38) Appendix (F), no. 46, T. Butler, Capt. 40th Reg. Commandant, 'Report on Macquarie Harbour', para. 9.

28. J. Reynolds, 'The Penal Stations of New South Wales and Van Diemen's Land: The Reality behind the Legend', *Journal of the Royal Australian Historical Society*, vol. 67, no. 4 (1982), pp. 354–63; C. Smith, *Shadow over Tasmania* (Hobart, Waltch, 1941), p. 37; Hirst, *Convict Society*, p. 65; Hughes, *Fatal Shore*, pp. 371–80.

29. T.L. Lempriere, *The Penal Settlements of Van Diemen's Land* (Launceston, Royal Society of Tasmania, 1954), pp. 40–1.

30. *Hobart Town Gazette*, Supplements: 29 April 1825; 12 Nov. 1825; and 11 March 1826.

31. PP, XII (1837–38), Appendix (F), no. 46, para. 7.

32. PP, XIX (1837), Appendix no. 1, Correspondence Respecting Secondary Punishment, The report of a Visit to the Penal Settlement of Macquarie Harbour, Van Diemen's Land, by James Backhouse and George Washington Walker, p. 7; and PP, XII (1837–38), Testimony of John Barnes Esq, p. 44.

33. 234G Robert Greenfield per *Countess Harcourt*, 2 Sept. 1829, 'wilfully impeding the work of one of the mills by misscrewing part of the machinery – 25 lashes'; 13V John Vickers per *Lady Ridley*, 29 Nov. 1822, 'Destroying some of the working tools at Gordon River & endeavouring to persuade some of his fellow prisoners not to work – 50 lashes'.

34. See for example the following offences: 360H Thomas Hemming per *Malabar*, and 636S Samuel Smith per *Princess Charlotte*, both tried 23 Oct. 1828, 'Giving in his nails short of the proper quantity – To make up the deficiency and 100 extra nails daily'; 280D Thomas Davis per *Caledonia* (2), 27 Nov. 1824, 'Using improper language when his timber was being measured – 25 lashes'.

35. PP, XIX (1837), Appendix no. 1, p. 7.

36. Calculated at: 6 × metal workers; 4 × tanners; 2 × masons; 2 × bricklayers; 2 × bakers; 2 × cooks; 2 × gardeners (1 Sarah Island, the other Garden Island and Farm Bay); and 2 × clerks (Commandant's office and Commissariat). Lower bound estimate = 22.

37. Calculated at: 1 × superintendent; 3 × overseer (one per gang); 3 × coxswain; 4 × constable (one for each gang plus one to check arriving and departing boats); 4 × watchmen; and 3 × signalmen (one at the heads, one on Sarah Island, one within sight of the out gangs). Lower bound estimate = 18.

38. Calculated at: 18 × sawyers (Lempriere claims there were 9 or 10 pairs, *Penal Settlements*, p. 39); 6 × nailers; 4 × treenail mooters (wooden ships require vast numbers of wooden plugs, treenails, for fastening. Treenails are also amongst the list of items exported to Hobart: Lempriere, *Penal Settlements*, p. 42); 7 × servants (one for each civil and military officer); 2 × storeman; 1 × hospital orderly; 2 × firewood cutters; 2 × water carriers; 12 × timber fellers; 2 × charcoal burners. Lower bound estimate = 56.

39. PP, XII (1837–38), Appendix to Report: Enclosure (A); PRO, HO/10/46. Estimate of mean population calculated from returns for the years 1823, 1824, 1825, 1826 and 1830.

40. Lempriere, *Penal Settlements*, pp. 27–51.

41. Lempriere, *Penal Settlements*, pp. 108–10; I. Brand, *Port Arthur 1830–1870* (Tasmania, Jason, 1978), pp. 29–35 and 52–4.

42. Lempriere, *Penal Settlements*, pp. 53–7.

43. See Robson, *Convict Settlers*, pp. 157–8.

44. H. Maxwell-Stewart, 'The Bushrangers and the Convict System of Van Diemen's Land', PhD thesis, University of Edinburgh (1990), pp. 148–9.

45. Compared to a comparative sample of convicts arriving in Australia in the early 1820s, rural workers were underrepresented at Macquarie Harbour. There is an observed occurrence of 14 per cent compared to an expected 38 per cent, a staggering 24-point difference.

46. For an account of just how important economic activity is to the prisoner see R.A. Radford, 'The Economic Organisation of a P.O.W. Camp', *Economica*, vol. 12 (1945), pp. 189–201.

47. Examples include 213G William Garrett per *Juliana*, 17 July 1826, 'Making a copper kettle contrary to orders – 75 lashes & dismissed as overseer of blacksmiths'; 448H George Hill per *Caledonia* (2), 15 Dec. 1829, 'Making a box when employed in the lumber yard without orders – 6 days solitary confinement on bread and water'; 38F Leslie Fergusson per *Minerva*, 4 Oct. 1825, 'Making & selling a box contr^y to orders – 25 lashes and to be dismissed as overseer of carpenters, corporal punishment remitted' and 3 Dec. 1825, 'Making cabinet furniture – 50 lashes'; 210C William Crafts per *Dromedary*, 8 March 1828, 'Offering brooms for sale – 12 lashes remitted'. Note also that the black economy embraced employment: 388B William Budd per *Lady Ridley*, 15 Aug. 1826, 'Employing a carpenter contrary to orders – 18 lashes'. Some of this trade was moneyed although legal tender was not always supplied: 91N James Newcombe per *Surrey* (NSW) and *Elizabeth Henrietta* (VDL), 9 Aug. 1823, 'Paying away forged notes to Elizabeth Slater – 25 lashes'.

48. 124K William Kelly per *Lady Ridley*, 2 Jan. 1831, 'Having a swan skin in his possession & offering the same for sale – 5 days solt^y on bread and water'; 225C Thomas Clay per *Dromedary* (4), Nov. 1829, 'Bringing a kangaroo skin to the settlement contrary to orders when returning from an out gang – 4 days solt^y on bread and water'; 316S Richard Sheridan per *Medway*, 13 Sept. 1827, 'Bartering kangaroo skins in the Tannery – 50 lashes'.

49. M. Cash, *Martin Cash the Bushranger of Van Diemen's Land* (Hobart, Waltch, no date), pp. 57–8. Macquarie Harbour examples include 559H William Harrison per *Sir Godfrey Webster*, 25 Jan. 1830, 'Robbing the bakehouse of a quantity of flour the property of Gov^t which had been issued to be baked into bread for the prisoners of the settlement – 100 lashes & Small Island'; 173F Samuel Fergusson per *Lord Hungerford*, 22 July 1824, 'Receiving beef from the cookhouse knowing it to be stolen – 25 lashes & dismissed as constable'.

50. S. Nicholas, 'The Care and Feeding of Convicts', *Convict Workers*, p. 186; Lempriere, *The Penal Settlements*, p. 48; Diary of James Cubbiston Sutherland, 23 Oct. 1824, AOT, N/61; A.A. Paul and D.A.T. Southgate, *McCane and Widdowson's The Composition of Foods* (London, HMSO, 1978). Note: all meat values calculated as off the bone and assumed to be salt pork (Macquarie

Harbour), fresh beef or mutton (assignees). Poorest quality cuts were selected in all cases and method of cooking assumed to be boiling. The results of this calculation were: Macquarie Harbour gang diet, lower bound, 2956 calories, upper bound 3084; Sutherland's assignees (including top-up incentives) lower bound, 4054, and upper bound, 4353.

51. Evans and Thorpe, 'Power, Punishment and Penal Labour', p. 105.

52. P.A. David, *Reckoning with Slavery: A Critical Study in Quantitative History of American Negro Slavery* (New York, Oxford University Press, 1976), pp. 265–8.

53. Lieutenant Governor Sorell to Commandant Cuthbertson, 8 Dec., 1821. Quoted in Hughes, *The Fatal Shore*, p.372.

54. PP, XIX (1837), Appendix no. 1, p. 6. If official estimates of deaths among absconders are taken into account this figure rises to perhaps as high as 84 per 1000. PP, XII (1837–38), Appendix no. 56, enclosures (A) and (B); PRO, HO/10/47 and HO/10/48.

55. P. Curtin, *Death by Migration: Europe's Encounter with the Tropical World in the Nineteenth Century* (Cambridge, Cambridge University Press, 1989), p. 194.

56. C. Roland and H. Shannon, 'Patterns of Disease among World War II Prisoners of the Japanese: Hunger, Weight Loss and Deficiency Diseases in Two Camps', *Journal of the History of Medicine*, vol. 46, no. 1 (1991), p. 83. In percentage terms Roland and Shannon report death rates of between 20 and 35 per cent for Allied POWs in the Far East, pp. 68–7. This compares with 7 per cent for Macquarie Harbour rising to 23 per cent if non-apprehended absconders are counted as deaths. My estimate for non-apprehended absconders is based on reported rates for the years 1822 to 1827.

57. PP, XIX (1837), Appendix no. 1, p. 6.

58. PP, XII (1837–38), Testimony of John Barnes Esq p. 46. and Appendix (F), no. 46, para. 8.

59. Lempriere, *Penal Settlements*, pp. 36–7.

60. To provide just a short list of examples: 388B William Budd per *Lady Ridley*, 16 Nov. 1829, 'Attempting to make away with vegetables from the Garden & for having a quantity of potatoes concealed in his hat'; 305F Patrick Feagan per *Andromeda*, 6 May 1830, 'Breaking into the Sawyer's hut at Kelly Basin & stealing a piece of pork & 3 loaves of bread'; and 340D Robert Dudlow per *Phoenix* (2), 4 June 1825, 'Having fat in his possession supposed to have been stolen'.

61. Lempriere, *Penal Settlements*, p.11.

62. Examples include: 635S Thomas Small per *Princess Charlotte*, 23 July 1829, 'Falsely reporting himself sick to the Ass^t Surgeon – 4 days solt^y confinement'; 194A John Allsop per *Chapman* (1), 28 Dec. 1827, 'Leaving his gang & coming to the settlement under the pretence of being sick – 25 lashes'; 241L Henry Leonard per *Morley*, 11 Feb. 1829, 'Refusing to work under pretence of being ill – 25 lashes'; and 58T John Thompson per *Surrey*, 17 Sept. 1828, 'Feigning extreme illness – 18 lashes'.

63. 550S John Salmon per *Commodore Hayes*, 13 June 1828.

64. 185M James Mason per *Dromedary*, 22 Nov. 1822.

65. Genovese, *Roll Jordan Roll*, p. 15. See also M. Craton, *Testing the Chains: Resistance*

to Slavery in the British West Indies (London, Cornell University Press, 1982), p. 41.

66. 42A Joseph Armstrong per *Surrey*, 12 April 1830.

67. 258C James Crawford per *Prince Regent*, 2 Nov. 1822 – '100 lashes and to work in irons until further orders'; 843S Joshua Seaburn per *Asia* (2), 23 July 1831 – '150 lashes & to work in irons during pleasure 50 lashes remitted'.

68. *Hobart Town Gazette*, 3 Sept. 1825.

69. 278D James Dalway per *Caledonia* (2), 19 Oct. 1827; Lempriere, *Penal Settlements*, p.31, and Hughes, *Fatal Shore*, p. 379.

70. 420H William Hopper per *Phoenix*, 18 May 1827, 'chain gang 3 months'.

71. 257S John Smith per *Caledonia*, 10 Dec. 1829, 'to be returned to his party & worked in irons until he can be sent'.

72. 504B Henry Jones Batchelor per *Richmond*, 30 Jan. 1827, 'Altering in the Police Office Register the date of the year in which John Vie a convict was sentenced to transportation for 7 yrs with intent to benefit the said Vie by making it appear that he had been tried in 1820 when in fact he (Vie) was tried in 1823'. See also AONSW, Musters and other papers *re* Convict Ships, Reel no. 2427.

73. 13 days of this sentence to solitary confinement was remitted by the Commandant.

74. Evans and Thorpe, 'Power, Punishment and Penal Labour', pp. 108–9.

75. S. Nicholas, 'The Convict Labour Market' in *Convict Workers*, pp. 113–20. Note that the Nicholas model of the convict labour market can be improved by: (a) ignoring the inelastic condition for the public labour supply (here Nicholas appears to confuse labour power and labour); (b) redrawing all labour supply curves as backward bending (this allows for the effects of incentive bargaining to be built into the model).

Part 3

Classifying Bodies

CHAPTER NINE

The Genealogy of the Modern Subject: Indian Convicts in Mauritius, 1814–1853

Clare Anderson

A quelque distance, trois cents Indiens d'une haute stature, la tête
envelopée d'une espèce de turban, n'ayant d'autres vêtements que quelques
haillons autour des reins, s'avançaient à pas lents vers le port, attachés deux
à deux par une longue chaîne qui traînait de leur cou jusqu'à terre: on me
dit que ces malheureux n'étaient qu'une partie d'un régiment sipahis, qui,
pour le crime de révolte contre les Anglais, avaient été condamnés à la
déportation et aux travaux publics pour un temps illimité.[1]

In 1816 the first Indian convicts were transported from the East India Company's
Presidency of Bengal across the *kala pani* (black water) to the island of Mauritius.
Lying 800 km east of Madagascar in the Indian Ocean, and measuring just 58 km
from north to south and 47 km from east to west, over the next 20 years this
British colony was to receive well over a thousand convicts from India, until the
practice of transporting them to the island was abandoned in 1837. During this
period, the convicts became a valuable workforce, playing a vital role in both
public works projects and private agricultural enterprise, building and repairing
the roads and bridges of the island and employed within the expanding
plantation economy. In a society desperately short of labour, the diminution of
the convict labour supply was greatly lamented as transportation ceased.

An examination of the discourse surrounding those convicts transported from
India to Mauritius during the first half of the nineteenth century provides an
ideal opportunity to explore some of the imperatives in the work of the French
philosopher Michel Foucault, whose focus has largely been on the relationship
between specific scientific disciplines and particular social practices in the
modern age.[2] Foucault identifies such scientific disciplines, with their origins in
the mid-eighteenth century, in the development of the human sciences which, he
argues, are significant as 'technologies', techniques appropriated in the 'bio-
(technico-)power' of a society concerned with the ordering, classification and

control of individuals. In diagnosing the development of this bio-power, Foucault produces a reading of Nietzsche's 'genealogy', describing the way in which power uses the illusion of meaning to further itself, in focusing upon the play of force relations as they exist in society. It is here that the relationship between scientific disciplines and social practices is implicated, as the enmeshment of power and knowledge is seen as integral to modern society. It is not a causal, but a correlative relationship, with power and knowledge operating in a mutually generative fashion, where knowledge of all sorts is thoroughly enmeshed in all forms of power, and power is enmeshed in all forms of knowledge:

> We should admit ... power and knowledge directly imply one another; that there is no power relation without the correlative constitution of a field of knowledge, nor any knowledge that does not presuppose and constitute at the same time power relations.[3]

The implication of the nature of such power-knowledge is that it is relations of confrontation, domination and subjection which characterize the social web. However, although power weaves its way into society in this way, it cannot be monopolized by an agent. Power is a strategy, but only in terms of the level of effect within a particular field in which a particular set of power relations are played out.[4] In this sense, the technologies of power and knowledge cannot be localized in a particular type of institution or state apparatus, although the development of the technology of power was clearly political in that it was intimately related to the development of capitalism as an economic venture, as we will see.

In analysing the social relations of domination and subjection, Foucault attempts to locate historically and then to analyse the strands of discourse which deal with the individual, the knowledge of that individual and the power relations between individuals in society. His 'genealogical' approach seeks to construct a mode of analysis of those social practices where power and knowledge intertwine to shape the modern individual as both object and subject.[5] In this sense, power-knowledge is at once both individualizing and totalizing in its implications. That is to say an attempt (and only an attempt, for power is open to resistance) is made to mould the individual in society into a subject of knowledge and then transform that individual from a subject (of that knowledge) into an object of the (totalizing) power of that knowledge, in what is essentially a duality of genealogical praxis. Moreover, for Foucault, the bio-power which is described is concerned with the categorization of populations through the use of the individual body as an object to be manipulated, a place where human science as a local practice reflects the nature of extraneous power relations.

There are three aspects to the genealogical process through which the individual subject is transformed into an object of power relations. Firstly, dividing practices form and give an identity to individuals within a group and, in so doing, force a sense of social exclusion on those groups within the general population. Secondly, these divisions are mediated and consolidated through the use of scientific classifications. Finally, in a paradoxical twist to the tale, individuals transform themselves into an object of their own subjectification.[6] This process of subjectification takes on a dual meaning for each individual: 'subject to someone else by control and dependence, and tied to his own identity by a conscience or self-knowledge. Both meanings suggest a form of power which subjugates and makes subject to'.[7]

An exploration of the relationship between power, knowledge and body and its implications for the division, classification and subjectification of individuals in society is highly relevant to the practice surrounding the experience of convictism, taking place as it did within an emergent colonial economy. However, such an exploration also illuminates the lacunae in Foucault's work. Not only does he fail to explore the relationship of the social practices which he describes to their economic context in a truly satisfactory way, he also overlooks the ways in which colonial knowledge itself was sometimes inaccurate and thus ineffective. It is to these issues that I will return later in this chapter. To begin, however, with some more conventional genealogical analysis: who were the convicts transported to Mauritius?

A few convicts were apparently brought to Mauritius from Batavia and China by the Dutch who settled in Mauritius intermittently, between 1638 and 1710, a practice which was discontinued by the French during their subsequent period of rule. However, soon after the British gained control of the island in 1810, the Governor of the colony, Sir Robert Townsend Farquhar, wrote to the Governor-General of Bengal, requesting that a supply of convicts be sent to Mauritius in order to meet the labour shortage on public works projects. Initially, a proposal for the employment of between 1500 and 2000 convicts from India was submitted.[8] However, the Earl of Moira, the Governor-General, replied that the 'too inconsiderable' number of convicts who could be sent under the provisions of Act 53, Section 121, which only permitted the transportation of convicts overseas if they had been sentenced to transportation for life with hard labour, was so insignificant as to render the proposed scheme unfeasible.[9] As a result, Farquhar scaled down his request and expressed his desire 'to be furnished as soon as possible with 500 Convicts'.[10]

It is perhaps unsurprising that Farquhar desired such a supply of convict labour. At the time of his request, the colonial government was using 'government slaves' on public works projects, largely clearing the streets of Port Louis and building or repairing roads. These slaves had either been 'inherited' from the French colonial administration, or were 'Prize Negroes', seized from slave ships captured by the British in their attempts to suppress the slave-trade (illegal in British colonies under the Abolition Act of 1807).[11] In addition, and for the same purpose, each planter was obliged to furnish a certain number of slaves proportionate to the number they owned as corvée labour for a period of four days labour per slave per year. The abolition of the slave-trade, coinciding with the expansion of cane growing in Mauritius, precipitated a massive labour shortage. The introduction of a replacement source was seen as crucial to the stamping out of illegal slave importations.[12] But why did Farquhar request a supply of convict labour, and why convicts from Bengal? The British had long since adopted the Indian practice of using coerced labour (*begar*) in India itself to clear roads and carry their supplies. Moreover, prior to its establishment by the East India Company as a Presidency in 1805, Farquhar had been the Lieutenant-Governor of Pulo Penang, a small island just off the west coast of the Malay Peninsula, a place which had been receiving Bengali convicts on a regular basis since 1790 to work on various public projects.[13] Farquhar was, it would seem, well aware of the utility of Indian convict labour.[14]

So, after an agreement that the total cost of the shipping of the transportees and their subsistence upon arrival in the colony was to be borne by the Mauritian authorities, the first convicts, a combination of 'Hindoos' and 'Musselmen', arrived in the colony from Bengal in January 1816, on board the ships *Lady Barlow* and *Helen*.[15] Fifteen additional convicts under sentence of transportation for life in Alypur later embarked on the ship *Charlotte*, with 'thirty or forty' more ready to sail on the *Discovery*,[16] making a total of 537 arrivals during 1816.[17] The transportation of convicts from Bengal was to continue until the mid-1820s, after which the supply was replaced by convicts from Bombay until 1837, when transportation from India to Mauritius ceased.[18] These convicts had been convicted of a variety of crimes, including: political offences; dacoity; and thuggee.[19] With the arrival of the Indian convicts on the island, in lieu of providing corvée labour, the plantation owners were called upon to take a certain number of convicts as labourers in each quarter or parish, and were financially responsible for the cost of their maintenance.[20] In this way, not only did the convicts ameliorate the labour shortage on the island, but the colonial government also largely washed its hands of the labour costs of public works.[21]

A return of the number of Indian convicts in Mauritius, prepared for the Commission of Eastern Enquiry in 1828, states that a total of 1018 Indian convicts had been brought to the island, with a total of 381 having died since their arrival. Six hundred were listed as fit for labour, with about one-third of their number either masons, stonecutters, weavers or carpenters. Records also relate the arrival of blacksmiths, gardeners, tailors, bricklayers, basketmakers, opium planters, braziers, a baker, a pastry cook and a silk and cotton spinner.[22]

Such indents should not, however, be taken at face value. Working horses were not used in India which makes it extremely unlikely that any of the Indian convicts were, in fact, blacksmiths. Similarly, the strict rules of Hinduism concerning 'pollution' and food preparation meant that professional bakers and pastry cooks simply did not exist in India at this time. The transportation of several hundred more convicts was to boost this number during the 1830s, with the largest number of convicts in the colony at any one time peaking at 986 in 1834.[23] The number of female convicts was never numerically significant, despite Farquhar's initial concern that 'the natural proportion of the Sexes would be preserved as far as it may be found practicable'.[24] It was said that the nature of the sentences passed on Indian female felons usually precluded the possibility of transporting them, which 'rendered it impracticable for us to comply' with Farquhar's wish.[25] As a result, the total number of Indian convict women transported to Mauritius appears to have been just six, one from Bengal and five from Bombay.[26]

Initially, the convicts were put to work clearing the harbour and demolishing old buildings in Port Louis.[27] Placed under the control of the newly set up Convict Department, by 1823 it was reported that 500 men were employed in the construction and repair of roads in the eight districts of the island, with the remainder employed in the public works of Port Louis itself, under the control of the Civil Engineer.[28] By 1825, the use of corvée labour on public works projects had been abolished altogether, first in the country districts and later in Port Louis, having been completely replaced by Indian convict labour.[29] After this date, many of the convicts transported to Mauritius continued to work on public works projects, whether at the Civil Engineer's Department in Port Louis or in the outlying districts of the colony under the Department of Roads and Bridges.[30] Others were said to have been employed at the *batelage* (loading and unloading ships) under the directions of the Collector of Customs and Harbour Master,[31] with a significant number also allocated to private individuals such as Monsieur de Chazal and Mr Hughes, who were silk cultivators, and the (largely French) owners of the large sugar estates.[32] In 1818, for example, almost 100 of the convicts were employed on the Belombre and D'Unienville plantations alone.[33] Indeed, the labour supply on the island was so short that individuals made continual requests to the governor either to allocate them convict labour or to write to the Indian government requesting such labour on their behalf.[34]

The transportation of Indian convicts onto the island ceased in 1837, with those who had been transported prior to that date retained as unfree labourers in the colony until 1847. It was then recommended that, as soon as the necessary permission was granted from the government of India, all convicts who had served over 30 years in the colony or were more than 65 years old and who bore 'good character' be liberated, with the option of a free return passage to India or continuing under the charge of the government if remaining in the colony and unable to gain their own livelihood.[35] On 11 April 1853, Governor Higginson reported having liberated all the Indian convicts except for two who were undergoing sentences of imprisonment for secondary offences committed in the colony. Some of the convicts were pensioned and, at the time of the *Report of the Royal Commissioners* in 1875, ten or twelve were said to remain there, receiving rations and lodgings. One had even established himself as a shopkeeper.[36] Although the Indian government had initial reservations about receiving its emancipated convicts back, most eventually did return.

* * *

Although the study of Indian convicts transported to Mauritius has not yet been the subject of systematic scholarly attention, this does not reflect a lack of historical sources. Not only were the convicts frequently mentioned in the travel literature of this period, but the colonial government itself was concerned with the documentation of each individual convict. This began with the creation of indents as each convict embarked on board ship and arrived in the colony,[37] and continued in the records of the regular musters and inspections which ensued. It is from such records that one can extract a great deal of extremely interesting 'bio-data' about the convicts, their names (and often, by implication, their occupations/castes), places of origin, probable ages, crimes for which transported and their occupations in the colony. However, it is also possible to look at such documentation, indeed documentation in general, as 'bio-power', a form of discourse exemplifying the web of power-knowledge as Foucault describes it. Indeed, Foucault argues that the accumulation of documentation makes possible 'the measurement of overall phenomena, the description of groups, the characterisation of collective facts, the calculation of the gaps between individuals, and their distribution in a given "population", in other words, makes possible the division and classification of individuals into groups'.[38] In this sense, such 'bio-data/power' is part of the social relations of domination and subjection through which individuals are at once both individualized and totalized in society. At work within these particular convict records, then, is an example of the dividing practices central to Foucault's 'genealogy of the modern subject'.

At one level it seems clear that the ethnocentric British colonial eye homogenized the 'racial' and ethnic diversity of the convicts into the categories of 'Indian' and 'convict', individuals within a collective 'they'. However, implicit to this process was the fact that at another level, colonial discourse, in its concern to categorize and classify groups, was forced to specify the individuality of each convict. In this sense, the totalization of the convicts into a population depended upon the specification of the individuality of each:

Before seeing these people I had no idea that the inhabitants of India were such noble looking men; their skin is extremely dark, and many of the older men had large moustachios and beards of a snow white colour; this, together with the fire of their expressions, gave to them an aspect quite imposing.[39]

So wrote Charles Darwin upon his first sighting of the Indian convicts in Mauritius: the physical appearance (noble-looking, complete with fiery expression) of 'these people' as an *homogenized* group was taken as significant in creating '*an aspect* quite imposing', a sense of the character of *the men*. Although rather less sympathetic in his observations, James Holman, the author of many travelogues during this period, wrote in a similar fashion:

> *These people* are brought from Bombay, and are rendered very useful in this Colony; but *they* are most determined thieves, and may be considered to have a fish-hook attached to the end of every finger, stealing any thing that can either be converted into money, or turned to any use ... *they* are very idle when employed on public works.[40]

It has also been argued that this abstracted he/they situated the individual subject in a timeless present tense, characterizing individual action not as a particular historical event, but as an instance of a pregiven custom or trait, which transforms the individual into 'a *sui generis* configuration'.[41] Indeed, in a perfect illustration of this, the Revd Patrick Beaton wrote of the convicts in 1859:

> In physical organisation and general intelligence they are far superior to their Coolie countrymen. One fine old man, living in the hut nearest to the sea, might sit as a model for one of the patriarchs. His Oriental features, tall, erect figure, flashing eyes, and flowing beard, recall the pictures of Abraham by the old masters.[42]

The judgement of character according to physical appearance was, of course, nothing new, but what was significant was that it coincided with the development of particular human sciences which sought to divide, categorize and classify groups of individuals via at least perceived physical characteristics. In this way, concepts of the criminal class, the criminal caste and the criminal tribe were developing to take a place in the 'scientific' discourse of 'race', exemplified by anthropometry in which Charles Darwin himself, of course, was a key player.[43] Integral to this process of scientific ordering was the creation and appropriation of 'knowledge' of individuals where scientific categories were becoming, for the first time in the late eighteenth and early nineteenth centuries, the object of systematic political attention in their intervention in the systematization of the division of populations. It is against this background that both the writing on and the documentation of the convicts must be understood. Such documentation, in its description of each convict, exemplifies the 'bio-power' of a colonial state concerned with classification, order and control. Such 'bio-politics of the population' were distinct from those 'anatomo-politics of the human body' which had been the focus of earlier forms of power. That focus on the individual body had become less necessary to the apparatus of control as societal power had developed to control the whole population.[44] However, paradoxically, the power of the state to produce an increasingly totalizing web of control over entire populations was increasingly intertwined with and dependent on its ability to produce a specification of such individuality, as 'the state's power (and that's one of the reasons for its strength) is both an individualizing and a totalizing form of power'.[45] It is this which was so significant in the division of convicts, with the authorities clearly concerned with the compilation of information, the harnessing of power through the creation of knowledge.[46]

How then might we see these attempts at the physical description of the convicts by the state? Clearly, some sort of description was necessary in order to recognize each convict.[47] However, this need to identify – this individualizing creation of knowledge – was only really appropriate in a society concerned to recognize; in this case recognition served the dual purpose of the allocation of labourers to appropriate work tasks as active participants in the colonial economy and the identification of them as individuals in the event of their resistance to it.[48] It is not unreasonable to suggest that, as elsewhere, convict labour was crucial in constructing the infrastructure of Mauritius during the early years of British rule.[49] The Indian convicts built and repaired many of the quays, canals, roads and bridges throughout the island, as well as carrying out other vital roles as agricultural labourers for private individuals. Indeed, the benefits which the convicts could bring to the island were something which Farquhar was well aware of when he instigated the scheme. In a letter to the Bengal Judicial Department of 11 September 1815, it was agreed that '*as the whole measure is intended for the benefit of the island*', Mauritius should bear the charge of shipping the convicts to Mauritius and 'the providing of food, clothing, medical and, safe custody, and all incidental expenses from the period at which they may reach the Colony until their death'.[50] Later correspondence of Mauritian officials with the Calcutta authorities confirms that the measure was '*calculated to promote in a very material degree, the prosperity of the Mauritius*'.[51] In this context, an obsession with cost-effectiveness permeated the whole exercise. At the very onset of transportation, in correspondence with Farquhar, the Earl of Bathurst wrote:

The Employment of Indian Convicts in the Colony may I am aware lead to all the beneficial results which you anticipate from it, and *should the Expense*

*of the Maintenance not exceed what the work on which they are employed would
otherwise require*, I shall readily sanction the transportation of a further
number hereafter.[52]

He later warned Governor Darling, who required a further labour supply in
1819:

I see no objection also to you obtaining from the Government of India
such a further supply [of convicts] as may be consistent with the means of
the Colony to maintain, provided it shall appear to you that their services
can be made essentially useful, — You will, however, consider previously to
taking measures for procuring [the convicts], how far the temporary
convenience of having their aid in rebuilding the town and repairing the
roads, will counterbalance the inconvenience of entailing upon the
Government a permanent charge for the maintenance of so large a number
of individuals.[53]

As transportation from India to Mauritius reached its zenith, the utility of it
and *skilled* convict labour was realized, and requests for a further supply of men
from India specified that it was 'most advisable' that 'stout able bodied male
convicts, capable of being employed on the roads and not exceeding about 35
years of age (of whom it is very desirable that as many as possible should be
artificers, such as masons, smiths, carpenters &c.)' should be selected for
transportation.[54] Again, the Governor was mistaken in his belief that 'smiths' as
such *were* obtainable. A specific request was later made for convicts to be sent
who were skilled in the processes involved in the manufacture of silk, either in
the cultivation of the mulberry, in the rearing of the silkworm, or in the spinning
of the silk itself.[55] Such age and occupation-specific concerns in the recruitment
of labour would seem to be a hallmark of organized migration streams.[56]
Convict migration itself would appear to be no exception.

It seems that the Indian convicts fulfilled their useful role in building and
repairing public works in Mauritius. As the supply began to tail off, there were
complaints that the roads were in want of repair through the decrease in use of
convict road gangs.[57] This, together with the high wages being demanded by
ex-slaves in the colony, led to a call from the Protector of Immigrants in 1858 to
propose a scheme to reintroduce convicts from India. It was said that the
planters themselves had no objections to such action, as they 'formerly caused
no disorders' and that there was a great shortage in household servants:

It would be a great boon to persons living in Port Louis to get convict
servants allowed to engage as a reward for good behaviour, and who, from
fear of being sent back on the roads, would continue to behave well.[58]

It is not unlikely that Mauritius's experience of the utility of Indian convict labour helped to inform the decision, after slave emancipation in 1834, to import Indians under terms of indenture to work on the plantations.[59] Indeed, the *Commission of Enquiry* in 1875 reported that convict 'forced labour' meant that the Indian indentured labourer 'was not the entire stranger he was in the West Indies and Demerara'.[60]

* * *

It seems clear that although the accumulation of knowledge was neither a catalyst nor did it directly cause the development of capitalism, it was clearly at least a prerequisite. As Foucault states in *Discipline and Punish*, 'the accumulation of men and the accumulation of capital were inseparable' as 'the techniques that made the cumulative multiplicity of men useful accelerated the accumulation of capital'.[61] Within an emergent colonial economy, it was such a precise 'accumulation' of the Indian convicts, the recording of their age and fitness for labour and their occupational skills, which allowed the government to recognize each individual and to allocate every one to appropriate work tasks accordingly. Indeed, it was their later division into 'classes' as 'effective', 'half-effective' and 'invalid' that also allowed the colonial government to conclude in 1847 that their maintenance was no longer a cost-effective exercise.[62]

Discipline and particular spatial arrangements were also necessary to effect the capitalist work process, with disciplined and orderly individuals inserted into a machinery of production, parallel to their fixation, control and rational distribution as a population within the developing colonial economy. The fixation, control and rational distribution of populations built on what was perceived to be a statistical knowledge of them was crucial to the mutual dependence of disciplinary strategies and capitalism. Convict labour was no exception, with convicts allocated to work tasks, surveyed and disciplined by their overseers. In 1823 the Convict Establishment in Mauritius was made up of a General Superintendent, three Lieutenants, a Chief Overseer, and 21 ordinary overseers belonging to three 'classes'. The General Superintendent's duties were to ensure that the convicts performed their work and 'that justice is done in every respect with regard to the food, clothing, medical care and general treatment of the convicts'.[63] The Lieutenants were charged with the immediate superintendence of the work in progress, making weekly and monthly reports to the head of the Convict Establishment. The Chief Overseer, who had a knowledge of the 'Hindoo Language', was to enquire into complaints made by the convicts against the authorities. The Overseers, meanwhile, were:

entrusted with the *immediate surveillance* of the Convicts employed on the roads in the different Districts of the Island – Their duties are extremely arduous, as in order to *preserve Discipline* and ensure the performance of the

Labour required — they are with the convicts day and night, and are consequently much exposed to the Weather and Heat of the Sun. The Overseers must be *extremely vigilant* at night to prevent the Convicts dispersing themselves in the Country which might easily be done as they are Hutted in open Camps.[64]

The convicts were to be constantly surveyed and disciplined, as subjects of the colonial panopticon eye.

It seems clear, then, that the Indian convicts in Mauritius were divided as individuals within a (total) population in order to be disciplined and controlled in a way which reflected the needs of the colonial economy. However, the power relations within this particular society also illustrate the process by which the individual becomes subjectified, that is controlled by and dependent on a third party and tied to a sense of his or her own identity. Evidently, convicts were always dependent upon the state for their basic subsistence needs such as their accommodation and rations. Moreover, it was to the convict's own advantage to work within the system, to accept his or her identity as a convict and to use it to best advantage. As in the management of Indian convicts in the Straits Settlements, convict commanders were integral to the working of the convict gangs, a position which could be reached after several years of 'good behaviour'.[65] Such incentives were key instruments in the successful extraction of labour from convicts' labour power, with convicts also permitted to hire out their labour once their government tasks had been completed, and sometimes paid a small gratuity for government labour itself.[66]

* * *

It is noticeable that among nineteenth-century travellers to Mauritius, most observers were not unsympathetic towards the convicts whom they saw. James Backhouse, during a visit to Mauritius in the month of March 1838, wrote in his *Narrative* that:

What renders [the convicts] particular objects of sympathy is, that they were sent hither for life, and no hope of any remission of sentence is held out to them for good conduct. There are among them persons who were so young when transported, that in their offences, they could only be looked upon as the dupes of those who were older; and many of them bear good characters.[67]

Charles Darwin also wrote that:

These convicts are generally quiet & well conducted; from their outward conduct, their cleanliness, and faithful observance of their strange religious enactments, it was impossible to look at these men with the same eyes as our wretched convicts in New South Wales.[68]

Similarly, the *Report of the Royal Commissioners* in 1875 noted:

Many of these men, particularly among the first introduced, were very desperate characters; but considering the depôt in which they were housed at Black River was admittedly incapable of keeping them in safe custody, and that the camps they were in when at work on the roads were no more places of security than are the straw huts of the present immigrants, it appears extraordinary that more complaints were not made of their conduct; in fact it is wonderful that they should have behaved themselves so well.[69]

Such sympathetic descriptions of the convicts can be juxtaposed against earlier representations of them to reveal something of the imperatives of colonial labour. At the onset of transportation, correspondence contained in the *Bengal Judicial Consultations* described the 'turbulent nature' and 'desperate character' of the convicts,[70] whilst Governor Hall wrote at the beginning of 1818 that the extreme 'prejudice against the convicts in this Island is to that Extent that the Planters will not hire them'.[71] However, as the demand for labour grew and the plantocracy began to realize the potential utility of the convicts for private enterprise, demand was such that later in the same year Farquhar wrote that he had received 'numerous and incessant applications from the planters to be permitted to employ them, in agriculture, and other new branches of industry'.[72] It was at this point that the representation of the convicts seems to have begun to change, with the convicts transformed, at least in the colonial eye, from 'dangerous dacoits' and 'violent thugs' into docile and useful workers. How could they be perceived in any other way in an economy in such desperate need of their labour power? Their 'manners ... far from that atrocious ferocity which individuals, misled by delusive theories, may appear to apprehend' became 'generally submissive, and inoffensive'.[73] Moreover, their 'moral improvement' was perceived as having taken place in the very act of their transportation, assured as they crossed the Indian Ocean to be transplanted onto British soil; an act which broke their 'vicious habits and associations':[74]

It may be observed that it has been found by experience that the Indian Convicts transported to the Mauritius have been most successfully cut off from ... improper communication with their former associates of other Indian Tribes, and that generally speaking their condition, and morals have been much improved by the discipline under which they are governed in the Colony.[75]

It is in the representation of the Indian convicts in Mauritius that we see the extent to which the development of colonial knowledge was inevitably both partial and incomplete. Charles Darwin, for example, described one convict that he saw as 'a confirmed opium eater, of which fact his emaciated body and strange drowsy expression bore witness',[76] in a misunderstanding of Indian practices surrounding the use of the drug. And what are we to make of Holman's observations that the convicts were 'most determined thieves' and, moreover, 'very idle when employed on public works'?[77] Another observer was to write in a similar fashion:

> One has only, as one drives along, to watch the gangs of convicts working on the roads. Here is forced labour, by the side of yonder labour in the cane-fields which is *paid*. I do not mean to say you often perceive, even in the last, much genuine alacrity, unless it be when the sugar carts are unloading, – that work goes on briskly; but the way in which the men condemned to the roads [the convicts] creep along with their baskets on their heads, and sleepily tilt over the contents at a given spot, at once convinces you on which side the superiority lies ... It has been calculated that at Portland the prisoners do about 40 per cent. of the quantity of work which would be performed, in the like time, by the like number of free hands. I know not what the proportion may be here, but at the most limited computation it must be something like the above.[78]

Such observations might well tell us something about the nature of convict 'resistance', but, in their classically orientalist fashion, they also tell us a great deal about colonial perceptions which saw only the negative 'alacrity' of the Indian labour process, rather than understood the nature of that process itself.

There is an obvious need for further research into the representation of the convicts transported to Mauritius. It seems possible, however, that the colonial eye showed a certain short-sightedness in its evaluation of the nature of Indian cultural practices, resulting in an imperfect 'knowledge' of the convicts themselves. This has profound ramifications for Foucault's interpretation of the nature of power relations in society. If it is true that power and knowledge are mutually reinforcing, it could be suggested that where knowledge has no real basis, the nature of power itself must also be seriously reconsidered. That is to say, in this case, efforts to order and control the convict subject within an emergent colonial economy could never be totalizing as the web of power relations was not ineluctable. Or, as another critic has put it, although colonialism was certainly dominant, it was not necessarily hegemonic.[79] Thus the colonial state might seem all-power*ful*, but the colonial subject is not, however, rendered totally power*less*.[80]

Notes

1. François Jacques Marie Auguste Billiard, *Voyages aux colonies orientales ou Lettres écrites des Îles de France et de Bourbon pendant 1817, 1818, 1819 et 1820 à M. le comte de Montalivet* (Paris, Librairie Française de l'Advocat, 1829), p. 31.

2. Although Foucault's work exhibits a continuity at this level, it also shows a clear methodological shift. His early work – *The Order of Things: An Archaeology of the Human Sciences* (London, Tavistock, 1970); *The Archaeology of Knowledge* (London, Tavistock, 1972), *Madness and Civilization: A History of Insanity in the Age of Reason* (New York, Vintage/Random House, 1973); and *The Birth of the Clinic: An Archaeology of Medical Perception* (London, Tavistock, 1973) – could be described as neo-structuralist in its focus upon the 'hermeneutics of suspicion', the recovery of the deep, hidden meanings and truths ('epistemic rules') which Foucault saw as regulating and governing the discursive practices of the human sciences. In this sense, social practice was subordinated to a determining theoretical social structure, with the discourse of human sciences producing the subject within an autonomous rule-governed system. A turning-point seems to have come with the essay 'Nietzsche, Genealogy, History', and was developed in his subsequent works *Discipline and Punish: The Birth of the Prison* (London, Allen Lane, 1977), *The History of Sexuality: Volume 1* (New York, Pantheon, 1978) and the collection in *Power/Knowledge: Selected Interviews and Other Writings by Michel Foucault, 1972–1977* (New York, Pantheon, 1980), in which Foucault's concerns shift from a focus upon theory to one on practice. This later work is still 'archaeological' in the sense that he isolates the discursive practices of the human sciences, but is post-structural (and post-hermeneutic) in the sense that rather than locating them as a product of hidden epistemic rules, his focus turns to their social effects, their role in the organized and organizing practices of society, in whose spread they play a crucial role. The whole concept of deep meaning itself comes to be viewed as a cultural construction. See Hubert L. Dreyfus and Paul Rabinow, *Michel Foucault: Beyond Structuralism and Hermeneutics* (Brighton, The Harvester Press, 1982).

3. Foucault, *Discipline and Punish*, p. 27.

4. Barry Smart, 'On Discipline and Social Regulation: A Review of Foucault's Genealogical Analysis' in David Garland and Peter Young (eds), *The Power To Punish* (Aldershot, Ashgate Publishing, 1992), p. 77.

5. Dreyfus and Rabinow, *Michel Foucault*, p. 123, term this approach 'interpretive analytics'.

6. Michel Foucault, 'The Subject and Power' in Dreyfus and Rabinow, *Michel Foucault*, p. 208. An analogy between Foucault's concern with the conception of the human subject and that of Nietzsche has also been drawn here – implicit to both is the assumption that only the status and capacities of the subject can define the capacities of that subject to domination and freedom. Barry Smart, 'On Discipline and Social Regulation', p. 64.

7. Foucault, 'The Subject and Power', p. 212.

8. India Office Library, London (henceforth IOL), E/4/695, *Extracts of Bengal Judicial Consultations*, Despatch from Governor Farquhar to the Earl of Moira, Governor-General-in-Council, 29 Dec. 1814, p. 10.

9. IOL F/4/534, *Board's Collections* 12,853, *Correspondence with Governor Farquhar relative to the measure of supplying the Island of Mauritius with Convicts sentenced to transportation for Life by the Courts of Criminal Judicature under this Presidency*, Despatch from the Earl of Moira to Governor Farquhar, 1817, pp. 13 and 5.

10. Ibid., pp. 2 and 18.

11. Moses D.E. Nwulia, *The History of Slavery in Mauritius and the Seychelles, 1810–1875* (New Jersey, Associated University Presses, 1981), p. 71.

12. Public Record Office, London (henceforth PRO), Colonial Office (henceforth CO) archives 167/57. In this later despatch (no. 19) to Bathurst, 14 March 1821, in suggesting that a further number of convicts be introduced into Mauritius, Farquhar wrote: 'The inhabitants of this Island feel most sensibly the want of working hands, and this has been one of the great inducements to the infraction of the Abolition Laws – a larger portion of convicts, therefore, introduced and distributed, without expense to this Government, would proportionally lessen the temptation to those Crimes'.

13. Kernial Singh Sandu, *Indians in Malaya: Some Aspects of Their Immigration and Settlement* (Cambridge, Cambridge University Press, 1969), pp. 132–40; Kernial Singh Sandu, 'Tamil and Other Indian Convicts in the Straits Settlements, A.D. 1790–1873', *Proceedings of the First International Conference Seminar of Tamil Studies*, vol. 1 (Kuala Lumpur, International Association of Tamil Research, 1968), p. 203; N. Rajendra, 'Transmarine Convicts in the Straits Settlements', *Asian Profile*, vol. 11, no. 5 (Oct. 1983), pp. 510–11.

14. PRO CO 167/41, Despatch from Farquhar to Bathurst, 18 July 1818, enclosing a *Minute on the Employment of Convicts from India*, which stated: 'His Excellency [Farquhar], from a long experience in Prince of Wales Island [Pulo Penang], where, under the immediate authority of the Governor General of India, he made similar allotments of Convicts to public works, and to individuals who undertook to introduce new branches of industry, and new modes of agriculture, can speak with confidence of the happy results of their extensive employment'.

15. IOL E/4/695, *Extracts*, 13 Sept. 1815, *Magistrate of the Suburbs of Calcutta to the Acting Secretary of the Judicial Department at Fort William*, p. 135.

16. IOL F/4/534, *Board's Collections, Correspondence between the Magistrates of the Suburbs of Calcutta and the Judicial Department at Fort William*, 21 Sept. 1815, pp. 196–205.

17. PRO CO 167/29, Despatch no. 45, Farquhar, Port Louis to Bathurst, London, 1 Nov. 1816.

18. PRO CO 167/287, *Report of the Committee Appointed to Inquire into the Present State of the Indian Convicts and the Most Expedient Mode of Employing them now that the Effectives are so Reduced in Number*, Port Louis, 20 July 1847, *Appendix No. 1: List of Surviving Convicts in April 1847*.

19. Ibid. An analysis of the crimes of the Indian convicts is extremely interesting in its implications for the definition and labelling of normative behaviour and crime by the British in India during this period. Secondary literature of interest includes Basudev Chatterji, 'The Darogah and the Countryside: The Imposition of Police Control in Bengal and its Impact (1793–1837)', *The Indian Economic and Social History Review*, vol. XVIII, no. 1 (1981), pp. 19–42; Stewart N. Gordon, 'Scarf and

Sword: Thugs, Marauders, and State-formation in 18th Century Malwa', *The Indian Economic and Social History Review*, vol. VI (1969), pp. 403–29; Radhika Singha, '"Providential Circumstances": The Thuggee Campaign of the 1830s and Legal Innovation', *Modern Asian Studies*, vol. 27, no. 1 (1993), pp. 83–146; and Anand A. Yang (ed.), *Crime and Criminality in British India* (Tucson, University of Arizona Press, 1985), pp. 140–63.

20. PRO CO 167/41, *Minute on the Employment of Convicts in Mauritius*, Despatch from Farquhar to Bathurst, 18 July 1818.

21. PRO CO 167/41, Despatch from Farquhar to Bathurst, 18 July 1818. Indeed, it would seem that this was a concern dear to Farquhar's heart. In an earlier pamphlet, *Suggestions, Arising from the Abolition of the African Slave Trade, for Supplying the Demands of the West India Colonies with Agricultural Labourers* (London, John Stockdale, 1807), p. 37, he suggested that Chinese labourers be imported into the West Indies at the expense of the plantation owners who would, he argued, realize that it was in their own interest to do so.

22. PRO CO 167/124, *Commissioners of Eastern Enquiry 1828, Vol. I, Mauritius Finances and Establishments, Appendix No. 23: Return of the Number of Indian Convicts at Mauritius 30th October 1828, Distinguishing their Trades and the Number who have Left Families in India.*

23. PRO CO 167/287, *Report of the Committee Appointed to inquire into the present state of the Indian Convicts*, and ibid., *Appendix No. 1.*

24. IOL E/4/695, *Bengal Despatches*, Correspondence from Governor Farquhar to the Earl of Moira, 27 May 1815.

25. IOL E/4/695, *Bengal Despatches*, Correspondence from the Earl of Moira to Governor Farquhar, 11 Sept. 1815.

26. *The Report of the Royal Commissioners Appointed to Enquire into the Treatment of Immigrants in Mauritius, 1875, Vol XXXIV*, p. 26.

27. PRO CO 167/41, Despatch from Farquhar to Bathurst, 18 July 1818.

28. PRO CO 172/44, *Blue Book 1823*, para. 85.

29. PRO CO 167/82, Despatch no. 4 from Governor Cole to Bathurst, 1 Feb. 1825.

30. See R.R. Kuczynski, *Demographic Survey of the British Colonial Empire*, vol. 2 (London, Oxford University Press, 1948), pp. 767–97.

31. Ibid., p. 771.

32. *Report of the Royal Commissioners*, 1875, p. 26.

33. PRO CO 167/40, *Convict Department, 21st Sept. 1818. An Enclosed Return Shewing the Number of Convicts Employed with Individuals During the Months of February, March, April, May, June and July 1817* shows another 150 were employed by other individuals.

34. PRO CO 167/56, Despatch no. 19 from Farquhar to Bathurst, 14 March 1821.

35. PRO CO 167/287, *Report of the Committee Appointed to inquire into the present state of the Indian Convicts*, 20 July 1847.

36. *Report of the Royal Commissioners*, 1875, p. 27.

37. See *Passenger Lists, Inward*, Mauritian Archives.

38. Foucault, *Discipline and Punish*, p. 190.

39. Nora Barlow (ed.), *Charles Darwin's Diary of the Voyage of the H.M.S. 'Beagle'* (Cambridge, Cambridge University Press, 1933), pp. 401–2.

40. James Holman, *A Voyage Around the World, Including Travels in Africa, Asia, Australasia, America, etc. etc. from MDCCCXXVII to MDCCCXXXII*, vol. III (London, Smith, Elder and Co., 1834), p. 129 (emphases added).

41. Mary Louis Pratt, 'Scratches on the Face of the Country: or, What Mr Barrow Saw in the Land of the Bushmen' in Henry L. Gates (ed.), *'Race', Writing and Difference* (Illinois, University of Chicago Press, 1991), p. 139.

42. Revd Patrick Beaton, *Creoles and Coolies: Or, Five Years in Mauritius* (New York, Kennikat Press, 1971; first published in 1859), p. 179. By the date of first publication all the convicts had been emancipated.

43. See, for example, Crispin Bates, 'Race, Caste and Tribe in Central India: The Early Origins of Indian Anthropometry' in P. Robb (ed.), *The Concept of Race in South Asia* (New Delhi, Oxford University Press, 1995). There is a plethora of literature on the importance attached to 'race' in the recruitment of labour. See, for example, Syed Hussein Alatas, *The Myth of the Lazy Native: A Study of the Image of the Malays, Filipinos, and Javanese from the Sixteenth to the Twentieth Century and its Functions in the Ideology of Colonial Capitalism* (London, Frank Cass, 1977); David Dabydeen and Brinsley Samaroo (eds), *India in the Caribbean* (London, Hansib, 1987); and P.C. Emmer, 'The Meek Hindu: The Recruitment of Indian Indentured Labourers for Service Overseas, 1870–1916' in P.C. Emmer (ed.), *Colonialism and Migration: Indentured Labour before and after Slavery* (Dordrecht, Martinus Nijhoff, 1986). Jan Bremen, *Taming the Coolie Beast: Plantation Society and the Colonial Order in Southeast Asia* (New Delhi, Oxford University Press, 1989) and C.C. Crais, *White Supremacy and Black Resistance in Pre-Industrial South Africa: The Making of the Colonial Order in the Eastern Cape, 1770–1865* (Cambridge, Cambridge University Press, 1992) both discuss the importance attached to 'race' in the organization of the labour process. The author hopes to explore these issues in more depth at a later date.

44. See Foucault, *The History of Sexuality*, p. 143, on 'anatomo-politics' and 'bio-power'. In his earlier *Discipline and Punish*, he juxtaposes the image of the gruesome execution of the regicide Damiens with Jeremy Bentham's Panopticon prison, which illustrates the same point – a shift from the focus on individual bodies to a focus on the discipline and control of the individual within a whole population.

45. Foucault, 'The Subject and Power', p. 213.

46. In Mauritius during this period, *The Establishment of the Colonial Archives and Domain of the Crown*, under Baron D'Unienville, was instructed to undertake 'the delivery and authorisation of documents, ... comparison, computing and extracting from the originals deposited in the archives, for the use of the courts, the government or individuals'. PRO CO 172/45, *Blue Book 1824*, para. 70.

47. Photography was not used for such purposes until the 1850s. See J. Falconer, 'Photography in the Nineteenth Century' in C.A. Bayly (ed.), *The Raj: India and the British, 1600–1947* (London, National Portrait Gallery, 1991), pp. 264–77.

48. Constrictions of space do not allow a more detailed discussion of the exact nature of the colonial economy, particularly in relation to the theoretical problematics concerning the role of 'unfree' labour within a capitalist system. However, as Ernesto Laclau argues in *Politics and Ideology in Marxist Theory* (London, NLB, 1977), in

conceiving of concrete economic realities it is also necessary to conceive of those economies as systems of relations constituted by the articulation of different modes of production within a world capitalist economic system. In this way, one can draw a clear distinction between 'economic systems' and 'modes of production', in order to analyse particular economic systems within a broadly capitalist framework. Thus, in the colonial plantation economies, the dominant mode of production was 'formally' capitalist, in that its plantocracy participated in the world market in which the dominant productive sectors were already capitalist, enabling them to participate in the general movement of the capitalist system without, however, their particular mode of production necessarily being capitalist: pp. 25 and 41–2.

49. This was also true in Australia. See, for example, R. Evans and W. Thorpe, 'Power, Punishment and Penal Labour: *Convict Workers* and Moreton Bay', *Australian Historical Studies*, vol. 25, no. 98 (April 1992); Hamish Maxwell-Stewart, 'The Bushrangers and the Convict System of Van Diemen's Land, 1803–1846', PhD thesis, University of Edinburgh (1990); and Stephen Nicholas (ed.), *Convict Workers: Reinterpreting Australia's Past* (Cambridge, Cambridge University Press, 1988). Nicholas and Shergold also argue that 'the growth of Gibraltar, Bermuda, Penang, Malacca and Mauritius would have been retarded without a source of bonded, criminal labour': Stephen Nicholas and Peter R. Shergold, 'Transportation as Global Migration' in Nicholas (ed.), *Convict Workers*, p. 37. One might add Singapore to this list. Similarly, Robert Miles in *Capitalism and Unfree Labour: Anomaly or Necessity?* (London, Tavistock, 1987), particularly pp. 198–9, cites the example of the convicts transported to Australia in arguing that where certain historical conditions are absent, labour power cannot be made available and distributed by a purely economic mechanism and some form of politico-legal intervention and/or compulsion becomes necessary. Thus, under certain conditions, unfree labour is necessary for the global expansion of capitalism.

50. IOL E/4/695, *Bengal Despatches*, 15 Jan. 1819–24 Feb. 1819, pp. 656–7 (emphasized in original).

51. IOL F/4/534, *Board's Collections, Correspondence with Governor Farquhar relative to the measure of supplying the Island of Mauritius with Convicts Sentenced to Transportation for Life by the Courts of Criminal Judicature under this Presidency*, p. 3 (emphasized in original).

52. PRO CO 168/3, Despatch from Earl Bathurst to Farquhar, 4 Aug. 1817 (emphasis added).

53. Ibid., Despatch from Earl Bathurst to Major-General Darling, 20 Oct. 1819.

54. PRO CO 167/86, Despatch no. 100 from Governor Cole to Earl Bathurst, 15 Dec. 1826, Enclosure no. 1: Minute 26, Reduit, 19 Feb. 1825.

55. Ibid., Enclosures in Enclosure no. 4, *To our Governor General in Council at Fort William in Bengal, from the Judicial Department, London*, 31 Aug. 1825 and a letter from H. Shakespear (Secretary to the Governor) to the Superintendent at Allypore Jail, 2 March 1826.

56. A point made by Crispin Bates and Marina Carter in referring to the recruitment of indentured labourers for Mauritius later on in the nineteenth century: see 'Tribal and Indentured Migrants in Colonial India: Modes of Recruitment and Forms of

Incorporation' in P. Robb (ed.), *Dalit Movements and the Meanings of Labour in India* (Oxford University Press, New Delhi, 1993), p. 161. As the demand for indentured labourers gathered momentum in the 1830s, the colonial government actively encouraged the recruitment of tribals from Calcutta, considering them best adapted for plantation labour in the colony. See Crispin Bates and Marina Carter, 'Tribal Migration in India and Beyond' in Gyan Prakash (ed.), *The World of the Rural Labourer in Colonial India* (New Delhi, Oxford University Press, 1992), p. 232.

57. PRO CO 714/99, *Analytical Index, 1811–1849*, 25 March 1841.

58. *Report of the Royal Commissioners, 1875*, p. 27, recalled the 1858 debate.

59. On this point, see Nicholas and Shergold, 'Transportation as Global Migration', p. 32.

60. *Report of the Royal Commissioners, 1875*, p. 27.

61. Foucault, *Discipline and Punish*, p. 221.

62. PRO CO 167/287.

63. PRO CO 172/43, *Blue Book 1823*, para. 85.

64. Ibid., paras 31 and 85 (emphasis added).

65. PRO CO167/67, 30 Aug. 1823, Despatch no. 8 from Cole to Bathurst.

66. PRO CO 167/45, Despatch from Governor Darling to Bathurst, 6 May 1819, enclosing a letter from the Civil Engineer's Office, 11 March 1819. James Holman, *A Voyage Around the World*, p. 129, also noted that 'some of them are not long in the Colony before they contrive to gain a little fortune'.

67. James Backhouse, *A Narrative of A Visit to The Mauritius and South Africa* (London, Hamilton, Adams and Co., 1844), p. 35.

68. Barlow (ed.), *Charles Darwin's Diary*, p. 402.

69. *Report of the Royal Commissioners, 1875*, pp. 26–7.

70. IOL E/4/695, *Bengal Despatches*, p. 125.

71. PRO CO 167/37, Despatch from Governor Hall to Earl Bathurst, 28 Jan. 1818.

72. PRO CO 167/41, Despatch from Farquhar to Bathurst, 18 July 1818.

73. Ibid.

74. PRO CO 167/56, Despatch no. 19 from Farquhar to Bathurst, 14 March 1821, enclosing a letter from W. May to Farquhar, 6 Sept. 1820, requesting the allocation of 200 convicts for his own private use.

75. PRO CO 167/86, Despatch no. 100 from Governor Cole to Bathurst, 15 Dec. 1826, Enclosure in Enclosure no. 4, from H. Shakespear (Secretary to the Governor, Fort William) to G.A. Barry (Chief Secretary to the Government of Mauritius), 13 July 1826.

76. Barlow (ed.), *Charles Darwin's Diary*, p. 402.

77. Cited in P.J. Barnwell (ed.), *Visits and Despatches, Mauritius, 1598–1948* (Port Louis, Standard Printing Establishment, 1948), p. 235.

78. Charles John Boyle, *Far Away: Or, Sketches of Scenery and Society in Mauritius* (London, Chapman and Hall, 1867), p. 109.

79. Ranajit Guha, 'Dominance without Hegemony and its Historiography' in Ranajit Guha (ed.), *Subaltern Studies: Writings on South Asian History VI* (New Delhi, Oxford University Press, 1989), pp. 210–310.

80. I would like to thank Crispin Bates and Ian Duffield for their comments on earlier drafts of this chapter.

CHAPTER TEN

Embodied Explorations: Investigating Convict Tattoos and the Transportation System

James Bradley and Hamish Maxwell-Stewart

We had our bodies tattooed with adornments so that the flower and scroll would be set in a framework worthy of them. Some were cruelly branded with brutal signs that ate away their flesh like lovers' initials graven on aloe leaves. I would gaze with anguish at the men who were devoured by drawings as the crews of galleys were by salt, for the tattoos were the mark — stylized, ornate and flowery, as all marks become, whether they grow more intricate or less — of the wounds they would suffer later on, sometimes in the heart, sometimes on their flesh, whereas in days of old, on the galley, pirates had those frightful ornaments all over their body, so that life in society became impossible for them. Having willed that impossibility themselves, they suffered less from the rigour of fate. They willed it, limited their universe in its space and comfort. (Jean Genet)[1]

Power, punishment and post-modernism

Convict bodies have occupied an unspoken but implicit position in the historiography of transportation. Before 1988 debates centred upon the criminality of the transportees, while their bodies were entangled in arguments about the extent of brutality within the system.[2] The publication of *Convict Workers* in 1988 altered this position.[3] Its deployment of human capital theory to demonstrate the economic effectiveness of transportation gave the convict body new life as an input in a growth model. Traditionally perceived both as passive surfaces on which punishment was inflicted and as symbols of moral degeneracy, convict bodies were now transformed into useful economic factors, preformed for productive roles in the new colonial economy.[4] By concentrating upon the twin issues of morality and criminality, the storm which greeted *Convict Workers* recapitulated old arguments.[5] It took four years for constructive criticism to appear in the shape of Evans and Thorpe's article 'Power, Punishment and Penal Labour'.[6] They focused upon the use made of the convict indents by the *Convict Workers* team. The transportation of the convict produced this trace which encapsulated knowledge the state found useful about each transportee. Evans and Thorpe believed that Nicholas *et al.* had used these documents uncritically, failing to acknowledge that these traces were the product of discourse — the state's attempt to classify the penal subject within the power/knowledge dichotomy. Instead the nature of punishment, as well as the convicts and their culture, could only be understood by locating a convict 'voice' in 'autobiographical' narratives. These revealed the psychological terror and physical brutality underpinning transportation.[7] Furthermore, focusing on the penal settlement of Moreton Bay, they argued that the use of physical punishment on the few provoked fear in the minds of the many — the convict body was thus transformed into a subject of disciplinary knowledge and an object of state-power.[8]

This chapter aims to explore the place of convict bodies within the punishment system by looking at the tattoos of convicts transported from Scotland. Between 1840 and 1853, 1226 male convicts, tried in Scotland, were transported to Van Diemen's Land (VDL). As with all convicts we can trace their journey through the penal system in a number of sources. Most importantly, upon arrival in VDL the indent and the shipboard inspection produced the Conduct Registers.[9] Among the standard anthropometric data, physical descriptions were provided. These can be placed into three categories. Firstly, there were general statements which described the most striking physical characteristics of each convict, including: 'nearly bald'; 'stout made hairy chest'; and 'freckled'. Secondly, observations of scarification and bodily change due to pathological conditions were recorded: '4 lancet marks right arm'; 'several scars on breast from being cupped'; 'scar from bleeding'; and 'pockpitted'. Finally, we find literal (and occasionally pictorial) representations of tattoos. We have descriptions of 1179 cohort members. Of these, 308 (or 26 per cent) sported some form of tattoo.[10]

While the study of scarification gives an insight into the incidence of disease and medical intrusion, and the general statements reveal fragments of the gaol keepers' mentalities, it is with the third of these categories that we are concerned. The existence of tattoos begs a whole range of questions. What were the Scottish convicts having inscribed upon their bodies? What does this reveal about their culture? How do the tattoo descriptions relate to the punishment of convicts? Central to these problems is the location of the convict body within the transportation system. The tattooed body of the convict was one intentionally marked, neither by lash nor branding iron, but through voluntary surrender to the tattooer's needles.[11] The tattooed body is generated by the social, cultural and self identities of the transportees. But it is transformed through the system's observational powers into a subject of disciplinary knowledge.

What follows is an initial investigation into the relationship between tattoos, convicts and transportation. The scope is therefore limited and problematic. Two omissions should be highlighted. Firstly, this chapter analyses tattooed men and represents, therefore, only one half of the gender equation. The lack of tattooed women is a product of the data we had to hand. Thus we have been unable to explore the gendered dimensions of tattooing.[12] Secondly, the cohort consists exclusively of prisoners convicted in Scotland. It does not, therefore, include those convicts transported on the same ships but prosecuted elsewhere in the British Isles, preventing us from carrying out meaningful statistical analysis on the incidence of tattoos and the clustering of tattoo designs.[13] Besides these gaps, the tattoo data are highly complex. The convict clerks, who observed and reported the tattoos, used words not pictures, rarely allowing the differentiation between a composition and elements of that composition. In some descriptions several elements are grouped together in a tableau portraying a single concept, for example scenes from the fall of man. Uncovering an underlying syntax for the rest was, however, fraught with difficulty.[14] While these problems are considerable they are not insurmountable. Furthermore, the main intention here is to open up the subject for further exploration. In the process we hope to relocate the convict, body and voice, within the system of transportation, while questioning existing sociological perspectives on the body.

Unwritten histories, silent sociologies and enthusiastic amateurs

Why do people get tattooed? What does the act of tattooing mean? How does it relate to social practice? These are good questions; but neither historians nor the majority of social scientists can provide satisfactory answers. Tattoos are beyond the boundaries of disciplinary discourse for most. Virtually no historiography exists,[15] while sociology, despite the recent problematization of the body, proves a frustrating field of engagement.[16] Thus, Chris Shilling's review of the body in social theory mentions many of the ways that the body can be 'artificially' transformed and shaped, including plastic surgery, fitness regimes and dieting.[17] He does not, however, cite tattooing, one of the most common 'artificial' body transformations. Elsewhere, Bryan S. Turner in his review essay 'Recent Developments in the Theory of the Body' managed the insight that 'Tattooing has become part of fashion rather than a necessary aspect of religious culture or the stratification system'.[18] The book in which this quotation is located, *The Body: Social Process and Cultural Theory*, yields no more. Of all the disciplines, anthropology is the most forthcoming, but the focus on tattoos produced within pre-capitalist societies and their relationship to social practice and cosmological beliefs is unhelpful.[19]

To make any sense of the history and culture of tattooing we have to turn to books written by enthusiasts. These all tell a similar story. While tattooing was a common practice in most pre-capitalist societies, it had disappeared in Europe under pressure from the Catholic Church, aside from a few pilgrims to Jerusalem who returned with a tattoo to mark their religious devotion. Modern European tattooing was, instead, an import from the South Pacific; the result of enthusiastic sailors on James Cook's 1770 voyage seeing Polynesian tattoos and deciding, in the now time-honoured fashion, that they wanted one too. Mysteriously the abstract Polynesian-style designs, which stylistically consisted of blue spiral markings etched on the buttocks, arms or face, transformed themselves into the symbolic tattooing described in the conduct registers.[20] We do not believe this convenient story.[21]

Along with attempts to create a history of tattooing, the enthusiasts have also tried to explain the practice itself. Thus Samuel Steward, tattooist and author of *Bad Boys and Tough Tattoos*, created an exhaustive taxonomy with a cornucopia of categories, including: decoration; herd instinct; narcissism; exhibitionism; homosexuality; crypto-homosexuality; manhood initiation rite; masculine status; and national and ethnic origins.[22] Steward's main purpose appears to have been to demonize his clientele by appealing to Freudian psychology and Lombrosian criminology.[23] Scutt and Gotch, although more sympathetic to the practice, also see sexual motivation in the desire for tattoos, although they also ascribe roles to superstition, occupational custom and sentimentality.[24] Ultimately, however, these attempted explanations founder due to their failure to connect tattoos to wider social processes.

How is it possible then to theorize the dynamics which occur in the triangulation of convict body, tattoo and indent? While there is no scholarly tradition with which to play academic follow-my-leader, the discovery of the body and its relation to society by sociologists means that there is plenty of theory with which to play fast and loose.

Theory surfing

Despite the lack of explicit work on tattooing, there is a surfeit of social theory which potentially provides insights into the practice. Of all recent approaches the most promising sees the body as socially constructed, 'shaped, constrained and even invented by society'.[25] Nineteenth-century tattoos might invest the body with meaning as part of the process of conditioning, defining and demarcating individuals. Foucault is the most obvious starting place, not least because his attempt at dissecting the micro-politics of power resulted in *Discipline and Punish*, one of the most influential recent contributions to the history of punishment. Furthermore, his approach (or at least *our* Foucault's approach) was to see the body as the product of discourse, related conglomerations of knowledge which 'underpin, generate and establish relations between all that can be seen, thought and said'.[26] At the same time he was interested in tracing the relationships between institutions, power and the body. The body becomes a focus of discourse — the link between social practice and the exercise of power. Thus, *Discipline* locates the birth of 'carceral society' in a mutation of discourse. In the pre-industrial age punishment was symbolic; the public display of torture, recantation and execution functioned as a metaphor for the attack by the criminal on the organic hierarchy of society and the natural authority of the state embodied (mostly) in the figure of the king. The Enlightenment transformed punishment, focusing on the soul of the criminal and the submission of the criminal body 'through the control of ideas'.[27] Thus carceral society was born. Midwife to the birth was the desire of institutions (governments, prisons, hospitals) to 'know' the subject — to observe, categorize and classify. In this way knowledge was produced which was used to regulate the lives of individual agents enmeshed in the distribution of power.

Classification, codification and taxonomy (placed under the umbrella of individualization) are a prerequisite to understanding convict records. Concentration, however, upon monolithic power and the groups which exercise it places far too much emphasis on structure and far too little upon agency. An apt critique of Foucault focuses upon the totalizing power of his system and the powerlessness of subjects (and the reader) in the face of it.[28] While he allowed local resistances to the power/knowledge duality, the overwhelming nature of discourse allows them only in terms of that discourse itself. Similar criticisms must apply Turner's reformulation of individualization. Following Foucault, Turner described 'individuation', an evolution of *Discipline*-cum-*Sexuality*-Foucauldianism. The categorization of bodies through knowledge leads to individuation: a process by which individuals 'are identified and separated by marks, numbers, signs and codes which are derived from knowledge of the population and related to the establishment of norms'.[29] Individuation is at the heart of the surveillance of populations. In *The Body and Society* Turner subordinated individuation to a wider problem: the relationship between the control of bodies and the creation and maintenance of social order: 'Every society is confronted by four tasks: the reproduction of populations in time, the regulation of bodies in space, the restraint of the "interior" body through discipline, and the representation of the "exterior" body in social space'.[30]

Individuation now plays one part in a range of societal tasks. Furthermore, the introduction of the representation of the 'exterior' body within social space might have some use for the problematization of convict tattoos. Clearly, the transportees were using tattoos as a mode of representation. However, if this is true in its most simple formulation, it becomes less so if we look at the mechanics of the argument. Turner draws a fine distinction between representation in the modern and pre-modern worlds. Prior to the modern era, status in Western societies was ascribed through visible symbols.[31] By contrast, in the twentieth century 'self and the presentation of self become dependent on style and fashion rather than symbols of class or hierarchical status'.[32] Representation is intertwined with consumption and 'social success depends on an ability to manage self by the adoption of appropriate interpersonal skills and success hinges crucially on the presentation of an acceptable image'.[33] Turner fails, however, to explain the dynamics of change from pre-modern to modern forms. Thus the convicts of the 1840s cannot be placed in the pre-modern age because the visible symbols of ascription (characterized as a 'status shield' by Turner) were becoming blurred in the maelstrom of industrialization. Intuitively one might follow Turner's thesis, with tattoos functioning as a bodily demarcator of status in pre-industrial society. But the 1840s do not belong to the pre-modern age and there is no evidence that at the time tattoos were constructed as a visible sign of class membership, criminal or social. Neither were the transportees consumers in the modern or post-modern senses. The very idea of one of our cohort possessing the bourgeois conceptions of social success or interpersonal skills borders upon the surreal.

At the heart of the problems which convict tattoos pose for Turner's conception of bodily and societal order still lurks (ironically) the beast of a dominant ideology not that distinct from Foucault's totalizing discourse of power/knowledge.[34] Despite the introduction of agency through representation, he explains how society regulates itself through the control of bodies, and not how bodies choose to shape and transform themselves within structural constraints. Nevertheless, both Foucault and Turner provide valuable insights into the creation and use of state records and the surveillance and regimentation of bodies documented in these sources. This must, however, be tempered with a conception of the interaction of structure and agency. A number of solutions have been suggested for overcoming the structure versus agency duality. We will briefly examine three: Arthur W. Frank's typology of body use in action; Pierre Bourdieu's demonstration of the embodiment of culture; and the body as project, outlined by Chris Shilling.

Frank, in 'For a Sociology of the Body', attempts to map the relationship between bodies, action and society. His starting place is the obverse of Turner's. Rather than looking at the body as a functional problem for society, Frank emphasizes the 'action problem' of 'how the body is a problem for *itself*'.[35] Frank then outlines four action problems that the body confronts as it goes about its daily business: control (the predictability of an individual body in carrying out a specific task); desire (whether the body lacks or produces desire); other-relatedness (does the body see itself as monadic, closed in upon itself, or dyadic, 'in relation of mutual constitution with others'?); and finally, self-relatedness ('does the body consciousness associate itself with its own being, particularly its surface, or dissociate itself from that corporeality?').[36] These resolve themselves into four different body types. The disciplined (regimented) body finds its clearest expression in military or monastic orders. The mirroring (consuming) body narcissistically reflects all around it through consumption.[37] The dominating (forceful) body is warlike, male and compensates for its lack of desire through murder, torture and other acts of soldierly nastiness.[38] Finally, the communicative (recognitive) body is more a future possibility than a present reality: the nearest to its realization can be found in the work of carers and the choreography of post-modern dance.[39]

We find Frank's typology problematic. Clearly bodies can be different types at different times, according to problems faced. Is it possible to be more than one type at one time? Where do we place bodies confronted with (albeit) nebulous emotions, like love? The body in love, in Frank's own terms, might be nearer to the communicative body than the movement-centred post-modern body of contemporary dance. As Shilling comments, 'it gives us little explanation as to *why* people should chose to adopt particular relations to their bodies, *how* individuals are able to change between styles of body usage, or what wider *historical conditions* could influence their adoption of certain styles rather than others'.[40] From our perspective, tattooed convict bodies were the outcome of any number of 'action problems' (imprisonment, separation, loyalty). Thus, Frank's typology is too rigid to cope with a tattoo which both transforms the body and is the result of a transaction between two individuals (tattooer and tattooed) functioning within different social spaces and historical contexts. To understand the significance of the tattoos we need a less functional approach to the interaction body, culture and (convict) system.

Pierre Bourdieu provides a more sensitive and useful approach. He believes that bodies are the product of social class. Modes of behaving, life-style, manners and gestures are learned from an early age and expressed through the body. Class becomes embodied through three factors: the material capital individuals possess (their social location); the 'habitus' (a world-view produced through social location and manifested through gesture, habits and preferences);[41] and taste, a visible expression (often through the body) of the agents' culture, itself the product of social context and 'habitus'. The body becomes a site where culture and class are produced and reproduced.[42] Bourdieu's exploration of these issues in *Distinction: A Social Critique of the Judgement of Taste* centred primarily on class attitudes to cultural artefacts (like different pieces of music). While tattoos are removed from these artefacts (although in contemporary Western culture not so far removed from clothing and fashion), it is the sense of the reproduction of culture through the body that is relevant to us.[43]

Deriving from Bourdieu, Shilling schematically presents the body in modern society as a 'project'. He points out that in 'the affluent West, there is a tendency for the body to be seen as an entity which is in the process of becoming; a project which should be worked at and accomplished as part of an individual's self-identity'. Thus recognizing 'that the body has become a project for many modern persons entails accepting that its appearance, size, shape, and even its contents, are potentially open to reconstruction in line with the designs of its owner'.[44] Shilling specifically means body-building, plastic surgery and lesser interventions like aerobics, colonic irrigation and other fitness fads. He is neither thinking of nineteenth-century bodies nor of tattoos. Nevertheless, his assertion that the body is an unfinished project allows for transformation through tattooing, and if the body is unfinished at birth in late twentieth-century society, this is as true in the era of early industrial capitalism. Cf course, the transformations were different in content and meaning; the social construction of tattooing has changed in the last few years and will have shifted many times before.

Sociology has failed to deal with the existence of the tattoo, perhaps as the result of an historical silence. The tattoo has been physically concealed by clothes and socially hidden through a taboo which has constructed it as criminal and unnatural in Western societies.[45] We have been fortunate in two senses. Firstly, the dictates of current fashion have removed the taboo, constructing skin-art as an object of desire. From an academic perspective this has a contemporary sexiness. Secondly, the discovery of the descriptions was accidental: we were using the source for a completely different purpose.[46] We must now turn to the production of these descriptions.

Surveillance

The detailed register descriptions, of which the tattoos form a part, were taken from each convict for surveillance purposes. In the days before mass photography the transportee had to be portrayed in words. The information was gathered at the individual shipboard inspection of each transportee which preceded disembarkation; a process which served as the gateway to a new penal existence and placed the convicts within the system of production and discipline by assessing their occupational skills and informing them of their role as objects of disciplinary knowledge.[47] The dynamics of the inspection are highlighted by William Gates and Linus Miller, two of the Canadian patriots (albeit immigrants from the United States) transported for their part in the Upper Canada revolt of 1837. Gates describes the Board of Health, presided over by Chief Superintendent William Gunn. A number of clerks were in attendance to note the details of a 'most searching' examination.[48] Then:

> Questions were asked, and answers given – as to our names, ages, trades, nativity, religion, whether, married, if so, where lived the wife – what the number of children – their sex and ages – whether our parents were alive – their ages, religion, residence – place of nativity – amount of education – whether we could read and write ourselves – where arrested – where, and when, and for what tried – how long sentenced ... and what scars on our persons.[49]

This bombardment of questions over, the physical examination proceeded:

> We were taken into another room, stripped of our clothing, and a minute description of every scar, blemish or mole on our persons, placed on record. There was another officer among the rest, who eyed us most searchingly, and who also put on record a faithful description of our features, color of hair, eye-brows, eyes, number of teeth lost, appearance of nose, ears, chin, mouth, &c., together with our height and weight.[50]

Miller's descriptions of the process of recording convicts before they disembarked are equally revealing:

> the work of initiation into the mysteries of the penal colony commenced. William Gunn esq. took possession of the cabin. Proclamation was made that every prisoner should instantly make his appearance at the cabin door when called, under penalty of *'severe punishment'* ... Mr Gunn a very respectable looking man with but one arm, occupied the *uppermost* seat at the table, with an immense book before him in which he was writing *'remarks'*. The clerks, all of whom affected *importance*, were likewise employed. ... I was ordered to pull off my shoes and stockings, which being done, the 'measuring' rod was applied. 'Stand up straight, no shrinking, no stretching'. My height was declared to be 'jest six feet'. I was then commanded to strip to the waist, and my person was closely scrutinized for any *marks* or *scars* by which I might be identified in case I

became wicked and depraved enough to run away. After my hand had been minutely described, 'that will do' was pronounced in a condescending tone.[51]

As with all narratives, both require careful deconstruction. They are coloured by the political beliefs and social class of the two transportees. The artisan Gates's prose is plain and pointed, using the intensiveness of the interrogation to create a suffocating atmosphere of confinement through relentless questioning. The lawyer Miller, on the other hand, layers his account with irony and scorn. The use of the courtesy title 'esq.' for Gunn acknowledges the superintendent's respectability while mocking his grandiose demeanour. In opposition to Gunn are the socially inferior clerks who 'affected' an 'importance' that Miller believed was unjustified, a theme reiterated when he uses the pseudo-colloquial 'jest' to mimic the (presumably) Irish accent of the convict clerk measuring his height.[52] Miller attempts to illustrate the social distance between the other transportees and himself — re-emphasizing his lack of criminality while deriding Imperial justice.

Through the textual fog, however, the function of the inspection becomes clearer. While both prisoners appear detached from the process, they recount a more rigorous scrutiny than indicated by the surviving registers. Many of the questions they recall were either fictional or not routinely recorded by the clerks. Furthermore, Gates remembers being weighed, although this measurement is not found in surviving records. If intentional, this exaggeration functioned to make the system appear excessively oppressive. More likely it was the product of the subconscious, the inspection leaving an indelible impression of powerlessness in the face of the powerful, for it re-emphasized the degraded status of the transportees. In Miller's description, the interrogation inverts the judicial procedure. Gunn is seated like a judge, but acts as an attorney. The convict guard, although a transportee, bullies like a common gaoler. The prisoner should both be in awe of the system (which in Miller's account he patently is not) and aware that the system has complete knowledge of his or her characteristics, crimes, vital statistics and physiology.

Body texts

Surveillance, however, produced startling descriptions of individualistic tattoos. Twenty-two-year-old Alexander Anderson, a bricklayer, convicted for stealing a 'gun and 2 swords'. arrived in VDL with many tattoos among which was the heart-rending inscription — 'Oh My Mother'.[53] Henry McQuaid, a migrant labourer from Fermanagh, was charged at Lanark with attempted rape. On his right arm 'Napoleon and cannon shots' was portrayed.[54] Apprentice tailor Thomas McFarlane, a Glaswegian, convicted of housebreaking and the theft of jewellery and watches, sported the hanged man upon his arm.[55] John Maitland, a labourer from central Scotland, transported for the robbery of a silver watch, had a tattoo of a bird with a letter in its mouth.[56] The spectacular list goes on: a zebra with the word 'Zebra' written underneath; scenes from the fall of man and crucifixion; a bird in a cage; the nickname 'Barbary Inglis'; a woman resting her hand on a tomb in mourning; boxing matches and a cockfight; several instances of flowerpots; a man sitting on a cask of rum; a sailor with a straw hat and a glass; several Highlanders with and without weaponry; Masonic regalia; cutters, brigs, schooners and barques; and nationalist and unionist symbols, including the rose, thistle and shamrock, sometimes together and sometimes apart. But these are dwarfed by the numbers of anchors, hearts and darts and, most of all, initials. Of approximately 1500 recorded tattoo elements, we discoverd 116 designs involving anchors, 55 variations of heart motifs and at least 213 based upon initials or strings of letters.

How do we read these body texts? To the modern gaze this provides a clear opposition between the esoteric and the every day: so much that is drawn from a nascent working-class culture dominated by the Bible and Bunyan; but also so much that is normal, everyday and personal.[57] The complexity of the tattoo designs baffles, intrigues and ultimately frustrates. The temptation to impose a single meaning upon each piece of skin-art must be resisted – only shifting and competing readings emerge from the miscellanea of the record. We must be alive to the multiple possibilities which reverberate from the state records; and to the social dynamics which created the tattoos and the tattoo descriptions. We must be aware that these texts were embedded in living and breathing individuals who experienced emotion and physical sensation. We must also understand the technical, psychological and cultural nuances of the practice.

The tattooed

The 26 per cent who were tattooed are fairly representative of the whole cohort, although there are some subtle differences. They were younger than the non-tattooed (average age 24 as opposed to 27). In terms of occupation, comparing the distribution of members of each using the Nicholas–Shergold skills classification,[58] both groups have major clusters in the urban unskilled (26 and 27 per cent respectively) and the skilled manufacturers category (40 per cent for both). The only noticeable difference is that 2 per cent of the non-tattooed were drawn from the category which included sailors, seaman and soldiers, while 8 per cent of the tattooed were from this group, confirming the traditionally held view that early tattooing was centred upon the army and navy. It becomes apparent, however, that other groups were disproportionately represented, particularly construction workers and domestic servants. The rural unskilled, intermediate retailers (for example, drapers and butchers) and professionals were all underrepresented. Finally, if we look at literacy, we see that proportionally more of the tattooed were illiterate than the untattooed; but by the same token, more of the tattooed were fully, as opposed to partially, literate. Taking these statistics into consideration, we are left with the teasing impression of workers in certain sectors of the economy being more prone to tattooing than others. Aside from its connection with the armed services, tattooing seems to have been a more urban than rural phenomenon.[59] Furthermore the low returns for the intermediate and professional occupations are an indication that tattooing may have been connected with social class.

But one thing is shared by the tattooed of whatever social class or occupational category (and, for that matter, the non-tattooed alike): their experience of convictism and transportation tended to level other differences and reshaped them within the bounded structure of the penal system. This transformation exposed the transportees to a similar set of experiences, founded in incarceration and transportation (the sentence, the hulk, the voyage and the destination), which open up a possible reading of the tattoos further revealed by examining the relationship between the tattoo, the tattooer and the tattooed.

Time and space

Extracting meaning from our refracted texts relies on the distillation of a number of points: the identity and role of the tattooer; the 'contract' between tattooer and tattooed; and the context of the tattoos in time and space. The tattooer creates and executes the skin-art. He or she has been largely absent from our research. 'Professional' tattooists, individuals who earn a substantial part of their incomes from the practice, were at this time non-existent.[60] A large number, if not the majority, of our tattoo descriptions were probably self-creations like those of modern 'deviant' school kids (or 'dangerous' skinheads) using compasses (or Stanley knives) and ink. Nevertheless, many of the tattoos were executed by 'professors', individuals skilled in technical and artistic execution, in return for pecuniary or non-pecuniary payment. They will have had a favoured repertoire of designs, but will, no doubt, have executed requests. The hand of the professor can only be seen where unusual designs cluster on ships. Thus, at least five individuals arriving aboard the *Equestrian* (2) had tattoos depicting a sailor wearing a 'straw hat' with four of these figures holding a bottle or a flag.[61]

Where transportees have not inscribed themselves a contract has been struck between the tattooer and the tattooed. Either the tattooer will have suggested or the tattooed requested a specific design. Meanings are produced through and beyond this transaction. Balance between the desires and (relative) wealth of the client, the repertoire and skill of the executor, the audience for the product (which inevitably includes the client), and the subsequent history of the client who must live with the near-indelible mark and its backlog of reminders, make the tattoo an unstable and multidimensional object whose meanings shift in time and space. While the artist, therefore, had a place in the construction of meaning, it was not (and rarely is) the most prominent one. Even where the tattoo is a self-creation there remain the variable arenas of multiple audiences and the shifting contexts of time and space.

Separations and 'moorings'

Although the product of surveillance, the disciplinary function of tattoo descriptions is undermined in the dimensions of time and space. The tattoos themselves can be placed into three different categories: life events/personal histories; relationships; and culture. The first group of tattoos contains those which chart the major events in individual lives including birth, death, marriage, coming-of-age and military service. Notable in this group are birth and coming-of-age tattoos, the former of which include the date of birth and the latter objects of leisure, particularly smoking pipes and drinking glasses. But perhaps the most striking examples in this category are those which seem to note the year of incarceration, of which we have found at least five examples.

The second group portrays the relationships between the convict and others: wives, lovers, children, parents, regiments and ships. This is most clearly seen in the simple tattoos which consist of strings of letters. To abstract sense from these initial strings we undertook a crude pattern-matching exercise, comparing the names of the transportee with the initials inscribed upon their bodies. Of the 213 who had initial-string tattoos, 115 had their full initials inscribed. Furthermore, in at least 36 cases the initials were embedded within a longer string, often with the surname initial repeating two or more times. J. McQueen's 'DMCQJMCQMAW' is a typical example of this.[62] The effect of an initial string combined with other images is more explicitly poignant. William Thomson's 'woman and girl hand in hand', combined with hearts and darts and the initial string 'ETMTWT', can be interpreted as a portrait of wife and child.[63] William Paterson's tattoo seems, in contrast, more obscure: 'woman and girl, two birds, two thistles, WPEP anchor MG'.[64] Finally, Thomas Lawson, tattooed with a 'man and woman hand in hand MFTL', was wearing a permanent representation of himself and his lover/wife.[65] In a number of cases relationships are more clearly represented by names. Thus, William Martin had 'Agnes Steel Peter Nowland 1841' inscribed upon his arm.[66] Many of the strings of initials, however, bore no relationship to the names of the transportee. Some were related to other loyalties, for example, the individual who had 'HMB TWEED' tattooed on his arm. Most were not this revealing, but must be interpreted as references to relationships in the past life of the transportee.

The third group is perhaps the broadest, for in this sense culture relates to work, religion and leisure. Some instances of work-related tattoos were apparent, including John Ferguson, coachman and groom, who had 'a horse' tattooed on his right arm and 'mares' upon his left hand.[67] A more detailed analysis of occupational-related tattoos proved problematic.[68] Culture beyond work is, however, better represented. Religious imagery and pre-Darwinian cosmology are seen in many examples. The numerous crosses, images of the fall, crucifixion and apocalypse, and even the portrayal of the 'sun, moon and seven stars' reflect a pre-industrial world-view. More prosaically, examples abound of ordinary leisure pursuits, like drinking, hunting and blood sports. The tattooed body in these instances acts as a generative site of production and reproduction for nineteenth-century culture, inscribing in skin the everyday preoccupations of ordinary folk.

But such interpretations assume that the tattoos have only one possible reading. The context of transportation transforms the tattooed body. To understand this a more acute understanding of the timing of the tattoos is needed. Superficially, any reading of the tattoos must take into account the time at which the tattoo was created. A hulk or shipboard tattoo can be read quite clearly as an explicit comment upon the fate of the convict: an attempt to locate the self in the world and culture of the society from which he or she has been expelled. We would argue, however, that timing is relatively unimportant. Tattooing involves the embedding of a text beneath the skin. It is a drastic and painful operation and, in the nineteenth century, was virtually irreversible. The skin becomes a text which can be read and reread both by the self and society. The meaning of the text shifts with the changing context in which the body finds itself. A tattoo originally celebrating a relationship consummated in freedom takes on an entirely different construction following sentencing, transportation and separation. The tattoo therefore acts as what Toni Morrison, in another context, called a 'mooring': something to be used 'for the verification of some idea you wanted to keep alive'.[69] The tattooed body, by implicitly referring to freedom and its loss, becomes a reminder of its own status as controlled, regimented and dominated. It is also a constant and ever-present keepsake of the trauma of separation – the shattering of 'moorings'. But the tattooed body also offers the prospect of resistance, a culturally embodied slap in the face to authority and respectability – a site for the encoding of subversive texts.[70]

Culture versus discipline

Social theory helps us understand the creation of state records and their relationship to the functioning of convict society. And yet it is wrong to maintain (following Foucault) that the penal system in VDL was one characterized by a totalizing power which turned the convict subject of knowledge into an object of state power. From a practical perspective the administration of transportation was overloaded following the 1842 reforms; its need to know undermined by a huge increase in transportees and the bureaucratic nightmare of a fundamentally altered management system, the complex and, in the end, unworkable Probation System.[71] Indeed, after 1844 the physical descriptions of transportees deteriorate in detail (although interestingly, the quality of the tattoo data does not to the same degree). Furthermore, we must attempt to see through the eyes of the transportee.[72] The convict objects of power may have perceived and even accepted the legitimacy of state power. Nevertheless, they defined their position within that system through the actions and language of the pre-industrial 'moral economy'. In the end the state records, the actual means of categorization and classification, undermine the distribution of power within the system. An inherent paradox exists between the need to 'know' the convict — to place him or her within the disciplinary strait-jacket of discourse — and the revelations contained therein of both the convict's agency and, from the perspective of the state administrators, his alien culture.[73]

Fragments of social theory (particularly Bourdieu) do, however, allow us to balance convict agency against state power, regressing from the post-modern gaze to an early industrial-capitalist or even pre-capitalist world-view and to map the physically transformative power of the tattoo within the nineteenth-century societal web. The end-of-the-century post-modern (and Western) body is shaped by the discourse of consumerism. We see our bodies as prefabricated annexes (rather than temples) built from 'life-style', 'well-being' and the health/illness dichotomy. In the mid-nineteenth century, where poverty and social dislocation were not relative but absolute, the body was moulded more explicitly by a project called survival, with all that that entails. Nevertheless, in both ages the body is central to cultural reproduction and tattoos provide testimony to historical similarities and differences. Clearly, the need of agents in both societies to alter permanently their physical appearance is a significant phenomenon. Furthermore, tattoos chart both human relationships and loyalties. But whereas the post-modern tattoo is a highly stylized commodity, a cultural object at once criminalized and glamorized, a badge of belonging and outlawry, its early industrial counterpart signifies a culture dominated by a pre-Darwinian and pre-Freudian cosmology complete with a largely pre-industrial system of punishment.

Sociologists not only need to take an historical view of body development, they must also confront the awkward (and, perhaps, unwelcome) spectrum of human emotions. The convict tattoos were themselves an embodied and concrete display of emotion. Implied is the need for a closer analysis of the integration of brain and body, for the brain is the most important control-mechanism in the physical transformation of the body. Cultural practice is embedded in thought and memory; if Bourdieu's 'habitus' resides physically within the body it is 'hard-wired' into the neural networks of the brain (itself a physical process as synapses fire electro-chemical currents along pathways and across synaptic gaps). Body theorists will have to pay more attention to present and future developments within the domain of cognitive science.[74]

The tattoos not only challenge sociological approaches to the body, they have a powerful impact on the historiographical stramash[75] raging post-*Convict Workers*. We return to the tattoo stating 'Oh My Mother'. This plaintive statement reveals, not a member of a criminal class, with its eugenic undertones, as the historiographical consensus had it before the publication of *Convict Workers*, but an individual who committed crimes. 'Oh My Mother', the tattoos depicting the fall of man, the flowerpots, the zebra, the kilted Highlanders, the men and women hand in hand, the hearts, anchors and initials all have been recorded to aid the functioning of the penal system. Yet surely, they also reveal, through their location of the individual within the shifting culture of the nineteenth-century industrial working class, the 'convict voice' as much as any convict narrative, including those identified by Evans and Thorpe. Indeed, the tattoo descriptions were not reshaped in the same way as those narratives which were edited and published by the convict narrators' social superiors.[76] Furthermore, unlike convict petitions, they are not shaped into formulations appealing to the values and policies of men in authority. Enigmatic and susceptible to various readings though they are, it may thus be that the tattoo descriptions are the closest to the 'convict voice' that it is now possible to attain.

Notes

1. Jean Genet, *The Miracle of the Rose*, quoted in Robert Brain, *The Decorated Body* (London, Hutchison, 1979), pp. 159–60.
2. Significant among these are Lloyd Robson, *The Convict Settlers of Australia: An Enquiry into the Origin and Character of the Convicts Transported to New South Wales and Van Diemen's Land 1787–1852* (Carlton, Victoria, Melbourne University Press, 1965); A.G.L. Shaw, *Convicts and the Colonies: A Study of Penal Transportation from Great Britain and Ireland to Australia and Other Parts of the British Empire* (London, Faber, 1966); J.B. Hirst, *Convict Society and its Enemies: A History of Early New South Wales* (Sydney, George Allen and Unwin Australia, 1983); and Robert Hughes,

The Fatal Shore: A History of the Transportation of Convicts to Australia (London, Collins Harvill, 1987).

3. Stephen Nicholas (ed.), *Convict Workers: Reinterpreting Australia's Past* (Cambridge, Cambridge University Press, 1988).

4. Stephen Nicholas and Peter Shergold, 'Convicts as Workers', ibid., ch. 5.

5. In general, the *Convict Workers* argument seems to have been more palatable to British historians, not least because it dovetails neatly with the historiography of crime and punishment during the industrial revolution which has posited rising crime rates not as the product of the growth of the urban 'dangerous classes' but as a response to structural changes in the economy. This was stated dramatically by E.P. Thompson, *The Making of the English Working Class* (Harmondsworth, Penguin Books, 1968; first pub. London, Gollancz, 1963), pp. 63–6. More recently Peter Linebaugh, *The London Hanged: Crime and Civil Society in the Eighteenth Century* (London, Allen Lane, Penguin Press, 1991), has explored the shift from the moral to waged economy.

6. R. Evans and W. Thorpe, 'Power, Punishment and Penal Labour: *Convict Workers* and Moreton Bay', *Australian Historical Studies*, vol. 25, no. 98 (April 1992), pp. 90–111.

7. Ibid., pp. 94–6.

8. In making their argument they deployed the neo-structuralist Michel Foucault of *The Order of Things: An Archaeology of the Human Sciences* (London, Tavistock Publications, 1970). The post-structural Foucault of Power/Knowledge renown might have been more useful, particularly in *Discipline and Punish: The Birth of the Prison* (London, Allen Lane, 1977).

9. The convict indents, Archives Office of Tasmania (henceforth AOT), Con 14, were compiled prior to disembarkation in VDL. These documents did not contain physical descriptions. Many of the details contained in Con 14 were later incorporated into Con 33, the Conduct Registers, which were compiled on arrival in VDL and used as the primary means of documenting each convict's progress through the transportation system.

10. Of the missing 47, eleven died at sea, two died before inspection, one had been landed previously and no information was available on the remaining 33.

11. For description of how tattoos were done before the advent of the electric tattoo machine see: Surg.-Capt. R.W.B. Scutt and Christopher Gotch, *Art, Sex and Symbol: The Mystery of Tattooing* (Cranbury, NJ, Cornwall Books, 1986; 1st edn 1974), pp. 15–16; Ira Dye, 'Early American Seafarers', *Proceedings of the American Philosophical Society*, vol. 120, no. 5 (1976), p. 355.

12. Recent data collection has redressed the balance. At the conference 'Changing Organisms; Organisms of Change', University of Aberdeen (29 June to 1 July 1995), our unpublished paper 'Interdiscipline and Punish: Convict Tattoos and Transportation Trauma' addressed gender more emphatically.

13. Again recent data collection has gone a long way to solving this problem. Initial results were also presented at the 'Changing Organisms' conference, see note 12 above.

14. Our solution to this has been to treat each tattoo description atomically. But to

keep the data in a state where compositions consisting of several tattoos can be generated we numbered each in the order that they were reported. Using our software it is possible to recreate compositional groups when and where they are identified.

15. Dye, 'Early American Seafarers', is an honourable exception.

16. Brain, *The Decorated Body*, should also be regarded as an exception. The book contains ch. 2, 'The Tattooed Body', pp. 48–67, and ch. 9, 'The Social Body', pp. 158–63, which deals extensively with modern (i.e. late twentieth century) practices.

17. Chris Shilling, *The Body and Social Theory* (London, Sage, 1993), esp. pp. 6, 92 and 130–1.

18. Bryan S. Turner, 'Recent Developments in the Theory of the Body' in Mike Featherstone, Mike Hepworth and Bryan S. Turner (eds), *The Body: Social Process and Cultural Theory* (London, Sage, 1991), p. 6.

19. See Frances E. Mascia-Lees and Patricia Sharpe, *Tattoo, Torture, Mutilation, and Adornment: The Denaturalization of the Body in Culture and Text* (New York, State University of New York Press, 1992). For an early example of this type of work see W.D. Hambly, *The History of Tattooing and its Significance* (London, H.F. and G. Witherby, 1925), which concentrates almost exclusively on non-Western tattoos.

20. This account of the traditional history of tattooing is adapted from Scutt and Gotch, *Art, Sex and Symbol*, pp. 21–36, and Dr Stephen Oettermann, 'Introduction' in Stefan Richter, *Tattoo* (London, Quartet, 1985), pp. 12–14. Interestingly Brain, *The Decorated Body*, pp. 51–5, reproduces a very similar, if slightly more sophisticated, account.

21. Neither did Dye, 'Early American Seafarers', p. 354. In 1794, a mere 24 years after Cook's voyage, 25 per cent of seamen, applying for protection certificates to shield them from impressment by the British navy, were tattooed. 'The custom could hardly spread so far in so short a time', he comments.

22. Samuel M. Steward, *Bad Boys and Tough Tattoos: A Social History of the Tattoo with Gangs, Sailors and Street-Corner Punks 1950–1965* (New York, Harrington Park Press, 1966), pp. 45–80.

23. See Cesare Lombroso, 'Introduction' in Gina Lombroso Ferrero, *Criminal Man according to the Classification of Cesare Lombroso briefly summarized by his Daughter* (London, G.P. Putnam, 1911), p. xiii; see also pp. 45–8 and 232. This line was subsequently followed by the anthropologist Hambly, *The History of Tattooing*, pp. 194–7. Brain, *The Decorated Body*, p. 160, notes this process.

24. Scutt and Gotch, *Art, Sex and Symbol*, esp. p. 87.

25. Shilling, *The Body and Social Theory*, p. 70.

26. Ibid., p. 75.

27. Michel Foucault, *Discipline and Punish*, p. 101–2.

28. See discussions in J. G. Merquior, *Foucault* (London, Fontana, 1985), p. 116.

29. Shilling, *The Body and Social Theory*, p. 78.

30. Bryan S. Turner, *The Body and Society* (Oxford, Basil Blackwell, 1984), p. 3.

31. Ibid., pp. 108–10.

32. Ibid., p. 110.

33. Ibid., p. 114.

34. Ironic, given Turner's contribution to the debate about the function of dominant ideology. See Nicholas Abercrombie, Stephen Hill and Bryan S. Turner, *The Dominant Ideology Thesis* (London, Allen and Unwin, 1980).

35. Arthur W. Frank, 'For a Sociology of the Body: An Analytical Review' in Featherstone *et al.*, *The Body*, p. 47.

36. Ibid., p. 52.

37. Ibid., p. 61.

38. Ibid., p. 72.

39. Ibid., pp. 79–90. Regular (armchair) critics of post-modern dance will not recognize this description. Anyone unfortunate enough to see Lucinda Childs, the paradigm of post-modern dance (characterized by its repetitions, lack of visual and textual depth, pastiche of classical formalization and contemporary aesthetics, use of multi-media, Philip Glass score, etc.), at the 1994 Edinburgh International Festival will quietly giggle. It would, perhaps, be kindest to say that it left the audience monadic!

40. Shilling, *The Body and Social Theory*, p. 98.

41. Such a preference included whether an individual chooses to play football or rugby. See Pierre Bourdieu, 'Sport and Social Class', *Social Science Information*, vol. 17, no. 6 (1978), p. 833.

42. We have relied on Shilling for this synopsis, *The Body and Social Theory*, pp. 128–9.

43. Pierre Bourdieu, *Distinction: A Social Critique of the Judgement of Taste* (London, Routledge, 1994; first published in English 1984). See, for example, his rank ordering of films seen by secondary teachers, professions and industrial and commercial employers (p. 271) or, more relevant to this chapter, the social breakdown of 'the value placed by Frenchwomen on body, beauty and beauty care' (p. 203).

44. Shilling, *The Body and Social Theory*, p. 5.

45. This taboo has waxed and waned in intensity. The late nineteenth and early twentieth centuries saw a tattooing craze, where even kings and princes sported tattoos. It has also been a socially acceptable practice for all ranks of the British army during the twentieth century.

46. Hamish Maxwell-Stewart's project on convict height required analysis of convict indents and registers. In the process of researching these sources his attention was again drawn to the physical descriptions which he originally noted when researching his doctoral thesis, 'The Bushrangers and the Convict System of Van Diemen's Land, 1803–1846', University of Edinburgh (1990).

47. A similar process occurred for convicts entering New South Wales.

48. William Gates (ed. by George Mackannes), *Recollections of a Life in Van Diemen's Land*, Australian Historical Monographs, no. 40 (Sydney, D.S. Ford, 1961; originally published in 1850), p. 39; Linus W. Miller, *Notes of an Exile to Van Diemen's Land* (New York, Social Science Research Council of Canada *et al.*, 1968; facsimile reprint of Toronto, 1846 edition), pp. 255–6.

49. Gates, *Recollections of a Life in Van Diemen's Land*, p. 39.

50. Ibid., p. 40.

51. Miller, *Notes of an Exile to Van Diemen's Land*, pp. 257–8.

52. The vast majority of Convict Department clerks were convicts themselves who had been employed in the occupation prior to their sentencing to transportation. They appear to be a category of convicts whose occupational skills and experience were far too scarce and valuable in the penal colonies to be overlooked on the grounds of purely penal considerations.

53. 26412 Alexander Anderson per *Lady Montague*, AOT, Con 33. All subsequent references to convicts from this source will be cited thus: police number; convict name; and ship on which transported.

54. 2370 Henry McQuaid per *Layton* (4).

55. 17374 Thomas McFarlane per *Pestonjee Bomanjee*.

56. 13532 John Maitland per *Maria Soames* (1).

57. A culture which has been analysed in some detail. Most notably Thompson, *History of the English Working Class*, pp. 34–58, details the relationship between radical politics, nascent working-class culture and the Bible and Bunyan. It is also implicit in Linebaugh, *The London Hanged* and Iain McCalman, *The Radical Underworld: Prophets, Revolutionaries and Pornographers in London, 1795–1840* (Cambridge, Cambridge University Press, 1988).

58. For the Nicholas–Shergold skill classification, see Nicholas (ed.), *Convict Workers*, pp. 223–4.

59. The figure for the services was a considerable underrepresentation; many of the soldiers were encouraged to give their civilian occupations.

60. Dye, 'Early American Merchant Seafarers', p. 355, notes that the professional tattooist 'came on the scene in American (and British seaports) around 1870–1880', and also observes that 'Mayhew, in his exhaustive 1850 survey of the detailed occupational specialities of London's lower classes does not mention the tattooist'.

61. *Equestrian* (2), 15 Oct. 1845. Other examples include the *Hindoostan*, 19 Jan. 1841, where at least eight variations are found around the theme of wreath, crown and/or moon. Of these six were teenagers convicted in Edinburgh on the same day. Equally, on the *Gilmore* (3), 20 Aug. 1843, five crucifixions are found and four bracelets.

62. 14566 John McQueen per *Lord Auckland* (1).

63. 11036 William Thomson per *Henrietta*.

64. 12319 William Paterson per *Duke of Richmond*.

65. 12286 Thomas Lawson per *Duke of Richmond*.

66. 4584 William Martin per *John Brewer*.

67. 25590 John Ferguson per *Fairlie* (4).

68. A classification scheme was developed for the tattoos. When cross-tabulated with the Nicholas–Shergold classification the results were unedifying. To be fully effective a far larger sample of tattoos and a more sophisticated codification scheme is needed.

69. Toni Morrison, *Song of Solomon* (London, Picador, 1989), p. 13.

70. It is possible to read this in some of the religious and symbolic tattoos. But more

than this the reference to exile, reminders of freedom, and a world lost undermines the authority of the state.

71. See Shaw, *Convicts and the Colonies*, pp. 295–301.

72. Kirsty Reid, '"Contumacious, Ungovernable and Incorrigible": Convict Women and Workplace Resistance, Van Diemen's Land, 1820–1839', in this volume, exemplifies this approach.

73. A similar argument is made by Clare Anderson in her contribution to this volume, 'The Genealogy of the Modern Subject: Indian Convicts in Mauritius, 1814–1853'.

74. This should not, however, be taken as endorsement of the position of socio-biologists, particularly evolutionary psychologists. Indeed, this chapter can be read as a refutation of the socio-biological premiss that all social development is a function of biological programming. Rather, we are suggesting that cognitive science is starting to reveal the way in which such vital social mechanisms as memory function. The insistence of cognitive scientists that the brain is a physical organ, with its somatic 'qualities' reduced to functionary status, may open up a way of reintegrating mind and body.

75. The Scots word 'stramash', meaning a heated dispute (with hints of a potential for outbreaks of fisticuffs), is highly appropriate here – indeed, in view of the pugnaciousness of *Convict Workers* itself and the hostile reactions by many reviewers, one might almost say that the appropriate Scots word is 'bruilzies', meaning affrays.

76. This problem in understanding convict narratives is extensively discussed in Ian Duffield, 'Problematic Passages: "Jack Bushman's" Convict Narrative', in this book.

CHAPTER ELEVEN

'What punishment will be sufficient for these rebellious hussies?' Headshaving and Convict Women in the Female Factories, 1820s–1840s

Joy Damousi

Following a riot in the female factory in 1839 at Parramatta in New South Wales, the *Colonial Times* lamented the fact that the factory had yet again proven to be an inadequate form of discipline, punishment or reform of convict women. 'What punishment', despaired the editor, 'will be sufficient for these rebellious hussies?'[1] One issue agreed upon was that 'a more refined system of discipline ... should be enforced in the case of females'.[2] The question of women and punishment was a constant source of frustration for the colonial authorities because they had limited means by which to punish recalcitrant women. Flogging of women had been outlawed in Britain in 1817.[3] The female factories which were established in Australia served not only as prisons, but also as workhouses, as well as labour and marriage bureaux.

In this chapter, I consider the impact of one form of punishment inflicted on convict women – that of headshaving. While men, too, had their heads shaved, I want to examine the ways in which headshaving was a gendered activity, for headshaving *women* assumed a significance specific to the construction of femininity during the nineteenth century. The second point I pursue in relation to this is a concomitant issue – that of the broader relationship between the female factories and the 'outside' world of colonial society. I argue that we can understand convict women's violent response to headshaving through an analysis of the moment of transition between the outside and inside worlds of the prison and the society beyond its walls. For convict women, this moment of transition accentuated an anxiety about their femininity.

Australian historians have constructed the experiences of women within the female factories in a number of ways. These discussions have centred on whether or not the factories provided adequate or inadequate reform of convict women, or whether women preferred the camaraderie of the factory to what is often characterized as the violence and abuse outside of the factory. Implicit in some of these writings is an outside/inside dichotomy, where the two worlds were kept separate and distinctive.[4] For the purposes of this chapter, I want to concentrate on this crucial assumption that there was little interaction between the inside/ outside worlds of the prison. Our understanding of women's 'experience' becomes more complex if we consider the fluidity and interactive process in the movement between the two. The female factories, I would suggest, were not separate, independent institutions. The model of inside/outside is limiting particularly when analysing the space women occupied, moved between and transgressed. The nature of punishment of convict women meant that they were constantly moving between the inside and the outside worlds — between societies and spaces which defined and constructed their identities, behaviour and actions — in a way which forces us to reconceptualize how the prison operated. Rather than the factories revealing a static model of inside/outside, they were institutions which functioned along the model of *inside/out*: they were both defined by and were dependent on the outside, as the colonial society defined itself in relation to its carceral centre.

Diane Fuss has argued that the binaries of inside/outside operate as a site of 'meaning production', with each category defining the other.[5] The female factories were a site of production about femininity, but this was constantly constructed with reference to the 'outside'. In being such a 'site' the factories, in some respects, became 'female spaces' where women could transcend the expectations of the outside world, but were never entirely immune to the expectations imposed on them by this world. The practice of headshaving, as we shall see, was an illustration of this fluidity, for while the shaving took place *within* the secluded confines of the factory, clearly it was one of the most effective means of inscribing punishment on women's bodies and instilling shame. The subculture within the factory suggests the ways in which the milieu of the prison was influenced by women coming back and forth, and how the prison became a space where women could transcend the feminine ideal. Male prisons operated in similar ways. After the completion of convict barracks in 1819 in Hyde Park the male convicts worked for the government the entire day under constant surveillance. Men were also employed in private service. But while there was a similar movement for men, the meanings these spaces acquired were different. For women, this entailed a movement between *male* and *female* space and a process of *defining* the feminine in that interaction. Before examining the issue of headshaving and the relationship between the outside and inside worlds of female factories, some comment on punishment and women during the nineteenth century is necessary to contextualize these processes.

Punishment and women

In Australia, women were institutionalized within prisons in ways in that men did not experience. In the 1820s women's prisons were streamlined. Governor Macquarie had adopted a hierarchical model based on reward, good conduct and privileges. The General Class comprised of the aged, married and young women. Those in the Merit Class had behaved well for six months after their admission; and women in the Crime Class were distinguished by a badge which differentiated them from those in the Merit Class.[6] Governor Ralph Darling's reforms introduced during the 1820s further refined this classification system. The first comprised the recently arrived or the destitute (assigned labour was drawn from this class). The second class constituted those women who had returned to the factory after being assigned because of improper conduct, or those who had advanced from the third class. The third class was the penitentiary class: these women were subject to hard labour each morning.[7]

Like other penitentiaries established during the nineteenth century, this institution was based on an infantile system of reward and reduced the prisoners to the dependent status of children.[8] Such rigid and stark classification and identification reinforced humiliation and degradation within the factory and fixed their position in the hierarchy. The female factories then classified women, kept them under surveillance, ordered and structured their time and space, imposing the discipline of isolation, work and silence. But in other respects, they differed. The construction of the 'docile body', to which Foucault refers in his examination of discipline, operated differently when applied to female prisoners. Foucault considered the disciplinary practices and methods of punishment which produced the 'docile bodies' of modernity.[9] But the 'disciplinary practices' differed for women as they aimed not only to refine the processes of punishment and reform but also to reinforce the 'feminine'. The practice of headshaving was an obvious example of how the meanings of bodily inscriptions differed between men and women as this practice inscribed meanings of gender for women. Despite the insularity of the prisons, these practices within were influenced by meanings informed by the 'outside'. I will now turn to looking more specifically at headshaving.

Defeminizing convict women: the practice of headshaving

In Australia, the systematic practice of convict women having their hair cut short was introduced as a form of punishment by Governor Ralph Darling in 1826 for third-class women (and for 'incorrigibles') in the female factory in New South Wales. While the need to contain lice and uphold a standard of cleanliness was a consideration for Darling, he explicitly stipulated the purpose of the exercise was a form of punishment for women 'in their second committment to the Penitentiary', who were to have their hair close cut and 'kept so during the period of their confinement'.[10] While the authorities attempted to feminize convict women through domestic service, headshaving was the inverse of this procedure: a method of defeminization which was not lost on contemporary commentators. James O'Connell, a clergyman, readily made the association between this and masculine activity: 'when convicts are degraded from the second to the third class, employment suited to their sex ceases; their heads are shaved, and they are set to breaking stone, wheeling earth, and cultivating the grounds about the factory'.[11] Interestingly, such a punishment did not disrupt women's effectiveness as *workers* within the prison: they may have been removed, but they could be returned to their workplace. James Backhouse, the Quaker missionary, noted that on 'being sent hither for misconduct, the women are dressed in a prison garb and have their hair cut off, which they esteem a great punishment'.[12] As a bodily inscription, headshaving was both a sign of punishment and an outward symbol of moral corruption and weak character. In a practical way, it meant the prisoners' potential for success in acting as prostitutes may have been diminished, as was their ability to secure a husband – both essential for women's economic survival in the colony. Crucially, it also denoted feminine shame – with their vanity undermined the women were desexed and defeminized. Elizabeth Fry made these intentions clear when she entered the prisons to reform them. Feminine adornment was prohibited and earrings, dress and finery were confiscated from female prisoners. To further engender the 'humiliation of spirit', women's hair was cut close and they were issued with white uniforms. These dresses were modelled on the plain dresses worn by Quaker women.[13]

Contemporary commentators such as Fry noted the effectiveness of the punishment. For Fry, short hair was a 'certain, yet harmless punishment' and promoted 'that humiliation of spirit which ... is an indispensable step to improvement and reformation'.[14] James Mudie, the marine lieutenant and colonial magistrate, observed that headshaving particularly distressed these women. He told the Molesworth Committee on Transportation 'I believe that there is nothing that mortifies a convict woman, if she is a young woman and has good hair, more than shaving her head; I think that annoys them more than any mode of punishment'.[15]

In 1841, Josiah Spode, the Principal Superintendent of convicts in Van Diemen's Land, lamented that the practice of headshaving had been abandoned. It was, he reported, 'adopted in cases of disorderly conduct in the House of Correction and ... was found to be very effective'. It was abandoned as a punishment 'about five years since', but he was of the 'opinion that it would be advisable to resume that custom'.[16] The custom was identified as an appropriate form of punishment for all women, irrespective of their age. Inmates at the Female Orphan school were punished in this way. In 1821, Sarah Patfield was headshaved for selling garments to her sister outside the school. In order that some 'proper example ... be made of her before the other children', the Committee of the school deemed it appropriate that:

> a suit of Factory clothing be provided for her – a collar of wood marked Thief to be worn day and night – that her head be shaved in the presence of the other Girls – and that solitary confinement and bread and water be continued 'till the next meeting – and that she be brought down to prayers in that disgraceful manner night and morning.[17]

Headshaving elicited a violent response and was often a catalyst for rebellion. In 1827, the superintendent of the Hobart factory received the following reception when she told the assigned convict Ann Bruin that she was to be shorn for absconding from her master:

> She screamed most violently, and swore that no one should cut off her hair ... She then entered my Sitting Room screaming, swearing, and jumping about the Room as if bereft of her sense. She had a pair of Scissors in her hand and commenced cutting off her own hair ... Coming before the window of my Sitting Room [she] thrust her clenched fist through three panes of glass in succession ... With a Bucket [she] broke some more panes of glass and the Bottom Sash of the window Frame.[18]

Robert Hughes is right to suggest that this was a 'protest of a woman whose physical rights were brutally transgressed'.[19] Bruin's seizure of scissors was a particularly potent act of empowerment.

Headshaving could also precipitate riot. In March 1833, at the female factory in Parramatta, the monitress from the first class refused to cut hair. Samuel Marsden, the Anglican clergyman and member of the board of management of the Parramatta prison, reported that they were 'very determined not to submit to [their hair being cut]' and

> The women had collected large heaps of stones, and as soon as we entered the third class they threw a shower of stones as fast as they possibly could at the whole of us – at last they were overcome ... and at length their hair was cut ... All the three classes were under great excitement. It will never do to show them any Clemency – they must be kept under ... but they must not do as they please ... all the officers who saw their riotous

conduct will be convinced of the necessity of keeping them under by the hand of power'.[20]

Headshaving was often appropriated by women as a symbol of resistance. In February 1831, when women of the third class attempted to escape from the prison, they seized the superintendent, Mrs Gordon, and had her 'hair ... shaved or closely cropped'. The 'chief of the insurgents were heard to say that if they got to Sydney, they would shave the heads of the Governor and his mob'.[21] This performance disrupted the distinction between the 'public' and 'private' spaces. In this theatrical resistance, what Butler would call 'theatrical rage', the women mimicked their oppressors.[22] Why were women so resistant to such punishments?

Headshaving was a way in which women's *feminine* dignity was undermined. Humiliation and disgrace was the aim of this punishment, as the Judge-Advocate David Collins observed of a convict woman who had been shorn in December 1788:

> one of the [women was] made a public example of, to deter others from offending in the like manner. The convicts being all assembled for muster, she was directed to stand forward, and, her head having been previously deprived of its natural covering, she was clothed with a canvas frock, on which was painted, in large characters, R.S.G. [receiver of stolen goods] ... This was done in the hope that shame might operate, at least with the female part of the prisoners, to the prevention of crimes.[23]

Through this practice, colonial authorities attempted to instil 'shame' in women – who they believed were otherwise immune to such humiliation. Their sexual licence and drunkenness, as well as their resistance to authority, convinced them that these women were 'shameless', lacking any sense of decency and virtue, qualities required to feel a natural sense of 'shame'. This view legitimized repressing and containing women's behaviour. It made their punishment different from that of men, who were emasculated through whippings and the lash – it made it more difficult, because many of these women were perceived to be 'depraved' beyond redemption.[24] For convict women who absconded from their masters, or attempted to escape, headshaving tainted and stigmatized them. Catherine Reily was charged in January 1822, with 'making her escape from the ... Factory and when being apprehended by a constable attempted to stab him with a knife'. She was ordered to live on bread and water for a month and 'to have her head shaved, to wear a Log and Cap of Disgrace being incorrigible'.[25] When the convict woman entered the factory it was her vanity which was gradually eroded when her head was shaved. As the visitor to the colony, John Henderson, noted 'When the convict receives sentence of solitary confinement, the depriving her of her hair, is ever considered, by the new comer, as the most severe portion of the punishment, for vanity is still her ruling passion'.[26]

Within the prisons and amongst groups of women, 'femininity' assumed a particular meaning. Women's networks and subculture were sites of an exchange for their colonial survival knowledge and skills, as well as an opportunity for women to reject the passivity and modesty of ideal femininity.[27] Mary Haigh, who had been sentenced to seven years' transportation, was an inmate of the Cascades female factory near Hobart. She noted that food, clothing and other items from the outside were exchanged within the prison. Time was passed singing, dancing, playing cards and talking about the tricks of survival in the colony. 'The women', she asserted, 'named the bad services and advised each other not to go to them.' 'Bad' services were considered those where women were well kept and clothed, but 'coerced'; those where women were 'allowed to do as they pleased' were held to be 'good' ones.[28] Women also exchanged information about where they could obtain liquor on the sly, or in which houses they could obtain shelter when they absconded. Smoking and the consumption of rum were both common within the factory. The well conducted were berated and were 'sworn at and struck if they found fault with the other women'. The 'Flash Mob', wearing handkerchiefs, earrings and rings, who in particular influenced the young girls, were the 'greatest blackguards in the buildings'.[29] Their influence within the prisons could be detrimental: 'some of the women are very bad there by whom the young girls are led away'. The prevalence of lesbianism, the use of abusive, 'masculine' language, fighting amongst themselves and rejection of submissiveness and passivity by refusing to work, all suggested ways in which the factory allowed women a space to transcend feminine expectations of them. Responses, however, to headshaving indicated that convict women's feminine identity was not fixed or static but shaped by movement in and out of these public and private spaces.

While punishment took place within the factory, true shame and humiliation occurred when these women entered the 'male dominated space' beyond the factory walls. The gaze of men outside of the prisons (unlike that within its walls which was predominately female) engendered a particular anxiety. Some women experienced this point as a moment of anxiety and fear about their femininity. It was no wonder that women attempted to retrieve the remnants of their hair when they ventured outside the factory. After having their heads shaved, wigs could be worn when the women left the factory.[30] Convict women could make a wig from their locks which had been shorn, thus giving an impression that they had not been punished, and saving them a sense of humiliation and disgrace. The *Sydney Gazette* noted that:

We have always remarked that on the return of a female from the Factory after having served her time of incarceration ... that she invariably appears as if her hair had *grown* considerably longer in front, while the back part of the head being carefully covered with a cap, conceals the wiry appearance that would otherwise be exposed to the vulgar gaze.[31]

As the *Gazette* noted in disgust, some women managed to retrieve their locks, and when they were released from the factory, these locks made 'a nice little plait for the front, which gives her all the fascinating appearance of having long hair, and of course of not having been punished'.

The paper expressed its protest at allowing this practice because, in doing so, women appeared not to have been punished. 'This is not quite correct', notes the paper, 'for as the present punishment for the women principally consists in "close shaving," they should not be allowed to make themselves appear as if they had not been relieved of the exuberance of this "female ornament".' It was such practices that led the paper to condemn the punishment of convict women as 'mere farce'.[32] Indeed, some of the women made a concerted effort to conceal this bodily inscription. Others, however, had become immune to its taint. Mary Orange, transported for seven years and an assigned servant to John Wild, was accused of 'insolence and repeated neglect of duty' by her master. When threatened with punishment because of her 'grossly insolent' behaviour, she:

commenced a torrent of abuse ... and said she had been treated worse than a dog in the place and that she wished to be sent to the factory, that her head had been shaved too often for her to mind it now, and made use of many impertinent expressions.[33]

Her 'torrent of abuse' had the desired effect: she was sentenced to the third class in the female factory for two months and returned to the government at the end of that service. For Orange, the very site of punishment – headshaving – became the basis for opposition. But it appeared that few women exercised their agency by reinscribing its meaning in this way.

The act of hair cutting was a violation of convict women's femininity, and thus of their identity. It has been argued that middle-class women's identity was defined by their beauty and many nineteenth-century publications assigned beauty to women as a way of controlling their bodies.[34] Equally, for working-class women, the violation of their body engendered an anxiety and fear about their feminine identity. Although there are very few sketches of convict women, we can gain an impression of their appearance from remaining records, especially from absconding notices in the colonial press. Many were pockpitted or marked with scars on their arms and faces. Some had rings pin-pricked on their fingers and tattoos of letters. A few had their ears pierced and it was common for them to have lost a number of teeth, through either poor diet or dental neglect. On one convict ship, the *Harmony*, Phillip Tardif estimates that the grin of every fifth woman was marred by at least one missing tooth.[35] Absconding notices provide a glimpse into the appearance of some. Margaret McKee, a 44-year-old servant who escaped from the factory, had a pale freckled complexion.[36] Ellen Sheehan, a 20-year-old laundry maid, had a fresh pockpitted complexion.[37] Similarly, Sarah Gardener had a sallow and pockpitted face.[38] The description of sallow or pockpitted complexions seems to have been used to characterize convict women of all ages: some as young as the 15-year-old servant Ann Ross, whose complexion was described as sallow and freckled, to Eliza Hargraves, over double her age at 31, who was 'ruddy' and pockpitted.[39] While their skin texture may have been predominantly sallow, their hair remained their crowning glory. The pockpitted and/or sallow complexion, however, also characterized the appearance of middle-class women. The difference between them was that bourgeois women, as well as being able to retain their hair, had access to facial adornment which concealed such imperfections.

The iconography and symbolism associated with cutting hair was related to controlling and disciplining women by undermining their femininity. This was also a way of containing what were perceived to be their 'wild animal passions and impulses', which were identified as the source of disorder, since they unsettled the state, society and nature. In response to women's recalcitrant behaviour, the authorities sought to defeminize and masculinize them. Convict women's responses suggests the way in which their feminine identity was not static or fixed and was defined by the two worlds they inhabited.

Although there may have been a subculture within the factory which may have challenged broadly received ideas about femininity, notions of feminine appearance were at the same time not immune from the standards imposed by society at large. The theatre of headshaving stripped women of their feminine attributes, defeminized and desexed them and for this reason was, as the surgeon Robert Espie noted in 1822, 'to be the only [punishment] they regard'.[40]

Notes

1. *Colonial Times*, 7 May 1839, p. 2.
2. 'Report of the Committe into Convict Discipline 1843', Archives Office of Tasmania (henceforth AOT), CSO 22/50.
3. John Hirst, *Convict Society and its Enemies: A History of Early New South Wales* (Sydney, Allen and Unwin, 1983), p. 17.
4. Hilary Weddaburn, 'The Female Factory' in Judy Mackinolty and Heather Radi (eds), *In Pursuit of Justice: Australian Women and the Law, 1788–1979* (Sydney, Hale

and Iremonger, 1979), p. 26; Laren Heath, 'The Female Convict Factories in New South Wales and Van Diemen's Land: An Examination of their Role in the Control, Punishment and the Reformation of Prisoners between 1804 and 1854', MA thesis, Australian National University (1978); Anne Summers, *Damned Whores and God's Police: The Colonization of Women in Australia* (Harmondsworth, Penguin, 1975), p. 282.

5. Diana Fuss, 'Inside/Out' in Diana Fuss (ed.), *Inside/Out: Lesbian Theories, Gay Theories* (London, Routledge, 1991), p. 1.

6. Lachlan Macquarie, 'Rules and Regulations for the Management of the Female Convicts in the New Factory at Parrammatta', Sydney, 1821, pp. 1–11.

7. 'Rules and Regulations for the Conduct of the Female Factory and recommended by the Committee of Inquiry in their report', 12 April 1826, Governor's Minutes 1826, Archives Office of New South Wales (henceforth AONSW), 4/990.

8. For the comparative point, see Michael Ignatieff, *A Just Measure of Pain: The Penitentiary in the Industrial Revolution, 1750–1850* (New York, Pantheon, 1978), p. 75.

9. Michel Foucault, *Discipline and Punish: The Birth of the Prison* (Harmondsworth, Penguin, 1991; first published London, Allen Lane, 1977), pp. 135–69.

10. 'Rules and Regulations for the Conduct of the Female Factory and Recommended by the Committee of Inquiry in their Report', in Governor's Minutes 1826, AONSW, 4/990.

11. James F. O'Connell, *A Residence of Eleven Years in New Holland and the Caroline Islands* (Boston, B.B. Mussey, 1836), p. 68.

12. James Backhouse, *A Narrative of a Visit to the Australian Colonies* (London, Adams and Co., 1843), p. 21.

13. Ignatieff, *A Just Measure of Pain*, pp. 143–4.

14. R.P. Dobash, R.E. Dobash and S. Gutteridge, *The Imprisonment of Women* (London, Basil Blackwell, 1986), p. 54.

15. 'Report from the Select Committee on Transportation 1837–1838', *British Parliamentary Papers*, vol. 2, Session 1837, p. 49.

16. 'Report of the Committee of Inquiry into Convict Discipline', AOT, CSO 22/50.

17. 'Female Orphan School', p. 77, 17 Oct. 1821, AONSW, 4/403.

18. Quoted in Robert Hughes, *The Fatal Shore: A History of the Transportation of Convicts to Australia, 1787–1868* (London, Collins Harvill, 1987), pp. 257–8.

19. Ibid., p. 258.

20. Samuel Marsden, 7 March 1833, Colonial Secretary, Inward Letters, 1833, AONSW, 4/2191.3.

21. *Sydney Monitor*, 5 Feb. 1831, p. 2.

22. Judith Butler, *Bodies That Matter: On the Discursive Limits of 'Sex'* (London, Routledge, 1993), p. 233.

23. David Collins, *An Account of the English Colony in New South Wales*, vol. 1 (London, T. Cadell Jun. and W. Davies, 1798; reprint Sydney, Reed, 1975) p. 39.

24. For an analysis along these lines of women, crime and punishment, see Dobash *et al.*, *The Imprisonment of Women*, pp. 104–8.

25. 'Return of Proceedings taken at the Magistrates Court at Parramatta for the Quarter ending 30 September 1822', NSW Archives Office, Reel 660.

26. John Henderson, *Observations on the Colonies of New South Wales and Van Diemen's Land* (Calcutta, Baptist Mission Press, 1832), p. 20.

27. See Kay Daniels, 'The Flash Mob: Rebellion, Rough Culture and Sexuality in the Female Factories of Van Diemen's Land', *Australian Feminist Studies*, vol. 18 (Summer 1993), pp.133–50.

28. The question of workplace resistance by Van Diemen's Land convict women is discussed at length by Kirsty Reid in her contribution to this volume.

29. AOT, CSO 22/50.

30. R.C. Hutchinson, 'Mrs Hutchinson and the Female Felonies of Early Australia', *Tasmanian Historical Research Association*, vol. 11, no. 2 (Dec. 1963), p. 57.

31. Sydney Gazette, 29 Dec. 1836, p. 3.

32. Ibid.

33. Bench book, Stonequarry, 4 Aug. 1831–9 Dec. 1833, AONSW, 4/7573, Reel 672.

34. Robyn Cooper, 'Victorian Discourses on Women and Beauty: The Alexander Walker Texts', *Gender and History*, vol. 5, no. 1 (Spring 1993), pp. 34–55.

35. Phillip Tardif, *Notorious Strumpets and Dangerous Girls: Convict Women in Van Diemen's Land 1803–1829* (Sydney, Angus and Robertson, 1990), p. 9.

36. *Sydney Gazette*, 17 Sept. 1828, p. 14.

37. *Sydney Gazette*, 22 Oct. 1827, p. 4.

38. *Sydney Gazette*, 2 Dec. 1826, p. 4.

39. *Sydney Gazette*, 5 Nov. 1827, p. 3.

40. Robert Espie, *Journal of Robert Espie*, Lord Sidmouth, 22 Aug. 1822–1 March 1823, AONSW, PRO 3201.

Bibliography

Printed works to 1900

'Jack Bushman', *Passages from the Life of a 'Lifer'*, serialized in the *Moreton Bay Courier*, 2, 9, 16, 23 and 30 April 1859.

Anon., 'Criminal Women', *Cornhill Magazine*, vol. 14 (Aug. 1866).

Backhouse, James, *A Narrative of a Visit to the Australian Colonies* (London, Adams and Co., 1843).

Backhouse, James, *A Narrative of A Visit to The Mauritius and South Africa* (London, Hamilton, Adams and Co., 1844).

Beaton, Revd Patrick, *Creoles and Coolies: Or, Five Years in Mauritius* (New York, Kennikat Press, 1971; first published in 1859).

Becke, Louis, 'Introduction' in William Derrincourt, *Old Convict Days* (London, Fisher Unwin, 1899).

Billiard, François Jacques Marie Auguste, *Voyages aux colonies orientales ou Lettres écrites des Îles de France et de Bourbon pendant 1817, 1818, 1819 et 1820 à M. le comte de Montalivet* (Paris, Libraire Française de l'Advocat, 1829).

Bowes Smyth, A., *The Journal of Arthur Bowes Smyth* (Sydney, Library of Australian History, 1979; facsimile ed. by P.G. Fidlon and R.J. Ryan).

Boyle, Charles John, *Far Away: Or, Sketches of Scenery and Society in Mauritius* (London, Chapman and Hall, 1867).

Cash, M., *Martin Cash the Bushranger of Van Diemen's Land* (Hobart, Waltch, no date).

Cobbold, R.S., *Margaret Catchpole: History of a Suffolk Girl* (London, Henry Colburn, 1845).

Cobbold, R.S., *Margaret* (London, Simpkin Marshall, 1858).

Collins, David, *An Account of the English Colony in New South Wales: With Remarks on the Dispositions, Customs, Manners etc of the Native Inhabitants of that Country*, vol. 1 (London, 1798; 2nd edn – with introduction by Brian H. Fletcher – Sydney, A.H. and W.A. Reed in association with the Royal Australian Historical Society, 1975).

Coote, W., *History of the Colony of Queensland* (Brisbane, William Thorne, 1882).

Ellis, Mrs S., *The Mothers of England: Their Influence and Responsibility* (London, Fisher, Son and Co., 1843).

Ellis, Mrs S., *The Wives of England: Their Relative Duties, Domestic Influence and Social Obligations* (London, Fisher, Son and Co., c.1843).

Farquhar, Robert Townsend, *Suggestions, Arising from the Abolition of the African Slave Trade, for Supplying the Demands of the West India Colonies with Agricultural Labourers* (London, John Stockdale, 1807).

Fenton, Elizabeth, *The Journal of Mrs Fenton: A Narrative of her life in India, the Isle of France, and Tasmania during the years 1826–1830* (London, Edward Arnold, 1901).

Gates, William (ed. by George Mackannes), *Recollections of a Life in Van Diemen's Land, Australian Historical Monographs*, no. 40 (Sydney, D.S. Ford, 1961; 1st edn, Lockport, NY, D.S. Crandall, 1850).

Gowring, R., *Public Men of Ipswich and East Suffolk: A Series of Personal Sketches* (Ipswich, W.J. Scopes, 1875).

Griffiths, A., *Memorials of Millbank and Chapters in Prison History* (London, Chapman and Hall, 1884).

Henderson, John, *Observations on the Colonies of New South Wales and Van Diemen's Land* (Calcutta, Baptist Mission Press, 1832).

Holman, James, *A Voyage Around the World, Including Travels in Africa, Asia, Australasia, America, etc. etc. from MDCCCXXVII to MDCCCXXXII*, vol. III (London, Smith, Elder and Co., 1834).

Jorgenson, Jorgen, *The Convict King: Being the Life and Adventures of Jorgen Jorgenson retold by James Francis Hogan* (London, Ward and Downey, 1891).

Knight, J.J., *In the Early Days: History and Incident in Pioneer Queensland* (Brisbane, Sapsford, 1898).

Mayhew, H. and Binny, J., *The Criminal Prisons of London and Scenes of Prison Life* (London, 1862).

Miller, Linus W., *Notes of an Exile to Van Diemen's Land* (New York, Social Science Research Council of Canada *et al.*, 1968; facsimile reprint of Toronto, 1846 edn).

Mitchell, John, *Jail Journal, with an Introductory Narrative of Transactions in Ireland*, serialized in *The Citizen* (New York), 14 Jan. to 19 Aug. 1854 (reprinted London, Sphere, 1983).

Morrison, W.F., *The Aldine History of Queensland* (Sydney, Aldine Company, 1888).

O'Connell, James F., *A Residence of Eleven Years in New Holland and the Caroline Islands* (Boston, B.B. Mussey, 1836).

'Queensland 1900', *A Narrative of her Past, Together with Biographies of her Leading Men* (Brisbane, Alcazar Press, 1900).

Robinson, F.W., *Female Life in Prison by a Prison Matron* (London, 1862).

Suffolk, Owen, *Days of Crime and Years of Suffering*, serialized weekly in the *Australasian*, Jan.–Oct. 1867.

Traill, W.H., 'Historical Sketch of Queensland' in Andrew Garran (ed.), *Picturesque Atlas of Australia* (Sydney, Lansdowne Press, 1974; facsimile of Sydney, 1886 edn).

Trollope, Anthony, *The Macdermotts of Ballycloran* (London, Penguin, 1993; facsimile of 1847 edn).

Ullathorne, W., *The Horrors of Transportation* (Dublin, Richard Coyne, 1838).

West, J., *The History of Tasmania*, vol. 2 (Launceston, Dowling, 1852).

Printed works after 1900

Abbott, G.J., 'The Botany Bay Decision', *Journal of Australian Studies*, vol. 16 (May 1985).

Abercrombie, Nicholas, Hill, Stephen and Turner, Bryan S., *The Dominant Ideology Thesis* (London, Allen and Unwin, 1980).

Alatas, Syed Hussein, *The Myth of the Lazy Native: A Study of the Image of the Malays, Filipinos, and Javanese from the Sixteenth to the Twentieth Century and its Functions in the Ideology of Colonial Capitalism* (London, Frank Cass, 1977).

Alford, Katrina, *Production or Reproduction? An Economic History of Women in Australia, 1788–1850* (Melbourne, Oxford University Press, 1984).

Allport, Henry, 'Gould, William Buelow (1801–1853)' in *Australian Dictionary of Biography*, vol. 1, *1788–1850*.

Anderson, Benedict, *Imagined Communities: Reflections on the Origin and Spread of Nationalism* (London, Verso, 1983), p. 91.

Andrews, William L., *To Tell a Free Story: The First Century of Afro-American Autobiography* (Urbana and Chicago, University of Illinois Press, 1986).

Atkinson, Alan, 'Four Patterns of Convict Protest', *Labour History*, vol. 37 (1979).

Atkinson, Alan, 'Convicts and Courtship' in Patricia Grimshaw *et al.* (eds), *Families in Colonial Australia* (Sydney and London, Allen and Unwin, 1985).

Atkinson, Alan, *Camden: Farm and Village Life in New South Wales* (Melbourne, Oxford University Press, 1988).

Aveling (now Quartly), Marion, 'She Only Married to be Free: or Cleopatra Vindicated' in Norma Grieve and Patricia Grimshaw (eds), *Australian Women: Feminist Perspectives* (Melbourne, Oxford University Press, 1981).

Aveling, Marion, 'The Action of Gender in Early New South Wales Society', *Push from the Bush*, 24 (April 1987).

Aveling, Marion, 'Bending the Bars: Convict Women and the State' in Saunders and Evans (eds), *Gender Relations in Australia* (1992).

Aveling, Marion, 'Imagining New South Wales as a Gendered Society, 1783–1821', *Australian Historical Studies*, vol. 25, no. 98 (1992).

Baker, A.W., *Death is a Good Solution: The Convict Experience in Early Australia* (St Lucia, University of Queensland Press, 1984).

Baker, D.W.A., *Days of Wrath: A Life of John Dunmore Lang* (Carlton, Victoria, Melbourne University Press, 1985).

Baker, Houston A., *The Journey Back: Issues in Black Literature and Criticism* (Chicago and London, University of Chicago Press, 1980).

Bank, Andrew, *The Decline of Urban Slavery at the Cape, 1806 to 1843* (Cape Town, University of Cape Town Communications no. 21, 1991).

Barber, Richard, 'The Real Margaret Catchpole' in R.S. Cobbold, *Margaret Catchpole* (Ipswich, Boydell Press, 1979; reprint of 1971 facsimile of 5th edn of 1847).

Barlow, Nora (ed.), *Charles Darwin's Diary of the Voyage of the H.M.S. 'Beagle'* (Cambridge, Cambridge University Press, 1933).

Barnwell, P.J. (ed.), *Visits and Despatches, Mauritius, 1598–1948* (Port Louis, Standard Printing Establishment, 1948).

Bates, Crispin, 'Race, Caste and Tribe in Central India: The Early Origins of Indian Anthropometry' in P. Robb (ed.), *The Concept of Race in South Asia* (New Delhi, Oxford University Press, 1995).

Bates, Crispin and Carter, Marina, 'Tribal Migration in India and Beyond' in Gyan Prakash (ed.), *The World of the Rural Labourer in Colonial India* (1992).

Bates, Crispin and Carter, Marina, 'Tribal and Indentured Migrants in Colonial India: Modes of Recruitment and Forms of Incorporation' in P. Robb (ed.), *Dalit Movements and the Meanings of Labour in India* (1993).

Bateson, C., *Patrick Logan* (Sydney, Ure Smith, 1966).

Bateson, Charles, *The Convict Ships, 1787–1868* (Glasgow, Brown, Son and Ferguson, 1959).

Baxter, C.J. (ed.), *General Muster and Land and Stock Muster of New South Wales, 1822* (Sydney, ABGR in association with the Society of Australian Genealogists, 1988).

Beattie, J.M., 'The Pattern of Crime in England 1600–1800', *Past and Present*, vol. 62 (1974).

Beattie, J.M., *Crime and the Courts in England, 1660–1800* (Oxford, Clarendon, 1986).

Beddoe, Deidre, *Welsh Convict Women: A Study of Women Transported from Wales to Australia, 1787–1852* (Wales, Stewart Williams, 1979).

Bennet, J. M., 'Feminism and History', *Gender and History*, vol. 1, no. 3 (Autumn 1989).

Block, G., 'Women's History and Gender History; Aspects of an International Debate', *Gender and History*, vol. 1, no. 1 (Spring 1988).

Blythe, R., 'Introduction' in Cobbold, *Margaret Catchpole* (Ipswich, 1979).

Bourdieu, Pierre, 'Sport and Social Class', *Social Science Information*, vol. 17, no. 6 (1978).

Bourdieu, Pierre, *Distinction: A Social Critique of the Judgement of Taste* (London, Routledge, 1984).

Bradley, William, *A Voyage to New South Wales 1786–1792* (Sydney, William Dixson Foundation Publication no. 11, 1969).

Brain, Robert, *The Decorated Body* (London, Hutchison, 1979).

Brand, I., *Port Arthur 1830–1870* (Tasmania, Jason, 1978).

Brass, Tom, 'Review Essay: Slavery Now: Unfree Labour and Modern Capitalism', *Slavery & Abolition*, vol. 9, no. 2 (Sept. 1988).

Brass, Tom, 'Contextualising Sugar Production in Nineteenth-Century Queensland', *Slavery & Abolition*, vol. 15, no. 1 (April 1994).

Bremen, Jan, *Taming the Coolie Beast: Plantation Society and the Colonial Order in Southeast Asia* (New Delhi, Oxford University Press, 1989).

Brereton, Bridget, 'Searching for the Invisible Woman', *Slavery & Abolition*, vol. 13, no. 2 (1992).

Bush, Barbara, *Slave Women in Caribbean Society 1650–1838* (London, James Currey, 1990).

Butler, James D., 'British Convicts Shipped to American Colonies', *American Historical Review*, vol. II (1896).

Butler, Judith, *Bodies That Matter: On the Discursive Limits of 'Sex'* (London, Routledge, 1993).

Butlin, N.G., *Forming a Colonial Economy: Australia, 1810–1850* (Cambridge, Cambridge University Press, 1994).

Byrne, Paula Jane, *Criminal Law and Colonial Subject: New South Wales 1810–1830* (Cambridge, Cambridge University Press, 1993).

Bythell, Duncan, *The Handloom Weavers: A Study of the English Cotton Industry* (London, Cambridge University Press, 1969).

Canarella, G. and Tomaske, J.A., 'The Optimal Utilization of Slaves', *Journal of Economic History*, vol. 35 (1975).

Carter, George G., *Margaret Catchpole, the Girl from Wolfkettel* (London, Constable & Co., 1949).

Carter, Marina, 'The Transition from Slave to Indentured Labour in Mauritius', *Slavery & Abolition*, vol. 14, no. 1 (1993).

Carter, Marina and Gerbeau, Hubert, 'Covert Slaves and Coveted Coolies in the Early Nineteenth-Century Mascareignes' in W.G. Clarence-Smith (ed.), *The Economics of the Indian Ocean Slave Trade in the Nineteenth Century* (London, Frank Cass, 1989).

Chatterji, Basudev, 'The Darogah and the Countryside: The Imposition of Police Control in Bengal and its Impact (1793–1837)', *The Indian Economic and Social History Review*, vol. XVIII, no. 1 (1981).

Christchurch Mansion Museum, *Ipswich: A Brief History and Guide* (Ipswich, Ipswich Museum Committee, 1964).

Cilento, R. and Lack, C., *Triumph in the Tropics: An Historical Sketch of Queensland* (Brisbane, Smith and Paterson, 1959).

Clark, C.M.H., 'The Origins of the Convicts Transported to Eastern Australia, 1787–1852', *Historical Studies: Australia and New Zealand*, vol. 7, nos 26 and 27 (1956).

Clark, C.M.H., *A History of Australia*, vol. 1, *From Earliest Times to the Age of Macquarie* (Melbourne, Melbourne University Press, 1962).

Clark, C.M.H., *A History of Australia*, vol. 2, *New South Wales and Van Diemen's Land, 1822–1838* (Melbourne, Melbourne University Press, 1968).

Clark, Ralph (ed. by Paul G. Fidlon and R.J. Ryan), *The Journal and Letters of Ralph Clark* (Sydney, Library of Australian History, 1981).

Clune, F., *Rascals, Ruffians and Rebels* (New South Wales, Angus and Robertson, 1987).

Cobley, John (ed.), *The Crimes of the First Fleet Convicts* (Sydney, Angus and Robertson, 1970).

Cobley, John, *Sydney Cove, 1788–1792*, 3 vols (London, Angus and Robertson, 1980).

Coldham, Peter W., 'Transportation of English Felons', *National Geographic Society Quarterly*, vol. LXIII (1975).

Conlon, A., '"Mine is a Sad Yet True Story": Convict Narratives 1818–1850', *Royal Australian Historical Society Journal*, vol. 55 (1969).

Connell, R.W. and Irving, T.H., *Class Structure in Australian History: Documents, Narrative and Argument* (Melbourne, Longman Cheshire, 1980).

Cook, Ron and Wertenbaker, Timberlake, 'Dramatic Convictions: Dialogue between Playwright Timberlake Wertenbaker and Actor Ron Cook', *The Listener*, 30 Nov. 1989.

Cooper, Robyn, 'Victorian Discourses on Women and Beauty: The Alexander Walker Texts', *Gender and History*, vol. 5, no. 1 (Spring 1993).

Costanza, Angelo, *Surprising Narrative: Olaudah Equiano and the Beginnings of Black Autobiography* (London and New York, Greenwood, 1987).

Craig, W.W., *Moreton Bay Settlement, or Queensland before Separation 1770–1859* (Brisbane, Watson, Ferguson, 1925).

Crais, Clifton C., *White Supremacy and Black Resistance in Pre-Industrial South Africa: The Making of the Colonial Order in the Eastern Cape, 1770–1865* (Cambridge, Cambridge University Press, 1992).

Cranfield, L., 'Early Commandants of Moreton Bay', *Royal Historical Society of Queensland Journal*, vol. 7, no. 2 (1963–64).

Craton, Michael, 'Hobbesian or Panglossian? The Two Extremes of Slave

Conditions in the British Caribbean, 1783–1834', *William & Mary Quarterly*, 3rd ser., vol. 35 (1978).

Craton, Michael, *Testing the Chains: Resistance to Slavery in the British West Indies* (London, Cornell University Press, 1982).

Craton, Michael, 'The Transition from Slavery to Free Wage Labour in the Caribbean, 1790–1890', *Slavery & Abolition*, vol. 13, no. 2 (Dec. 1992).

Craven, Paul and Hay, Douglas, 'The Criminalization of "Free" Labour: Master and Servant in Comparative Perspective' in Lovejoy and Rogers (eds), *Unfree Labour in the Development of the Atlantic World* (1994).

Cryle, Denis, *The Press in Colonial Queensland: A Social and Political History 1845–1875* (St Lucia, University of Queensland Press, 1989).

Curtin, P., *Death by Migration: Europe's Encounter with the Tropical World in the Nineteenth Century* (Cambridge, Cambridge University Press, 1989).

Curtin, P.D., *Africa Remembered: Narratives of Africans from the Era of the Slave Trade* (Madison, Wisconsin University Press, 1967).

Dabydeen, David and Samaroo, Brinsley (eds), *India in the Caribbean* (London, Hansib, 1987).

Dallas, K.M., *Trading Posts or Penal Colonies: The Commercial Significance of Cook's New Holland Route to the Pacific* (Hobart, Fuller's Bookshop Publishing Division, 1969).

Damousi, Joy, '"Depravity and Disorder": The Sexuality of Convict Women', *Labour History*, 68 (May 1995).

Daniels, Kay (ed.), *So Much Hard Work: Women and Prostitution in Australian History* (Sydney, Fontana, 1984).

Daniels, Kay, 'The Flash Mob: Rebellion, Rough Culture and Sexuality in the Female Factories of Van Diemen's Land', *Australian Feminist Studies*, vol. 18 (1993).

Daniels, Kay and Murnane, Mary (eds), *Uphill All the Way: A Documentary History of Women in Australia* (St Lucia, Queensland University Press, 1980).

Darby, Garry, *William Buelow Gould* (n.p., Copperfield Publishing Proprietary Co., 1980).

David, P.A., *Reckoning with Slavery: A Critical Study in Quantitative History of American Negro Slavery* (New York, Oxford University Press, 1976).

Davidoff, L., *The Best Circles* (London, Croom Helm, 1973).

Davidoff, L., 'Editorial: Why Gender and History?', *Gender and History*, vol. 1, no. 1 (Spring 1988).

Davidoff, Leonore and Hall, Catherine, *Family Fortunes: Men and Women of the English Middle Class 1780–1850* (London, Hutchinson, 1987).

Davidson, A., 'A Review of Convict Workers', *Australian Historical Studies*, vol. 24 (1989).

Davis, C.T. and Gates, H.L. Jr (eds), *The Slave's Narrative: Texts and Contexts* (New York and Oxford, Oxford University Press, 1985).

de Groot, J., '"Sex and Race": The Construction of Language and Image in the Nineteenth Century' in S. Mendus and J. Rendall, *Sexuality and Subordination: Interdisciplinary Studies of Gender in the Nineteenth Century* (London, Routledge, 1989).

Department of Main Roads, Tasmania, *Convicts and Carriageways: Tasmanian Road Development until 1830* (Hobart, Department of Main Roads, 1988).

Dixson, Miriam, *The Real Matilda: Woman and Identity in Australia 1788 to the Present* (Ringwood, Victoria, Penguin Books Australia, 1976).

Dobash, R.P., Dobash, R.E. and Gutteridge, S., *The Imprisonment of Women* (Oxford, Basil Blackwell, 1986).

Donzelot, J., *The Policing of Families* (London, Hutchinson, 1980; 'Foreword' by Gilles Deleuze).

Dreyfus, Hubert L. and Rabinow, Paul, *Michel Foucault: Beyond Structuralism and Hermeneutics* (Brighton, The Harvester Press, 1982).

Duffield, Ian, 'Alexander Harris's *The Emigrant Family* and Afro-Blacks in Colonial Australia' in David Dabydeen (ed.), *The Black Presence in English Literature* (Manchester University Press, Manchester, 1985).

Duffield, Ian, 'Martin Beck and Afro-Blacks in Colonial Australia', *Journal of Australian Studies*, vol. 16 (May 1985).

Duffield, Ian, 'From Slave Colonies to Penal Colonies: The West Indian Convict Transportees to Australia', *Slavery & Abolition*, vol. 7, no. 1 (May 1986).

Duffield, Ian, 'The Life and Death of "Black" John Goff: Aspects of the Black Convict Contribution to Resistance Patterns During the Convict Era in Eastern Australia', *Australian Journal of Politics and History*, vol. 33, no. 1 (1987).

Duffield, Ian, 'Blockbusting Transportation', *Australian Studies*, no. 1 (June 1988).

Duffield, Ian, 'Identity, Community and the Lived Experience of Black Scots from the Late Eighteenth to the Mid Nineteenth Centuries', *Immigrants and Minorities*, vol. 11, no. 2 (1992).

Duffield, Ian, 'Skilled Workers or Marginalized Poor? The African Population of the United Kingdom, 1815–1852' in David Killingray (ed.), *Africans in Britain* (Ilford, Frank Cass, 1994).

Duffield, Ian, 'Constructing and Reconstructing "Black" Caesar' in Paul Hulla (ed.), *Romanticism and Wild Places* (Quadriga, Edinburgh, 1996).

Duly, L.C. '"Hottentots to Hobart and Sydney": The Cape Supreme Court's Use of Transportation', *Australian Journal of Politics and History*, vol. 25, no. 3 (1979).

Duyker, Edward, *Of the Star and the Sea: Mauritius, Mauritians and Australia* (Sylvania, New South Wales, Australian Mauritian Research Group, 1988).

Dye, Ira, 'Early American Seafarers', *Proceedings of the American Philosophical Society*, vol. 120, no. 5 (1976).

Dyster, Barrie, 'Public Employment and Assignment to Private Masters, 1788–1821' in Nicholas (ed.), *Convict Workers* (1988).

Eakin, Paul John, 'Foreword' in Philippe Lejeune (ed. Paul John Eakin), *On Autobiography* (Minneapolis, University of Minnesota Press, 1989).

Egan, Susanna, *Patterns of Experience in Autobiography* (Chapel Hill, University of North Carolina Press, 1984).

Ekirch, A. Roger, 'Great Britain's Secret Convict Trade to Maryland, 1783–1784', *American Historical Review*, vol. LXXXIX (1984).

Ekirch, A. Roger, 'Bound for America: A Profile of British Convicts Transported to the Colonies, 1715–1775', *William & Mary Quarterly*, 3rd ser., vol. XLIII (1985).

Ekirch, A. Roger, 'The Transportation of Scottish Criminals to America during the Eighteenth Century', *Journal of British Studies*, vol. XXIV (1985).

Ekirch, A. Roger, *Bound for America: The Transportation of British Convicts to the Colonies, 1718–1775* (Oxford, Clarendon, 1987).

Ekirch, A. Roger, *Bound for the Colonies: The Transportation of British Convicts to the Colonies, 1718–1775* (New York, Oxford University Press, 1987).

Elbourne, Elizabeth, 'Freedom at Issue: Vagrancy Legislation and the Meaning of Freedom in Britain and the Cape Colony, 1799–1842' in Lovejoy and Rogers (eds), *Unfree Labour in the Development of the Atlantic World* (1994).

Eldredge, Elizabeth A. and Morton, Fred (eds), *Slavery in South Africa: Captive Labour on the Dutch Frontier* (Boulder and Oxford, Westview Press, 1994).

Eltis, David, 'Labour and Coercion in the English Atlantic World from the Seventeenth to the Early Twentieth Century', *Slavery & Abolition*, vol. 14, no. 1 (April 1993).

Emmer, P.C., 'The Meek Hindu: The Recruitment of Indian Indentured Labourers for Service Overseas, 1870–1916' in P.C. Emmer (ed.), *Colonialism and Migration: Indentured Labour before and after Slavery* (Dordrecht, Martinus Nijhoff, 1986).

Emsley, Clive, 'The Criminal Past: Crime in Nineteenth-Century Britain', *History Today*, April 1988.

Engerman, S., 'Some Considerations Relating to Property Rights in Man', *Journal of Economic History*, vol. 33 (1973).

English, David, 'History and the Refuge of Art: Thomas Keneally's Sense of the Past', *Meridian*, vol. 6, no. 1 (Melbourne, 1987).

Evans, R., '"The Blood Dimmed Tide": Frontier Violence and Aboriginal Resistance' in Evans *et al.*, *Race Relations in Colonial Queensland* (1975).

Evans, R., 'Harlots and Helots: Exploitation of the Aboriginal Remnant' in Evans *et al.*, *Race Relations in Colonial Queensland* (1975).

Evans, R., 'The Mogwi Take Mi-An-Jin. Race Relations at the Moreton Bay Penal Settlement: 1824–1842' in R. Fisher (ed.), *Brisbane: The Aboriginal Presence 1824–1860, Brisbane History Group Papers*, no. 11 (1992).

Evans, R., '"What Do You Want? Do You Wish to Kill Me?" Early Racial Contact and Conflict on Stradbroke Island' in Regina Ganter (ed.), *Whose Island? The Past and Future of North Stradbroke* (Griffith University, Queensland Study Centre, 1992).

Evans, R., 'Australian Historiography' in D.R. Woolf (ed.), *Making History* (New York, Garland, forthcoming 1997).

Evans, R., Saunders, K. and Cronin, K. (eds), *Race Relations in Colonial Queensland: A History of Exclusion, Exploitation and Extermination* (St Lucia, Queensland University Press, 1975).

Evans, R. and Thorpe, W., 'Power, Punishment and Penal Labour: *Convict Workers* and Moreton Bay', *Australian Historical Studies*, vol. 25, no. 98 (April 1992).

Evans, R. and Thorpe, W. 'Freedom and Unfreedom at Moreton Bay: The Structures and Relations of Secondary Punishment', paper presented at the conference 'Beyond *Convict Workers*' (University of New South Wales, Oct. 1995).

Faber, Richard, *Class in Victorian Fiction* (London, Faber and Faber, 1971).

Falconer, J., 'Photography in the Nineteenth Century' in C.A. Bayly (ed.), *The Raj: India and the British, 1600–1947* (London, National Portrait Gallery, 1991).

Faller, L., *Turned to Account: The Forms and Functions of Criminal Biography in Late Seventeenth and Early Eighteenth-Century England* (Cambridge, Cambridge University Press, 1987).

Featherstone, Mike, Hepworth, Mike and Turner, Bryan S. (eds), *The Body: Social Process and Cultural Theory* (London, Sage, 1991).

Fenoaltea, S., 'The Slave Debate: A Note from the Sidelines', *Explorations in Economic History*, vol. 18, no. 3 (1981).

Fenoaltea, S., 'Slavery and Supervision in Comparative Perspective: A Model', *Journal of Economic History*, vol. 44, no. 3 (1984).

Fesl, Eve Mumewa, *Conned!* (St Lucia, University of Queensland Press, 1993).

Findlay, R., 'Slavery, Incentives, and Manumission: A Theoretical Model', *Journal of Political Economy*, vol. 83 (1975).

Fitzgerald, Ross, *From the Dreaming to 1915: A History of Queensland* (St Lucia, University of Queensland Press, 1982).

Foucault, Michel, *The Order of Things: An Archaeology of the Human Sciences* (London, Tavistock, 1970).

Foucault, Michel, *The Archaeology of Knowledge* (London, Tavistock, 1972).

Foucault, Michel, *The Birth of the Clinic: An Archaeology of Medical Perception* (London, Tavistock, 1973).

Foucault, Michel, *Madness and Civilization: A History of Insanity in the Age of Reason* (New York, Vintage/Random House, 1973).

Foucault, Michel, *Discipline and Punish: The Birth of the Prison* (London, Allen Lane, 1977).

Foucault, Michel, *The History of Sexuality*, Volume 1 (New York, Pantheon, 1978).

Foucault, Michel, *Power/Knowledge: Selected Interviews and Other Writings by Michel Foucault, 1972–1977* (Brighton, Harvester Press, 1980).

Foucault, Michel, 'The Subject and Power' in Dreyfus and Rabinow, *Michel Foucault* (1982).

Fox-Genovese, Elizabeth, *Within the Plantation Household: Black and White Women of the Old South* (Chapel Hill, University of North Carolina Press, 1988).

Frank, Arthur W. 'For a Sociology of the Body: An Analytical Review' in Featherstone *et al.*, *The Body* (1991), p. 47.

Fraser, D.W., 'Early Public Service in Queensland', *Royal Historical Society of Queensland Journal*, vol. 7, no. 2 (1962–63).

Fraser, D.W., 'Settlement in the Logan Period', *Royal Historical Society of Queensland Journal*, vol. 7, no. 3 (1962–63).

Frost, Alan, *Convicts and Empire: A Naval Question, 1776–1811* (Melbourne, Oxford University Press, 1981).

Fuss, Diana, 'Inside/Out' in Diana Fuss (ed.), *Inside/Out: Lesbian Theories, Gay Theories* (London, Routledge, 1991).

Garton, S., 'The Convict Origins Debate: Historians and the Problem of the "Criminal Class"', *Australian and New Zealand Journal of Criminology*, vol. 24, no. 2 (1991).

Gates, H.L. Jr, *Black Literature and Literary Theory* (London, Methuen, 1984).

Gates, H.L. Jr (ed.), *The Classic Slave Narratives* (New York, Penguin, 1987).

Gates, H.L. Jr, *The Signifying Monkey: Theory of Afro-American Literary Criticism* (New York and Oxford, Oxford University Press, 1989).

Gatrell, V.A.C., *Crime and the Law: The Social History of Crime in Europe since 1500* (London, Europa, 1980).

Gatrell, V.A.C., *The Hanging Tree: Execution and the English People, 1770–1868* (Oxford, Oxford University Press, 1994).

Genovese, E.D., *Roll Jordan Roll: The World the Slaves Made* (New York, Pantheon, 1974).

Giddens, A., *Sociology* (Cambridge, Polity Press, 1990).

Gillen, Mollie, 'The Botany Bay Decision: Convicts not Empire', *English Historical Review*, vol. XCVII (1982).

Gillen, Mollie, *The Founders of Australia: A Biographical Dictionary of the First Fleet* (Sydney, Library of Australian History, 1989).

Gittings, Robert (ed.), *The Letters of John Keats: A New Selection* (London, Oxford University Press, 1970).

Gordon, D., 'Sickness and Death at the Moreton Bay Convict Settlement', *The Medical Journal of Australia*, vol. 11, no. 12 (1963).

Gordon, Stewart N., 'Scarf and Sword: Thugs, Marauders, and State-formation in 18th Century Malwa', *The Indian Economic and Social History Review*, vol. VI (1969).

Graves, Adrian, *Cane and Labour: The Political Economy of the Queensland Sugar Industry 1862–1905* (Edinburgh, Edinburgh University Press, 1993).

Griffiths, Tom, 'Past Silences: Aborigines and Convicts in Our History Making', *Australian Cultural History*, vol. 6 (1987).

Grimshaw, Patricia, 'Women and the Family in Australian History – A Reply to *The Real Matilda*', *Historical Studies, Australia and New Zealand*, vol. 18 (1978–79).

Guha, Ranajit, *Elementary Aspects of Peasant Insurgency in Colonial India* (Delhi, Oxford University Press, 1983).

Guha, Ranajit, 'The Prose of Counter-Insurgency' in Ranajit Guha (ed.), *Subaltern Studies: Writings on South Asian History II* (Delhi, Oxford University Press, 1983).

Guha, Ranajit, 'Dominance without Hegemony and its Historiography' in Ranajit Guha (ed.), *Subaltern Studies: Writings on South Asian History VI* (Delhi, Oxford University Press, 1989).

Gundara, Jagdish S. and Duffield, Ian (eds), *Essays on the History of Blacks in Britain from Roman Times to the Mid-Twentieth Century* (Aldershot, Avebury, 1992).

Hambly, W.D., *The History of Tattooing and its Significance* (London, H.F. and G. Witherby, 1925).

Hamilton, Paula, '"Tipperarifying the Moral Atmosphere": Irish Catholic Immigration and the State 1840–1860', in Sydney Labour History Group, *What Rough Beast? The State and Social Order in Australian History* (Sydney, Allen and Unwin for the Australian Society for the Study of Labour History, 1982).

Harries, Patrick, 'Slavery, Social Incorporation and Surplus Extraction: The Nature of Free and Unfree Labour in South-East Africa', *Journal of African History*, vol. 22 (1981).

Harris, Sally, *Smuggler's Girl* (Colchester, Anglia TV Books, 1991).

Harrison, Jennifer, '"The Very Worst Class": Irish Women Convicts at Moreton Bay' in Reece (ed.), *Irish Convict Lives* (1990).

Hassam, Andrew, *Sailing to Australia: Shipboard Diaries by Nineteenth-Century British Emigrants* (Manchester, Manchester University Press, 1994).

Hay, D., *et al.*, *Albion's Fatal Tree: Crime and Society in Eighteenth Century England* (London, Allen Lane, 1975).

Hergenham, L., *Unnatural Lives: Studies in Australian Fiction about the Convicts from James Tucker to Patrick White* (St Lucia, University of Queensland Press, 1983).

Hiener, J.E., 'Martin Cash: The Legend and the Man', *Tasmanian Historical Research Association — Journal and Proceedings*, vol. 14, no. 2 (1976).

Hiener, W. and J.E., 'Introduction' in Jeffrey Mark (ed. W. and J.E. Hiener), *A Burglar's Life* (Sydney, Angus and Robertson, 1968).

Hirst, J.B., *Convict Society and its Enemies: A History of Early New South Wales* (Sydney, George Allen and Unwin, 1983).

Hirst, J.B., 'Convicts and Crime', *Overland*, no. 113 (Dec. 1988).

Hirst, J.B., 'Convict Past Divides Historians', *The Age*, 21 Feb. 1989.

Holthouse, H., *An Illustrated History of Queensland* (Adelaide, Rigby, 1978).

Hopgood, Edwin, *A History of the Lancashire Cotton Industry and the Amalgamated Weavers' Association* (Manchester, Amalgamated Weavers' Association, 1969).

Horner, C.J. and Hadgraft, Cecil, 'Rowcroft, Charles, 1798–1856' in *Australian Dictionary of Biography*, vol. 2, *1788–1850*.

Houston, R. and Snell, K., 'Proto-industrialization? Cottage Industry, Social Change and Industrialization', *Historical Journal*, vol. 27 (1984).

Hughes, Robert, *The Fatal Shore: A History of the Transportation of Convicts to Australia, 1787–1868* (London, Collins Harvill, 1987).

Humphries, J., '"The Most Free from Objection": The Sexual Division of Labor and Women's Work in Nineteenth-Century England', *Journal of Economic History*, vol. 47, no. 4 (1987).

Hutchinson, R.C., 'Mrs Hutchinson and the Female Felonies of Early Australia', *Tasmanian Historical Research Association*, vol. 11, no. 2 (Dec. 1963).

Ignatieff, Michael, *A Just Measure of Pain: The Penitentiary in the Industrial Revolution, 1750–1850* (New York, Pantheon, 1978).

Jameson, Fredric, 'Marxism and Historicism' in Fredric Jameson, *The Ideologies of Theory: Essays, 1971–1986*, vol. 2, *Syntax of History* (London, Routledge, 1988).

Jebb, Mary Anne and Haebich, Anna, 'Across the Great Divide: Gender Relations on Australian Frontiers' in Saunders and Evans (eds), *Gender Relations in Australia* (1992).

Jeffrey, Walter James (ed.), *Illustrated Australian Encyclopaedia* (Sydney, Angus and Robertson, 1925).

Johnston, W.R., *Call of the Land: A History of Queensland to the Present Day* (Brisbane, Jacaranda Press, 1982).

Johnston, W.R., *Brisbane: The First Thirty Years* (Brisbane, Boolarong, 1988).

Jones, David, *Crime, Protest, Community and Police in Nineteenth Century England* (London, Routledge and Kegan Paul, 1982).

Katzman, David, *Seven Days a Week: Women and Domestic Service in Industrializing America* (New York, Oxford University Press, 1978).

Keneally, Thomas, *The Playmaker* (London and Sydney, Hodder and Stoughton, 1987).

Kent, David, 'Customary Behaviour Transported: A Note on the Parramatta Female Factory Riot of 1827', *Journal of Australian Studies*, vol. 40 (1994).

Kent, David and Townsend, Norma, 'Deborah Oxley's "Female Convicts": An Accurate View of Working-Class Women?', *Labour History*, 65 (Nov. 1993).

Klein, Martin, 'Slavery, the International Labour Market and the Emancipation of Slaves in the Nineteenth Century' in Lovejoy and Rogers (eds), *Unfree Labour in the Development of the Atlantic World* (1994).

Kociumbas, Jan, *The Oxford History of Australia*, vol. 2, *1770–1868: Possessions* (Melbourne and Oxford, Oxford University Press, 1992).

Kuczynski, R.R., *Demographic Survey of the British Colonial Empire*, vol. 2 (London, Oxford University Press, 1948).

Lack, Clem, *Queensland, Daughter of the Sun: A Record of a Century of Responsible Government* (Brisbane, Jacaranda, 1987).

Laclau, Ernesto, *Politics and Ideology in Marxist Theory* (London, NLB, 1977).

Lake, Marilyn, 'Convict Women as Objects of Male Vision: An Historiographical Review', *Bulletin of the Centre for Tasmanian Studies*, vol. 2, no. 1 (1988).

Lake, Marilyn, 'Women, Gender and History', *Australian Feminist Studies*, 7 and 8 (Summer 1988).

Lempriere, T.L., *The Penal Settlements of Van Diemen's Land* (Launceston, Royal Society of Tasmania, 1954).

Lerner, G. *The Majority Finds its Past: Placing Women in History* (Oxford, Oxford University Press, 1981).

Lerner, G., *The Creation of Patriarchy* (New York, Oxford University Press, 1986).

Levine, L.W., *Black Culture and Black Consciousness: Afro-American Folk Thought from Slavery to Freedom* (New York, Oxford University Press, 1977).

Linebaugh, Peter, 'The Ordinary of Newgate and his *Account*' in J.S. Cockburn (ed.), *Crime in England, 1550–1800* (London, Methuen, 1977).

Linebaugh, Peter, *The London Hanged: Crime and Civil Society in the Eighteenth Century* (London, Allen Lane, Penguin Press, 1991).

Lombroso, Cesare, 'Introduction' in Gina Lombroso Ferrero, *Criminal Man according to the Classification of Cesare Lombroso briefly summarized by his Daughter* (London, G.P. Putnam, 1911).

Lovejoy, Paul E. and Rogers, Nicholas (eds), *Unfree Labour in the Development of the Atlantic World*, special issue of *Slavery & Abolition*, vol. 15, no. 2 (Aug. 1994).

Lyotard, Jean-François, *The Postmodern Condition: A Report on Knowledge* (Minneapolis, University of Minnesota, 1984).

Lyotard, Jean-François, *The Differend: Phrases in Dispute* (Manchester, Manchester University Press, 1988).

McBride, Theresa, *The Domestic Revolution: The Modernisation of Household Service in England and France, 1820–1920* (London, Croom Helm, 1976).

McCalman, Iain, *The Radical Underworld: Prophets, Revolutionaries and Pornographers in London, 1795–1840* (Cambridge, Cambridge University Press, 1988).

MacFie, Peter, 'Dobbers and Cobbers: Informers and Mateship among Convicts, Officials and Settlers on the Grass Tree Hill Road, Tasmania 1830–1850', *Tasmanian Historical Research Association*, vol. 35, no. 3 (Sept. 1988).

McGrath, Ann, *'Born in the Cattle': Aborigines in Cattle Country* (Sydney and London, Allen and Unwin, 1987).

McGrath, Ann, 'The White Man's Looking Glass: Aboriginal–Colonial Gender Relations at Port Jackson', *Australian Historical Studies*, vol. 24, no. 95 (Oct. 1990).

McIntyre, Kenneth Gordon, *The Rebello Transcripts: Governor Phillip's Portuguese Interlude* (London, Souvenir, 1984).

Macintyre, Stuart, Review article of *Convict Workers*, *London Review of Books*, vol. 11, no. 18 (Sept. 1989).

Mackay, David, *A Place of Exile: The European Settlement of Australia* (Melbourne, Oxford University Press, 1985).

Mackinolty, Judy and Radi, Heather (eds), *In Pursuit of Justice: Australian Women and the Law 1788–1979* (Sydney, Hale and Iremonger, 1979).

McLachlan, Iaen, *Place of Banishment: Port Macquarie 1818–1832* (Marickville, NSW, Hale and Iremonger, 1988).

Malherbe, V.C., 'David Stuurman, the Last Chief of the Hottentots', *African Studies Quarterly Journal* (Johannesburg, Witwatersrand University Press, 1980).

Malherbe, V.C., 'Khoikhoi and the Question of Transportation from the Cape Colony', *South African Journal of History*, vol. 17 (1985).

Malouf, David, *Johnno* (Sydney, Pan, 1979).

Marshall, Hazel, 'Convict Pioneers and the Failure of the Management System on Melville Island, 1824–29', *Push from the Bush*, 29 (1991).

Martin, Ged (ed.), *The Founding of Australia: The Argument about Australia's Origins* (Sydney, Hale and Iremonger, 1978).

Martin, Ged, 'The Founding of New South Wales' in Pamela Statham (ed.), *The Origins of Australia's Capital Cities* (Cambridge, Cambridge University Press, 1989).

Mascia-Lees, Frances E. and Sharpe, Patricia, *Tattoo, Torture, Mutilation, and Adornment: The Denaturalization of the Body in Culture and Text* (New York, State University of New York Press, 1992).

Mendus, Susan and Rendall, Jane, *Sexuality and Subordination: Interdisciplinary Studies of Gender in the Nineteenth Century* (London, Routledge, 1989).

Merquior, J. G., *Foucault* (London, Fontana, 1985).

Meston, Archibald, *A Geographic History of Queensland* (Brisbane, Government Printer, 1995).

Miles, Robert, *Capitalism and Unfree Labour: Anomaly or Necessity?* (London, Tavistock, 1987).

Mintz, Stephen, *A Prison of Expectations: The Family in Victorian Culture* (New York, New York University Press, 1985).

Moore, J., *The Convicts of Van Diemen's Land, 1840–1853* (Hobart, Cat and Fiddle, 1976).

Morgan, Kenneth, 'The Organization of the Convict Trade to Maryland; Stevenson, Randolph and Cheston, 1768–1775', *William & Mary Quarterly*, 3rd ser., vol. XLII (1985).

Morrison, Toni, *Song of Solomon* (London, Picador, 1989).

Mulvaney, D.J., 'John Graham: The Convict as Aboriginal' in Reece (ed.), *Irish Convict Lives* (1990).

Murray, Norman, *The Scottish Handloom Weavers, 1790–1850: A Social History* (Edinburgh, Donald, 1978).

Neal, D., *The Rule of Law in a Penal Colony: Law and Power in New South Wales* (Cambridge, Cambridge University Press, 1991).

Neale, R.S., 'Class and Class Consciousness: Three Classes or Five?', *Victorian Studies*, 12 (1968–69).

Neale, R.S., *Class in English History, 1680–1850* (Oxford, Blackwell, 1981).

Newby, D., 'The Deferential Dialectic', *Comparative Studies in Society and History*, vol. 17 (1975).

Nichol, W., 'Malingering and Convict Protest', *Labour History*, vol. 47 (1984).

Nichol, W., 'Ideology and the Convict System in New South Wales, 1788–1820', *Historical Studies, Australia and New Zealand*, vol. 22, no. 86 (1986).

Nicholas, Stephen, 'The Care and Feeding of Convicts' in Nicholas (ed.), *Convict Workers* (1988).

Nicholas, Stephen, 'The Convict Labour Market' in Nicholas (ed.), *Convict Workers* (1988).

Nicholas, Stephen (ed.), *Convict Workers: Reinterpreting Australia's Past* (Cambridge, Cambridge University Press, 1988).

Nicholas, Stephen, 'The Organisation of Public Work' in Nicholas (ed.), *Convict Workers* (1988).

Nicholas, Stephen and Shergold, Peter R., 'Transportation as Global Migration' in Nicholas (ed.), *Convict Workers* (1988).

Nicholas, Stephen and Shergold, Peter R., 'Unshackling the Past' in Nicholas (ed.), *Convict Workers* (1988).

Nwulia, Moses D.E., *The History of Slavery in Mauritius and the Seychelles, 1810– 1875* (New Jersey, Associated University Presses, 1981).

O'Brien, Patrick and Quinault, Roland (eds), *The Industrial Revolution and British Society* (Cambridge, Cambridge University Press, 1993).

O'Donnell, Ruan, 'General Joseph Holt' in Reece (ed.), *Exiles from Erin* (1991).

O'Donoghue, F., 'Winding Down the Convict Machine: Brisbane 1838', *Push from the Bush*, 13 (Nov. 1982).

O'Keefe, M., *A Brief Account of the Moreton Bay Penal Settlement* (Brisbane, John Oxley Library, 1974).

O'Keefe, M., 'A Report of Missing Tools and Other Items – Moreton Bay Penal Settlement, 1928', *Queensland Heritage*, vol. 3, no. 2 (May 1975).

O'Keefe, M., 'The Runaway Convicts of Moreton Bay', *Royal Historical Society of Queensland Journal*, vol. 10, no. 1 (1975–76).

Oettermann, Stephen, 'Introduction' in Stefan Richter, *Tattoo* (London, Quartet, 1985).

Oldham, Wilfred, *Britain's Convicts to the Colonies* (Sydney, Library of Australian History, 1990).

Oxley, D., 'Female Convicts' in Nicholas (ed.), *Convict Workers* (1988).

Oxley, D., 'Women Transported: Gendered Images and Realities', *Australian and New Zealand Journal of Criminology*, vol. 24, no. 2 (1991).

Oxley, D., 'Exercising Agency', *Labour History*, 65 (Nov. 1993).

Oxley, D., 'Packing Her (Economic) Bags: Convict Women Workers', *Australian Historical Studies*, vol. 26, no. 102 (April 1994).

Oxley, D., *Convict Maids: The Forced Migration of Women to Australia* (Cambridge, Cambridge University Press, 1996).

Oxley, D. and Richards, E., 'Convict Women and Assisted Female Immigrants Compared: 1841 – a Turning Point?' in Eric Richards (ed.), *Visible Women: Female Immigrants in Colonial Australia* (Canberra, Australian National University, 1995).

Paquette, Robert, 'Slave Resistance and Social History', *Journal of Social History*, vol. 24, no. 3 (1991).

Pascale, Roy, *Design and Truth in Autobiography* (London, Routledge and Kegan Paul, 1960).

Paul, A.A. and Southgate, D.A.T., *McCane and Widdowson's The Composition of Foods* (London, HMSO, 1978).

Pearce, C., *Through the Eyes of Thomas Pamphlett, Convict and Castaway* (Brisbane, Boolarong, 1993).

Perrott, Monica, *A Tolerable Good Success: Economic Opportunities for Women in New South Wales 1788–1830* (Sydney, Hale and Ironmonger, 1983).

Philips, David, *Crime and Authority in Victorian England: The Black Country, 1835– 1860* (London, Croom Helm, 1977).

Philips, David, 'Moral Entrepreneurs and the Construction of a "Criminal Class" in England, c.1800–1840', unpublished paper presented to the Australian Historical Association Conference, (University of Sydney, 1988).

Philips, David, 'Crime, Law and Punishment in the Industrial Revolution' in O'Brien and Quinault (eds), *The Industrial Revolution and British Society* (1993).

Prakash, Gyan, *Bonded Histories: Genealogies of Labor Servitude in Colonial India* (Cambridge, Cambridge University Press, 1990).

Prakash, Gyan (ed.), *The World of Rural Labourers in Colonial India* (Delhi, Oxford University Press, 1992).

Pratt, Mary Louise, 'Scratches on the Face of the Country: or, What Mr Barrow Saw in the Land of the Bushmen' in Henry L. Gates (ed.), *'Race', Writing and Difference* (Illinois, University of Chicago Press, 1991).

Quartermaine, Peter, *Thomas Keneally* (London, Edward Arnold, 1991).

Radford, R.A., 'The Economic Organisation of a P.O.W. Camp', *Economica*, vol. 12 (1945).

Rajendra, N., 'Transmarine Convicts in the Straits Settlements', *Asian Profile*, vol. 11, no. 5 (Oct. 1983).

Rawlings, P., *Drunks, Whores and Idle Apprentices: Criminal Biographies of the Eighteenth Century* (London, Routledge, 1992).

Reece, Bob (ed.), *Irish Convict Lives* (Sydney, Crossing Press, 1990).

Reece, Bob (ed.), *Exiles from Erin: Convict Lives in Ireland and Australia* (Basingstoke, Macmillan Academic and Professional, 1991).

Reece, Bob, 'Frank the Poet' in Reece (ed.), *Exiles from Erin* (1991).

Reece, Bob, 'The True History of Bernard Reilly' in Reece (ed.), *Exiles from Erin* (1991).

Reynolds, Henry, '"That Hated Stain": The Aftermath of Transportation in Tasmania', *Historical Studies, Australia and New Zealand*, vol. 14, no. 53 (1969).

Reynolds, Henry, *The Other Side of the Frontier: Aboriginal Resistance to the European Invasion of Australia* (Ringwood, Victoria, Penguin Books Australia, 1982).

Reynolds, Henry, 'The Breaking of the Great Australian Silence: Aborigines in Australian Historiography 1955–1983', Trevor Reese Memorial Lecture (University of London Institute of Commonwealth Studies, Australian Studies Centre, 1984).

Reynolds, J., 'The Penal Stations of New South Wales and Van Diemen's Land: The Reality behind the Legend', *Journal of the Royal Australian Historical Society*, vol. 67, no. 4 (1982).

Richards, Eric, 'Margins of the Industrial Revolution' in O'Brien and Quinault (eds), *The Industrial Revolution and British Society* (1993).

Ripley, P.C. *et al.* (eds), *Witness for Freedom: African American Voices on Race, Slavery and Emancipation* (Chapel Hill and London, University of North Carolina Press, 1993).

Ritchie, John, *Punishment and Profit: The Reports of Commissioner Bigge* (Carlton, Victoria, Melbourne University Press, 1970).

Ritchie, John, 'John Thomas Bigge and his Reports on New South Wales', *Royal Australian Historical Society Journal and Proceedings*, vol. 60, no. 1 (1974).

Robb, Peter (ed.), *Dalit Movements and the Meanings of Labour* (Delhi, Oxford University Press, 1993).

Robinson, Portia, 'The First Forty Years' in Mackinolty and Radi (eds), *In Pursuit of Justice* (1979).

Robinson, Portia, *The Hatch and Brood of Time: A Study of the First Generation of Native-Born White Australians* (Melbourne, Oxford University Press, 1985).

Robinson, Portia, *The Women of Botany Bay: A Reinterpretation of the Role of Women in the Origins of Australian Society* (North Ryde, Macquarie Library, 1988).

Robinson, Portia, 'Getting a Nation's Record Straight?', *The Age – Arts and Books*, 21 Jan. 1989.

Robson, L.L., 'The Origins of the Women Convicts Sent to Australia, 1787– 1852', *Historical Studies, Australia and New Zealand*, vol. 11, no. 41 (1963).

Robson, L.L., *The Convict Settlers of Australia: An Enquiry into the Origin and Character of the Convicts Transported to New South Wales and Van Diemen's Land 1787–1852* (Carlton, Victoria, Melbourne University Press, 1965).

Roe, M., 'Colonial Society in Embryo', *Historical Studies*, vol. 7, no. 26 (1956).

Rogers, Nicholas, 'Vagrancy, Impressment and the Regulation of Labour in Eighteenth-Century Britain' in Lovejoy and Rogers (eds), *Unfree Labour in the Development of the Atlantic World* (1994).

Roland, C. and Shannon, H., 'Patterns of Disease among World War II Prisoners of the Japanese: Hunger, Weight Loss and Deficiency Diseases in Two Camps', *Journal of the History of Medicine*, vol. 46, no. 1 (1991).

Ross, Robert, 'Emancipation and the Economy of the Cape Colony', *Slavery & Abolition*, vol. 14, no. 1 (1989).

Rudé, George, *Criminal and Victim: Crime and Civil Society in Early Nineteenth Century England* (Oxford, Clarendon Press, 1985).

Russell, Penny, '"For *better* and for *worse*": Love, Power and Sexuality in Upper Class Marriages in Melbourne, 1860–1880', *Australian Feminist Studies*, 7 and 8 (Summer 1988).

Sainty, M.R. and Johnstone, K.A. (eds), *Census of New South Wales November 1828* (Sydney, Library of Australian History, 1985).

Sandu, Kernial Singh, 'Tamil and Other Indian Convicts in the Straits Settlements, A.D. 1790–1873', *Proceedings of the First International*

Conference Seminar of Tamil Studies, vol. 1 (Kuala Lumpur, International Association of Tamil Research, 1968).

Sandu, Kernial Singh, *Indians in Malaya: Some Aspects of Their Immigration and Settlement* (Cambridge, Cambridge University Press, 1969).

Saunders, Kay, *Workers in Bondage: The Origins and Bases of Unfree Labour in Queensland 1824–1916* (Brisbane, University of Queensland Press, 1982).

Saunders, Kay and Evans, R. (eds), *Gender Relations in Australia: Domination and Negotiation* (Sydney and London, Harcourt Brace Jovanovich, 1992).

Schlegel, Katharina, 'Mistress and Servant in Nineteenth-Century Hamburg: Employer/Employee Relationships in Domestic Service, 1880–1914', *History Workshop Journal*, vol. 15 (1983).

Schofield, R.S., 'Dimensions of Illiteracy, 1750–1850', *Explorations in Economic History*, vol. 20 (1973).

Scott, James C., *Weapons of the Weak: Everyday Forms of Peasant Resistance* (New Haven, Yale University Press, 1985).

Scott, James C., *Domination and the Arts of Resistance: Hidden Transcripts* (New York, Yale University Press, 1990).

Scutt, Surg.-Capt. R.W.B. and Gotch, Christopher, *Art, Sex and Symbol: The Mystery of Tattooing* (Cranbury, NJ, Cornwall Books, 1986; 1st edn. 1974).

Sekora, J. and Turner, D.T. (eds), *The Art of Slave Narrative: Original Essays in Criticism and Theory* (Macomb, IL, Western Illinois University Press, 1982).

Shaw, A.G.L, *Convicts and the Colonies: A Study of Penal Transportation from Great Britain and Ireland to Australia and Other Parts of the Empire* (London, Faber, 1966).

Shaw, A.G.L., 'Review of Convict Workers', *Victorian Historical Magazine*, no. 61 (May 1990).

Shaw, A.G.L. and Clarke, C.M.C. (eds), *Australian Dictionary of Biography* (Melbourne, Melbourne University Press, 1966).

Shilling, Chris, *The Body and Social Theory* (London, Sage, 1993).

Shlomowitz, Ralph, 'Convict Workers: A Review Article', *Australian Economic History Review*, vol. 30, no. 2 (1990).

Shlomowitz, Ralph, 'Convict Transportees: Casual or Professional Criminals?', *Australian Economic History Review*, vol. 31, no. 2 (Sept. 1991).

Shorter, C., 'Introduction' in R.S. Cobbold, *Margaret Catchpole* (London, Henry Frowde and Co., 1907).

Shubert, A., 'Private Initiative in Law Enforcement: Associations for the Prosecution of Felons, 1744–1856' in V. Bailey (ed.), *Police and Punishment in Nineteenth Century Britain* (London, Croom Helm, 1981).

Singha, Radhika, '"Providential Circumstances": The Thuggee Campaign of the 1830s and Legal Innovation', *Modern Asian Studies*, vol. 27, no. 1 (1993).

Smart, Barry, 'On Discipline and Social Regulation: A Review of Foucault's

Genealogical Analysis' in David Garland and Peter Young (eds), *The Power to Punish* (Aldershot, Ashgate Publishing, 1992).

Smith, Bernard, 'The Fatal Subject', *Scripsi*, vol. 4, no. 4 (1987).

Smith, C., *Shadow over Tasmania* (Hobart, Waltch, 1941).

Smith, F.B., 'Beyond the Uninviting Shore', *Times Literary Supplement*, 9–15 March 1990.

Sollers, Basil, 'Transported Convict Laborers in Maryland during the Colonial Period', *Maryland Historical Magazine*, vol. 2 (1907).

Stafford, Barbara Maria, *Body Criticism: Imaging the Unseen in Enlightenment Arts and Medicine* (Cambridge, MA, MIT Press, 1991).

Stafford-Clark, Max, *Letters from George* (London, Nick Hern Books, 1989).

Starling, Marion Wilson, *The Slave Narrative: Its Place in American Literary History* (Washington, DC, Harvard University Press, 1988).

Steele, J.G., *Brisbane Town in Convict Days, 1824–1842* (Brisbane, University of Queensland Press, 1975).

Stephen, Leslie and Lee, Sidney (eds), *Dictionary of National Biography* (Oxford, Oxford University Press, 1959–60 reprint).

Stepto, R.B., *From Behind the Veil: A Study of Afro-American Literary History* (Urbana and Chicago, University of Illinois Press, 1979).

Steward, Samuel M., *Bad Boys and Tough Tattoos: A Social History of the Tattoo with Gangs, Sailors and Street-Corner Punks 1950–1965* (New York, Harrington Park Press, 1966).

Stoler, A., 'Sexual Affronts and Racial Frontiers: European Identities and the Politics of Sexual Exclusivism in Colonial South-East Asia', *Comparative Studies in Society and History*, vol. 34, no. 3 (July 1992).

Sturma, Michael, 'Eye of the Beholder: The Stereotype of Women Convicts, 1788–1852', *Labour History*, vol. 34 (May 1978).

Sturma, Michael, *Vice in a Vicious Society: Crime and Convicts in Mid-Nineteenth Century New South Wales* (St Lucia, Queensland University Press, 1983).

Sturrock, John, *The Language of Autobiography: Studies in the First Person Singular* (Cambridge, Cambridge University Press, 1993).

Summers, Anne, *Damned Whores and God's Police: The Colonization of Women in Australia* (Ringwood, Victoria, Penguin Books Australia, 1975).

Summers, Anne, 'Hidden from History: Women Victims of Crime' in Satyanshu Mukherjee and Jocelynne Scutt (eds), *Women and Crime* (Sydney, George Allen and Unwin, 1981).

Tardif, Phillip, *Notorious Strumpets and Dangerous Girls: Convict Women in Van Diemen's Land, 1803–1829* (Sydney, Angus and Robertson, 1990).

Thompson, E.P., *The Making of the English Working Class* (London, Gollancz, 1963).

Thompson, E.P., 'Patrician Society, Plebeian Culture', *Journal of Social History*, vol. 7, no. 4 (1974).

Thompson, E.P., *The Poverty of Theory and Other Essays* (London, Merlin Press, 1978).

Thomson, Alistair, *Anzac Memories: Living with the Legend* (Melbourne, Oxford University Press, 1994).

Townsend, Norma, '"The Clamour of ... Inconsistent Persons": Attitudes to Transportation in New South Wales in the 1830s', *Australian Journal of Politics and History*, vol. 25, no. 3 (1979).

Townsend, Norma, 'A "Mere Lottery": The Convict System in New South Wales through the Eyes of the Molesworth Committee', *Push from the Bush*, 21 (1985).

Tunzelmann, G.N. von, 'Technological and Organizational Change During the Industrial Revolution' in O'Brien and Quinault (eds), *The Industrial Revolution and British Society* (1993).

Turner, Bryan S., *The Body and Society* (Oxford, Basil Blackwell, 1984).

Turner, Bryan S., 'Recent Developments in the Theory of the Body' in Featherstone *et al.* (eds), *The Body* (1991).

Turner, Mary, 'Slave Workers, Subsistence and Labour Bargaining: Amity Hall, Jamaica, 1805–1832', *Slavery & Abolition*, vol. 12, no. 1 (1991).

Twaddle, Michael (ed.), *The Wages of Slavery: From Chattel Slavery to Wage Labour in Africa, the Caribbean and England* (London, Frank Cass, 1993).

Walker, Jan, *Jondaryan Station: The Relationship Between Pastoral Capital and Pastoral Labour 1840–1890* (St Lucia, University of Queensland Press, 1988).

Ward, Russel, *The Australian Legend* (Melbourne, Melbourne University Press, 1958).

Watson, R.L., *The Slave Question: Liberty and Property in South Africa* (Hanover, NH, University Press of New England, 1990).

Weddaburn, Hilary, 'The Female Factory' in Mackinolty and Radi (eds), *In Pursuit of Justice* (1979).

Wertenbaker, Timberlake, *Our Country's Good* (London, Methuen Drama, 1991).

Whittaker, Howard, 'Victoria's Convicts by Another Name', *Royal Historical Society of Victoria*, vol. 55, no. 4 (1984).

Wilson, Ann, '*Our Country's Good*: Theatre, Colony and Nation in Wertenbaker's Adaptation of *The Playmaker*', *Modern Drama*, vol. 34, no. 1 (Toronto, March 1991).

Worden, Nigel, 'Diverging Histories: Slavery and its Aftermath in the Cape Colony and Mauritius', *South African Historical Journal*, vol. 27 (1992).

Wynd, Ian, 'The Pentonvillians', *Victorian Historical Journal*, vol. 60 (Sept. 1989).

Yang, Anand A. (ed.), *Crime and Criminality in British India* (Tucson, University of Arizona Press, 1985).

Unpublished theses

Connors, L., 'The Birth of the Prison and the Death of Convictism: The Operation of Law in Pre-Separation Queensland, 1839–1859', PhD thesis, University of Queensland (1990).

Heath, Laren, 'The Female Convict Factories in New South Wales and Van Diemen's Land: An Examination of their Role in the Control, Punishment and the Reformation of Prisoners between 1804 and 1854', MA thesis, Australian National University (1978).

Johnston, W.R., 'A Study of the Relationship between Law and the Community in Colonial Queensland', MA thesis, University of Queensland (1964).

Maxwell-Stewart, Hamish, 'The Bushrangers and the Convict System of Van Diemen's Land, 1803–1846', PhD thesis, University of Edinburgh (1990).

O'Connor, Tamsin, 'Power and Punishment: The Limits of Resistance; The Moreton Bay Penal Settlement 1824–1842', BA (Hons) thesis, University of Queensland (1994).

Oxley, Deborah, 'Convict Maids', PhD thesis, University of New South Wales (1991).

Reid, Kirsty, 'Work, Sexuality and Resistance; The Convict Women of Van Diemen's Land, 1820–1839', PhD thesis, University of Edinburgh (1995).

Index